ENCYCLOPEDIA OF
ROCK MUSIC ON FILM

ENCYCLOPEDIA OF ROCK MUSIC ON FILM

A Viewer's Guide to Three Decades of Musicals, Concerts, Documentaries and Soundtracks 1955-1986

Linda J. Sandahl

BLANDFORD PRESS
POOLE · NEW YORK · SYDNEY

First published in the UK 1987 by Blandford Press
Link House, West Street, Poole, Dorset BH15 1LL

Copyright © 1987 Linda J. Sandahl

Distributed in Australia by
Capricorn Link (Australia) Pty Ltd
PO Box 665, Lane Cove, NSW 2066

British Library Cataloguing in Publication Data

Sandahl, Linda J.
Encyclopedia of rock music : a viewer's
guide to three decades of rock 'n' roll musicals,
concerts, documentaries and soundtracks 1955-
1986.
1. Moving-picture music — Dictionaries
2. Rock music — Dictionaries
I. Title
791.43'09'09357   ML2075

ISBN 0 7137 1685 1 (Hardback)
ISBN 0 7137 1923 0 (Paperback)

All rights reserved. No part of this book may be
reproduced or transmitted in any form or by any means,
electronic or mechanical, including photocopying,
recording or any information storage and retrieval
system, without permission in writing from the
Publisher.

Typeset by Asco Trade Typesetting Ltd., Hong Kong
Printed in Great Britain by Bath Press Ltd., Avon

Contents

Introduction	7
MUSICALS	9
CONCERTS AND DOCUMENTARIES	131
SOUNDTRACKS	177
Index of Film Titles	201
Index of Names	204
Index of Song Titles	222

Introduction

Within this book, rock feature films have been divided into three categories: first musicals, then concerts and documentaries, and then soundtracks. Each type of film makes up a section of the book; each section is arranged in alphabetical order by title.

MUSICALS
These are defined as films in which actors perform musically in some way (or are *seen* to, which includes mimed and dubbed singing or playing and animated films like *AMERICAN POP*), or in which musicians also act (even if they play themselves, like Chuck Berry in *AMERICAN HOT WAX*). But *HAVING A WILD WEEKEND*, for example, will be found under SOUNDTRACKS because, although the film stars the Dave Clark Five, and their songs are heard in the background, they do *not* perform. Dance musicals, such as *FOOTLOOSE*, in which the musical performances are choreographed dance routines rather than singing or playing, *are* included as proper musicals. Not so films with just one rock number, even if it is performed; this omits such movies as *CAT PEOPLE, HIGH SCHOOL CONFIDENTIAL* and *BACK TO THE FUTURE*, excellent though their single songs are.

In this section, each entry contains: original title (and alternative titles), year of first release in the country of origin, company, length, important production credits (director, producer, screenplay), other various credits if they are interesting or memorable (such as choreography, musical direction, technical advisor, etc.), cast, musical performers, songs performed (indicating *by whom* when the information is obtainable), soundtrack songs if any, soundtrack and video availability in the US and UK, and a *brief* critical plot summary.

CONCERTS AND DOCUMENTARIES
This is a fairly clear category; however, only those documentaries where performances are seen as well as heard are listed here. Documentaries with rock scores are included under SOUNDTRACKS.

In this section, entries contain: original title (and alternative titles), year of first release in the country of origin, company, length, important production credits (director, producer), other credits (if they're of interest – musical director, etc.), musical performers, songs performed (and by whom, if the information is available), soundtrack songs if any, soundtrack and video availability in the UK and US, and a brief critical summary.

INTRODUCTION

SOUNDTRACKS
This section includes films with scores that are at least *mostly* rock and those with scores written or performed by rock musicians; examples are *AMERICAN GRAFFITI* or *THE FAMILY WAY*.

Entries in this section contain: original title (and alternative titles), date of first release in the country of origin, company, length, important production credits (director, producer), other interesting credits (composer, musical director, etc.), soundtrack songs (and performers where the information is available), and soundtrack availability in the US and UK.

Only films at least 50 minutes in length and originally made in English are included. Films are listed by the title used in the country of first release; alternative titles are listed separately (thus: *FURY UNLEASHED see HOT ROD GANG*). Three indexes are provided at the back of the book: an Index of Film Titles, in which all the films are listed alphabetically; an Index of Names, which gives personal names of performers and production personnel *and* band names; and an Index of Song Titles, which explains itself.

HOW TO USE THIS BOOK
As a viewer, you might wish to find the entry for a particular film, say one of the beach movies of the Sixties, but cannot remember the title. You know it will be in the MUSICALS section, but where? If you can *only* remember the plot – perhaps it's the one where a foreign princess appears – you'll have to browse through the section, reading the synopses for beach movies. But if you can remember that the princess is played by Luciana Paluzzi, just look in the Index of Names at the back of the book, where you will find that she stars in *MUSCLE BEACH PARTY*. However, maybe you want to find the one where Little Stevie Wonder performs *Fingertips*. In that case, look in the Index of Song Titles for *Fingertips*; Stevie appeared in more than one beach movie, believe it or not, but that particular song is in *BIKINI BEACH*.

MUSICALS

ALICE'S RESTAURANT   1969
United Artists, color, 111 minutes

DIRECTOR: Arthur Penn
PRODUCERS: Hillard Elkins, Joe Manduke
SCREENPLAY: Vanavle Herndon
CAST: Arlo Guthrie, James Broderick, Pat Quinn, Pete Seeger
SONGS PERFORMED: *Alice's Restaurant, Amazing Grace, Car Song, Pastures of Plenty, Songs to Ageing Children*
SOUNDTRACK: United Artists
VIDEO: Twentieth Century Fox – US

ALICE'S RESTAURANT   Arlo Guthrie and friend.

Still a pretty good representation of American hippiedom in its first blush – casual, mildly political, disorganised and good-natured. With a cast mainly of non-actors, Penn directs the story of the 'Alice's restaurant massacree' almost like a home movie, and as such it can be very enjoyable.

AMERICAN HOT WAX   1976
Paramount Pictures, color, 91 minutes

DIRECTOR: Floyd Mutrux
PRODUCER: Art Linson
SCREENPLAY: John Kaye
MUSICAL SUPERVISION: Kenny Vance

ALICE'S RESTAURANT London poster, 1970.

CAST: Tim McIntire, Fran Drescher, Jay Lenno, Laraine Newman
MUSICAL PERFORMERS: Chuck Berry, the Chesterfields, the Delights, Screamin' Jay Hawkins, Jerry Lee Lewis, Clark Otis (Charles Green), the Planotones, Timmy and the Tangerines
SONGS PERFORMED: *Reelin' and Rockin'*, *Roll Over Beethoven*, *Sweet Little Sixteen*, Chuck Berry; *The ABC of Love*, *Since I Don't Have You*, *That Is Rock and Roll*, *Why Do Fools Fall In Love?*, the Chesterfields; *Mr Lee*, the Delights; *I Put a Spell On You*, Screamin' Jay Hawkins; *Great Balls of Fire*, *Whole Lotta Shakin' Goin' On*, Jerry Lee Lewis; *Hey Little Girl*, Clark Otis; *Rock and Roll Is Here to Stay*, the Planotones; *Mister Blue*, Timmy and the Tangerines
SOUNDTRACK SONGS: *Zoom*, the Cadillacs; *Charlie Brown*, the Coasters; *Summertime Blues*, Eddie Cochran; *Splish Splash*, Bobby Darin; *Whispering Bells*, the Del Vikings; *Little Darlin'*, the Diamonds; *Honky Tonk part 2*, the Bill Doggett Trio; *Sixty Minute Man*, the Dominoes; *There Goes My Baby*, the Drifters; *Little Star*, the Elegants; *Bye Bye Love*, the Everly Brothers; *Sea Cruise*, Frankie Ford; *Do You Wanna Dance?*, Bobby Freeman; *A Thousand Miles Away*, the Heartbeats; *Oh Boy*, *Rave On*, Buddy Holly; *Tutti Frutti*, Little Richard; *Sincerely*, the Moonglows; *Hushabye*, the Mystics; *Willie and the Hand Jive*, Johnny Otis; *Goodnight, It's Time to Go*, the Spaniels; *When You Dance*, the Turbans; *La Bamba*, Ritchie Valens; *Stay*, Maurice Williams and the Zodiacs; *That's Why*, Jackie Wilson
SOUNDTRACK: A&M

Slight but engaging fictionalized story of the

ALICE'S RESTAURANT   Arlo and friend (Geoff Outlaw, left) are arrested for littering.

AMERICAN HOT WAX   Jerry Lee Lewis rips it up.

fall of the great American disc jockey Alan Freed, whose honesty under pressure and real love for rock music are well conveyed by McIntire. Most of the other characters are little more than cameos; standouts are a humorous Jay Lenno and a touching Laraine Newman. Some rock giants play themselves in a massive concert sequence, to exhilarating effect.

AMERICAN POP   1981
Columbia Pictures, animated, color, 97 minutes

DIRECTOR: Ralph Bakshi
PRODUCERS: Ralph Bakshi, Martin Ransohoff
SCREENPLAY: Ronni Kern
SONGS PERFORMED: *Hell Is For Children*, Pat Benatar; *People Are Strange*, the Doors; *Turn Me Loose*, Fabian; *Summertime*, Janis Joplin, Big Brother and the Holding Company; *Night Moves*, Bob Seger
SOUNDTRACK: MCA

Rather half-baked pop 'history' of American music, from vaudeville to rock'n'roll. The animation is brilliant, but unfortunately the idea just doesn't work; the music chosen is neither spectacularly good nor representative.

AMERICATHON   1979
United Artists, color, 85 minutes

DIRECTOR: Neil Israel
PRODUCER: Joe Roth
SCREENPLAY: Neil Israel, Monica Johnson, Michael Mislowe
CAST: John Ritter, Chief Dan George, Harvey Korman, Fred Willard
MUSICAL PERFORMERS: Elvis Costello, Eddie Money
SONGS PERFORMED: *Crawlin' to the USA*, *(I Don't Want to Go To) Chelsea*, Elvis Costello; *Get a Move On*, *Open Up Your Heart*, Eddie Money
SOUNDTRACK SONGS: *It's a Beautiful Day*, the Beach Boys; *Without Love*, Nick Lowe; *Car Wars*, Tom Scott
SOUNDTRACK: Columbia – US; CBS – UK
VIDEO: Lorimar – US

Generally unfunny adolescent humor with a few numbers thrown in, notably Elvis Costello. Not a bad idea, though; the US goes bankrupt and holds a ludicrous telethon to raise money. But it doesn't work. Ritter is quite good as the ineffectual president.

ATTACK OF THE PHANTOMS   see KISS MEETS THE PHANTOM

BALLAD IN BLUE   see BLUES FOR LOVERS

BE MY GUEST   1965
Rank Films, black & white, 82 minutes

DIRECTOR: Lance Comfort
PRODUCER: Lance Comfort
SCREENPLAY: Lyn Fairhurst
CAST: David Hemmings, Avril Angers, Joyce Blair, Steve Marriott
MUSICAL PERFORMERS: Kenny and the Wranglers, Jerry Lee Lewis, the Nashville Teens, the Nightshades, the Zephyrs
SONGS PERFORMED: *Be My Guest*, *No One But Me*, *She Laughed*, *Somebody Help Me*, *Watcha Gonna Do*

One of a string of mild teen-oriented musicals from Rank in the Sixties, several of them starring a young Hemmings. This one takes place at a seaside resort hotel – now how did Jerry Lee get there?

BEACH BALL   1964
Paramount Pictures, color, 107 minutes

DIRECTOR: Lennie Weinrib
PRODUCER: Bart Patton
SCREENPLAY: David Malcolm

BE MY GUEST The kids decide to put on a show! David Hemmings (third from left).

CAST: Edd Byrnes, Chris Noel, Gail Gilmore, Robert Logan
MUSICAL PERFORMERS: the Four Seasons, the Hondells, Jerry Lee Lewis, the Nashville Teens, the Righteous Brothers, the Supremes, the Walker Brothers
SONGS PERFORMED: *Dawn*, the Four Seasons; *My Buddy Seat*, the Hondells; *Baby, What You Want Me to Do?*, the Righteous Brothers; *Beach Ball, Surfer Boy*, the Supremes

Rotten semi-beach movie without the usual cast. Most of it concerns an ersatz college band called the Wiggles, but it does have some great guest stars, if you can stand the wait to see them.

BEACH BLANKET BINGO 1965
American International Pictures, color, 98 minutes

DIRECTOR: William Asher
PRODUCERS: Samuel Z. Arkoff, James H. Nicholson

BEACH BALL Guest stars the Supremes: Florence Ballard (top), Diana Ross (right), Mary Wilson (left).

BEACH PARTY Frankie Avalon in a publicity still before 1959.

SCREENPLAY: William Asher, Leo Townsend
CAST: Frankie Avalon, Annette Funicello, Linda Evans, Harvey Lembeck, Donna Loren, the Hondells
SONGS PERFORMED: *The Good Times*, Frankie Avalon; *Beach Blanket Bingo*, Avalon and Funicello; *Fly Boy*, *New Love*, Linda Evans; *You'll Never Change Him*, Annette Funicello; *I Think You Think*, *The Cycle Set*, the Hondells; *I Am My Ideal*, Harvey Lembeck; *It Only Hurts When I Cry*, Donna Loren
SOUNDTRACK: American International – US

The usual extremely thin plot involves sky-diving and a girl lifeguard. Songs appear and

Annette and Frankie sing a duet on the way to the BEACH PARTY.

disappear with little logic or purpose, but at least Erich Von Zipper performs one. And yes, it is that Linda Evans, and she looks better *now*.

BEACH PARTY   1963
American International Pictures, color, 101 minutes

DIRECTOR: William Asher
PRODUCERS: James H. Nicholson, Samuel Z. Arkoff
SCREENPLAY: Lou Rusoff
SONGS BY: Roger Christian and Gary Usher
CAST: Frankie Avalon, Annette Funicello, Bob Cummings, Harvey Lembeck, Dorothy Malone, Eva Six
MUSICAL PERFORMERS: Frankie Avalon, Dick Dale and the Deltones, Annette Funicello
SONGS PERFORMED: *Don't Stop Now*, Frankie Avalon; *Beach Party*, Avalon and Funicello; *Surfin' and A Swingin'*, *Secret Surfin'*, Dick Dale

and the Deltones; *Promise Me Anything, Treat Him Nicely*, Annette Funicello
SOUNDTRACK: American International – US
VIDEO: WEA – US

This one is pretty amusing, actually, in a mindless sort of way – an anthropologist analyses the denizens of Annette-and-Frankie-dom through a telescope; the legendary Erich Von Zipper and his gang arrive on the scene and raise some havoc. Watchable, at least.

BEAT GIRL A.K.A. WILD FOR KICKS
1960
Times Films, black & white, 92 minutes

DIRECTOR: Edmond T. Greville
PRODUCER: George Willoughby
SCREENPLAY: Dail Ambler
MUSICAL DIRECTOR: John Barry
CAST: Adam Faith, Noelle Adam, David Farrar, Gillian Hills, Shirley Ann Field, Christopher Lee
MUSICAL PERFORMERS: Adam Faith, the John Barry Seven
SONGS PERFORMED: *The Stripper*, the John Barry Seven; *Beat Girl Song, I Did What You Told Me, It's Legal, Made You*, Adam Faith
SOUNDTRACK: Columbia – UK

Stylish if ultimately silly attempt to mix rock'n'roll with the kitchen-sink drama of the time. It works in a sleazy kind of way; Noelle Adam is pretty boring as the sulky teen heroine who flips out when her father remarries, but Faith, as always, shows undeniable charisma, and the supporting cast is good. Worth seeing.

BEAT GIRL Adam Faith.

BECAUSE THEY'RE YOUNG   1960
Columbia Pictures, black & white, 102 minutes

DIRECTOR: Robert Peterson
PRODUCER: Jerry Bresler
SCREENPLAY: James Gunn
CAST: Dick Clark, Michael Callan, Tuesday Weld, Warren Berlinger, Victoria Shaw
MUSICAL PERFORMERS: James Darren, Duane Eddy and the Rebels, Bobby Rydell
SONGS PERFORMED: *Because They're Young*, James Darren; *Shazam*, Duane Eddy and the Rebels; *Swingin' School*, Bobby Rydell

MUSICALS

BECAUSE THEY'RE YOUNG Michael Callan, a teen heart-throb whose talent as a dancer was sadly under-used by the movies.

Dull and serious-minded drama of misunderstood teens with nothing but general early Sixties' atmosphere going for it. The liberal, concerned hero-teacher is played by American TV host and producer Dick Clark, who looks exactly the same now.

THE BIG BEAT   1957
Universal International Pictures, color, 82 minutes

DIRECTOR: Will Cowan
PRODUCER: Will Cowan
SCREENPLAY: David P. Harmon
CAST: Gogi Grant, William Campbell, William Reynolds, Ansra Martin, Jeffrey Stone
MUSICAL PERFORMERS: Charlie Barnet, Count Basie, the Del Vikings, the Diamonds, Fats Domino, The Four Aces, Harry James, the Mills Brothers, George Shearing
SONGS PERFORMED: *Can't Wait, Come Go With Me*, the Del Vikings; *Little Darlin', Where May Go, Go I*, the Diamonds; *The Big Beat, I'm Walkin'*, Fats Domino

The scion of a recording company saves the family business by signing new pop acts. End of plot. A weird mix of jazz and pop which pleased fans of neither, probably.

BIKINI BEACH   1964
American International Pictures, color, 100 minutes

DIRECTOR: William Asher
PRODUCERS: James Nicholson, Samuel Z. Arkoff
SCREENPLAY: William Asher, Leo Townsend, Robert Dillon
CAST: Frankie Avalon, Annette Funicello, Martha Hyer, Harvey Lembeck, Don Rickles, Keenan Wynn
MUSICAL PERFORMERS: Frankie Avalon, the Exciters, Annette Funicello, Donna Loren, the Pyramids, Little Stevie Wonder
SONGS PERFORMED: *Bikini Beach*, Frankie Avalon; *Gotcha Where I Want You*, the Exciters; *Because You're You, Gimme Your Love, How About That, Secret Weapon, This Time It's Love*, Annette Funicello, Donna Loren; *Record Run*, the Pyramids; *Fingertips*, Stevie Wonder
VIDEO: Ablay – US

Pretty horrible 'surfers strike back at the Beatles' idea behind this one – Frankie disguises himself as Potato Bug, the English teen idol. Unfortunately, Frankie had very little talent for comedy. The usual great acts are slotted into the plot with no rationale at all.

BIRTH OF THE BEATLES 1979
Dick Clark Productions, made for TV, color, 104 minutes

DIRECTOR: Richard Marquand
PRODUCER: Tony Bishop
SCREENPLAY: John Kurland, Jacob Erskender
MUSICAL DIRECTOR: Carl Davis
CAST: Stephen McKenna, Rod Culbertson, John Altman, Ray Ashcroft, Nigel Havers
MUSICAL PERFORMERS: Rain
SONGS PERFORMED: *Can't Buy Me Love, I Wanna Hold Your Hand, She Loves You* etc.

This was actually not at all bad. It's perhaps overly sincere and not very *funny*, which the real Beatles always were; but the story of their early days is quite touching in the light of the event of the next year. The young actors playing the 'fab four' are naturally overshadowed by our knowledge of the real people, but Nigel Havers is fine as Brian Epstein. I have to admit to an enjoyable personal nostalgia – I remember some of these stories, like George setting the Hamburg hotel on fire, from *Tiger Beat* magazine.

BLUE HAWAII 1961
Paramount Pictures, color, 101 minutes

DIRECTOR: Norman Taurog
PRODUCER: Hal Wallis
SCREENPLAY: Hal Kanter
SCORE: Joseph J. Lilly
CHOREOGRAPHY: Charles O'Curran
CAST: Elvis Presley, Joan Blackman, Angela Lansbury, Jenny Maxwell, Nancy Walters
MUSICAL PERFORMERS: Elvis Presley, the Jordanaires
SONGS PERFORMED: *Almost Always True, Aloha*

BLUE HAWAII   Elvis hits the tropics.

MUSICALS

One of the best things about THE BLUES BROTHERS — James Brown.

The Blues Brothers onstage with their all-star band.

Oe, Beach Boy Blues, Blue Hawaii, Can't Help Falling in Love, Hawaiian Sunset, Hawaiian Wedding Song, Island of Love, Ito Eats, Ku-u-i-po, Moonlight Swim, No More, Rock-a Hula Baby, Shave and a Haircut Two Bits, Slicin' Sand, Stepping Out of Line
SOUNDTRACK: RCA – US, UK
VIDEO: Heron – UK; Key – US

Elvis movies had lost their bite by this time, but this one is still pretty enjoyable. Here El breaks away from his wealthy family background (convincing, huh?) to be his own man as a tour guide. The scenery is great and there's a song approximately every six minutes.

THE BLUES BROTHERS 1980
Universal International Pictures, color, 133 minutes

DIRECTOR: John Landis
PRODUCER: Robert K. Weiss
SCREENPLAY: Dan Ackroyd, John Landis
MUSICAL DIRECTOR: Ira Newborn
CAST: John Belushi, Dan Ackroyd, Kathleen Freeman, Henry Gibson
MUSICAL PERFORMERS: Dan Ackroyd, John Belushi, James Brown, Cab Calloway, Ray Charles, Aretha Franklin, John Lee Hooker, the Blues Brothers Band: Steve Cropper, Duck Dunn, Murphy Dunne, Willie Hall, Lou

BODY ROCK Teen-oriented dance musicals were a craze in the early Eighties.

Marini, Tom Malone, Matt Murphy, Alan Rubin
SONGS PERFORMED: *Everybody Needs Someone to Love, Gimme Some Lovin', Jailhouse Rock, She Caught the Katy, Sweet Home Chicago, Theme from Rawhide,* Dan Ackroyd, John Belushi; *The Old Landmark,* James Brown; *Minnie the Moocher,* Cab Calloway; *Shake Your Tailfeathers,* Ray Charles; *Think,* Aretha Franklin; *Boogie Children,* John Lee Hooker
SOUNDTRACK SONGS: *I'm Walkin',* Fats Domino; *Shake Your Moneymaker,* Elmore James; *Let the Good Times Roll,* Louis Jordan; *Hold On, I'm Comin', Soothe Me,* Sam and Dave
SOUNDTRACK: Atlantic
VIDEO: CIC – UK; MCA – US

Overblown, over-long, and certainly over-expensive, this is still not totally awful, though perhaps John Landis might have realized that we would rather see James Brown perform than reaction shots of the audience. But they never *do* realize that, do they? Jake and Elmore are at least real characters, and they have great taste in music. It's hard to choose, but Aretha really steals it. Look out for John Lee Hooker too.

BLUES FOR LOVERS A.K.A. BALLAD IN BLUE   1964
Twentieth Century Fox, black & white, 89 minutes

DIRECTOR: Paul Henried
PRODUCER: Herman Blaser
SCREENPLAY: Burton Wohl
CAST: Ray Charles, Tom Bell, Mary Peach, Dawn Addams
MUSICAL PERFORMERS: Ray Charles and the Raelettes
SONGS PERFORMED: *Careless Love, Cry, Hallelujah, I Love Her So, I Got a Woman, Let the Good Times Roll, Light Out of Darkness, Talkin' About You, That Lucky Old Sun, Unchain My Heart, What'd I Say*

Sentimental soap opera of a blind child who finds a friend in Ray Charles (who just happens to be in London) and his concerned parents. The story is goopy but the music is great.

BODY ROCK   1984
New World Pictures, color, 90 minutes

DIRECTOR: Marcelo Epstein
PRODUCER: Jeffrey Schechtman
SCREENPLAY: Desmond Nakano
GRAFFITI ARTIST: Brim
MUSIC COMPOSED BY: Sylvester Levay
MUSICAL SUPERVISOR: Gaylon Horton
SOUNDTRACK SUPERVISED BY: Phil Ramone
CAST: Lorenzo Lamas, Vicki Frederick, Cameron Dye, Michelle Nicastro, Ray Sharkey
SONGS: *Drastic Measures, Everybody's Breakin',* Josie Aiello; *The Closest to Love, Do You Know Who I Am,* Ashford and Simpson; *Sharpshooter,* Laura Branigan; *Deliver,* Martin Briley; *One Thing Leads to Another,* Roberta Flack; *Fools Like Us, Smooth Talker,* Lorenzo Lamas; *Spray It On, Let Your Body Rock,* Ralph MacDonald; *Vanishing Point,* Baxter Robinson; *Smooth Talker,* Cruz Sembello; *Why You Wanna Break My Heart,* Dwight Twilley; *Body Rock,* Maria Vidal
SOUNDTRACK: EMI
VIDEO: Thorn–EMI

The usual healthy, tanned, freshly-scrubbed dancing 'street kids' – the Hollywood version – struggle to make it in show biz. Just about average for this type of movie, though there are nice shots of graffiti-covered walls and some good breakdancing, featuring the Rhythm Nation and Skeleton Dancers.

BREAKDANCE – THE MOVIE   1984
Cannon Films, color, 88 minutes

DIRECTOR: Joel Silberg
PRODUCERS: Allen De Bevoise, David Zito
SCREENPLAY: Allen De Bevoise, Charles Parker, Gerald Scaife

MUSICALS

MUSICAL NUMBERS STAGED BY: Jaime Rogers
CHOREOGRAPHY BY: Jaime Rogers
CAST: Shabba-Doo (Adolfo Quinones), Lucinda Dickey, Ben Lokey, Phineas Newborn III, Boogaloo Shrimp (Michael Chambers), Christopher McDonald
SOUNDTRACK SONGS: *Beat Box*, the Art of Noise; *Freakshow On the Dancefloor*, the Bar-Kays; *Lil' Lockers*, Matthew Ender, Stephen Elowe, Doug Lunn; *Street People*, Fire Fox; *Body Work*, Hot Streak; *Reckless, Tibetan Jam*, Ice T; *Boogie Down*, Al Jarreau; *Tour De France*, Kraftwerk; *There's No Stoppin' Us*, Ollie and Jerry; *Cut it*, Re-Flex; *Ain't Nobody*, Rufus with Chaka Khan; *Heart of the Beat, Three V; 99½*, Carol Lynn Townes
SOUNDTRACK: Polydor
VIDEO: Guild – UK

A very lively dance musical – the unoriginal script draws together a middle-class girl and two street performers and sends them along to the usual dance contest (which they naturally win, being the good guys). But the film's major asset is the brilliant dancing of Shabba-Doo, who also seems to have a certain flair for acting – too much talent for one man!

Two earnest punks – Hazel O'Connor and Phil Daniels – in BREAKING GLASS ...

... then Hazel is corrupted into a soul-less mega-star by the music industry.

BREAKING GLASS 1980
Paramount Pictures, color, 104 minutes

DIRECTOR: Brian Gibson
PRODUCERS: Davina Belling, Clive Parsons
SCREENPLAY: Brian Gibson
MUSIC AND LYRICS: Hazel O'Connor
MUSICAL DIRECTOR: Tony Visconti
CAST: Hazel O'Connor, Phil Daniels, Jonathan Pryce, Jon Finch, Peter-Hugo Daly, Mark Wingett
MUSICAL PERFORMERS: Hazel O'Connor, Victy Silva
SONGS PERFORMED: *Big Brother, Black Man, Calls the Tune, Come Into the Air, Eighth Day, Give Me an Inch, Monsters in Disguise, Top of the Wheel, Who Needs It?, Will You, Writing on the Wall,* Hazel O'Connor; *One More Time,* Victy Silva
SOUNDTRACK: A & M
VIDEO: Paramount – US

Colorful but not very street-credible attempt to put punk in the movies. Hazel O'Connor has rather too much weight to carry; the entire plot concerns her sufferings as an innocent primal punk co-opted by the music business. Other more interesting characters, like Jonathan Pryce's sax player, gradually disappear; Jon Finch is also interesting as a slimy producer. But the whole thing lacks drama and, worse, the music is pretty dull.

Gary Busey gave a brilliant performance in the title role of THE BUDDY HOLLY STORY.

THE BUDDY HOLLY STORY   1978
Columbia Pictures, color, 114 minutes

DIRECTOR: Steve Rash
PRODUCER: Freddy Bauer
SCREENPLAY: Robert Gitler
MUSICAL DIRECTOR: Joe Renzetti
CHOREOGRAPHER: Maggie Rash
CAST: Gary Busey, Maria Richwine, Don Stroud, Charles Martin Smith, Conrad Janis
MUSICAL PERFORMERS: Gary Busey, Gailard Sartain, Jerry Zaremba
SONGS PERFORMED: *Everyday, I'm Gonna Love You Too, Its So Easy, Listen To Me, Maybe Baby, Not Fade Away, Oh Boy, Peggy Sue, Rave On, Rock Around With Ollie Vee, That'll Be the Day, True Love Ways, Well All Right, Words of Love,* Gary Busey; *Chantilly Lace,* Gailard Sartain; *Whole Lotta Shakin' Goin' On,* Jerry Zaremba
SOUNDTRACK: Epic – US; Warwick – UK

The entire force of this film is due to Gary Busey's terrific performance as Holly; the script is banal and worse, the production shows *no* feeling for the era, and the music is not even well done, though at least it was recorded live. But somehow the story of that dynamic young Lubbock rocker remains compelling and, in the end, touching.

CAN'T STOP THE MUSIC   1980
AFD, color, 124 minutes

DIRECTOR: Nancy Walker
PRODUCER: Allen Carr
SCREENPLAY: Bronte Woodard, Allen Carr
SONGS BY: Jacques Morali
CAST: the Village People, Bruce Jenner, Valerie Perrine, Steve Guttenberg, Paul Sand, Tammy Grimes, June Havoc
MUSICAL PERFORMERS: David London, the Ritchie Family, the Village People
SONGS PERFORMED: *Sound of the City, Samantha,* David London; *Gimme a Break, Sophistication,* the Ritchie Family; *Can't Stop the Music, I Love You to Death, Liberation, Magic Night,*

CAN'T STOP THE MUSIC   Luckily Valerie Perrine's involvement with this complete turkey didn't destroy her career.

The Village People were unlikely and unsuitable movie stars in CAN'T STOP THE MUSIC.

Milkshake, *YMCA*, the Village People
SOUNDTRACK: Casablanca – US; Mercury – UK
VIDEO: Thorn – US

Absolutely dreadful attempt to make movie stars out of the faceless Village People, not to mention talentless decathlon champ Jenner. A must to avoid.

CARNIVAL ROCK   1957
Howco, black & white, 75 minutes

DIRECTOR: Roger Corman
PRODUCER: Roger Corman
SCREENPLAY: Leo Lieberman
CAST: Susan Cabot, David J. Stewart, Dick Miller, Brian Hutton, Ed Nelson
MUSICAL PERFORMERS: the Blockbusters, Susan Cabot, David Houston, Bob Luman, the Platters, the Shadows
SONGS PERFORMED: *Carnival Rock*, the Blockbusters; *Ou-Shoo-Bla-Dee*, *There's No Place Without You*, Susan Cabot; *Only One*, *Teenage Frankie and Johnny*, *This Is the Night*, David Houston, Bob Luman; *Remember When*, the Platters; *The Creep*, the Shadows

Comic loves a girl singer and sacrifices all. Roger Corman gets sentimental, and it's a bad mistake. This film would be greatly improved by the addition of some nice zombies, or at least monsters from outer space.

CATALINA CAPER   1967
Crown-International, color, 84 minutes

DIRECTOR: Lee Sholem
PRODUCERS: Bond Blackman, Jack Bartlett
SCREENPLAY: Clyde Ware
CAST: Tommy Kirk, Del Moore, Peter Duryea, Lyle Wagoner
MUSICAL PERFORMERS: the Cascades, Carol Connors, Little Richard, Mary Wells
SONGS PERFORMED: *There's a New World Opening for Me*, the Cascades; *Book of Love*, Carol Connors; *Scuba Party*, Little Richard; *Catalin Caper*, Mary Wells

Teens turn detective and foil art thieves. Pretty unexciting stuff, but some of the guest stars are great. (Do you think Little Richard sang *Scuba Party* from personal experience? Wouldn't the goggles mess up the hair?)

Richie Havens as Othello in CATCH MY SOUL.

CATCH MY SOUL   1974
Twentieth Century Fox, color, 95 minutes

DIRECTOR: Patrick McGoohan
PRODUCERS: Jack Good, Richard Rosenbloom
SCREENPLAY: Jack Good, from Shakespeare's *Othello*
SONGS: Jack Good, Delaney Bramlett
SCORE: Tony Joe White
CAST: Richie Havens, Season Hubley, Lance Le Gault, Susan Tyrell, Tony Joe White, Bonnie Bramlett. Delaney Bramlett
MUSICAL PERFORMERS: Delaney and Bonnie, Richie Havens, Lance Le Gault, Tony Joe White
SONGS PERFORMED: *Chug a Lug*, Bonnie Bramlett; *I Found Jesus, That's What God Said*, Delaney Bramlett; *Book of Prophecy, Open Our Eyes, Put Out the Light, Run, Shaker, Run, Working on a Building*, Richie Havens; *Backwoods Preacher, Looking Back, Othello, Wash Us Clean*, Tony Joe White
SOUNDTRACK: Metromedia – US; RCA – UK

Weird (and failed) attempt to put the story of Othello into the setting of a commune. Part of the problem is that singers generally can't act, and Othello is a pretty heavy plot to explicate. It comes out looking quite disorganized and scrappy, though the music is quite good.

CHANGE OF HABIT   1969
Universal International Pictures, color, 93 minutes

DIRECTOR: William Graham
PRODUCER: Joe Connelly
SCREENPLAY: Eric Bercovici, James Lee, S. S. Schweitzer
CAST: Elvis Presley, Mary Tyler Moore, Barbara McNair, Edward Asner
MUSICAL PERFORMER: Elvis Presley
SONGS PERFORMED: *Change of Habit, Have a Happy, Let Us Pray, Let's Be Friends, Rubberneckin'*

Truly, one of the worst Elvis movies, which is really saying something. It's only saved from being the worst by Mary and Barbara McNair, who actually have personalities, unlike most of the girls El co-starred with. But El as a doctor (well, he certainly knew enough about pharmaceuticals) and those two as nuns – ugh!

MUSICALS

CLAMBAKE   1967
United Artists, color, 100 minutes

DIRECTOR: Arthur H. Nadel
PRODUCERS: Arthur Gardner, Arnold Laven, Jules Levy
SCREENPLAY: Arthur Browne Jr
CHOREOGRAPHER: Alex Romero
CAST: Elvis Presley, Bill Bixby, Shelley Fabares, Will Hutchins
MUSICAL PERFORMER: Elvis Presley
SONGS PERFORMED: *A House That Has Everything, Clambake, Confidence, Hey Hey Hey, Who Needs Money?, You Don't Know Me, The Girl I Never Loved*
SOUNDTRACK: RCA

El is a millionaire who masquerades as a waterskiing instructor. Got it so far? Because that's the plot. Again, it's not *quite* the worst, largely because of a supporting cast who can actually act.

COLLEGE CONFIDENTIAL   1959
Universal International Pictures, black & white, 91 minutes

DIRECTOR: Albert Zugsmith
PRODUCER: Albert Zugsmith
SCREENPLAY: Irving Shullman
CAST: Steve Allen, Jayne Meadows, Cathy Crosby, Sheilah Graham, Rocky Marciano, Mickey Shaughnessey, Randy Sparks, Conway Twitty, Mamie Van Doren, Walter Winchell
MUSICAL PERFORMERS: Randy Sparks, Conway Twitty
SONGS PERFORMED: *College Confidential, Playmates*, Randy Sparks; *College Confidential Ball*, Conway Twitty
SOUNDTRACK: Chancellor – US

A steamy Sixties' soap opera with some rock music thrown in for some mysterious reason. A liberal sociology professor gets involved in his students' private lives (and one of them is Mamie Van Doren!). Steve Allen has been known as a rock hater ever since – maybe this is what did it.

C'MON LET'S LIVE A LITTLE   1967
Paramount Pictures, color, 85 minutes

DIRECTOR: David Butler
PRODUCERS: John Hertelandy, June Starr
SCREENPLAY: June Starr
CAST: Bobby Vee, Jackie De Shannon, Eddie Hodges, Suzie Kaye
MUSICAL PERFORMERS: Jackie De Shannon, Bobby Vee
SONGS PERFORMED: *Baker Man, For Granted*, Jackie De Shannon; *Instant Girl, What Fool This Mortal Be*, Bobby Vee; *Back Talk, C'mon Let's Live a Little, Let's Go Go, Over and Over, Tonight's the Night, Way Back Home*
SOUNDTRACK: Liberty – US

A young singer goes to college and meets the dean's daughter, who is also a singer. What a coincidence! This is a movie that stars Bobby Vee, so over to you, the viewer.

THE COOL ONES   1967
Warner Brothers, color, 95 minutes

DIRECTOR: Gene Nelson
PRODUCER: William Conrad
SCREENPLAY: Joyce Geller
MUSICAL SUPERVISOR: Lee Hazelwood
SCORE: Ernie Freeman
CHOREOGRAPHY: Toni Basil
CAST: Debby Watson, Gil Peterson, Roddy McDowell, Phil Harris, Robert Coote, Mrs Miller
MUSICAL PERFORMERS: the Bantams, Glen Campbell, the Leaves, T. J. and the Foundations
SONGS PERFORMED: *A Bad Woman's Love, Baby Baby Your Love Is All I Need, The Cool Ones, Hands, High, It's Magic, It's Your World, Tantrum, This Town, Up Your Totem Pole With Love, Where Did I Go Wrong?*

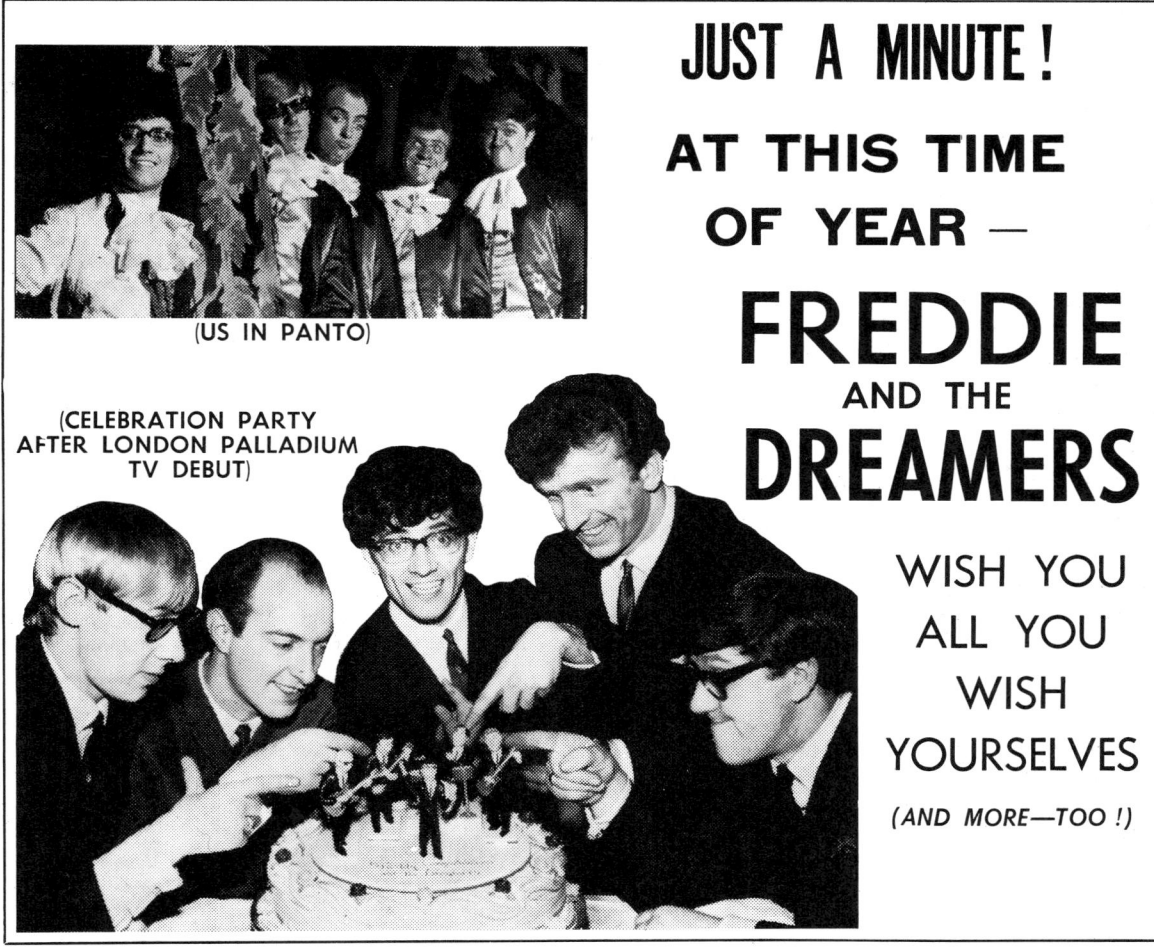

CUKOO PATROL (*Above*) Freddie and the Dreamers Christmas advert; (*below*) Before their first hit record.

Terrible movie about a go-go dancer reaching for the top of her profession. Bad idea, bad script, bad acting. But what a great title!

CUKOO PATROL 1965
Grand National, black & white, 76 minutes

DIRECTOR: Duncan Wood
PRODUCER: Maurice J. Wilson
SCREENPLAY: Lew Schwarz
CAST: Freddie and the Dreamers, Kenneth Connor, John Le Mesurier, Victor Maddern, Arthur Mullard
MUSICAL PERFORMERS: Freddie and the Dreamers

DATELINE DIAMONDS Stolen goods end up on a pirate radio ship.

DON'T KNOCK THE ROCK

Freddie and the Dreamers join the Boy Scouts. It might be all right for very small children with no discrimination, but I wouldn't count on it.

DATELINE DIAMONDS   1965
Rank Films, black & white, 70 minutes

DIRECTOR: Jeremy Summers
PRODUCER: Harry Benn
SCREENPLAY: Tudor Gates
CAST: William Lucas, Kenneth Cope, George Mikell, Conrad Phillips, Patsy Rowlands, Kenny Everett
MUSICAL PERFORMERS: The Chantelles, Kiki Dee, the Small Faces

The only rock movie, such as it is, to feature a pirate-radio ship, a unique phenomenon unknown in the US. That's just about the only outstanding feature, though it might be fun to see the Small Faces in 1965. Otherwise, it's feeble.

DISC JOCKEY JAMBOREE   see JAMBOREE

DON'T KNOCK THE ROCK   1956
Columbia Pictures, black & white, 84 minutes

DIRECTOR: Fred F. Sears
PRODUCER: Sam Katzman
SCREENPLAY: Robert E. Kent
CAST: Alan Dale, Alan Freed, Bill Haley and His Comets, Little Richard, the Treniers
SONGS PERFORMED: *Calling All Comets, Don't Knock the Rock, Hook Line and Sinker, Hot Dog Buddy Buddy*, Bill Haley and His Comets; *Long Tall Sally, Rip It Up, Tutti Frutti*, Little Richard

In this one, local kids put on a show to demonstrate that rock'n'roll is no worse than the Charleston craze, which is perfectly true.

There is some *terrific* dancing here, most of it unfortunately uncredited. Alan Dale is a highly unconvincing teen idol, but Freed collects some great guest stars, as usual.

DON'T KNOCK THE TWIST   1962
Columbia Pictures, black & white, 87 minutes

DIRECTOR: Oscar Rudolph
PRODUCER: Sam Katzman
SCREENPLAY: James B. Gordon
CAST: Chubby Checker, Mari Blanchard, Lang Jeffries
MUSICAL PERFORMERS: Chubby Checker, Gene Chandler, the Carroll Brothers, Vic Dana, the Dovells, Dee Dee Sharp, Linda Scott
SONGS PERFORMED: *Bo Diddley*, the Carroll Brothers; *Duke of Earl*, Gene Chandler; *Don't Knock the Twist, The Fly, I Love to Twist, La Paloma Twist*, Chubby Checker; *Slow Twist*, Chubby Checker and Dee Dee Sharp; *Little Altar Boy*, Vic Dana; *Bristol Stomp, Do the New Continental*, the Dovells; *Mashed Potato Time*, Dee Dee Sharp; *Yesiree*, Linda Scott
SOUNDTRACK: Parkway – US; Columbia – UK

DON'T KNOCK THE TWIST   A portrait of Chubby Checker.

MUSICALS

An extremely silly plot is just an excuse to string together a bunch of pretty good twist numbers; a TV executive races to put on a show before a rival station. Naturally, he does. End of plot. See if you can figure out the words to *Duke of Earl*, though, which makes even less sense when you see Gene Chandler crooning it clad in white tails and a monocle.

DOUBLE TROUBLE 1962   see SWINGING ALONG

DOUBLE TROUBLE 1968
Metro Goldwyn Mayer, color, 90 minutes

DIRECTOR: Norman Taurog
PRODUCERS: Judd Bernard, Irwin Winkler
SCREENPLAY: Jo Heins
TECHNICAL DIRECTOR: Col. Tom Parker
CHOREOGRAPHY: Alex Romero
CAST: Elvis Presley, Annette Day, John Williams, Yvonne Romain, the Wiere Brothers
MUSICAL PERFORMER: Elvis Presley
SONGS PERFORMED: *Baby If You Give Me All Your Love*, *City By Night*, *Could I Fall In Love?*, *Double Trouble*, *I Love Only One Girl*, *Long Legged Girl*, *Old Macdonald*, *There's So Much World To See*
SOUNDTRACK: RCA
VIDEO: MGM–UA – US

El is torn between two girls and, in the meantime, goes to Antwerp and solves a murder plot. This is certainly not one of the few *good* Elvis musicals, but it is mildly enjoyable for some reason, and at least it doesn't make you cringe.

DR GOLDFOOT AND THE GIRL BOMBS 1966
Color, 85 minutes

DIRECTOR: Mario Bava
MUSICAL DIRECTOR: Mike Curb
CAST: Vincent Price, Fabian, Franco Franchi, Carlo Ciccio, Laura Antonelli
MUSICAL PERFORMERS: the Candles, Bobby Lile, Paul and the Pack, the Sloopys, Terry Stafford
SONGS PERFORMED: *This I Say*, the Candles; *They Just Don't Make 'Em Like Her Anymore*, Bobby Lile; *Hidin' From Myself*, Paul and the Pack; *Dr Goldfoot and the Girl Bombs*, the Sloopys; *Try My World Little Girl*, Terry Stafford
SOUNDTRACK: Tower – US

Dr Goldfoot movies have a certain charm; they mix the stupidity of the beach-party pictures with the goofy, tongue-in-cheek sci-fi of James Bond. In this one, time-bombs are affixed to the navels of bikini-clad young ladies. The music is rotten, but look at the musical director, promoter of the Osmonds.

EASY COME EASY GO 1967
Paramount Pictures, color, 97 minutes

DIRECTOR: John Rich
PRODUCER: Hal Wallis
SCREENPLAY: Anthony Lawrence, Allan Weiss
CAST: Elvis Presley, Dodie Marshall, Pat Priest, Elsa Lanchester
MUSICAL PERFORMER: Elvis Presley
SONGS PERFORMED: *Easy Come Easy Go*, *I'll Take Love*, *She's a Machine*, *Sing You Children*, *The Love Machine*, *Yoga Is as Yoga Does*, *You Gotta Stop*
SOUNDTRACK: RCA; EP in the UK

Here El is a treasure-hunting deep-sea diver. Pretty poor cast, feeble music.

ELVIS – THE MOVIE 1979
Dick Clark Films, color, 119 minutes

DIRECTOR: John Carpenter
PRODUCERS: Dick Clark, Anthony Lawrence
SCREENPLAY: Anthony Lawrence
MUSICAL DIRECTOR: Joe Renzetti
SPECIAL CONSULTANT: Sam Phillips

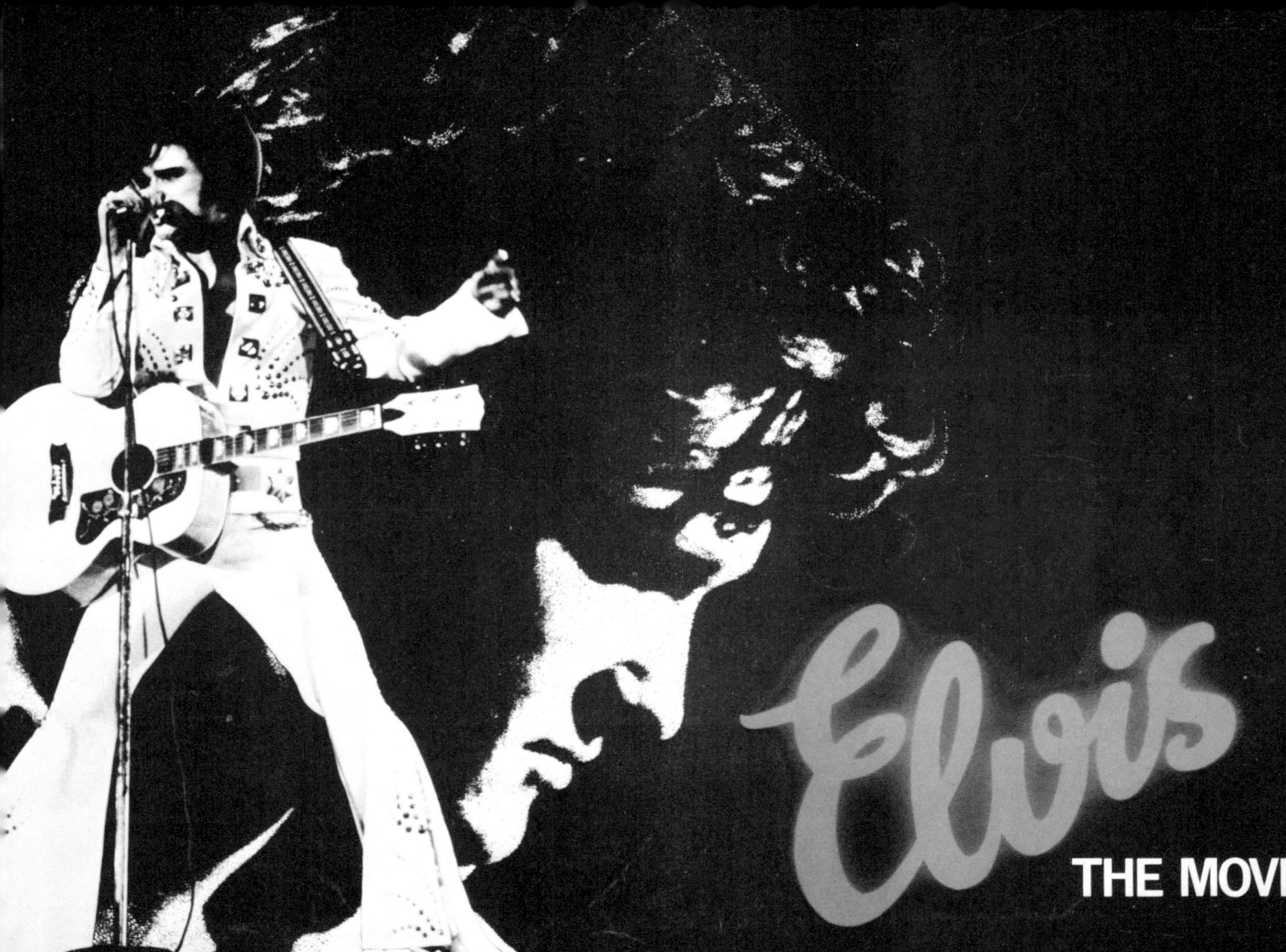

Kurt Russell did a fine job in ELVIS – THE MOVIE, but the film wasn't much.

CAST: Kurt Russell, Season Hubley, Shelley Winters, Bing Russell

MUSICAL PERFORMERS: the voice of Ronnie McDowell as Elvis; David Briggs, Bobby Ogden, keyboards; Buddy Harmon, drums; Mike Leach, bass; Charlie McCoy, harmonica; Dale Sellars, Chip Young, guitars; the Jordanaires

SONGS PERFORMED: *Are You Lonesome Tonight?, Battle Hymn of the Republic, Blue Moon of Kentucky, Blue Suede Shoes, Burnin' Love, Crying in the Chapel, Dixie, Fool Such As I, Heartbreak Hotel, Lawdy Miss Clawdy, Long Tall Sally, Love Me Tender, My Happiness, Mystery Train, Pledging My Love, Old Shep, Rip It Up, Separate Ways, Shake Rattle and Roll, Suspicious Minds, That's All Right, The Wonder of You, Until It's Time For You to Go*

SOUNDTRACK: Dick Clark Productions – US; Arcade – UK

Sincere but all too respectful biopic with fine performance, especially by Russell as Elvis and Shelley Winters as his mother (always a rather sad character). The very early scenes of his troubled teen years and professional start in Memphis are quite good, but the mushy treatment of his later days (the film ends in 1968) washes that out. You just can't discuss the strains of Elvis's life *without* discussing drugs and the questionable nature of the involvement of Col. Tom Parker in his life and career. This film does neither and collapses accordingly.

MUSICALS

EVERY DAY'S A HOLIDAY   Advertisement.

EVERY DAY'S A HOLIDAY A.K.A. SEASIDE SWINGERS   1965
Embassy Pictures, color, 94 minutes

DIRECTOR: James Hill
PRODUCERS: Ronald J. Kahn, Maurice J. Wilson
SCREENPLAY: James Hill, Jeri Matos, Anthony Marriot
CAST: Freddie and the Dreamers (Freddie Garrity, Pete Birrell, Roy Crewsdon, Bernie Quinn), Liz Fraser, John Leyton, Ron Moody, Mike Sarne
MUSICAL PERFORMERS: Freddie and the Dreamers, John Leyton, Grazina Frame
SONGS PERFORMED: *Don't Do That To Me, What's Cooking?*, Freddie and the Dreamers; *All I Want Is You, Crazy Horse Saloon,* John Leyton; *A Boy Needs a Girl*, John Leyton, Grazina Frame

An untrustworthy Bongo (Cliff Richard) turns on his fast-talking agent (Lawrence Harvey) in EXPRESSO BONGO.

SOUNDTRACK: Mercury – US

A bunch of teenagers goes to a seaside resort to enter a talent contest (a time-honored, not to say hoary, plot). Pretty awful, and so is the music.

EXPRESSO BONGO   1959
Continental Pictures, black & white, 111 minutes

DIRECTOR: Val Guest
PRODUCER: Val Guest
SCREENPLAY: Wolf Mankowitz, from his stage play
CAST: Laurence Harvey, Sylvia Sims, Cliff Richard, Yolande Donlan, Hank B. Marvin, Wilfred Owen

EXPRESSO BONGO   A brooding young Cliff Richard.

36

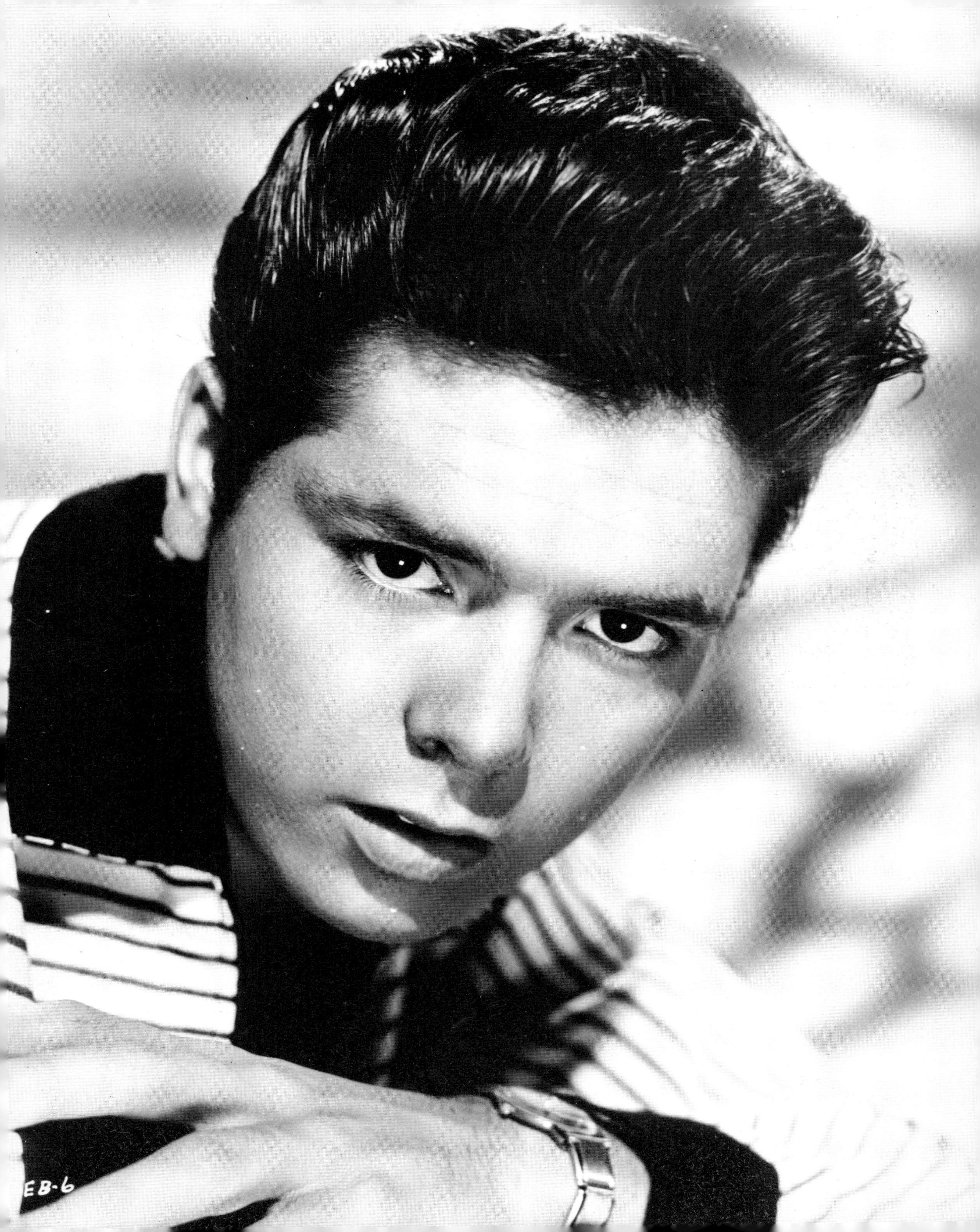
EB-6

MUSICALS

MUSICAL PERFORMERS: Cliff Richard and the Shadows
SONGS PERFORMED: *Bongo Blues, Love, The Shrine On The Second Floor, A Voice In the Wilderness*
SOUNDTRACK: Columbia EP in the UK
VIDEO: Videomedia – UK

Like *The Girl Can't Help It*, this is an anti-rock diatribe disguised as a musical. The makers manage to have their cake and eat it too by despising the music while exploiting it to the hilt. That said, it *is* a slick and enjoyable film, with a surprisingly surly young Cliff and the whole cast giving fine performances. The story concerns a slimy down-and-out agent who discovers this new youth music (in the person of Cliff) at a coffee bar and guides him to stardom. Memorable scenes include one with Wilfred Owen as Cliff's horrible old father, and Hank B. Marvin recommending 'bint' as the solution to all his ills.

FAME 1980
Metro Goldwyn Mayer, color, 133 minutes

DIRECTOR: Alan Parker
PRODUCER: David de Silva, Alan Marshall
SCREENPLAY: Christopher Gore
SONGS: Lesley and Michael Gore, Dean Pitchford
CAST: Irene Cara, Lee Curreri, Linda Clifford, Laura Dean, Antonia Franceschi, Paul McCrane, Gene Anthony Ray
SONGS PERFORMED: *Dogs In the Yard, Fame, Hot Lunch Jam, I Sing the Body Electric, Is It Okay If I Call You Mine?, Out Here On My Own, Ralph and Monty, Red Light*
SOUNDTRACK: RSO
VIDEO: MGM–UA – US

Worthy attempt to make a modern musical out of the lives of the teenage students at New York's High School for the Performing Arts. Quite entertaining, with some dynamic dance numbers and a colorful New York flavor; however, it's much softened and sentimentalized from the real place, and the eventual

FAME   Dancer Gene Anthony Ray.

Irene Cara sings in FAME.

38

TV series was even more softened. And everyone knows that teenagers in 1980 were *not* listening to music like this wimp rock.

FAST FORWARD 1984
Columbia Pictures, color, 110 minutes

DIRECTOR: Sidney Poitier
PRODUCER: John Patrick Veitch
SCREENPLAY: Richard Wesley
STORY: Timothy March
EXECUTIVE MUSIC PRODUCER: Quincy Jones
SCORE: Tom Scott, Jack Hayes
CHOREOGRAPHY: Rick Atwell
CAST: John Scott Clough, Don Franklin, Tamara Mark, Tracy Silver, Irene Worth, Constande Towers, Sam McMurray
SONGS PERFORMED: *Breakin' Out, Survive,* John Scott Clough; *Fast Forward, How Do You Do, Showdown,* John Scott Clough and Kip Lennon; *Curves, Taste,* Deco; *Do You Want It Right Now,* Siedah Garrett; *That's Just the Way It Is,* Narada Michael Williams
SOUNDTRACK: Quest – US
VIDEO: Columbia

Another teen-oriented dance musical, with a group of ambitious kids running away from their mid-western home to compete in a big dance contest in New York. The dancers are very good, though the score is a bit ordinary. Pleasant and fast-moving.

THE FASTEST GUITAR ALIVE 1966
Metro Goldwyn Mayer, color, 87 minutes

DIRECTOR: Michael Moore
PRODUCER: Sam Katzman
SCREENPLAY: Robert E. Kent
SONGS: Bill Dees, Roy Orbison
CAST: Roy Orbison, Joan Freeman, Sammy Jackson, Maggie Pierce, Sam ('the Sham') Scaduto
MUSICAL PERFORMER: Roy Orbison
SONGS PERFORMED: *The Fastest Guitar Alive, Good*

THE FASTEST GUITAR ALIVE Roy Orbison shows just how dangerous rock'n'roll can be.

Time Party, Medicine Man, Pistolero, River, Rollin' On, Snuggle Huggle, Whirlwind
SOUNDTRACK: MGM

A movie so silly that even Elvis wouldn't do it! Eventually the script was dusted off and offered to Roy Orbison; it concerns a Confederate soldier who tries to restore some stolen gold to the US Treasury, pursued by robbers. Somehow several songs are worked into this plot. But best of all, Orbison conceals a rifle *inside his guitar*, which can be clearly seen in stills from the film. Totally nonsensical.

FERRY CROSS THE MERSEY 1964
United Artists, black & white, 88 minutes

DIRECTOR: Jeremy Summers

MUSICALS

PRODUCER: Michael Holden
SCREENPLAY: David Franden
SONGS: Gerry Marsden
MUSICAL DIRECTOR: George Warren
CAST: Gerry Marsden, Cilla Black, George A. Cooper, Deryck Guyler, Jimmy Savile, the Pacemakers
MUSICAL PERFORMERS: Cilla Black, the Black Knights, the Blackwells, the Fourmost, Gerry and the Pacemakers, Earl Royce and the Olympics
SONGS PERFORMED: *Is It Love?*, Cilla Black; *I Got a Woman*, the Black Knights; *Why Don't You Love Me?*, the Blackwells; *I Love You Too*, the Fourmost; *Baby You're So Good To Me, Fall In Love, Ferry 'Cross the Mersey, I'll Wait For You, It's Gonna Be All Right, She's the Only Girl For Me, This Thing Called Love, Why Oh Why*, Gerry and the Pacemakers; *Shake a Tail Feather*, Earl Royce and the Olympics
SOUNDTRACK: Columbia – UK; United Artists – US

A nice simple plot line – Liverpool band competes in song contest – provides the framework for lots of Pacemaker numbers. Quite enjoyable, and the music is good. Gerry always had charisma.

FINDERS KEEPERS 1967
United Artists, color, 94 minutes

DIRECTOR: Sidney Hayers
PRODUCER: George H. Brown
SCREENPLAY: Michael Pertwee
STORY: George H. Brown
MUSICAL DIRECTOR: Norrie Paramour
CAST: Cliff Richard, Robert Morley, Peggy Mount, the Shadows
MUSICAL PERFORMERS: Cliff Richard and the Shadows
SONGS PERFORMED: *Fiesta, Finders Keepers, La La Song, My Way, Oh Senorita, Paella, This Day, Time Drags By, Washerwoman*
SOUNDTRACK: Columbia – UK

FINDERS KEEPERS Cliff (left) and the Shadows rest up.

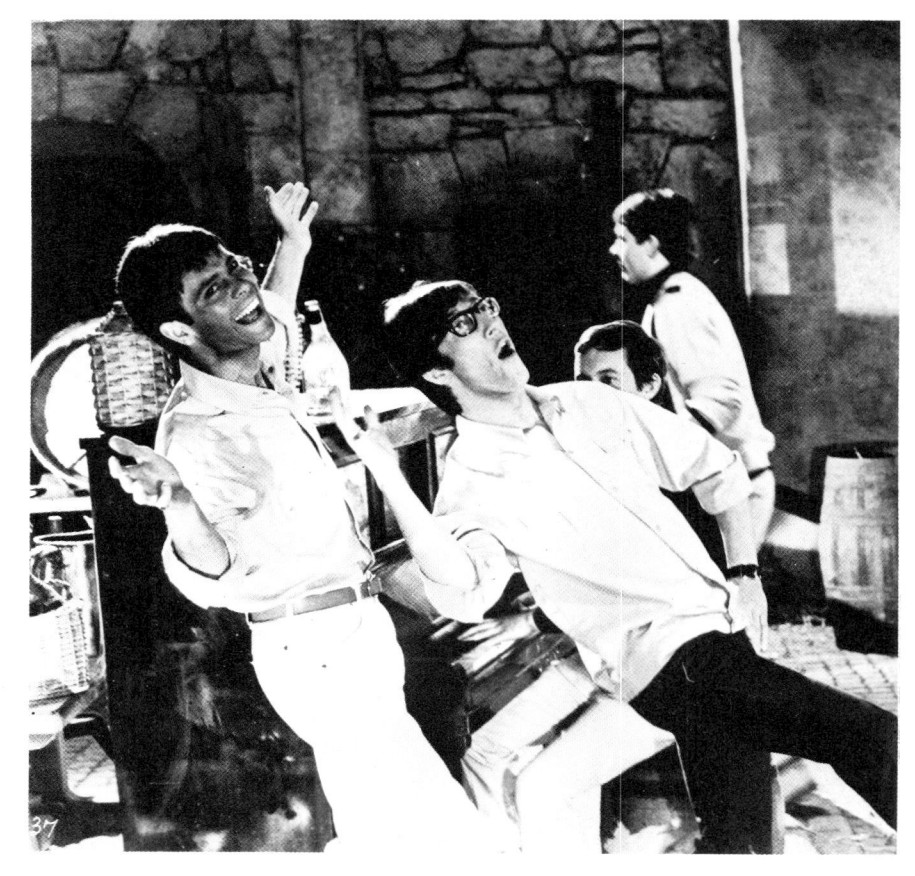

FINDERS KEEPERS Cliff and Hank B. Marvin.

40

Cliff and the Shadows go to Spain and recover a lost atom bomb. What?! Anyway there's lots of nice scenery, but not much sense.

FLAME 1974
VPS, color, 91 minutes

DIRECTOR: Richard Loncraine
PRODUCERS: Chas Chandler, John Steel
CAST: Slade, Tom Conti, Kenneth Colley, Alan Lake, Rosco, Johnny Shannon, Tommy Vance
MUSICAL PERFORMERS: Slade
SONGS PERFORMED: *Far Far Away, Heaven Knows, How Does It Feel, Lay It Down, O.K. Yesterday Was Yesterday, So Far So Good, Standing On the Corner, Summer Song, Them Monkeys Can't Swing, This Girl*
SOUNDTRACK: Warner Brothers – US: Polydor – UK

Yes, there *is* a Slade musical. Surprised? And it's quite good, too, as the boys in the band struggle with unsympathetic management. Although it takes place in the Sixties, the music and atmosphere have a nice early Seventies' feel.

FLAMING STAR 1960
Twentieth Century Fox, color, 101 minutes

DIRECTOR: Don Siegel
PRODUCER: David Weisbart
SCREENPLAY: Clair Huffaker, Nunnally Johnson
CAST: Elvis Presley, Dolores Del Rio, Barbara Eden, Steve Forrest
MUSICAL PERFORMER: Elvis Presley
SONGS PERFORMED: *Britches, A Cane and a High Starched Collar, Flaming Star, Summer Kisses Winter Tears*
VIDEO: Key – US

This *is* one of the good Elvis movies – it's more a straight western than a musical, with only a few songs. Don Siegel coaxes a good performance out of his star, who plays a half-breed (Dolores Del Rio is his mother) caught up in conflict between white settlers and renegade Kiowas. Fast and taut.

FLAMING STAR Elvis shoots it up.

MUSICALS

Elvis plays a half-breed in FLAMING STAR.

FLASHDANCE 1983
Paramount Pictures, color, 100 minutes

DIRECTOR: Adrian Lyle
PRODUCERS: Jerry Bruckheimer, Don Simpson
SCREENPLAY: Joe Esterhaus, Tom Hedley
SCORE: Giorgio Moroder
MUSICAL SUPERVISION: Joey Ramone
CAST: Jennifer Beals, Michael Nouri
DANCE DOUBLE: Marin Jahan
SOUNDTRACK SONGS: *Imagination*, Laura Branigan; *I'll Be Where the Heart Is*, Kim Carnes; *Seduce Me Tonight*, Cycle V; *What a Feeling*, Irene Cara; *Lady L*, Joe Esposito; *Mahuny*, Karen Kamon; *Maniac*, Michael Sembello; *He's a Dream*, Helen St. John; *Romeo*, Donna Summer
VIDEO: CIC – UK; Paramount – US

Style triumphs over substance in this rather foolish dance musical soap opera, about a girl steelworker who dances in nightclubs in her spare time and longs to become a ballet dancer. The choreography and photography are very effective, as is the actual dancing (*not* by Miss Beals, by the way); and there is a certain charm to the local color. But it is undeniably silly.

FOLLOW THAT DREAM 1962
United Artists, color, 110 minutes

DIRECTOR: Gordon Douglas
PRODUCER: David Weisbart
SCREENPLAY: Charles Lederer
FROM: the novel *Pioneer Go Home* by Richard Powell
MUSIC: Hans J. Salter
CAST: Elvis Presley, Anne Helm, Joanna Moore, Arthur O'Connell, Jack Kruschen, Simon Oakland
MUSICAL PERFORMER: Elvis Presley
SONGS PERFORMED: *Angel, Follow That Dream, Home Is Where the Heart Is, I'm Not the*

FLASHDANCE   The street girl (Jennifer Beals) among the ballerinas.

Marrying Kind, On Top Of Old Smokey, Sound Advice, What a Wonderful Life
SOUNDTRACK: RCA

Hillbillies move to Florida and fight with the locals. At least it's an original idea with a workmanlike script by Hollywood veteran Charles Lederer. Not great, but not horrendous either.

FOLLOW THE BOYS   1962
MGM, color, 95 minutes

DIRECTOR: Richard Thorpe
PRODUCER: Lawrence P. Bachman
CAST: Connie Francis, Paula Prentiss, Dany Robin, Russ Tamblyn
MUSICAL PERFORMER: Connie Francis
SONGS PERFORMED: *Follow the Boys, Intrigue, Italian Lullaby, Sleepyland, Tonight's My Night, Waiting for Billy*
SOUNDTRACK: MGM

Light, scenic (it takes place in the south of France), tuneful and pointless; Connie and the girls literally follow their boys from port to port.

FOOTLOOSE   1984
Paramount Pictures, color, 99 minutes

DIRECTOR: Herbert Ross
PRODUCERS: Lewis J. Rachmil, Craig Zadan
SCREENPLAY: Dean Pitchford
MUSICAL SUPERVISION: Becky Shargo
CHOREOGRAPHY: Lynne Taylor-Corbett
CAST: Kevin Bacon, Lori Singer, Dianne Wiest, John Lithgow, Christopher Penn
STUNT DANCER: Peter Tramm
SONGS PERFORMED: *Somebody's Eyes*, Karla Bonoff; *The Girl Gets Around*, Sammy Hagar; *Footloose, I'm Free (Heaven Help the Man)*, Kenny Loggins; *Never*, Moving Pictures; *Almost Paradise*, Mike Reno and Ann Wilson; *Dancing In the Streets*, Shalamar; *Holding Out For a Hero*, Bonnie Tyler; *Let's Hear It For the Boys*, Deniece Williams
SOUNDTRACK SONGS: *Hurts So Good*, John Cougar; *Waiting For a Girl Like You*, Foreigner; *Bang Your Head*, Quiet Riot
SOUNDTRACK: Columbia – US
VIDEO: CIC – UK; Paramount – US

43

MUSICALS

FOOTLOOSE   Lori Singer, Kevin Bacon.

Energetic and enjoyable dance musical with the most unlikely premise that there could be a mid-western town so backward that the kids don't even have rock'n'roll. Kevin Bacon, the new kid from the big city, moves in, his car stereo blasting *Bang Your Head*, and all hell breaks loose. The young lead players all have verve and personality, and there are some excellent dance numbers (ill-photographed as usual by Herbert Ross, who showed in *TURNING POINT* that he had no feel for dance). The best performance is by John Lithgow, as a troubled but repressive minister.

FOREVER YOUNG 1983
Goldcrest Films, color, 84 minutes

DIRECTOR: David Drury
PRODUCER: Chris Griffin
SCREENPLAY: Ray Connolly
MUSIC ARRANGED BY: Anthony King
CAST: James Aubrey, Nicholas Gecks, Julian Firth, Jason Carter, Alec McCowan, Karen Archer, Liam Holt
MUSICAL PERFORMERS: James Aubrey, Nicholas Gecks
SONGS PERFORMED: *Baby What You Want Me to Do, Donna, Forever Young, Honeybee, Leave My Woman Alone, Locomotion, Lonely Afternoon, Searchin', To Know Him Is to Love Him*, James Aubrey, Nicholas Gecks
SOUNDTRACK SONGS: *Be Bop a Lula, Bo Diddley, Raunchy, Saturday Night*, James Aubrey, Nicholas Gecks
VIDEO: Thorn–EMI – UK

Rather wimpy and humorless story of two might-have-beens. A young priest and a university teacher who, as teenagers, aspired to become the British Everly Brothers meet again after many years, remember their past, and become involved in the lives of a mother and her young son. That's about it, really. The music is extremely well done, but the plot completely lacks excitement or surprises.

FRANKIE AND JOHNNY 1966
United Artists, color, 87 minutes

DIRECTOR: Frederick de Cordova
PRODUCER: Edward Small
SCREENPLAY: Alex Gottlieb
CAST: Elvis Presley, Donna Douglas, Nancy Kovack, Sue Ann Langdon
MUSICAL PERFORMER: Elvis Presley
SONGS PERFORMED: *Beginner's Luck, Chesay, Come Along, Down By the Riverside, Everybody Come Aboard, Frankie and Johnny, Hard Luck, Look*

FOREVER YOUNG

MUSICALS

Out Broadway, Petunia the Gardener's Daughter, Please Don't Stop Loving Me, Shout It Out, What Every Woman Longs For, When the Saints Go Marching In

Scenic but flavorless musical, with Elvis as a riverboat gambler (reminding one irresistibly of Gaylord Mitty) who joins a show boat and eventually hits the big time as an entertainer. Not the worst but not the best, either.

FUN IN ACAPULCO   1963
Paramount Pictures, color, 98 minutes

DIRECTOR: Richard Thorpe
PRODUCER: Hal B. Wallis
SCREENPLAY: Allan Weiss
MUSICAL NUMBERS STAGED BY: Charles O' Curran
SCORE: Joseph J. Lilley
TECHNICAL ADVISOR: Col. Tom Parker
CAST: Elvis Presley, Ursula Andress, Elsa Cardenas, Paul Lukas, Alejandro Rey
MUSICAL PERFORMERS: Elvis Presley, the Jordanaires, the Four Amigos, Mariachi Aguila, Mariachi Los Vaqueros
SONGS PERFORMED: *Bossa Nova Baby, The Bullfighter Was a Lady, El Toro, Fun In Acapulco, Guadalajara, I Think I'm Gonna Like It Here, Marguerita, Mexico, No Room to Rhumba In a Sports Car, Vino Dinero Y Amor, You Can't Say No In Acapulco,* Elvis Presley
SOUNDTRACK: RCA
VIDEO: Heron – UK

FRANKIE AND JOHNNY   Donna Douglas and Elvis.

FUN IN ACAPULCO Advertisement.

Some semblance of a plot here; Elvis arrives in Acapulco with a secret – he's the scion of a family of trapeze artists who suffers from loss of nerve after a tragic accident. This moderately interesting idea is soon submerged in a sea of froth, though, and the usual mixed up love life. Also the usual watered-down score, this time using real Mariachi bands. He even does a number in Spanish, but it doesn't help.

FURY UNLEASHED see **HOT ROD GANG**

G.I. BLUES 1960
Paramount Pictures, color, 104 minutes

DIRECTOR: Norman Taurog
PRODUCER: Hal Wallis
SCREENPLAY: Edmund Belan, Henry Garson
CHOREOGRAPHY: Charles O'Curran
CAST: Elvis Presley, James Douglas, Robert Ivers, Juliet Prowse, Leticia Roman, Sigrid Maier
MUSICAL PERFORMERS: Elvis Presley, the Jordanaires
SONGS PERFORMED: *Big Boots, Didya Ever, Doin' the Best I Can, Frankfurt Special, G.I. Blues, Pocketful of Rainbows, Shoppin' Around, Tonight Is So Right For Love, What's She Really Like, Wooden Heart*
SOUNDTRACK: RCA
VIDEO: Heron – UK; Key – US

Another fairly dumb Elvis flick; this time he's a soldier stationed in West Germany with a yen for a nightclub dancer. Songs and misunderstandings follow but everything comes out all right in the end.

MUSICALS

G.I. BLUES Elvis meets Juliet Prowse.

GAS! OR IT BECAME NECESSARY ...
1970
American International Pictures, color, 79 minutes

DIRECTOR: Roger Corman
PRODUCER: Roger Corman
SCREENPLAY: George Armitage
MUSIC: Barry Metton
CAST: Robert Corff, Bud Cort, Talia Coppola(Shire), Elaine Giftos, Country Joe MacDonald, Ben Vereen, Cindy Williams
MUSICAL PERFORMERS: Country Joe and the Fish, Robert Corff, Gourmet's Delight, Johnny and the Tornadoes

SONGS PERFORMED: *Don't Chase Me Around, Got To Get Moving, I'm Looking For a World, Maybe It Wasn't Really Love, Please Don't Bury My Soul, World That We All Dream Of,* Country Joe and the Fish; *This Is the Beginning,* Robert Corff; *First Time Last Time, Today Is Where, Gourmet's Delight; Bubble Gum Girl, Castles, Cry a Little, Gas Man, Juke Box Serenade, The Pueblo Pool,* Johnny and the Tornadoes
SOUNDTRACK: American International – US
VIDEO: Paramount – US

Everyone over twenty-five dies when poison gas is accidentally released. One of the last gasps of counter-culture satire, this is loose but fun, with lots of music and Country Joe McDonald playing a disc jockey whose program is always on the air.

GET YOURSELF A COLLEGE GIRL
1964
Metro Goldwyn Mayer, color, 88 minutes

DIRECTOR: Sid Miller
PRODUCER: Sam Katzman
SCREENPLAY: Robert E. Kent
CHOREOGRAPHY: Hal Belfer
CAST: Mary Ann Mobley, Chad Everett, Joan O'Brien, Nancy Sinatra
MUSICAL PERFORMERS: the Animals, Freddy Bell and the Bellboys, Donnie Brooks, the Dave

GET YOURSELF A COLLEGE GIRL
The Animals guested ...

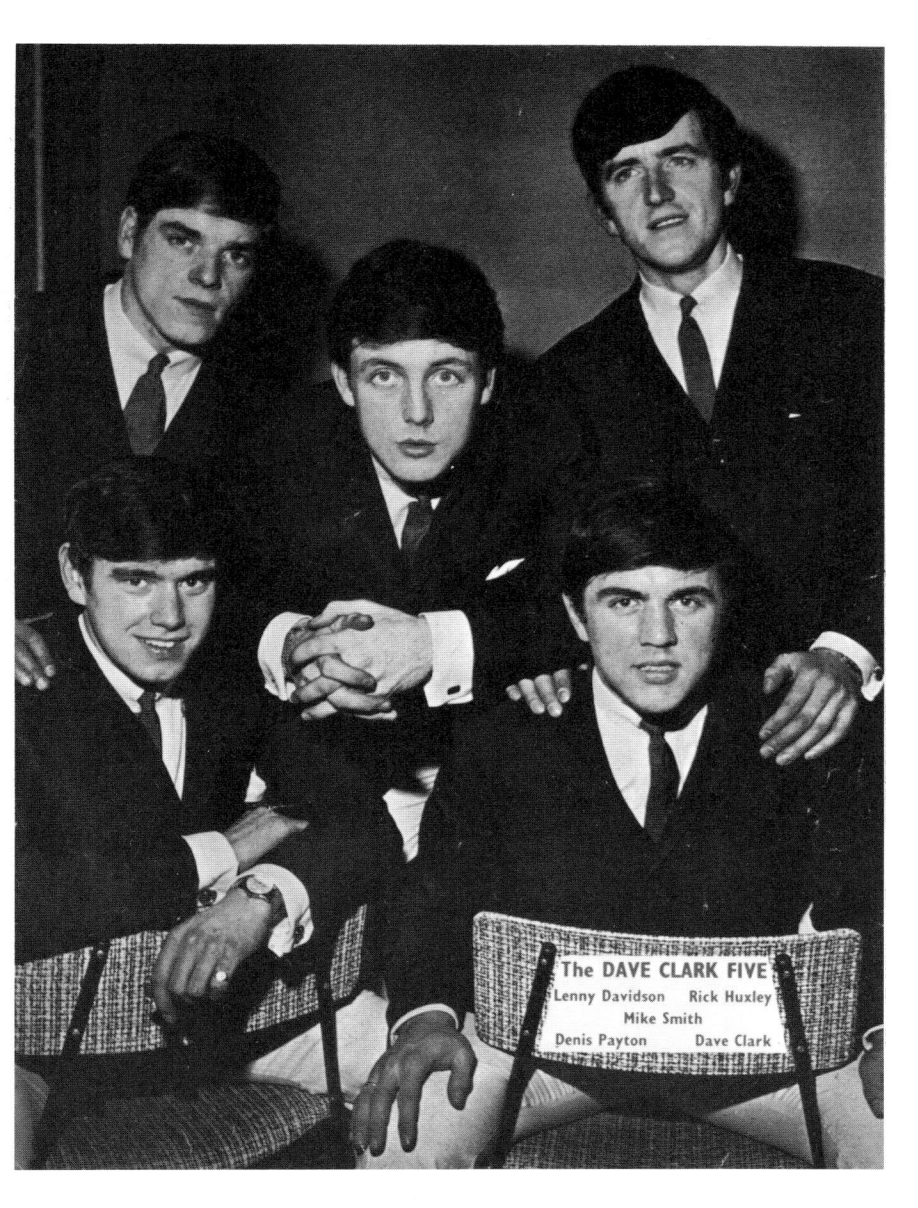

Comin' Home Johnny, *The Sermon*, the Jimmy Smith Trio; *Boney Moronie*, *The Swim*, the Standells
SOUNDTRACK: MGM

A girl student at an Ivy League school gets in trouble for writing pop songs. This slight framework supports *lots* of musical numbers, including a giant watusi (the dance, not the tribe) production number.

THE GHOST IN THE INVISIBLE BIKINI   1966
American International Pictures, color, 82 minutes

DIRECTOR: Don Weis
PRODUCERS: Samuel Z. Arkoff, James H. Nicholson
SCREENPLAY: Louis M. Heyward, Elwood Ullman
MUSIC: Les Baxter
CAST: Deborah Walley, Tommy Kirk, Boris Karloff, Harvey Lembeck, Basil Rathbone, Francis X. Bushman
MUSICAL PERFORMERS: the Bobby Fuller Four, Piccola Puppa, Nancy Sinatra
SONGS PERFORMED: *Make the Music Pretty*, *Swing-A-Ma-Thing*, the Bobby Fuller Four; *Stand Up and Fight*, Piccola Puppa; *Geronimo*, Nancy Sinatra

A new standard in teen exploitation – whether it's a high or low point is debatable – as AIP mix their monster and beach formats. Karloff somehow always manages to be authoritative, and at least Erich Von Zipper appears.

THE GHOST OF DRAGSTRIP HOLLOW   1959
AIP, black & white, 65 minutes

DIRECTOR: William Junior
PRODUCER: Lou Rusoff
SCREENPLAY: Lou Rusoff

... and so did the Dave Clark Five.

Clark Five, Roberta Linn, Mary Ann Mobley, the Jimmy Smith Trio, the Standells
SONGS PERFORMED: *Around and Around*, *Blue Feeling*, the Animals; *Talkin' About Love*, Roberta Linn, Freddy Bell and the Bellboys; *How Would You Like It*, *Sloppy Sue*, *The Swingin' Set*, Donnie Brooks; *Thinking of You Baby*, *Whenever You're Around*, the Dave Clark Five; *Get Yourself a College Girl*, Mary Ann Mobley;

MUSICALS

MUSIC: Alexander Courage, Ron Goodwin
SONGS: Bruce Johnstone, Nik Venet
CAST: Russ Bender, Jody Farr, Henry McCann, Leon Tyler
SONGS PERFORMED: *Charge*, *Geronimo*, *Ghost Train*, *He's My Guy*, *Tongue Tied*

This is really one of the worst, practically unwatchable. For one thing, *no one* in the cast can act. The story, such as it is, concerns a drag-racing club who establish their headquarters in a haunted house. It's all downhill from there.

THE GIRL CAN'T HELP IT 1956
Twentieth Century Fox, Color(Cinemascope), 99 minutes

DIRECTOR: Frank Tashlin
PRODUCER: Frank Tashlin
SCREENPLAY: Herbert Baker, Frank Tashlin
STORY: Garson Kanin
CAST: Jayne Mansfield, Tom Ewell, Edmond O'Brien, John Emery
MUSICAL PERFORMERS: Ray Anthony (for Edmond O'Brien), the Chuckles, Eddie Cochran, Fats Domino, Eddie Fontaine, Abbey Lincoln, Little Richard, Julie London, Johnny Olen, the Platters, Nino Tempo, the Treniers, Gene Vincent and His Blue Caps
SONGS PERFORMED: *Rock Around the Rock Pile*, Ray Anthony; *Cinnamon Sinner*, the Chuckles; *Twenty Flight Rock*, Eddie Cochran; *Blue Monday*, Fats Domino; *Cool It Baby*, Eddie Fontaine; *Spread the Word*, Abbey Lincoln; *The Girl Can't Help It*, *Ready Teddy*, *She's Got It*,

THE GIRL CAN'T HELP IT   The terrific Treniers rehearse.

Little Richard; *Cry Me a River*, Julie London; *My Idea of Love*, Johnny Olen; *You'll Never Know*, the Platters; *Tempo's Tempo*, Nino Tempo; *Rockin' Is Our Business*, the Treniers; *Be Bop A Lula*, Gene Vincent and His Blue Caps

Like EXPRESSO BONGO, this is basically an anti-rock movie; the final point is that you don't need talent to succeed in rock'n'roll (demonstrated by shots of Eddie Cochran). However, the film in general is a lot of fun, mainly relying on the charm – bodily and otherwise – of Jayne Mansfield, who is delightful as always. O'Brien is amusingly over the top as a gangster who hires an agent (Ewell) to make his girlfriend a star, though all she wants is a home and family. They visit nightclub after nightclub, catching performances by Little Richard, Fats Domino, the Platters etc, most of them marred for the rock fan by intercut conversations and reaction shots. But oh well, it *is* the only place you're going to see Gene Vincent and the original Blue Caps in color.

GIRL HAPPY 1965
Metro Goldwyn Mayer, color, 96 minutes

DIRECTOR: Boris Sagal
PRODUCER: Joe Pasternak
SCREENPLAY: R. S. Allen, Harvey Bullock
CAST: Elvis Presley, Shelley Fabares, Gary Crosby, Harold J. Stone
MUSICAL PERFORMER: Elvis Presley
SONGS PERFORMED: *Cross My Heart and Hope to Die, Do Not Disturb, Do the Clam, Fort Lauderdale Chamber of Commerce, Girl Happy, I've Got To Find My Baby, Puppet On a String, She's the Meanest Girl In Town, Spring Fever, Startin' Tonight, Wolf Call*
SOUNDTRACK: RCA

Yet another dumb Elvis vehicle – somebody hires El as a chaperone (!) for a group of girls on a trip to Fort Lauderdale. *Do the Clam* is a strong contender for the worst Elvis song title, too.

GIRL'S TOWN A.K.A. THE INNOCENT AND THE DAMNED 1959
Metro Goldwyn Mayer, black & white, 92 minutes

DIRECTOR: Charles Haas
PRODUCER: Albert Zugsmith
SCREENPLAY: Robert Smith
SONGS: Paul Anka
CAST: Mamie Van Doren, Mel Tormé, Paul Anka
MUSICAL PERFORMERS: Paul Anka, the Platters, Mamie Van Doren
SONGS PERFORMED: *Ave Maria, Lonely Boy, Time to Cry*, Paul Anka; *Girls' Town*, Mamie Van Doren and Paul Anka; *Wish It Were Me*, the Platters; *Hey Mama*, Mamie Van Doren

Amazing film in which Mamie Van Doren is sent to a prison farm run by *nuns*. The musical numbers make absolutely no sense. This is a really classic exploitationer, and nobody could

GIRL'S TOWN   Paul Anka appeared briefly in this exploitation flick.

MUSICALS

take it seriously today. The question is, could they ever?

GIRLS GIRLS GIRLS 1962
Paramount Pictures, color, 106 minutes

DIRECTOR: Norman Taurog
PRODUCER: Hal B. Wallis
SCREENPLAY: Anthony Wallace, Allan Weiss
SCORE: Joseph J. Lilley
MUSICAL NUMBERS STAGED BY: Charles O'Curran
TECHNICAL ADVISOR: Col. Tom Parker
CAST: Elvis Presley, Stella Stevens, Laurel Goodwin, Benson Fong, Beulah Quo, Jeremy Slate
MUSICAL PERFORMERS: Elvis Presley, the Jordanaires, Stella Stevens
SONGS PERFORMED: *A Boy Like Me A Girl Like You, Dainty Little Moonbeam, Earth Boy, Girls Girls Girls, I Don't Wanna Be Tied, Return to Sender, Thanks to the Rolling Sea, Song of the Shrimp, The Walls Have Ears, We'll Be Together, We're Comin' In Loaded, Where Do You Come From,* Elvis Presley; *The Nearness of You, Never Let Me Go,* Stella Stevens
SOUNDTRACK: RCA
VIDEO: Heron – UK; Key – US

Elvis is surprisingly vital in this one, singing and dancing up a storm. It's hard to see why, since it's the usual slight story, about a fisherman who works as a nightclub singer to earn money to buy his own boat. There are the usual complications with girls, of course, and I'm afraid he does sing a number with cute children. But best of all, there is the terrific *Return to Sender*, and El is a live wire throughout.

GIRLS ON THE BEACH 1965
Paramount Pictures, color, 85 minutes

DIRECTOR: William M. Witney
PRODUCER: Harvey Jacobson
SCREENPLAY: David Malcolm
MUSIC: Gary Usher

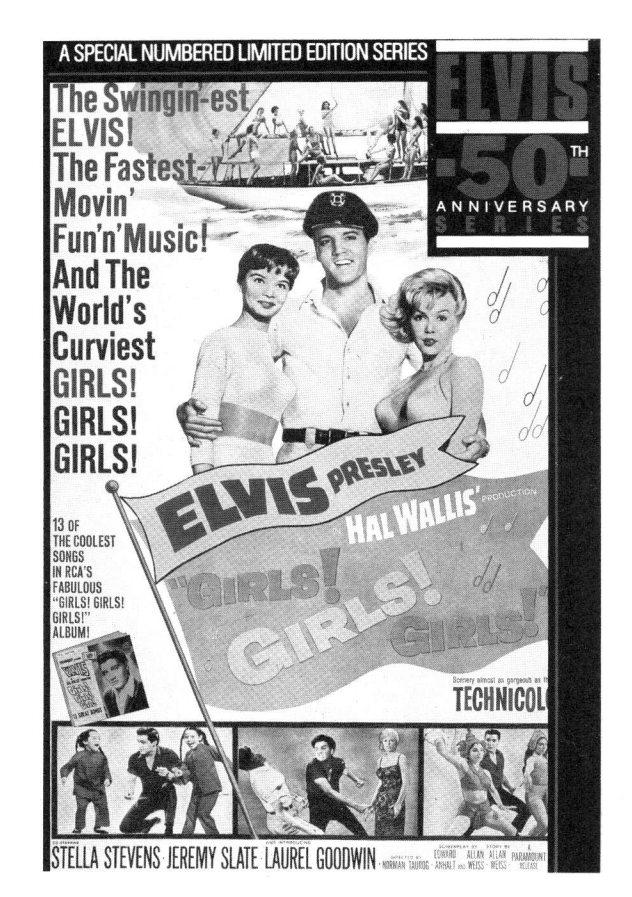

GIRLS GIRLS GIRLS

MUSICAL SUPERVISION: Nik Venet
CAST: Noreen Corcoran, Martin West, Peter Brooks, Lana Wood
MUSICAL PERFORMERS: the Beach Boys, the Crickets, Lesley Gore
SONGS PERFORMED: *The Girls On the Beach, Little Honda, The Lonely Sea,* the Beach Boys; *La Bamba,* the Crickets; *I Don't Want To Be a Loser, It's Gotta Be You, Leave Me Alone,* Lesley Gore

Girl students organize a rock concert to raise funds for their sorority; they think they've booked the Beatles (notice how a lot of these pictures work the Beatles in without our actually seeing them?) but they haven't. They get the Beach Boys instead and all is eventually well.

GIVE MY REGARDS TO BROAD STREET 1985
Thorn-EMI Pictures, color, 102 minutes

DIRECTOR: Peter Webb
PRODUCER: Andros Eraminondas
SCREENPLAY: Paul McCartney
MUSIC: Paul McCartney
MUSIC PRODUCED AND DIRECTED BY: George Martin
COSTUMES: David Toguri
CAST: Paul McCartney, Bryan Brown, Barbara Bach, Ringo Starr, Linda McCartney, Tracey Ullman, Ralph Richardson, George Martin
MUSICAL PERFORMERS: Paul McCartney and Band consisting of Ringo Starr, Dave Edmunds, John Paul Jones, Linda McCartney, Chris Spedding, Eric Stewart
SONGS PERFORMED: *Ballroom Dancing, Eleanor Rigby, For No One, Medley: Good Day Sunshine, Yesterday, Here There and Everywhere, No More Lonely Nights, Not Such a Bad Boy, Silly Love Songs, So Bad, Wanderlust*
SOUNDTRACK SONGS: *Band On the Run, The Long and Winding Road*
VIDEO: Thorn–EMI – UK; Twentieth Century Fox – US

String of videos loosely strung together by a story about some lost master tapes for an album. Some of the videos are excellent, in fact, especially a futuristic version of *Silly Love Songs*, but the connecting plotline is limp. It isn't a bad idea, but very badly written by McCartney himself; it's more a sketch than a script. That said, the movie isn't unenjoyable, and the music is the best he's done in years.

GO JOHNNY GO 1958
Hal Roach Releases, black & white, 75 minutes

DIRECTOR: Paul Landres
PRODUCER: Alan Freed
SCREENPLAY: Gary Alexander
CAST: Alan Freed, Chuck Berry, Jimmy Clanton, Sandy Stewart, Herb Vigran
MUSICAL PERFORMERS: Chuck Berry, the Cadillacs, Jo-Ann Campbell, Jimmy Clanton, Eddie Cochran, the Flamingos, Harvey Fuqua, Sandy Stewart, Ritchie Valens, Jackie Wilson
SONGS PERFORMED: *Go Johnny Go, Little Queenie, Memphis Tennessee*, Chuck Berry; *Jay Walker, Please Mr Johnson*, the Cadillacs; *Momma Can I Go Out?*, Jo-Ann Campbell; *Angel Face, It Takes A Long Time, My Love Is True, Ship On a Stormy Sea*, Jimmy Clanton; *Teenage Heaven*, Eddie Cochran; *Jump Children*, the Flamingos; *Don't Be Afraid to Love Me*, Harvey Fuqua; *Heavenly Father, Playmate*, Sandie Stewart; *Once Again*, Sandie Stewart, Jimmy Clanton; *Ooh My Head*, Ritchie Valens; *You'd Better Know It*, Jackie Wilson

GO JOHNNY GO (left to right) Chuck Berry, Sandie Stewart, Alan Freed, Jimmy Clanton.

This is a real beaut from Alan Freed, in which Jimmy Clanton is an ex-choirboy (he gets kicked out of the choir for singing jungle music) who eventually becomes a singing star. There is a host of terrific guest stars, as in all Freed pictures, and Clanton is pretty good too. But best of all, Chuck Berry plays himself in a speaking role, and shows that if life were fair he could have been a movie star too. And watch for the scene, set in a nightclub after hours, where Alan Freed plays drums with Berry's combo and enjoys himself mightily. He deserved it.

MUSICALS

GODSPELL 1973
Columbia-Warner, color, 110 minutes

DIRECTOR: David Greene
PRODUCER: Edgar Lansbury
SCREENPLAY: John-Michael Tebelak
MUSIC AND LYRICS: Stephen Schwarz
CAST: Victor Garber, David Haskell, Jerry Sroka, Lynne Thigpen
SONGS PERFORMED: *All For the Best, Beautiful City, Bless the Lord, By My Side, Christ the Clown, Day By Day, Turn Back O Man*
SOUNDTRACK: Bell

Admittedly this has some good tunes, but the exposition is relentlessly cutesy and flower-power. There is nothing worse than a Jesus-freak who is also a hippie.

Advertisement for GODSPELL.

GODSPELL Jesus and Judas.

THE GOLDEN DISC

THE GOLDEN DISC Terry Dene...

...and Nancy Whiskey.

CHRISTMAS GREETINGS

to all of you who helped make 1958 a wonderful year for me — may 1959 be as bright for you

NANCY WHISKEY

Direction: SONNY ZAHL, KAVANAGH PRODUCTIONS, 201 Regent St., London, W.1

THE GOLDEN DISC 1958
Butcher's, black & white, 78 minutes

DIRECTOR: Don Sharp
PRODUCER: W. G. Chambers
STORY: Gee Nichol
MUSICAL DIRECTOR: Philip Green
CAST: Terry Dene, Lee Patterson, Mary Steele
MUSICAL PERFORMERS: Terry Dene, the Terry Kennedy Group, the Sonny Stewart Skiffle Group, Nancy Whiskey
SONGS PERFORMED: *Before We Say Goodbye, Candy Floss, Charm, C'Mon and Be Loved, Golden Age, I'm Gonna Wrap You Up, In-Between Age, Johnny O, Let Me Lie*

Slight story about coffee-bar owners who form a record company to support their oddly assorted mix of musical performers. Not exactly thrilling.

GONKS GO BEAT Lulu and the Luvvers guested on this one.

A MERRY VERY TO EACH AND EVERY

LULU AND **THE LUVVERS**

55

GONKS GO BEAT 1965
Warner Brothers, color, 92 minutes

DIRECTOR: Robert Hartford-Davis
PRODUCERS: Robert Hartford-Davis, Peter Newbrook
SCREENPLAY: Robert Hartford-Davis, Peter Newbrook, Jimmy Watson
CAST: Kenneth Connor, Jerry Desmonds, Terry Scott, Frank Thornton, Barbara Brown
MUSICAL PERFORMERS: Alan David, Elaine and Derek, the Graham Bond Organization, Ray Lewis and the Trekkers, the Long and the Short, Lulu and the Luvvers, the Troles, the Vacqueros

With a title like that you just know it's going to be terrible, and it *is*. It involves emissaries from the planet Gonk who stop a war between 'Beatland' and 'Balladisle' – yuck.

GOOD TIMES 1967
Columbia Pictures, color, 91 minutes

DIRECTOR: William Friedkin
PRODUCER: Lindsley Parsons
SCREENPLAY: Tony Barrett
MUSIC: Sonny Bono

GOOD TIMES Sonny and Cher.

CHOREOGRAPHY: Andre Taylor
COSTUMES: Leah Rhodes
CAST: Sonny and Cher Bono, George Sanders, Larry Duran, Norman Alden, Edy Williams
MUSICAL PERFORMERS: Sonny and Cher
SONGS PERFORMED: *Bang Bang, Don't Talk To Strangers, Good Times, I Got You Babe, I'm Gonna Love You, It's the Little Things, Just a Name, Trust Me*
SOUNDTRACK: Atco – US

Sonny and Cher decide to make a movie and dream up all the films they *could* make, including westerns, detective movies and a Tarzan picture. Pretty cute all around, with good music and a firm visual guide in director William Friedkin.

GREASE 1978
Paramount Pictures, color, 110 minutes

DIRECTOR: Randal Kleiser
PRODUCERS: Allen Carr, Robert Stigwood
SCREENPLAY: Bronté Woodard
FROM THE STAGE MUSICAL BY: Warren Casey, Jim Jacobs
CHOREOGRAPHY: Patricia Birch
CAST: John Travolta, Olivia Newton-John, Stockard Channing, Jeff Conaway, Lorenzo Lamas, Frankie Avalon, Edd Byrnes
MUSICAL PERFORMERS: Frankie Avalon, Stockard Channing, Olivia Newton-John, Sha-Na-Na, Louis St Louis, John Travolta, Frankie Valli
SONGS PERFORMED: *Beauty School Dropout*, Frankie Avalon; *Look At Me, I'm Sandra Dee*, Stockard Channing; *Hopelessly Devoted to You*, Olivia Newton-John; *Summer Nights, You're the One That I Want, We Go Together*, Olivia Newton-John and John Travolta; *Rock'n'Roll Party Queen*, Louis St Louis; *Sandy*, John Travolta; *Blue Moon, Born to Hand Jive, Hound Dog, Rock'n'Roll Is Here to Stay, Tears On My Pillow, Those Magic Changes*, Sha-Na-Na; *Grease*, Frankie Valli

Olivia Newton-John and John Travolta in GREASE.

GREASE

MUSICALS

SOUNDTRACK: RSO
VIDEO: CIC – UK; Paramount – US

Somebody really tried with this one – true, they lost the period feel of the original musical by adding modern songs, and the production is too overblown to retain much intimacy, but Travolta and Newton-John are just right for their parts, and Jeff Conaway and Stockard Channing are also very good as the best friend and the tough girl. An appearance (literally) by Frankie Avalon as a sort of angel singing *Beauty School Dropout* is irresistible in its good nature.

THE GROOVE TUBE   1974
GTO, color, 75 minutes

DIRECTOR: Ken Shapiro
PRODUCER: Ken Shapiro
SCREENPLAY: Lane Sarasohn, Ken Shapiro
CAST: Richard Baier, Richard Belzer, Chevy Chase, Berkeley Harris, Buzzy Linhart, Mary Mendham, Lane Sarasohn, Ken Shapiro
MUSICAL PERFORMERS: the Dreams, Buzzy Linhart, Curtis Mayfield
SONGS PERFORMED: *The Dealer's Theme*, the Dreams; *Fingers*, Buzzy Linhart; *Move On Up*, Curtis Mayfield
VIDEO: Media – US

A series of satiric sketches and blackouts, with Buzzy Linhart in an acting role as well as performing a song. This is a largely hit-and-miss affair; some bits are hilarious and some fall flat. It can't be all bad with Richard Belzer in it, though.

HAIR   1979
United Artists, color, 121 minutes

DIRECTOR: Milos Foreman
PRODUCERS: Michael Butler, Lester Persky
SCREENPLAY: Michael Weller
FROM: the Broadway musical

MUSIC: Galt McDermot
LYRICS: James Rado, Gerome Ragni
CHOREOGRAPHY: Twyla Tharp
CAST: John Savage, Treat Williams, Beverly D'Angelo, Annie Golden, Nicholas Ray, Donnie Dacus
SONGS PERFORMED: *Abie Baby, Air, Don't Put It Down, Donna, Easy To Be Hard, Electric Blues, Flesh Departures, Fourscore, Frank Mills, Good Morning Starshine, Hair, Hare Krishna, Hashish, I'm Black, I Got Life, L.B.J., Let the Sunshine In, Manchester, My Conviction, Old Fashioned Melody, Party Music, Sodomy, Somebody To Hold, Somebody To Love, 3-5-0-0, Walking In Space, What a Piece of Work Is Man, Where Do I Go*
SOUNDTRACK: RCA
VIDEO: Twentieth Century Fox – US

Treat Williams and Annie Golden in HAIR.

A very strange choice for director Milos Foreman, this belated tribute to anti-war protest and the counter-culture in America is nevertheless very interesting and watchable. It is a kind of elegy for hippiedom, set in 1968. We see a young conscript on his way to report for duty in the army (and, we conclude, be sent to Vietnam). On his way he falls in with a magical series of flower-power characters; he almost floats around New York, which looks beautiful and mysterious, for his last day of freedom. The cinematography and off-beat choreography by Twyla Tharp (look for the dancing police horses) create a dream-like feeling of powerful nostalgia for the days when people really believed in the Age of Aquarius.

A HARD DAY'S NIGHT 1964
United Artists, black & white, 85 minutes

DIRECTOR: Richard Lester
PRODUCER: Walter Shenson
SCREENPLAY: Alun Owen
MUSIC: John Lennon, Paul McCartney
MUSICAL DIRECTOR: George Martin
CAST: John Lennon, Paul McCartney, George Harrison, Ringo Starr, Wilfred Brambell, Norman Rossington, John Junkin, Victor Spinetti, Anna Quale
MUSICAL PERFORMERS: the Beatles
SONGS PERFORMED: *And I Love Her, Can't Buy Me Love, A Hard Day's Night, I Should Have Known Better, I'll Cry Instead, I'm Happy Just to Dance With You, If I Fell, Tell Me Why*
SOUNDTRACK SONGS: *Any Time At All, I Wanna Hold Your Hand, She Loves You*
SOUNDTRACK: United Artists – US; Parlophone – UK
VIDEO: Vintage – US

A HARD DAY'S NIGHT (left to right) George, Ringo, Paul and John: 'Please mister, can we have our ball back?'

A HARD DAY'S NIGHT Wilfred Brambell and Ringo.

Everything is just right about this film – the music, the performances, the fresh, sharp direction. The script by Alun Owen, basically the events of one day in the progress of a tour, provides a framework on which to display each Beatle personality in turn, and they shine. So does the supporting cast, with Victor Spinetti a standout as a very nervous television director. One of the best.

THE HARDER THEY COME 1972
New World Films, color, 110 minutes

DIRECTOR: Perry Henzell
PRODUCER: Perry Henzell
SCREENPLAY: Perry Henzell, Trevor Rhone
CAST: Jimmy Cliff, Janet Barkley, Carl Bradshaw, Bobby Charlton, Ras Daniel Hartman, Winston Stona

MUSICALS

UK advertisement for THE HARDER THEY COME.

MUSICAL PERFORMER: Jimmy Cliff
SONGS PERFORMED: *The Harder They Come, Many Rivers to Cross, Sitting In Limbo, You Can Get It If You Really Want It*
SOUNDTRACK SONGS: *Shanty Town*, Desmond Dekker; *Pressure Drop, Sweet and Dandy*, the Maytals; *Rivers of Babylon*, the Melodians; *Draw Your Brakes*, Scotty; *Johnny Too Bad*, the Slickers
SOUNDTRACK: Mango – US; Island – UK
VIDEO: Thorn – US

Gritty and colorful story of corruption in the Jamaican music business, with Cliff as a young reggae singer fighting his way to the top and running into trouble. The music is great and the drama compelling.

HAREM HOLIDAY see **HARUM SCARUM**

HARUM SCARUM A.K.A **HAREM HOLIDAY** 1965
Metro Goldwyn Mayer, color, 95 minutes

DIRECTOR: Gene Nelson
PRODUCER: Sam Katzman
CAST: Elvis Presley, Mary Ann Mobley, Michael Ansara, Fran Jeffries
MUSICAL PERFORMER: Elvis Presley
SONGS PERFORMED: *Go East Young Man, Golden Coins, Harem Holiday, Hey Little Girl, Kismet, Mirage, My Desert Serenade, Shake the Tambourine, So Close and Yet So Far (From Paradise)*
SOUNDTRACK: RCA
VIDEO: MGM–UA – US

Really stupid idea – Elvis gets involved in an attempted assassination of a Middle-Eastern ruler. There's not really much else to say about it, is there? And no good songs.

HARUM SCARUM   Elvis looks ridiculous in a turban and . . .

HURUM SCARUM ... there he is in action.

HEAD Peter Tork.

HEAD 1968
Columbia Pictures, color, 86 minutes

DIRECTOR: Bob Rafelson
PRODUCERS: Jack Nicholson, Bob Rafelson, Bert Schneider
SCREENPLAY: Jack Nicholson, Bob Rafelson
CHOREOGRAPHY: Toni Basil
CAST: the Monkees (Mickey Dolenz, Davy Jones, Michael Nesmith, Peter Tork (Torokvei)), Timothy Carey, Annette Funicello, Sonny Liston, Victor Mature, Frank Zappa, Jack Nicholson, Bob Rafelson
MUSICAL PERFORMERS: the Monkees
SONGS PERFORMED: *As We Go Along, Can You Dig It?, Circle Sky, Daddy's Song, Long Title – Do I Have to Do This All Over Again?, Porpoise Song*
SOUNDTRACK: Colgems – US; RCA – UK

Very enjoyable and innocent trip-movie, a series of brief adventures in parody Westerns, prison movies, horror films, etc. The music isn't their best, but there's considerable nostalgia in this last gasp of sincere flower-power, before things began to go wrong.

Davy Jones in HEAD.

MUSICALS

A production shot from HEAD. Micky Dolenz submerges (left).

HEDY 1965
Filmmakers Co-Op, black & white, 70 minutes

DIRECTOR: Andy Warhol
PRODUCER: Andy Warhol
SCREENPLAY: Ronnie Tavel
IMPROVISED MUSIC: the Velvet Underground
CAST: Maria Montez, Mary Woronov, Jack Smith

Warhol and company re-tell the story of Hedy Lamarr's arrest for shoplifting. It's hard to see the point, beyond exploitation and general nastiness, but some people like that sort of thing.

HELP! 1965
United Artists, color, 92 minutes

DIRECTOR: Richard Lester
PRODUCER: Walter Shenson
SCREENPLAY: Marc Behm, Charles Wood
MUSICAL DIRECTOR: George Martin
CAST: John Lennon, Paul McCartney, George Harrison, Ringo Starr, Leo McKern, Eleanor Bron, Victor Spinetti, Roy Kinnear, Patrick Cargill
MUSICAL PERFORMERS: the Beatles
SONGS PERFORMED: *Another Girl, Help, I Need You, The Night Before, Ticket To Ride, You're Going To Lose That Girl, You've Got To Hide Your Love Away*
SOUNDTRACK: Capitol – US; Parlophone – UK

At the time of its release, everyone said this wasn't as good as *A HARD DAY'S NIGHT*.

HELP George Harrison, Eleanor Bron, Ringo Starr, Paul McCartney, John Lennon.

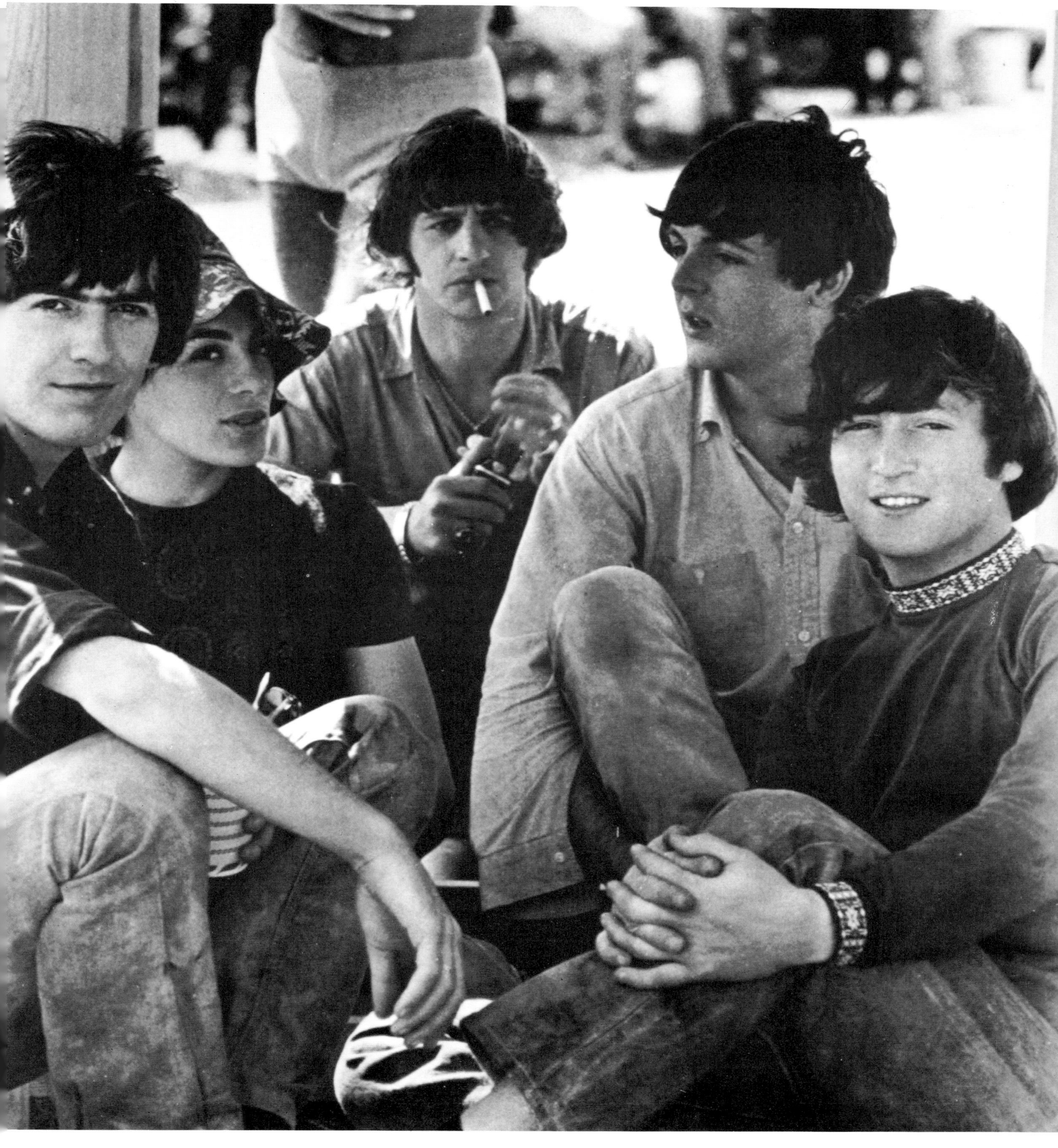

HELP! Leo McKern stepping on Eleanor Bron (left) and Ringo (right).

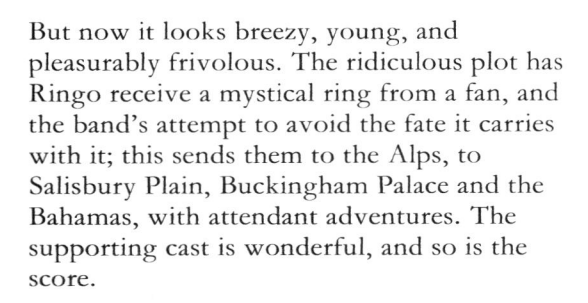

HOLD ON Starring Herman's Hermits.

But now it looks breezy, young, and pleasurably frivolous. The ridiculous plot has Ringo receive a mystical ring from a fan, and the band's attempt to avoid the fate it carries with it; this sends them to the Alps, to Salisbury Plain, Buckingham Palace and the Bahamas, with attendant adventures. The supporting cast is wonderful, and so is the score.

HEY LET'S TWIST   1961
Paramount Pictures, black & white, 80 minutes

DIRECTOR: Greg Garrison
PRODUCER: Harry Romm
CAST: Joey Dee, Zohra Lampert, Jo-Ann Campbell, Teddy Randazzo
MUSICAL PERFORMERS: Jo-Ann Campbell, Joey Dee and the Starlighters, Teddy Randazzo
SONGS PERFORMED: *Let's Do My Twist*, Jo-Ann Campbell; *Roly-Poly*, Joey Dee; *Hey Let's Twist, Peppermint Twist, Shout*, Joey Dee and the Starlighters; *Joey's Blues*, Dave and the Starlighters; *It's a Pity to Say Goodnight*, Teddy Randazzo
SOUNDTRACK: Roulette – US; Columbia – UK

This *sort* of takes place in the Peppermint Lounge, but that's about all the plot there is. It's a terrific song line-up, mostly by Joey Dee and the Starlighters, and Jo-Ann Campbell is always worth watching in her all-too-rare film appearances.

HOLD ON   1965
Metro Goldwyn Mayer, color, 86 minutes

DIRECTOR: Arthur Lubin
PRODUCER: Sam Katzman
SCREENPLAY: James B. Gordon
CHOREOGRAPHY: Wilda Taylor
CAST: Herman's Hermits (Peter Noone, Karl Green, Derek Leckenby, Barry Whitwam), Shelley Fabares, Sue Ann Langdon
MUSICAL PERFORMERS: Herman's Hermits
SONGS PERFORMED: *A Must To Avoid, All the Things I Do for You Baby, The George and Dragon, Got a Feeling, Gotta Get Away, Hold On, Leaning On the Lamppost, Make Me Happy, We Want You Herman, Where Were You When I Needed You, Wild Love*
SOUNDTRACK: MGM

Really ridiculous story which suggests that NASA would consider naming a spacecraft after Herman's Hermits. Pretty pathetic stuff. Sam Katzman had a lot to answer for, one way or another.

THE HORROR OF PARTY BEACH   1963
Twentieth Century Fox, black & white, 78 minutes

DIRECTOR: Del Tenney
PRODUCER: Del Tenney
SCREENPLAY: Richard L. Hilliard
CAST: John Scott, Alice Lyon, Marilyn Clark,

Allen Laurel, Eulabelle Moore
MUSICAL PERFORMERS: the Del-Aires
SONGS PERFORMED: *Drag, Wigglin'n'Wobblin', You Are Not a Summer Love, The Zombie Stomp*

This really *is* the worst. Lousy music, lousy cast, lousy everything. Quite unwatchable – however, it does at least have a real monster, who understandably attacks that rotten band.

HOT ROD GANG A.K.A. FURY UNLEASHED 1958
American International Pictures, black & white, 72 minutes

DIRECTOR: Lew Landers
PRODUCER: Buddy Rogers
SCREENPLAY: Lou Rusoff
CAST: John Ashley, Gene Vincent, Jody Farr
MUSICAL PERFORMERS: Gene Vincent and the Blue Caps
SONGS PERFORMED: *Baby Blue, Dance In the Streets, Dance to the Bop, Lovely Loretta*
SOUNDTRACK: EP   Capitol – US

Neat little teen exploitation flick which gives Gene Vincent his only speaking role: he's the hero's sidekick whose band raises entrance fee money for a hot-rod race. Vincent is very charming, and his four songs are among his best. It's hard to realize that this was considered dangerous rabble-rousing stuff at that time, and the British release was considerably delayed; note the title change, too. Apparently it was unthinkable to say 'hot rod' in public, for fear of arousing disorder.

HOUND DOG MAN 1959
Twentieth Century Fox, color, 87 minutes

DIRECTOR: Don Siegel
PRODUCER: Jerry Wald
SCREENPLAY: Fred Gipson, Walter Miller
FROM: a novel by Fred Gipson

HOUND DOG MAN   Fabian.

CAST: Stuart Whitman, Fabian, Carol Lynley
MUSICAL PERFORMER: Fabian
SONGS PERFORMED: *Hayfoot Strawfoot, Hilltop Song, Hound Dog Man, I'm Growing Up, Pretty Little Girl, Single, This Friendly World, What a Big Boy*

Mild backwoods drama set in 1912, which makes Fabian's songs rather out of place. Not a bad cast, but the story, about a drifter admired by local teenagers, is over-earnest and dull.

HOW TO STUFF A WILD BIKINI 1965
American International Pictures, color, 93 minutes

DIRECTOR: William Asher
PRODUCERS: Samuel Z. Arkoff, James H. Nicholson
SCREENPLAY: William Asher, Leo Townsend
CAST: Frankie Avalon, Annette Funicello, Dwayne Hickman, Buster Keaton, Harvey Lembeck, Mickey Rooney
MUSICAL PERFORMERS: Annette Funicello, the Kingsmen
SONGS PERFORMED: *Better Be Ready, The Perfect Boy*, Annette Funicello; *Give Her Lovin', How to Stuff a Wild Bikini*
SOUNDTRACK: Wand – US
VIDEO: WEA – US

Just about what you'd expect from a movie with this title – which has nothing to do with the plot, but how could it? Frankie joins the Navy Reserve and hires a witch-doctor to watch Annette; meanwhile, Erich Von Zipper gets up to his old tricks. The script isn't as cringe-making as usual, but the music is poor.

IDLE ON PARADE 1959
Columbia, black & white, 94 minutes

DIRECTOR: John Gilling
EXECUTIVE PRODUCERS: Irving Allen, Albert R. Broccoli
PRODUCER: Harold Huthe
SCREENPLAY: John Antrobus
FROM: a novel by John Camp
MUSIC: Bill Shepherd
CAST: Anthony Newley, Anne Aubrey, William Bendix, Sidney James, Lionel Jeffries, David Lodge
MUSICAL PERFORMER: Anthony Newley
SONGS PERFORMED: *Idle On Parade, Idle Rock A Boogie, I've Waited So Long, Saturday Night Rock A Boogie*

Awful attempt to pass Anthony Newley off as a rock star. No wonder Brits never made it in America until the Beatles. It's sort-of based on Elvis' induction into the Army, as Jeep Jones, teen idol (Newley), does his national service. The cast isn't all bad, but the songs are terrible.

THE IDOLMAKER 1980
United Artists, color, 116 minutes

DIRECTOR: Taylor Hackford
PRODUCERS: Gene Kirkwood, Howard W. Koch, Jr.
SCREENPLAY: Edward di Lorenzo
SONGS: Jeff Barry
TECHNICAL ADVISOR: Robert Marucci
CAST: Ray Sharkey, Paul Land, Peter Gallagher, Tovah Feldshuh
MUSICAL PERFORMERS: Jessie Frederick (for Paul Land), Peter Gallagher
SONGS PERFORMED: *Here Is My Love, Sweet Little Lover*, Jessie Frederick; *Baby, However Dark the Night*, Peter Gallagher
SOUNDTRACK SONGS: *I Can't Tell*, Colleen Fitzpatrick; *Ooo-Wee Baby*, Darlene Love; *A Boy and A Girl*, the Sweet Inspirations; *Come and Get It, I Believe It Can Be Done, I Know Where You're Goin'*, Nino Tempo
SOUNDTRACK: A&M – US
VIDEO: MGM–UA – UK

A good idea, with a fine performance by Ray Sharkey, is messed up as usual by the studio's totally failed attempt to get hit records out of the soundtrack. The film traces the career of the high-powered manager who makes stars out of inexperienced teenagers. This all takes place in about 1960, the era of Fabian and Ricky Nelson, but unfortunately the music is all soft-rock, semi-disco pap. Otherwise, it's very good, with Sharkey's Svengali frantically wheeling and dealing in his protegé's interest, only to be betrayed when they finally hit the top. Well worth watching, despite the songs.

THE INNOCENT AND THE DAMNED   see   GIRL'S TOWN

IT HAPPENED AT THE WORLD'S FAIR   1963
Metro Goldwyn Mayer, color, 105 minutes

DIRECTOR: Norman Taurog
PRODUCER: Ted Richmond
SCREENPLAY: Seamon Jacobs, Si Rose
CAST: Elvis Presley, Joan O'Brien, Gary Lockwood, Vicky Tu, H.M. Tynant
MUSICAL PERFORMER: Elvis Presley
SONGS PERFORMED: *Beyond the Bend, Cotton Candy Land, Happy Ending, How Would You Like To Be?, I'm Falling In Love Tonight, One Broken Heart, Relax, Take Me to the Fair, They Remind Me Too Much of You, A World of Our Own*
SOUNDTRACK: RCA
VIDEO: MGM–UA – US

Really the worst. El finds a cute lost child (ugh) at the Seattle World's Fair, and helps her find her family. Dim and dragging, with inferior songs.

IT'S A BIKINI WORLD   1967
Trans American Pictures, color, 86 minutes

DIRECTOR: Stephanie Rothman
PRODUCER: Charles S. Swartz
SCREENPLAY: Stephanie Rothman, Charles S. Swartz

CAST: Tommy Kirk, Deborah Walley, Suzie Kaye, Robert (Bobby 'Boris') Pickett
MUSICAL PERFORMERS: the Animals, the Castaways, the Gentrys, the Toys, Pat and Lolly Vegas
SONGS PERFORMED: *We Gotta Get Out of This Place*, the Animals; *I'll Be Unhappy*, the Castaways; *Peanut Butter and Jam*, the Gentrys; *Walk On*, Pat and Lolly Vegas; *All's Fair In Love and War*, the Toys

Dopey plot has Tommy Kirk masquerading as his own brother to prove he's a nice guy. Not funny, but some good music. I wonder what the Animals thought they were getting into.

IT'S ALL HAPPENING   1963
British Lion, black & white, 101 minutes

DIRECTOR: Don Sharp
PRODUCER: Norman Williams
MUSIC: Philip Green
LYRICS: Norman Newall
MUSICAL DIRECTOR: Philip Green
CAST: Tommy Steele, Angela Douglas, Michael Medwin, Shane Fenton, John Barry
MUSICAL PERFORMERS: John Barry, John Boulter, Clyde Valley Stompers, Russ Conway, Carol Deene, Shane Fenton and the Fentones, Dai Francis, Dick Kallman, Johnny de Little, Geoff Love, Tony Mercer, the George Mitchell Show, Marion Ryan, Tommy Steele, Danny Williams
SOUNDTRACK: Columbia – UK

A record company puts on a concert to raise funds for an orphanage. Fairly dull all around, with a strange mix of performers.

IT'S ALL OVER TOWN   1964
British Lion, 55 minutes

DIRECTOR: Douglas Hickox
PRODUCER: Jacques de Lane Lea
ADDITIONAL MATERIAL BY: Lance Percival, William Rushton

MUSICALS

IT'S ALL OVER TOWN   Dusty guested with the Springfields.

IT'S TRAD, DAD   Helen Shapiro was among many musical acts in this one.

MUSICAL DIRECTOR: Ivor Raymonde
CAST: Lance Percival, Willie Rushton, Acker Bilk
MUSICAL PERFORMERS: Acker Bilk, the Bachelors, Wayne Gibson and the Dynamite Sounds, the Hollies, the Springfields
SONGS PERFORMED: *Come On Let's Go*, Wayne Gibson and the Dynamite Sounds, *Now's the Time*, the Hollies; *Down and Out, Maraca Bamba*, the Springfields

Another loser with hardly any plot and an odd mix of musical styles. The Hollies and the Springfields (with Dusty) are worth seeing, that's all.

IT'S TRAD, DAD A.K.A. RING-A-DING RHYTHM   1962
Columbia Pictures, black & white, 78 minutes

DIRECTOR: Richard Lester
PRODUCER: Milton Subotsky
SCREENPLAY: Milton Subotsky

CAST: Craig Douglas, Felix Felton, Arthur Mullard, Helen Shapiro
MUSICAL PERFORMERS: Gary 'U.S.' Bonds, the Brook Brothers, Chubby Checker, Craig Douglas, John Leyton, Gene McDaniels, the Paris Sisters, Helen Shapiro, Del Shannon, Gene Vincent and Sounds Incorporated
SONGS PERFORMED: *Seven Day Weekend*, Gary 'U.S.' Bonds; *Lose Your Inhibition Twist*, Chubby Checker; *Rainbows, Ring-A-Ding Day*, Craig Douglas; *Lonely City*, John Leyton; *Another Tear Falls*, Gene McDaniels; *Let's Talk About Love, Sometime Yesterday*, Helen Shapiro; *You Never Talk About Me*, Del Shannon; *Space Ship to Mars*, Gene Vincent and Sounds Incorporated
SOUNDTRACK: Columbia

The usual let's-convince-the-grownups-that-rock-is-okay storyline, but directed with more flair than usual by Richard Lester. Fortunately a song comes along about every five minutes.

I'VE GOTTA HORSE 1965
Warner Brothers, color, 92 minutes

DIRECTOR: Kenneth Hulme
PRODUCER: Kenneth Hulme
SCREENPLAY: Ronald Chesney, Ronald Wolfe
STORY: Kenneth Hulme, Larry Parnes
CAST: Billy Fury, Amanda Barrie, Peter Gilmore, Michael Medwin
MUSICAL PERFORMERS: Billy Fury, the Gamblers
SONGS PERFORMED: *Do the Old Soft Shoe, Find Your Dream, I Like Animals, I've Gotta Horse, Stand By Me, Won't Somebody Tell Me Why, You've Got to Look Right For the Part*, Billy Fury; *I Cried All Night*, the Gamblers
SOUNDTRACK: Decca – UK

Amazingly banal tale of Fury's love for his racehorse. The script is feeble and so are the songs, unfortunately. Fury did make some good records but none of them can be heard here.

JAILHOUSE ROCK 1957
Metro Goldwyn Mayer, black & white, 97 minutes

DIRECTOR: Richard Thorpe
PRODUCER: Pandro S. Berman
SCREENPLAY: Guy Trosper
SONGS BY: Lieber and Stoller
MUSIC SUPERVISED BY: Jeff Alexander
TECHNICAL ADVISOR: Col. Tom Parker
CAST: Elvis Presley, Judy Tyler, Mickey Shaughnessy, Jennifer Holden, Dean Jones, Vaughn Taylor
MUSICAL PERFORMERS: Elvis Presley, the Jordanaires
SONGS PERFORMED: *Baby I Don't Care, Don't Leave Me Now, I Wanna Be Free, Jailhouse Rock,*

Elvis meets an uninterested starlet (Jennifer Holden) in JAILHOUSE ROCK.

MUSICALS

JAILHOUSE ROCK The big number – once seen, never forgotten.

One More Day, Treat Me Nice, Young and Beautiful
SOUNDTRACK: RCA (EP)
VIDEO: MGM–UA – UK

A strong contender for the *best* Elvis movie, rivalled only by *King Creole*. The script, though not exactly witty, actually tries to understand the new music and its appeal to young people; the story is of a talented young ex-con who makes his way to the top of the music business step by step, with the help of an attractive young manageress. Elvis gives some classic performances of classic songs, topped off by the tremendous title number; the design, choreography (unfortunately uncredited), and gorgeous black and white photography (by Robert Bronner) have had incalculable impact on rock styles ever since.

JAMBOREE   Jimmy Bowen.

JAMBOREE A.K.A. DISC JOCKEY JAMBOREE 1957
Warner Brothers, black & white, 87 minutes

DIRECTOR: Roy Lockwood
PRODUCERS: Max J. Rosenberg, Milton Subotsky
SCREENPLAY: Lenard Kantor
CAST: Kay Medford, Robert Pastine, Paul Carr, Freda Holloway
MUSICAL PERFORMERS: Frankie Avalon and Rocca and His Saints, Count Basie, Jimmy Bowen, Paul Carr and Connie Francis (for Freda Holloway), Fats Domino, the Four Coins, Charlie Gracie, Buddy Knox, Jerry Lee Lewis, Lewis Lymon and the Teenchords, Andy Martin, Carl Perkins, Jodie Sands, Slim Whitman, Joe Williams
SONGS PERFORMED: *Don't Wanna Be Teacher's Pet*, Frankie Avalon; *Cross Over*, Jimmy Bowen; *24 Hours a Day, Who Are We to Say?*, Paul Carr and Connie Francis; *Wait and See*, Fats Domino; *A Broken Promise*, the Four Coins; *Cool Baby*, Charlie Gracie; *Hula Love*, Buddy Knox; *Great Balls of Fire*, Jerry Lee Lewis; *Your Last Chance*, Lewis Lymon and the Teenchords; *Record Hop Tonight*, Andy Martin; *Glad All Over*, Carl Perkins

Two agents put their clients, a girl singer and a boy singer, together, and find love as well as a hit-making team. End of plot. Some terrific guest performances; Carl Perkins does *not* look very sober. Several popular disc jockeys appear; at the time, it was a big shock to some parents to find that a couple of them were black.

THE JAZZ SINGER 1980
Color, 116 minutes

DIRECTOR: Richard Fleischer
CAST: Neil Diamond, Lucy Arnaz, Laurence Olivier, Catlin Adams, Paul Nicholas
MUSICAL PERFORMER: Neil Diamond
SONGS PERFORMED: *Amazed and Confused, America, Acapulco, Adom Olom, Hey Louise, Hello Again, Kol Nidre, Love On the Rocks, My Name is Yussel, On the Robert E. Lee, Songs of Life, Summerlove, You Baby*
SOUNDTRACK: Capitol

VIDEO: Thorn–EMI – UK; Paramount – US

Incredibly pretentious and embarrassing remake of the old Al Jolson movie, which was dated and sentimental *then*. For those who don't know, it concerns a singer who defies his conservative Rabbi father to become a pop singer. One song – *Love On the Rocks* – is not bad, but the film is nearly two hours long. It's a long wait.

JESUS CHRIST SUPERSTAR 1973
Universal Pictures, color, 108 minutes

DIRECTOR: Norman Jewison
PRODUCER: Norman Jewison
SCREENPLAY: Norman Jewison, Robert Stigwood
LYRICS: Tim Rice
MUSIC: Andrew Lloyd Webber
MUSICAL DIRECTOR: Andre Previn
CAST: Ted Neeley, Carl Anderson, Bob Bingham, Barry Dennen, Yvonne Elliman
SONGS PERFORMED: *Heaven On Their Mind, Hosanna, I Don't Know How to Love Him, Last Supper, Poor Jerusalem, Simon Zealots, Strange Things Mystifying, Superstar, What's the Buzz?*
SOUNDTRACK: MCA
VIDEO: CIC – UK; MCA – US

The best thing about this is that it was shot on location in Israel, and it looks good; there are some good tunes, but it just doesn't add anything or ask any interesting questions about the Gospels. So it turns out to be rather dull.

JUBILEE 1978
Libra Films, color, 104 minutes

DIRECTOR: Derek Jarman
PRODUCERS: Howard Malin, James Whaley

JESUS CHRIST SUPERSTAR   Ted Neeley as Jesus (top); Jesus and the gang (bottom).

JUST FOR FUN

JUBILEE Adam Ant, Ian Charleston.

SCREENPLAY: Derek Jarman
SCORE: Brian Eno
CAST: Jenny Runacre, Little Nell, Hermine Demoriane, Ian Charleton, Toyah Wilcox, Neil Kennedy
MUSICAL PERFORMERS: Amilcar, Chelsea, Wayne County and the Electric Chairs, Suzi Pims, Siouxsie and the Banshees
SONGS PERFORMED: *Wargasm in Pornotopia*, Amilcar; *Right to Work*, Chelsea; *Paranoia Paradise*, Wayne County and the Electric Chairs; *Jerusalem*, *Rule Brittania*, Suzi Pims; *Love In a Void*, Siouxsie and the Banshees
SOUNDTRACK: Polydor – UK
VIDEO: VCL – UK, Media – US

Queen Elizabeth the First magically visits apocalyptic modern London and falls in with a group of murderous girl punks. Extraordinarily self-conscious and pretentious attempt to analyse – or is it exploit? – punk culture, this is far too glossy and stylish to really connect with the grimy but passionate reality.

JUKE BOX RHYTHM 1959
Columbia Pictures, black & white, 81 minutes

DIRECTOR: Arthur Driefuss
PRODUCER: Sam Katzman
SCREENPLAY: Earl Baldwin, Mary C. McCall Jr
STORY: Lou Morheim
MUSICAL DIRECTOR/CHOREOGRAPHY: Hal Belfer
CAST: Jack Jones, Brian Donlevy, Hans Conreid, Jo Morrow
MUSICAL PERFORMERS: Jack Jones, the Earl Grant Trio, Johnny Otis, the Treniers
SONGS PERFORMED: *The Freeze, Juke Box Rhythm, Make Room for Joy*, Jack Jones; *I Feel It Right Here, Last Night*, the Earl Grant Trio; *Willie and the Hand Jive*, Johnny Otis; *Get Out of the Car*, the Treniers

In which it is demonstrated that Jack Jones was not cut out to be a rocker. He plays Riff Martin, who raises money for his father to put on a hit show. Unexciting, but the Treniers are great.

JUST FOR FUN 1963
Columbia Pictures, black & white, 85 minutes

DIRECTOR: Gordon Flemyng

JUST FOR FUN The Spotniks, a Swedish group, were popular at the time and guest-starred in this teen special.

Cherry Roland and Mark Wynter co-starred in JUST FOR FUN.

JUST FOR FUN Other guest performers were Jet Harris and Tony Meehan.

PRODUCER: Milton Subotsky
SCREENPLAY: Milton Subotsky
PHOTOGRAPHY: Nicholas Roeg
CAST: Mark Wynter, Cherry Vernon, Reginald Beckwith, Richard Vernon, John Wood, Alan Freeman, Jimmy Saville
MUSICAL PERFORMERS: Joe Brown and the Breakaways, Freddie Cannon, the Crickets, Jet Harris, Ketty Lester, Tony Meehan, Brian Poole and the Tremeloes, Sounds Incorporated, Jimmy Powell, the Spotniks, the Springfields, Johnny Tillotson, the Tornados, Cherry Roland, Bobby Vee, Mark Wynter
SONGS PERFORMED: *What's the Name of the Game?*, Joe Brown; *Ups and Downs of Love*, Freddie Cannon; *My Little Girl*, the Crickets; *Man From Nowhere*, Jet Harris; *Doing the Hully Gully*, Jet Harris, Tony Meehan; *All On a Warm Summer Day*, Ketty Lester; *Keep On Dancin'*, Brian Poole and the Tremeloes; *Everybody But You*, Jimmy Powell; *Just For Fun*, Cherry Roland; *Go*, Sounds Incorporated; *My Bonnie*, the Spotniks; *Little Boat*, the Springfields; *Judy*, Johnny Tillotson; *All the Stars In the Sky*, the Tornados; *The Night Has a Thousand Eyes*, *Touch Me*, Bobby Vee; *Just For Fun*, Mark Wynter
SOUNDTRACK: Decca – UK

British teens enter politics and run for office. Meanwhile, there's a parade of pop stars, some of them rarely seen, like Jet Harris and the Springfields. Pretty good overview of the early Sixties' scene just before the Beatles; after they hit, a lot of these people were never heard from again.

KEEP IT COOL see **LET'S ROCK**

KID GALAHAD   1962
Paramount Pictures, color, 95 minutes

DIRECTOR: Phil Karlson
PRODUCER: Hal Wallis
SCREENPLAY: William Fay
CAST: Elvis Presley, Gig Young, Lola Albright, Joan Blackman, Charles Bronson
MUSICAL PERFORMER: Elvis Presley
SONGS PERFORMED: *Home Is Where the Heart Is, I Got Lucky, King of the Whole Wide World, Riding the Rainbow, This Is Living, A Whistling Tune*
SOUNDTRACK: RCA (EP)

One of the middle-range of Elvis films, not truly dire but not *KING CREOLE* either. It's a remake of the 1937 Warner Brothers' movie of the same name, which has been re-made about seven times under different titles. Elvis plays a young boxer who gets mixed up with a crooked manager, his mistress, and his innocent young sister. The story is stronger than the music, which is rather second-rate, and a fine supporting cast helps.

KING CREOLE   1958
Paramount Pictures, black & white, 116 minutes

DIRECTOR: Michael Curtiz
PRODUCER: Hal Wallis
SCREENPLAY: Herbert Baker, Michael Vincent Gazzo
FROM: the novel *A Stone For Danny Fisher* by Harold Robbins
CHOREOGRAPHY: Charles O'Curran
CAST: Elvis Presley, Carolyn Jones, Walter Matthau, Dolores Hart, Dean Jagger, Vic Morrow, Paul Stewart
MUSICAL PERFORMERS: Elvis Presley, Kitty White, the Jordanaires
SONGS PERFORMED: *As Long As I Have You, Crawfish* (with Kitty White), *Dixieland Rock, Don't Ask Me Why, Hard Headed Woman, King Creole, Lover Doll, New Orleans, Steadfast Loyal and True, Trouble, Turtles Berries and Gumbo, Young Dreams*
SOUNDTRACK: RCA
VIDEO: Heron – UK; Key – US

Probably Elvis' best film, an excellent marrying of Harold Robbins tough novel of rebel youth with a New Orleans setting better suited to the Presley style. He plays a young singer who gets mixed up with a gangster (terrific Matthau) and his sultry moll. Mike Curtiz' long experience of gangster movies stands everyone in good stead; he keeps it taut, gritty, and dark. Some great music and electrifying performances by the King Himself.

KISS MEETS THE PHANTOM A.K.A. ATTACK OF THE PHANTOMS 1978
Hanna-Barbera, Kiss-Aucoin Productions made for TV, color, 104 minutes

DIRECTOR: Gordon Hessler
PRODUCERS: Joseph Barbera, William M. Aucoin
CAST: Anthony Zerbe, Deborah Ryan, Kiss (Gene Simmons, Peter Criss, Ace Freshley, Paul Stanley)
MUSICAL PERFORMERS: Kiss
SONGS PERFORMED: *Almost Human, Beth, Easy Thing, Fractured Mirror, Hold Me, Touch Me, Hooked On Rock'n'Roll, I Stole Your Love, Love In Chains, Man of 1000 Faces, Mr Make Believe, New York Groove, Radioactive, Rip and Destroy, Rock'n'Roll All Night, Shout It Out Loud, That's the Kind of Sugar Papa Likes*

A madman (Zerbe, of course) plans to replace Kiss with robots. Extremely flimsy excuse to string together many, many Kiss numbers. It's not very entertaining, either, except to die-hard fans, of whom there must have been quite a few *once*.

KISSIN' COUSINS 1964
Metro Goldwyn Mayer, color, 76 minutes

DIRECTOR: Gene Nelson
PRODUCER: Sam Katzman
SCREENPLAY: Gerald Adams, Gene Nelson
CAST: Elvis Presley, Arthur O'Connell, Yvonne Craig, Glenda Farrell
MUSICAL PERFORMER: Elvis Presley
SONGS PERFORMED: *Anyone, Barefoot Ballad, Catchin' On Fast, Kissin' Cousins, Once Is Enough, One Boy Two Little Girls, Smokey Mountain Boy, Tender Feeling, There's Gold In the Mountains*
SOUNDTRACK: RCA

Elvis plays twins, one a hillbilly and one an Air Force pilot, in this mild comedy; one of him tries to stop the government from building on virgin land. In general, the Norman Taurog series was better than the Gene Nelson series of middle-of-the-road Elvis flicks; Nelson had no feel at all for rock, and El was in danger of turning into a second-string Bing Crosby. Feeble music, too.

LET'S ROCK A.K.A. KEEP IT COOL 1958
Columbia Pictures, black & white, 80 minutes

LET'S ROCK   This was an ill-fated attempt to make Julius La Rosa a teen idol.

Paul Nicholas as Wagner in LISZTOMANIA.

LaRosa, Della Reese, the Royal Teens, the Tyrones
SONGS PERFORMED: *I'll Be Waiting There For You*, Paul Anka; *At the Hop*, Danny and the Juniors; *Here Comes Love, Secret Path of Love*, Roy Hamilton; *Casual, Crazy Party Crazy, Perfect Strangers, There Are Times*, Julius LaRosa; *Lonelyville*, Della Reese; *Short Shorts*, the Royal Teens; *Blast Off*, the Tyrones

Julius LaRosa was never exactly going to be a big threat to Elvis; in this, a crooner is taught to rock by his girlfriend (Phyllis Newman). Hardly enlivening, but you can see two classics performed: *At the Hop* and the unforgettable *Short Shorts*.

LISZTOMANIA 1975
Warner Brothers, color, 105 minutes

DIRECTOR: Ken Russell
PRODUCER: Roy Baird
SCREENPLAY: Ken Russell
MUSIC ARRANGED BY: Rick Wakeman
CAST: Roger Daltrey, Fiona Lewis, Paul Nicholas, Sarah Kestelman
SONGS PERFORMED: *Love's Dream, Orpheus Song, Peace At Last*, Roger Daltrey; *Hell*, Fiona Lewis; *Excelsior Song*, Paul Nicholas
SOUNDTRACK: A & M
VIDEO: WEA – US

Sure, it's wildly overblown, garish, and maniacal; but there is something enjoyable about Russell's view of Liszt as the first pop

Roger Daltrey in Ken Russell's LISZTOMANIA.

DIRECTOR: Harry Foster
PRODUCER: Harry Foster
SCREENPLAY: Hal Hackady
CHOREOGRAPHY: Peter Gennaro
CAST: Julius LaRosa, Phyllis Newman, Conrad Janis, Joy Harmon
MUSICAL PERFORMERS: Paul Anka, Danny and the Juniors, Roy Hamilton and the Cues, Julius

idol. It makes no sense at all, of course, but it's energetic.

LIVE A LITTLE, LOVE A LITTLE   1968
Metro Goldwyn Mayer, color, 90 minutes

DIRECTOR: Norman Taurog
PRODUCER: Douglas Lawrence
SCREENPLAY: Dan Greenburg, Michael A. Hoey
FROM: the novel *Kiss My Firm But Pliant Lips* by Dan Greenburg
CAST: Elvis Presley, Michele Carey, Don Porter, Rudy Vallee
MUSICAL PERFORMER: Elvis Presley
SONGS PERFORMED: *Almost In Love, Edge of Reality, A Little Less Conversation, Wonderful World*

One of Elvis' real losers, in which he plays an advertising executive, none too convincingly. The songs are few and weak. Altogether a waste of time.

LIVE IT UP   1963
Universal International Pictures, black & white, 84 minutes

DIRECTOR: Lance Comfort
PRODUCER: Lance Comfort
SCREENPLAY: Lyn Fairbanks
SONGS BY: Joe Meek
CAST: David Hemmings, Veronica Hurst, Heinz Burt, Steve Marriott
MUSICAL PERFORMERS: Heinz Burt, Andy Cavett and the Saints, the Outlaws, Kim Roberts, Sounds Incorporated, Gene Vincent
SONGS PERFORMED: *Don't Take You From Me*, Andy Cavett and the Saints; *Don't You Understand, Live It Up*, Heinz; *Law and Order*, the Outlaws; *Loving Me This Way*, Kim Roberts; *Keep Moving*, Sounds Incorporated; *Temptation Baby*, Gene Vincent

Feeble pre-Beatles British teenpic with a group of postal workers forming a band and going

LIVE IT UP   A publicity shot of Sounds Incorporated.

into show-biz. Unexciting guest stars, with the exception of Gene Vincent, who does one of his lesser numbers, to say the least.

THE LIVELY SET   1964
Universal International Pictures, color, 95 minutes

DIRECTOR: Jack Arnold
PRODUCER: William Alland

THE LIVELY SET Pamela Tiffin and James Darren.

SCREENPLAY: Mel Goldburg
SONGS BY: Bobby Darin, Randy Newman and Terry Melcher
CAST: James Darren, Doug McClure, Pamela Tiffin, Joanie Summers
MUSICAL PERFORMERS: James Darren, the Surfaris, Joanie Summers
SONGS PERFORMED: *The Lively Set, Look at Me*, James Darren; *Boss Barracuda*, the Surfaris; *Casey Wake Up, If You Love Him*, Joanie Summers
SOUNDTRACK: Decca – US

James Darren fights with his girlfriend and becomes a drag-racer, finally (amazingly enough) winning the big race. Actually, this *is* pretty lively, compared with some of the competition, and it's not nearly as dopey as the beach pictures. Darren, McClure and Tiffin are all practically Oliviers compared to Annette and Frankie.

LOVE IN LAS VEGAS see **VIVA LAS VEGAS**

Elvis in his first film, LOVE ME TENDER, with Debra Paget.

LOVE ME TENDER 1956
Twentieth Century Fox, black & white, 89 minutes

DIRECTOR: Robert D. Webb
PRODUCER: David Weisbart
SCREENPLAY: Robert Buckner
CAST: Elvis Presley, Richard Egan, Debra Paget, Robert Middleton
MUSICAL PERFORMER: Elvis Presley
SONGS PERFORMED: *Let Me Be, Love Me Tender, Old Shep, Poor Boy, We're Gonna Move*
SOUNDTRACK: RCA (EP)
VIDEO: Key – US

Elvis' first picture, where he plays Richard Egan's younger brother; it's a Civil-War era western about three brothers; one gets mixed up in a robbery. The drama is no great shakes, and the few songs are rather downplayed but, when the Elvis character was killed, the teenage girls in the audience wept disconsolately (I have an eyewitness account of this), and the studio knew it had a real winner on its hands.

MUSICALS

LOVING YOU 1956
Paramount Pictures, color, 101 minutes

DIRECTOR: Hal Kanter
PRODUCER: Hal Wallis
SCREENPLAY: Herbert Baker, Hal Kanter
CAST: Elvis Presley, Lizabeth Scott, Wendell Corey, Dolores Hart
MUSICAL PERFORMER: Elvis Presley
SONGS PERFORMED: *Got a Lotta Livin' To Do, Hot Dog, Let's Have a Party, Lonesome Cowboy, Loving You, Mean Woman Blues, Teddy Bear*
SOUNDTRACK: RCA
VIDEO: WEA – US

A singing truck driver is discovered and guided to stardom by a female manager. One of the better Elvis vehicles, with dynamic Deke Rivers (Elvis) joining travelling hillbilly musician Tex Warner (Wendell Corey, who steals the picture), gradually surpassing him in popularity, getting a swelled head, and finally finding himself a nice girl (Hart). And much of the music is really exciting.

MAGICAL MYSTERY TOUR 1967
Apple Films, color, 60 minutes

DIRECTORS: the Beatles
PRODUCERS: the Beatles
CAST: the Beatles, Victor Spinetti, Jessie Robins, Derek Royle
MUSICAL PERFORMERS: the Beatles
SONGS PERFORMED: *All You Need Is Love, Baby You're a Rich Man, Blue Jay Way, The Fool On the Hill, Flying, Hello Goodbye, I Am the Walrus, Magical Mystery Tour, Penny Lane, Strawberry Fields Forever, Your Mother Should Know*
SOUNDTRACK: Capitol – US
VIDEO: Media – US

It's hard to see why this was so reviled when it was first broadcast; now that we are used to elaborate videos, these early ones by the 'fab four' look imaginative and entertaining. True, the connecting link of the bus tour is pretty silly, but the songs and production numbers are marvellous. No one ever surpassed those guys for variety.

MISTER ROCK AND ROLL 1957
Paramount Pictures, black & white, 86 minutes

DIRECTOR: Charles Dubin
PRODUCER: Ralph Siepe
SCREENPLAY: James Blumgarten
CAST: Alan Freed, Teddy Randazzo, Lois O'Brien, Rocky Graziano
MUSICAL PERFORMERS: LaVerne Baker, Chuck Berry, Brook Benton, Shayle Cogan, Lionel Hampton and His Orchestra, Ferlin Husky, Little Richard, Frankie Lymon and the Teenagers, Clyde McPhatter, the Moonglows

A lesser Alan Freed vehicle with the usual great line-up of guest stars. The script (what there is of it) re-tells the story of how DJ

A poster for MISTER ROCK AND ROLL, with Alan Freed.

Freed discovered rock'n'roll. The man certainly deserved that title.

THE MONSTER CLUB 1981
Color, 93 minutes

DIRECTOR: Roy Ward Baker
CAST: Vincent Price, Donald Pleasance, Britt Ekland
MUSICAL PERFORMERS: Night, B. A. Robertson, the Viewers
SONGS PERFORMED: *The Stripper*, Night; *Sucker For Your Love*, B. A. Robertson; *Monster Rule OK*, the Viewers
SOUNDTRACK SONGS: *Valentino Had Enough*, the Expressos; *The Monster Club*, the Pretty Things; *25 Per Cent*, UB40
SOUNDTRACK: Chips – UK
VIDEO: Trilion – US

The usual anthology of horror tales, linked together this time by the setting of a club for ghouls, where various bands can be seen and heard as an added bonus. Amusing but average.

MRS BROWN YOU'VE GOT A LOVELY DAUGHTER 1968
Metro Goldwyn Mayer, color, 95 minutes

DIRECTOR: Saul Swimmer
PRODUCER: Allen Klein
SCREENPLAY: Thaddeus Vane
CAST: Herman's Hermits (Peter Noone, Karl Green, Derek Leckenby, Barry Whitwam), Stanley Holloway, Mona Washbourne, Lance Percival
MUSICAL PERFORMERS: Herman's Hermits
SONGS PERFORMED: *Daisy Chain, Holiday Inn, It's Nice to Be Out In the Morning, Lemon and Lime, The Most Beautiful Thing In My Life, Mrs Brown You've Got a Lovely Daughter, Ooh She's Done It Again, There's a Kind of Hush All Over the World, The World Is For You*
SOUNDTRACK: MGM
VIDEO: MGM–UA – US

MRS BROWN YOU'VE GOT A LOVELY DAUGHTER Sheila White (left), Peter Noone (right).

MRS BROWN YOU'VE GOT A LOVELY DAUGHTER Here are Sheila White and Peter Noone with the greyhound which constitutes the plot.

Ridiculous story has the Hermits taking their greyhound to London for the big dog races. Talk about compelling drama! You know, when this came out, there were probably tens of thousands of little teeny-bop Herman fans who were absolutely thrilled by it. Where are they now?

MUSICALS

MUSCLE BEACH PARTY 1964
American International Pictures, color, 94 minutes

DIRECTOR: William Asher
PRODUCERS: Robert Dillon, James H. Nicholson
SCREENPLAY: Robert Dillon
CAST: Frankie Avalon, Annette Funicello, Luciana Paluzzi, Morey Amsterdam, Buddy Hackett
MUSICAL PERFORMERS: Frankie Avalon, Dick Dale and the Deltones, Annette Funicello, Donna Love, Little Stevie Wonder
SONGS PERFORMED: *A Boy Needs a Girl, Runnin' Wild*, Frankie Avalon; *Surfer's Holiday*, Frankie Avalon, Annette Funicello; *My First Love*, *Muscle Beach Party*, Dick Dale and the Deltones; *A Girl Needs a Boy*, Annette Funicello; *Muscle Bustle*, Donna Love; *Happy Street*, Little Stevie Wonder
SOUNDTRACK: AIP Records – US

Pretty pathetic beach flick – princess Luciana falls for Frankie (a likely story) and her body-building boyfriend gets mad. The addition of comedians Amsterdam and Hackett does *not* make up for the lack of Erich Von Zipper.

MUSCLE BEACH PARTY   Little Stevie Wonder appears briefly in this.

MUSCLE BEACH PARTY   The whole gang (left to right): Jody McCrea, Dick Dale, John Ashley, Frankie Avalon, Annette Funicello.

NEVER TOO YOUNG TO ROCK 1975
GTO, color, 99 minutes

DIRECTOR: Dennis Abey
PRODUCERS: Roy Inkpen, Greg Smith
SCREENPLAY: Dennis Abey, Roy Inkpen
CAST: Freddie Jones, Peter Denyer, John Clive, Joe Lyneh, Peter Noone, Sally James
MUSICAL PERFORMERS: the Glitter Band, Mud, the Rubettes, Slick
SONGS PERFORMED: *Angel Face, Just For You, Let's Get Together Again*, the Glitter Band; *Dyna-Mite, Tiger Feet*, Mud; *Boogiest Band In Town*, Slick; *Sugar Baby Love*, the Rubettes
SOUNDTRACK: GTO – UK

A TV station scours the country to find new

talent. This feeble excuse allows a long string of musical interludes. Some of these bands are seldom seen however, so it might be worth watching if you like that sort of thing.

ONE TRICK PONY 1980
Warner Brothers, color, 98 minutes

DIRECTOR: Robert M. Young
PRODUCER: Michael Tannen
SCREENPLAY: Paul Simon
CAST: Paul Simon, Blair Brown, Joan Hackett, Rip Torn, Lou Reed, Marc Winningham, Allen Goorwitz
MUSICAL PERFORMERS: the B52's, the Lovin' Spoonful, Sam and Dave, Paul Simon and band (Steve Gadd, Eric Gale, Tony Levin, Richard Tee)
SONGS PERFORMED: *Rock Lobster*, the B52's; *Do You Believe In Magic?*, the Lovin' Spoonful; *Soul Man*, Sam and Dave; *Ace In the Hole, God Bless the Absentee, How the Heart Approaches What It Yearns, Jonah, Late In the Evening, Long Long Day, Oh Marion, One-Trick Pony, Nobody, That's Why God Made the Movies*, Paul Simon
SOUNDTRACK: Warner Brothers
VIDEO: WEA –US

An honest attempt at making a real modern musical, this fails mainly because of its sad-sack hero, a touring musician whose career is on the wane and who faces a mid-life crisis. There are some very effective scenes, and Paul Simon's script is well done in general, but the story sags. Worth watching, though.

OUT OF SIGHT 1966
Universal International Pictures, color, 87 minutes

DIRECTOR: Lennie Weinrib
PRODUCER: Bart Patton
SCREENPLAY: Larry Hovis
CAST: Jonathan Daly, Karen Jensen, Robert Pine, Carole Shelyne
MUSICAL PERFORMERS: the Astronauts, Freddie and the Dreamers, Dobie Gray, the Knickerbockers, Gary Lewis and the Playboys, the Turtles
SONGS PERFORMED: *Baby Please Don't Go*, the Astronauts; *Funny Over You, A Love Like You*, Freddie and the Dreamers; *Out On the Floor*, Dobie Gray; *It's Not Unusual*, the Knickerbockers; *Malibu Run*, Gary Lewis and the Playboys; *She'll Come Back*, the Turtles
SOUNDTRACK: Decca – USA

All movies that Freddie and the Dreamers got anywhere *near* are terrible; the only thing that can be said for this is that it isn't as bad as the English ones. This one concerns a secret organization (F.L.U.S.H. – sigh) that wants to wipe out rock groups.

PAJAMA PARTY 1964
American International Pictures, color, 82 minutes

DIRECTOR: Don Weis
PRODUCERS: Samuel Z. Arkoff, James H. Nicholson

PAJAMA PARTY   Starlet Bobbi Shaw and Buster Keaton.

MUSICALS

SCREENPLAY: Louis M. Heyward
CHOREOGRAPHY: David Winters
CAST: Tommy Kirt, Annette Funicello, Elsa Lanchester, Harvey Lembeck, Buster Keaton
MUSICAL PERFORMERS: Tommy Kirk, Annette Funicello, the Nooney Rickett Four
SONGS PERFORMED: *Among the Young, Beach Ball, It's That Kind of Day, Pajama Party, Stuffed Animal, There Has To Be a Reason, Where Did I Go Wrong?*
SOUNDTRACK: Buena Vista – US

A Martian comes to earth as the spearhead of an invasion, but changes his mind when he meets Annette. Dumb plot and feeble songs.

PARADISE – HAWAIIAN STYLE

PARADISE – HAWAIIAN STYLE   1966
Paramount Pictures, color, 91 minutes

DIRECTOR: Michael Moore
PRODUCER: Hal Wallis
SCREENPLAY: Anthony Lawrence, Allan Weiss
STORY: Allan Weiss
MUSICAL NUMBERS STAGED BY: Jack Regas
CAST: Elvis Presley, James Shigeta, Suzanne Leigh, Donna Butterworth, Marianna Hill, Grady Sutton
MUSICAL PERFORMERS: Donna Butterworth, Elvis Presley and the Jordanaires, the Mellowmen
SONGS PERFORMED: *Bill Bailey*, Donna Butterworth; *Datin', A Dog's Life, Drums of the Islands, Hawaii USA, House of Sand, Paradise Hawaiian Style, Queenie Wahine's Papaya, Stop Where You Are, You Scratch My Back*, Elvis Presley
SOUNDTRACK: RCA
VIDEO: Heron – UK; Key – US

Mild but not too awful Elvis vehicle – here he is a helicopter pilot who starts his own business with pal James Shigeta. There is one excellent number, *Stop Where You Are*, towards the end, and El does an impressive production number at the Polynesian Cultural Center (they should have shot the whole movie there). It's interesting to note that, as late as 1966, the navel ban was still on – all the hula dancers had to wear one-piece bathing suits under their grass skirts.

PHANTOM OF THE PARADISE   1974
Twentieth Century Fox, color, 92 minutes

DIRECTOR: Brian De Palma
PRODUCER: Edward R. Pressman
SCREENPLAY: Brian De Palma
MUSIC AND LYRICS: Paul Williams
CAST: Paul Williams, William Findley, Jessica Harper, Gerrit Graham
MUSICAL PERFORMERS: Bill Finley, Archie Hahn and Harold Oblong, Jessica Harper, Ray Kennedy, Paul Williams

PHANTOM OF THE PARADISE

(*Top*) PHANTOM OF THE PARADISE   Gerrit Graham.

(*Left*) US advertisement for PHANTOM OF THE PARADISE.

(*Above*) William Findley (as the Phantom) and Paul Williams in PHANTOM OF THE PARADISE.

MUSICALS

SONGS PERFORMED: *Faust*, Bill Finley; *Goodbye Eddie Goodbye*, *Somebody Super Like You*, *Upholstery*, Archie Hahn and Harold Oblong; *Old Souls*, *Special To Me*, Jessica Harper; *Life At Last*, Ray Kennedy; *The Hell of It*, *Phantom's Theme*, Paul Williams
SOUNDTRACK: A & M

Stylish and funny take-off of THE PHANTOM OF THE OPERA, with Finley as a scarred musician wreaking revenge on the manager who ripped him off (Williams). The performances are ripe, to say the least, the design and direction striking and coherent. The music is serviceable rather than truly exciting, but that's nothing new in film musicals.

THE PIED PIPER   1971
Scotia-Barber, color, 90 minutes

DIRECTOR: Jacques Demy
PRODUCERS: Sanford Lieberson, David Puttnam
SCREENPLAY: Andrew Birkin, Jacques Demy, Mark Peploe
MUSICAL DIRECTOR: Kenneth Clayton
SCORE: Donovan
CAST: Donovan, Donald Pleasance, Diana Dors, Michael Hordern, John Hurt, Jack Wild
MUSICAL PERFORMER: Donovan

A terrible idea which went nowhere, this is a dim and disorganized retelling of the rat removal expert of tradition. The cast isn't bad, but the script and direction are awful.

PIPE DREAMS   1976
Avco Embassy Pictures, color, 89 minutes

DIRECTOR: Steven Verona
PRODUCER: Steven Verona
SCREENPLAY: Steven Verona
SCORE: Dominic Frontiere, Mike Masser
CAST: Gladys Knight, Barry Hankerson, Sherry Bain, Bruce French
MUSICAL PERFORMERS: Gladys Knight and the Pips

SONGS PERFORMED: *Alaskan Pipeline*, *Find a Way*, *Follow My Dreams*, *I'll Miss You*, *Nobody But You*, *Pipe Dreams*, *Pot of Jazz*, *So Sad the Spring*
SOUNDTRACK: Buddah

Gladys Knight follows her man to the brave new world of work on the Alaska pipeline. Not very dramatic material, though inoffensive. The songs are the same – nothing special, but not the worst.

PLATINUM HIGH SCHOOL A.K.A. TROUBLE AT 16; RICH YOUNG AND DEADLY   1960
Metro Goldwyn Mayer, black & white, 93 minutes

DIRECTOR: Charles Haas
PRODUCER: Albert Zugsmith
SCREENPLAY: Robert Smith
CAST: Mickey Rooney, Dan Duryea, Terry Moore, Yvette Mimieux
MUSICAL PERFORMER: Conway Twitty

A father investigates his son's death at a private school, where he runs into Yvette Mimieux, Terry Moore and *Conway Twitty*.

THE PIED PIPER Donovan charmed the rats in this unexciting re-telling.

Not much musically, but good Sixties' soap opera atmosphere.

PLAY IT COOL   1962
Allied Artists, black & white, 82 minutes

DIRECTOR: Michael Winner
PRODUCERS: Leslie Parkyn, Julian Wintle
SCREENPLAY: Jack Henry
CAST: Billy Fury, Anna Palk, Michael Anderson Jr., Dennis Price, Richard Wattis
MUSICAL PERFORMERS: Jimmy Crawford, Shane Fenton and the Fentones, Billy Fury, Helen Shapiro, Bobby Vee
SONGS PERFORMED: *Take It Easy*, Jimmy Crawford; *It's Gonna Take Magic*, Shane Fenton; *Once Upon a Dream*, *Play It Cool*, Billy Fury; *But I Don't Care*, *Cry My Heart Out*, Helen Shapiro; *Who Can Say?*, Bobby Vee

Good selection of early Sixties' performers strung along a slight plot about a bratty teenage rich girl looking for her boyfriend. Billy Fury is very acceptable in a speaking role.

PLAY IT COOL   Billy Fury starred . . .

. . . and Bobby Vee guested.

PRIVILEGE   1967
United International, color, 103 minutes

DIRECTOR: Peter Watkins
PRODUCER: John Heyman
SCREENPLAY: Norman Bogner, Peter Watkins
SONGS: Mark Leander, Mark London
CAST: Paul Jones, Jean Shrimpton, Mark London, Max Bacon
MUSICAL PERFORMERS: Paul Jones, the George Bean Group
SONGS PERFORMED: *Free Me*, *I've Been a Bad Bad Boy*, *Privilege*, Paul Jones; *Jerusalem*, *Onward Christian Soldiers*, the George Bean Group
SOUNDTRACK: UNI – US; HMV – UK

Fascinating examination of the subversion of rock'n'roll by big business, as a young, rebellious singer is almost turned into the next messiah by his managers. The production is gorgeous, with extraordinarily rich color and stylized design; the acting is excellent, especially Jones (but with the exception of Jean Shrimpton, who, though lovely, acts like a cardboard cut-out). But unfortunately, the music is uniformly awful, diluting the film's impact somewhat (these guys could not *possibly* become big stars, much less gods). Well worth

MUSICALS

seeing, and the point is still valid – in fact, nothing has changed.

PSYCH-OUT 1968
American International Pictures, color, 90 minutes

DIRECTOR: Richard Rush
PRODUCER: Dick Clark
SCREENPLAY: Betty Ulius, E. Hunter Willett
CAST: Susan Strasberg, Jack Nicholson, Bruce Dern, Dean Stockwell, Max Julien, Adam Roarke

A poster for PRIVILEGE.

The final rally in PRIVILEGE.

PSYCH-OUT

MUSICAL PERFORMERS: Boenzee Cryque, the Seeds, Strawberry Alarm Clock, the Storybook
SONGS PERFORMED: *Ashbury Wednesday*, Boenzee Cryque; *Two Fingers Pointing On You, Pushin' Too Hard*, the Seeds; *Incense and Peppermints, Rainy Day Mushroom Pillow, The World's On Fire*, Strawberry Alarm Clock; *Beads of Innocence, The Love Children, The Pretty Song, Psych-Out, Psych-Out Sanatorium*, the Storybook
SOUNDTRACK: Sidewalk

Terrific psychedelic musical drama about a deaf girl searching for her lost brother in the Haight Ashbury world of drug-crazed hippies. Unfortunately they cop out at the ending, but the cast is great; not only is this a real period piece, but the story is well told. The music is just right, too – good old Strawberry Alarm Clock.

Hippie Dean Stockwell smokes something pretty suspicious-looking in PSYCH-OUT.

The Strawberry Alarm Clock entertain a party of flower people in PSYCH-OUT; notice the light show behind them.

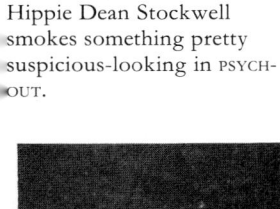

89

PURPLE RAIN   Prince in conce

Scene-stealers Jerome Benton and Morris Day in PURPLE RAIN.

PURPLE RAIN   1984
Warner Brothers, color, 90 minutes

DIRECTOR: Albert Magnoli
PRODUCERS: Robert Cavallo, Steven Fargnoli, Joseph Ruffalo
SCREENPLAY: William Blinn, Albert Magnoli
SONGS COMPOSED AND PRODUCED BY: Prince
SCORE: Michel Columbier
CAST: Prince, Apollonia Kotero, Clarence Williams III, Morris Day, Olga Karlatos, Jerome Benton
MUSICAL PERFORMERS: Morris Day, Apollonia Kotero, Prince, the Revolution, the Time
SONGS PERFORMED: *The Bird, Jungle Love,* Morris Day and the Time; *Sex Shooter,* Apollonia Kotero; *Take Me With U,* Apollonia Kotero, Prince; *Baby I'm a Star, The Beautiful Ones, Computer Blue, Darling Nikki, I Would Die 4 U, Let's Go Crazy, Purple Rain, When Doves Cry,* Prince
SOUNDTRACK: Warner Brothers
VIDEO: WEA – US

Straightforward rock musical in the mold of the best Presley films; Prince's tempestuous debut is simple but effective, with exciting music superbly performed and filmed. Surprisingly, given the star's salacious reputation, the story is not exploitative, but seems heartfelt; a young musician struggles to overcome a tragically unhappy family life, a stormy love affair, and his own ego problems. He's forced to grow up and finds success in the process. Clarence Williams III, as the tormented father, gives the best performance, and Morris Day is striking as Prince's wiseguy rival.

RENALDO AND CLARA   1977
Lombard Street Films, color, 235 minutes

DIRECTOR: Bob Dylan
PRODUCERS: Jack Baran, Mel Howard
SCREENPLAY: Bob Dylan, Sam Shepard
CAST: Bob Dylan, Joan Baez, Sara Dylan, Ronee Blakely, Ronnie Hawkins, Harry Dean Stanton, David Blue
MUSICAL PERFORMERS: Joan Baez, Ronee Blakely, Bob Dylan, the Eagles, Jack Elliot, Mama Maria Frasca, Hal Frazier, Leadbelly, Gordon Lightfoot, Roger McGuinn, Willie Nelson, Rob Stoner, Ann Waldman
SONGS PERFORMED: *Need a New Sun Rising,* Ronee Blakely; *Just Like A Woman,* Ronee Blakely, Bob Dylan; *Knocking On Heaven's Door,* Ronee Blakely, Joan Baez, Bob Dylan; *Diamonds and Rust, Suzanne,* Joan Baez; *A Hard Rain's A-Gonna Fall, House of the Rising Sun, Hurricane, I Want You, If You See Her Say Hello, Isis, It Ain't me Babe, It Takes a Lot To Laugh It Takes A Train To Cry, Kaw-Liga, Little Moses, One More Cup of Coffee, One Too Many Mornings, Patty's Gone to Laredo, People Get Ready, Romance In Durango, Sad-Eyed Lady of the Lowlands, Sara, She Belongs To Me, Tangled Up In Blue, What Will You Do When Jesus Comes?, When I Paint My Masterpiece,* Bob Dylan; *Hollywood Waltz,* the Eagles; *Mule Skinner Blues, Salt Pork West Virginia,* Jack Elliot; *Cucurrucucu Paloma, God and Mama, Mama's Lament,* Mama Maria Frasca; *In the Morning,* Hal Frazier; *In the Pines,* Leadbelly; *Ballad in Plain D,* Gordon Lightfoot; *Chestnut Mare,* Roger McGuinn; *Time of the Preacher,* Willie Nelson; *Catfish,* Rob Stoner; *Fast Speaking Woman,* Anne Waldman

RENALDO AND CLARA No one quite knew what Bob Dylan meant by this.

There's a lot of great music in this but unfortunately, at its full length of nearly four hours, it is almost unwatchable. The story is roughly about a tour and the events in the personal life of the main character; but it's hard to tell who is who – Dylan sometimes plays himself, and sometimes seems to be somebody else. Fascinating bits are spread rather thin over long dull stretches. A valuable document of *something*, but it's difficult to see what.

RICH YOUNG AND DEADLY see PLATINUM HIGH SCHOOL

RING-A-DING RHYTHM see IT'S TRAD DAD

ROADIE 1980
United Artists, color, 103 minutes

DIRECTOR: Alan Rudolph
PRODUCER: Carolyn Pfeiffer
SCREENPLAY: Big Boy Medlin, Michael Ventura
CAST: Meatloaf, Art Carney, Kaki Hunter, Gailard Sartain
MUSICAL PERFORMERS: Ray Benson, Blondie, Alice Cooper, Alvin Crow and the Pleasant Valley Boys, Ramblin' Jack Elliot, Emmylou Harris, Roy Orbison
SONGS PERFORMED: *Ring of Fire*, Blondie; *Pain, Road Rats*, Alice Cooper; *That Lovin' You Feelin' Again*, Roy Orbison, Emmylou Harris
SOUNDTRACK SONGS: *Me and You, Texas*, Asleep At the Wheel; *You Better Run*, Pat Benatar; *Your Precious Love*, Steven Bishop and Yvonne Elliman; *Everything Works If You Let It*, Cheap Trick; *Brainlock*, Joe Ely; *A Man Needs a Woman*, Jay Ferguson; *I'm a One Woman Man*, Jerry Lee Lewis; *Can't We Try*, Teddy Pendergrass; *Crystal Ball*, Styx; *Double Yellow Line*, Sue Saad and the Next
SOUNDTRACK: Warner Brothers

Vulgar and funny tale of a poor but mechanically inclined Texas boy (Meatloaf) whose dream in life is to be a roadie with Alice Cooper, which he finally achieves after various educational adventures. Undeniably ridiculous, but Meat Loaf has real personality and the performances and soundtrack keep song after song spinning along.

ROCK ALL NIGHT 1957
Allied Artists, black & white, 65 minutes

DIRECTOR: Roger Corman
PRODUCER: Roger Corman
SCREENPLAY: Charles B. Griffith
CAST: Abby Dalton, Kick Miller, Robin Morse
MUSICAL PERFORMERS: the Blockbusters, the Platters
SONGS PERFORMED: *I'm Sorry*, the Platters; *He's Mine*, the Blockbusters
SOUNDTRACK: Mercury – US

Somebody apparently thought Abby Dalton was a potential rock star, as she starred in several teen exploitation quickies. This one has elements of drama, as two gangsters hide out at a road house and hold the staff, including Abby, prisoner. Pretty forgettable.

Meatloaf was really funny in ROADIE.

MUSICALS

ROCK'N'ROLL HIGH SCHOOL 1979
New World Pictures, color, 93 minutes

DIRECTOR: Allan Arkush
PRODUCER: Michael Finnell
SCREENPLAY: Russ Dvonch, Joseph McBride, Richard Whitley
STORY: Allan Arkush
CAST: P. J. Soles, Vince Van Patten, Clint Howard, Dey Young, Paul Bartel
MUSICAL PERFORMERS: the Ramones
SONGS PERFORMED: *Blitzkrieg Bop, California Sun, I Just Wanna Have Something To Do, I Wanna Be Sedated, I Wanna Be Your Boyfriend, I Want You Around, Pinhead, Questionly, Teenage Lobotomy, Rock'n'Roll High School, She's the One, Sheena Is a Punk Rocker*
SOUNDTRACK SONGS: *Alley Cat*, Bent Fabric; *School Days*, Chuck Berry; *Smoking In the Boy's Room*, Brownsville Station; *School's Out*, Alice Cooper; *Come Back Jonee*, Devo; *Teenage Depression*, Eddie and the Hot Rods; *Energy Fools the Magician, M386, Spirits Drifting*, Brian Eno; *Albatross*, Fleetwood Mac; *So it Goes*, Nick Lowe; *High School*, the MC5; *C'mon Let's Go*, the Paley Brothers; *Do You Wanna Dance, Rock and Roll*, the Ramones; *A Dream Goes On Forever*, Todd Rundgren; *Rock'n'Roll*, the Velvet Underground; *Did We Meet Somewhere Before?*, Wings
SOUNDTRACK: Sire
VIDEO: WEA – US

Frivolous parody of Fifties' teen pics, with a whole class rebelling against authority and going wild at a Ramones concert. The script is amusing but not *that* witty, and the main attraction is the terrific soundtrack, good song after good song.

ROCK AROUND THE CLOCK 1956
Columbia Pictures, black & white, 77 minutes

DIRECTOR: Fred F. Sears
PRODUCER: Sam Katzman
SCREENPLAY: Robert E. Kent, James B. Gordon
CAST: Alan Dale, Lisa Gaye, Alix Tilton, Johnny Johnston, John Archer, Alan Freed
MUSICAL PERFORMERS: Freddy Bell and the Bellboys, Bill Haley and His Comets, Little Richard, Tony Martinez, the Platters
SONGS PERFORMED: *Giddy Up a Ding Dong, We're Gonna Teach You to Rock*, Freddy Bell and the Bellboys; *ABC Boogie, Happy Baby, Mambo Rock, R.O.C.K., Razzle Dazzle, Rock A Beatin' Boogie, Rock Around the Clock, Rudy's Rock, See You Later Alligator*, Bill Haley and His Comets; *The Great Pretender, Only You*, the Platters

Mild but important entry in Alan Freed's series of rock movies; the story is banal, as usual – a failing manager discovers that kids go wild over that new music (personified in Bill Haley and His Comets) – 'like hillbilly with a beat'. He signs the band and guides them to stardom with the help of his old pal Freed and two young dancers. So far, so dim, but the real importance of the film is that it is starring acts that are racially integrated. Freed was reknowned for never playing white cover versions of black hits, and though the Platters seem pop-oriented and harmless today, their appearances as stars on an equal footing with the other acts featured meant a great deal in 1956.

ROCK AROUND THE WORLD see THE TOMMY STEELE STORY

ROCK, BABY, ROCK IT
Freebar, black & white, 77 minutes

DIRECTOR: Murray Douglas Sporup
PRODUCER: J. G. Tiger
CAST: Johnny Carroll, Kay Wheeler
MUSICAL PERFORMERS: the Belew Twins, Johnny Carroll and His Hot Rocks, the Cell Block Seven, Don Coats, the Five Stars, Roscoe Gordon, Preacher Smith and the Deacons

SONGS PERFORMED: *Lonesome, Love Me Baby*, the Belew Twins; *Crazy Crazy Lovin', Rockin' Maybelle, Sugar Baby, Wild Wild Women*, Johnny Carroll; *Hot Rock, Rockin' Saints*, the Cell Block Seven; *China Star, Love Never Forgets, Stop the World*, Don Coats; *Funny Money, Hey Juanita, Love Is All I Need*, the Five Stars; *Boppin, Chicken In the Rough*, Roscoe Gordon; *Eat Your Heart Out, Roogie Oogie*, Preacher Smith and the Deacons

Dopey independently made feature with the usual 'hey let's put on a show' plot and a weird and obscure line up of acts. Johnny Carroll was a respectable minor rockabilly, but who ever heard of the Cell Block Seven?

John Saxon and Luana Patten find each other in ROCK PRETTY BABY.

ROCK PRETTY BABY 1956
Universal International Pictures, black & white, 89 minutes

DIRECTOR: Richard Barlett
PRODUCER: Edmond Chevis
SCREENPLAY: Herbert Margolis
CAST: Sal Mineo, John Saxon, Fay Wray, Shelley Fabares, Luana Patten
MUSICAL PERFORMERS: the Rod McKuen Group
SONGS PERFORMED: *Rock Pretty Baby*
SOUNDTRACK: Decca – US

Another band contest movie. Good cast, in its way – Luana Patten was always reliable – but dopey, and so is the music.

ROCK ROCK ROCK 1957
Directors Corporation of America, black & white, 83 minutes

DIRECTOR: Will Price
CAST: Tuesday Weld, Teddy Randazzo, Jacqueline Kerr, Ivy Schulman, Alan Freed
MUSICAL PERFORMERS: LaVerne Baker, the Bowties, Johnny Burnette and the Rock'n'Roll Trio, Jimmy Cavallo and His Houserockers, Chuck Berry, the Flamingos, Connie Francis (for Tuesday Weld), the Alan Freed Orchestra, Frankie Lymon and the Teenagers, the Moonglows, the Three Chuckles
SONGS PERFORMED: *Tra La La*, LaVerne Baker; *You Can't Catch Me*, Chuck Berry; *Ever Since I Can Remember*, the Bowties; *Rock Pretty Baby*, the Bowties with Ivy Schulman; *Lonesome Train*, Johnny Burnette and the Rock'n'Roll Trio; *The Big Beat, Rock Rock Rock*, Jimmy Cavallo and His Houserockers; *Would I Be Crying?*, the Flamingos; *I Never Had a Sweetheart, Little Blue Wren*, Connie Francis; *Right Now Right Now, Rock'n'Roll Boogie*, the Alan Freed Orchestra; *Baby Baby, I'm Not a Juvenile Delinquent*, Frankie Lymon and the Teenagers; *I Knew From the Start, Over and Over Again*, the Moonglows; *Thanks to You, The Things Your Heart Needs, We're Gonna Rock*

MUSICALS

Tonight, Won't You Give Me a Chance?, the Three Chuckles
SOUNDTRACK: Chess – US
VIDEO: Media – US

Yet ANOTHER band contest. But it's packed with great music, as well as the only appearance of Johnny Burnette and the Rock'n'Roll Trio. Alan Freed could always be relied upon to pull in the best acts.

ROCKERS   1979
Rockers Film Corporation, color, 100 minutes

DIRECTOR: Theodoras Bafoloukas
PRODUCER: Patrick Hulsey
SCREENPLAY: Theodoras Bafoloukas
CAST: Leroy Wallace, Richard Hall, Monica Craig, Jacob Miller, Big Youth, Errol Brown, Dillinger, Gregory Isaacs
MUSICAL PERFORMERS: Burning Spear, Junior Byles, the Heptones, Justin Hines and the Dominoes, Gregory Isaacs, Bunny Wailer
SONGS PERFORMED: *Jah No Dead*, Burning Spear; *Fade Away*, Junior Byles; *Book of Rules*, the Heptones; *Natty Takeover*, Justin Hines and the Dominoes; *Slave Master*, Gregory Isaacs; *Rockers*, Bunny Wailer
SOUNDTRACK SONGS: *Treasure Dub*, Joe Gibbs and the Professionals; *We a Rockers*, the Inner Circle; *Queen Majesty*, the Jays; *Graduation in Zion*, Kiddus-I; *Money Worries*, the Maytones; *Tenement Yard*, Jacob Miller and the Inner Circle; *Police and Thieves*, Junior Murvin; *Dread Lion*, Lee Perry and the Upsetters; *Satta Amasgana*, *Waiting For the Bus*, the Rockers All Stars; *Get Up and Get On Down*, Roundtree; *Stepping Razor*, Peter Tosh

Jamaican record-distributor musician gets into hassles with local gangsters. Not as grim and gritty as *THE HARDER THEY COME*, this is still entertaining and full of fine music.

THE ROCKY HORROR PICTURE SHOW   (left to right) Susan Sarandon, Tim Curry, Little Nell.

THE ROCKY HORROR PICTURE SHOW   1975
Twentieth Century Fox, color, 101 minutes

DIRECTOR: Jim Sharman
PRODUCERS: Lou Adler, Michael White
SCREENPLAY: Richard O'Brien, Jim Sharman
FROM: the musical *The Rocky Horror Picture Show* by Richard O'Brien
CAST: Tim Curry, Susan Sarandon, Barry Bostwick, Meatloaf, Richard O'Brien, Jonathan Adams, Little Nell, Charles Gray
SONGS PERFORMED: *Charles Atlas Song*, *Eddie's Teddy*, *I'm Going Home*, *It Was Great When It All Began*, *Over at the Frankenstein Place*, *Planet Schmanet*, *Science Fiction Double-Feature*, *Super-Heroes*, *Sweet Transvestite*, *The Sword of Damocles*, *The Time Warp*, *Toucha, Toucha, Touch Me*, *Wedding Song*
SOUNDTRACK: A&M

Fun camp musical, enjoyable mainly for the oddly touching lead performance by Tim Curry as extra-terrestrial mad scientist Dr Frank N. Furter, whose mysterious storm-

> "And if Tim Curry doesn't win an Academy Award for his performance as Frank, and the Time-Warp isn't the next dance craze I'll hang up my suspender belt. Miss it if you dare."
> Mick Brown – SOUNDS

Twentieth Century-Fox presents
A MICHAEL WHITE – LOU ADLER PRODUCTION

THE ROCKY HORROR PICTURE SHOW AA

TIM CURRY SUSAN SARANDON BARRY BOSTWICK

Original musical play, music & lyrics by RICHARD O'BRIEN Screenplay by JIM SHARMAN & RICHARD O'BRIEN
Executive Producer LOU ADLER Produced by MICHAEL WHITE Directed by JIM SHARMAN
EASTMAN COLOUR Original Film Soundtrack on ODE 77026 Released by FOX RANK Distributors
DOLBY SYSTEM Noise Reduction – High Fidelity

RIALTO COVENTRY ST 437 3488 BETWEEN PICCADILLY CIRCUS AND LEICESTER SQUARE | FROM AUG 14

swept castle is invaded by innocent all-American honeymooners. The music is more pop than rock, but the production numbers are vigorous and bright.

UK advertisement for THE ROCKY HORROR PICTURE SHOW.

THE ROSE 1979
Twentieth Century Fox, color 134 minutes

DIRECTOR: Mark Rydell
PRODUCERS: Aaron Russo, Marvin Worth
SCREENPLAY: Bo Goldman, Bill Kerby
MUSIC ARRANGED AND SUPERVISED BY: Paul Rothchild
CAST: Bette Midler, Alan Bates, Frederic Forrest, Harry Dean Stanton
MUSICAL PERFORMERS: Bette Midler, the Rose Band (Norton Buffalo, Robbie Buchanan, Pentti Glan, Steve Hunter, Jerome Jumonville, Mark Underwood, Danny Weiss), the Billy Ray Band (Doug Dillard, Rodney Dillard, Byron Berline), the Club 77 Band, Monty's Band
SONGS PERFORMED: *Camellia, Evil Lies, Fire Down Below, I've Written a Letter To Daddy, Keep On Rockin', Let Me Call You Sweetheart, The Night We Said Goodbye, The Rose, Stay With Me, Sold My Soul to Rock'n'Roll, When a Man Loves a Woman, Whose Side Are You On?,* Bette Midler
SOUNDTRACK: Atlantic

Cliché-ridden but very well done fictionalization of Janis Joplin's decline and death, with Midler fine as the confused and needy star. The acting and production are so good, giving a good picture of the seamy side of life on the road, that the basically unenlightening nature of the story doesn't become obvious until you think about it later. Bette is *not* a rock singer (though she has improved since then), but she is a real actress. She shows the character's helplessness *and* manipulativeness; her performance is more subtle and detailed than the script.

Bette Midler and the tour plane in a telling shot from THE ROSE.

Bette Midler and Alan Bates in THE ROSE.

ROUSTABOUT 1964
Paramount Pictures, color, 96 minutes

DIRECTOR: John Rich
PRODUCER: Hal Wallis
SCREENPLAY: Anthony Lawrence, Allan Weiss
STORY: Allan Weiss
MUSIC: Joseph E. Lilley
MUSICAL NUMBERS STAGED BY: Earl Barton
TECHNICAL ADVISER: Col. Tom Parker
CAST: Elvis Presley, Barbara Stanwyck, Joan Freeman, Leif Ericson, Sue Ann Langdon
MUSICAL PERFORMERS: Elvis Presley, the Jordanaires
SONGS PERFORMED: *Big Love Big Heartache, Carny Town, Hard Knocks, It's Carnival Time, It's a Wonderful World, Little Egypt, One Track Heart, Poison Ivy League, Roustabout, There's a Brand New Day on the Horizon, Wheels On My Heels*
SOUNDTRACK: RCA
VIDEO: Heron – UK; Key – US

Mid-range Presley, with an interesting background and one great song, Lieber and Stoller's *Little Egypt*, which he does very well. Otherwise, he plays the usual sulky loner who finally finds a home and a girl (surprise!) in a travelling carnival.

Barbara Stanwyck co-starred with Elvis in ROUSTABOUT (in a part first offered to Mae West!). Here she argues with veteran actor Dabs Greer.

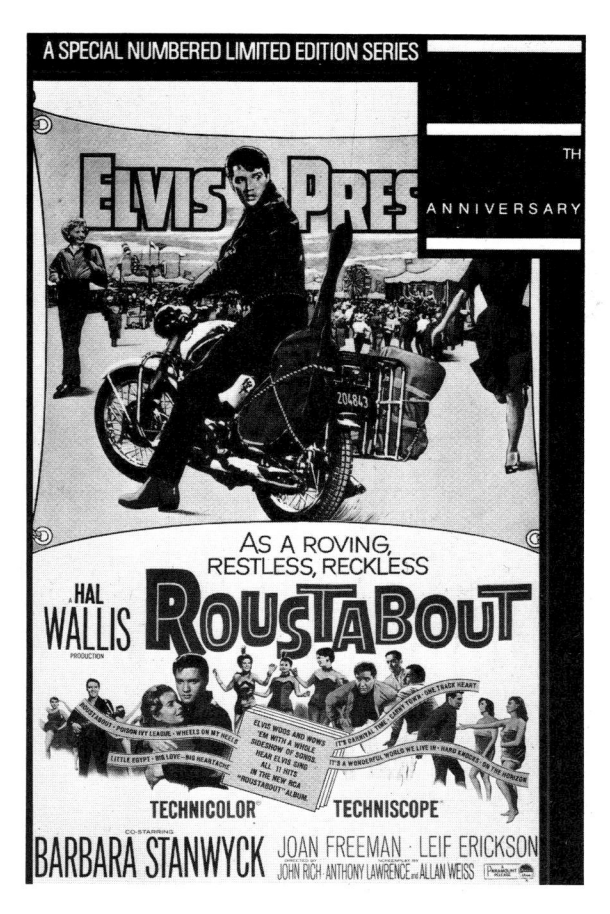

ROUSTABOUT

RUDE BOY 1980
Tigon, color, 133 minutes

DIRECTORS: Jack Hazan, David Mingay
PRODUCERS: Jack Hazan, David Mingay
SCREENPLAY: Ray Grange, Jack Hazan, David Mingay
CAST: Ray Grange, the Clash (Joe Strummer, Mick Jones, Nicky Headon, Paul Simonon), Barry Baker, Terry McQuade, Jimmy Pursey
MUSICAL PERFORMERS: the Clash
SONGS PERFORMED: *All the Young Punks, Complete Control, Garageland, I Fought the Law, Janie Jones, London's Burning, The Prisoner, Resolution Rock, Rudi Can't Fail, Safe European Home, Stay Free, Tommy Gun, USA, What's My Name, White Man at the Hammersmith Palais, White Riot*
SOUNDTRACK SONGS: *Johnny Too Bad*, the Slickers; *Wreck a Buddy*, the Soul Sisters; *No Reason*, Joe Strummer

Fascinating if depressing semi-improvised story of a punk with no future who becomes a roadie for the Clash. There are some excellent on-stage performances by the Clash, as well as

MUSICALS

(*Left*) An enthusiastic crowd of young punks in RUDE BOY.

(*Right*) SGT. PEPPER'S LONELY HEARTS CLUB BAND   A cast of thousands.

(*Right*) George Burns meets the Bee Gees in SGT. PEPPER'S LONELY HEARTS CLUB BAND.

(*Left*) Joe Strummer shows a lot of patience dealing with punk roadie Ray Grange in RUDE BOY.

some other bands. They were the most important band in England once; this is a good record of that era.

SEASIDE SWINGERS see **EVERY DAY'S A HOLIDAY**

SERIOUS CHARGE 1959
Eros Films, black & white, 99 minutes

DIRECTOR: Terence Young
PRODUCER: Mickey Delamar
SCREENPLAY: Guy Eames, Mickey Delamar
FROM: the play by Philip King
SONGS BY: Lionel Bart
CAST: Anthony Quayle, Sarah Churchill, Irene Browne, Cliff Richard
MUSICAL PERFORMER: Cliff Richard
SONGS PERFORMED: *Living Doll, Mad, No Turning Back*

Cunning attempt to make a youth-oriented Cliff musical out of a West End problem play; there's actually not much music in this, but the drama is pretty good if you like Fifties' soap opera. The plot involves the conflict between a vicar and the local tough kids (what, Cliff?!). Good earnest Fifties' atmosphere.

SGT. PEPPER'S LONELY HEARTS CLUB BAND 1978
Universal International Pictures, color, 111 minutes

DIRECTOR: Michael Schultz
PRODUCER: Robert Stigwood
SCREENPLAY: Henry Edwards, Tom O'Horgan, Robin Wagner
MUSICAL DIRECTOR: George Martin
CAST: the Bee Gees (Barry Gibb, Maurice Gibb, Robin Gibb), Frankie Howerd, Paul Nicholas, Donald Pleasance, Peter Frampton, George Burns
MUSICAL PERFORMERS: Aerosmith, the Bee Gees,

MUSICALS

Billy Preston in SGT. PEPPER'S LONELY HEARTS CLUB BAND.

George Burns, Alice Cooper, Earth Wind and Fire, Sandy Farina, Peter Frampton, Robin Gibb, Paul Nicholas, Donald Pleasance, Billy Preston, Jay MacIntosh, Stargard, Diane Steinberg, John Wheeler
SONGS PERFORMED: *Come Together*, Aerosmith; *A Day In the Life, Carry That Weight, Nowhere Man, Polythene Pam*, the Bee Gees; *Getting Better All the Time, She Came In Through the Bathroom Window, With a Little Help From My Friends*, the Bee Gees, Peter Frampton; *Being For the Benefit of Mr Kite*, the Bee Gees, George Burns, Peter Frampton; *Good Morning*, the Bee Gees, Peter Frampton, Paul Nicholas; *She's Leaving Home*, the Bee Gees, Jay MacIntosh, John Wheeler; *I Want You, She's So Heavy*, the Bee Gees, Paul Nicholas, Donald Pleasance, Stargard, Diane Steinberg; *Because*, Alice Cooper; *Got To Get You Into My Life*, Earth Wind and Fire; *Here Comes the Sun, Strawberry Fields Forever*, Sandy Farina; *Golden Slumbers, The Long and Winding Road*, Peter Frampton; *Oh Darling*, Robin Gibb; *You Never Give Me Your Money*, Paul Nicholas, Diane Steinberg; *Get Back*, Billy Preston; *Lucy In the Sky With Diamonds*, Stargard, Diane Steinberg; *Sgt. Pepper's Lonely Hearts Club Band*, cast
SOUNDTRACK: A & M
VIDEO: CIC – UK; MCA – US

Foolishly overproduced all-star jumble, as the good guys in Heartland fight off the villainy of Aerosmith. Even as a cartoon, this would have been silly. Among the vast numbers of performances, there are a few good ones, especially Alice Cooper doing *Because* and Earth, Wind and Fire with *Got To Get You Into My Life*. Much too long and loose to be much use, though.

SHAKE RATTLE AND ROCK 1956
American International Pictures, black & white, 75 minutes

DIRECTOR: Edward L. Cahn
PRODUCER: James H. Nicholson
SCREENPLAY: Lou Rusoff
CAST: Touch (Mike) Connors, Lisa Gaye, Paul Dubov, Douglas Dumbrille, Margaret Dumont, Sterling Holloway
MUSICAL PERFORMERS: Tommy Charles, Fats Domino, Annita Ray, Joe Turner
SONGS PERFORMED: *Sweet Love On My Mind*, Tommy Charles; *Ain't It a Shame, Honey Chile, I'm In Love Again*, Fats Domino; *Rockin' Saturday Night*, Annita Ray; *Feelin' Happy, Lipstick Powder and Paint*, Joe Turner

Kids, yet again, have to prove that rock does *not* cause decay and immorality. The baddies are unusually heavyweight – Margaret Dumont and Douglas Dumbrille! Some great stuff by Joe Turner, all too rarely seen in movies, and Fats Domino.

SING BOY SING 1958
Twentieth Century Fox, black & white, 90 minutes

DIRECTOR: Henry Ephron
PRODUCER: Henry Ephron
SCREENPLAY: Claude Binyon
FROM: a Kraft TV Playhouse production, *The Singing Idol*
CAST: Tommy Sands, Nick Adams, Lili Gentle, Edmond O'Brien, John McIntire
MUSICAL PERFORMER: Tommy Sands
SONGS PERFORMED: *A Little Bit More, Bundle of Dreams, Crazy Cause I Love You, Daddy Wants to Do Right, I'm Gonna Walk and Talk With My Lord, People In Love, Sing Boy Sing, Soda Pop Pop, Teenage Crush, That's All I Want From You, Who Baby?, Would I Love You*
SOUNDTRACK: Capitol

Quite a nifty little drama about the rise and struggles of a young Elvis-like singer. Tommy Sands was a little tame, but this one was unusually well-written, being from the Kraft TV Playhouse in the golden age of television.

6.5 SPECIAL 1957
Anglo Films, black & white, 85 minutes

DIRECTOR: Alfred Shaughnessy
PRODUCER: Herbert Smith
CAST: Diane Todd, Avril Leslie, Jo Douglas, Pete Murray, Freddie Mills
MUSICAL PERFORMERS: Petula Clark, Jim Dale, Johnny Dankworth, Lonnie Donegan, Jackie Dennis, Cleo Laine, the John Barry Seven

6.5 SPECIAL   Jim Dale and Avril Leslie.

6.5 SPECIAL   A portrait of guest star Lonnie Donegan.

Frankie Avalon and Dwayne Hickman in SKI PARTY.

SONGS PERFORMED: *Baby Lover*, Petula Clark; *Sugartime*, *The Train Kept A-Rollin'*, Jim Dale; *Grand Cooley Dam*, *Jack O'Diamonds*, Lonnie Donegan; *Lah Dee Dah*, Jackie Dennis

Lame-brained exploitation of the popular music TV programme, with two fans travelling by train to London and finding the coaches full of stars, for no discernable reason. The music is pretty lame too, with the brief exception of Lonnie Donegan.

SKI PARTY   1965
American International Pictures, color, 90 minutes

DIRECTOR: Alan Rafkin
PRODUCER: Gene Corman
SCREENPLAY: Robert Kaufman
CAST: Frankie Avalon, Deborah Walley, Dwayne Hickman, Yvonne Craig
MUSICAL PERFORMERS: Frankie Avalon, James Brown, Lesley Gore, the Hondells, Deborah Walley
SONGS PERFORMED: *Lots Lots More*, *Painting the Town*, Frankie Avalon; *I Got You*, James Brown; *Lollipops and Rainbows*, Lesley Gore; *The Gasser*, *Ski Party*, the Hondells; *You'll Never Change Them*, Deborah Walley

SKI PARTY   Dwayne Hickman (left) and Frankie Avalon (right) somehow deceive Deborah Walley (center) into believing that they are sorority girls.

Absurd change of pace from the beach movies, with the same cast; dopey Frankie and Dwayne disguise themselves as girls (most unconvincingly) to infiltrate a female dormitory. Unamusing except for a couple of good numbers: *I Got You*, by James Brown and *Lollipops and Rainbows* by Lesley Gore.

US advertisement for SON OF DRACULA.

SOME PEOPLE 1962
Anglo-Amalgamated, black & white, 93 minutes

DIRECTOR: Clive Donner
PRODUCER: James Archibald
CAST: Kenneth More, David Hemmings, Ray Brooks, Angela Douglas
MUSICAL PERFORMERS: the Eagles

Livelier than usual British teen flick about a couple of young motorcyclists who give up the road and form a band; Donner's direction and the better-than-average cast (catch Ray Brooks before *THE KNACK*) make it quite watchable. The music isn't much to write home about – no, of course it's not *those* Eagles.

SON OF DRACULA 1974
Cinemation, color, 90 minutes

DIRECTOR: Freddie Francis
PRODUCER: Ringo Starr
SCREENPLAY: Jay Fairbanks
SCORE: Harry Nilsson
CAST: Harry Nilsson, Ringo Starr, Freddie Jones, Dennis Price
MUSICAL PERFORMER: Harry Nilsson
SONGS PERFORMED: *At My Front Door, Daybreak, Down, Jump Into the Fire, The Moonbeam Song, Remember, Without You*
SOUNDTRACK: Rapple

Flimsy attempt to make a rock-horror musical, with Harry Nilsson as the vampire of the title. Director Freddie Francis couldn't bring the Hammer touch to this one, mainly due to lack of real actors. The music isn't bad, but it isn't very exciting, either.

MUSICALS

SPARKLE   1976
Warner Brothers, color, 98 minutes

DIRECTOR: Sam O'Steen
PRODUCER: Howard Rosenman
SCREENPLAY: Joel Schumaker
MUSIC: Curtis Mayfield
CAST: Lonette McKee, Irene Cara, Dawn Smith, Philip Michael Thomas
MUSICAL PERFORMERS: Irene Cara, Lonette McKee
SONGS PERFORMED: *Hooked On Your Love, Look Into Your Heart, Rock With Me, Sparkle*
VIDEO: WEA – US

Nifty low-budget musical drama of a black girl group based on the Supremes, their trials and tribulations, including the drug-addiction of one. The film is interesting mainly for the acting, by Lonette McKee and Irene Cara, who both have gone on to bigger things, and Philip Michael Thomas, before *MIAMI VICE*; the music is not too exciting, even if it *is* by Curtis Mayfield, and it's inappropriate to the period.

SPEEDWAY   1968
Metro Goldwyn Mayer, color, 94 minutes

DIRECTOR: Norman Taurog

SPEEDWAY   Elvis pursues a tax inspector in the person of Nancy Sinatra.

SPEEDWAY   Elvis complains about the government.

PRODUCER: Douglas Lawrence
SCREENPLAY: Philip Shuken
CAST: Elvis Presley, Nancy Sinatra, Bill Bixby, Gale Gordon
MUSICAL PERFORMERS: Elvis Presley, Nancy Sinatra
SONGS PERFORMED: *He's Your Uncle Not Your Dad, Let Yourself Go, Speedway, There Ain't Nothing Like a Song, Your Time Hasn't Come Yet Baby*, Elvis Presley; *Your Groovy Self*, Elvis Presley, Nancy Sinatra
SOUNDTRACK: RCA
VIDEO: MGM–UA – US

Definitely one of the worst Elvis musicals (though he liked the race-track ambience so much he used it twice – see *SPINOUT*); here he's a racing car driver who gets into trouble with a female Internal Revenue agent (a tax-inspector, to the British), played by Nancy Sinatra. They're quite good together, but this is a low-energy picture all the way.

A STAR IS BORN   Barbra Streisand.

SPINOUT   1966
Metro Goldwyn Mayer, color, 93 minutes

DIRECTOR: Norman Taurog
PRODUCER: Joe Pasternak
SCREENPLAY: Theodore J. Flicker, George Kirgo
CAST: Elvis Presley, Shelley Fabares, Diane McBain, Deborah Walley
MUSICAL PERFORMERS: Elvis Presley, the Jordanaires
SONGS PERFORMED: *Adam and Evil, All That I Am, Beach Shack, I'll Be Back, Never Say Yes, Smorgasbord, Spinout, Stop Look and Listen*
SOUNDTRACK: RCA

Here's El at the stock-car races again; this time there's even less plot than in *SPEEDWAY*, as he suffers from the usual girl trouble. The girls are better than usual, however; Shelley Fabares, Diane McBain and Deborah Walley all have a lot more character than the typical Elvis girl. But the story is dull and so is the music. *Smorgasbord* – I ask you.

A STAR IS BORN   1976
Warner Brothers, color, 140 minutes

DIRECTOR: Frank Pierson
PRODUCER: Jon Peters
SCREENPLAY: Joan Didion, John Gregory Dunne, Frank Pierson
STORY BY: Robert Carson, William Wellman
CAST: Barbra Streisand, Kris Kristofferson, Paul Mazursky, Gary Busey, Martha Heflin, Oliver Clark, Venetta Fields
MUSICAL PERFORMERS: Kris Kristofferson, Barbra Streisand, and back-up band (Stephen Bruton, Sammy Creason, Cleve Dupin, Donnie Fritts, Dean Hagen, Booker T. Jones, Jerry McGee, Art Munson, Charles Owens, Terry Paul, Jack Redmond, Bobby Shrew, Mike Utley)
SONGS PERFORMED: *Crippled Crow, Evergreen, Everything, Hellacious Acres, I Believe In Love, Lost Inside of You, Queen Bee, Spanish Lies, Watch*

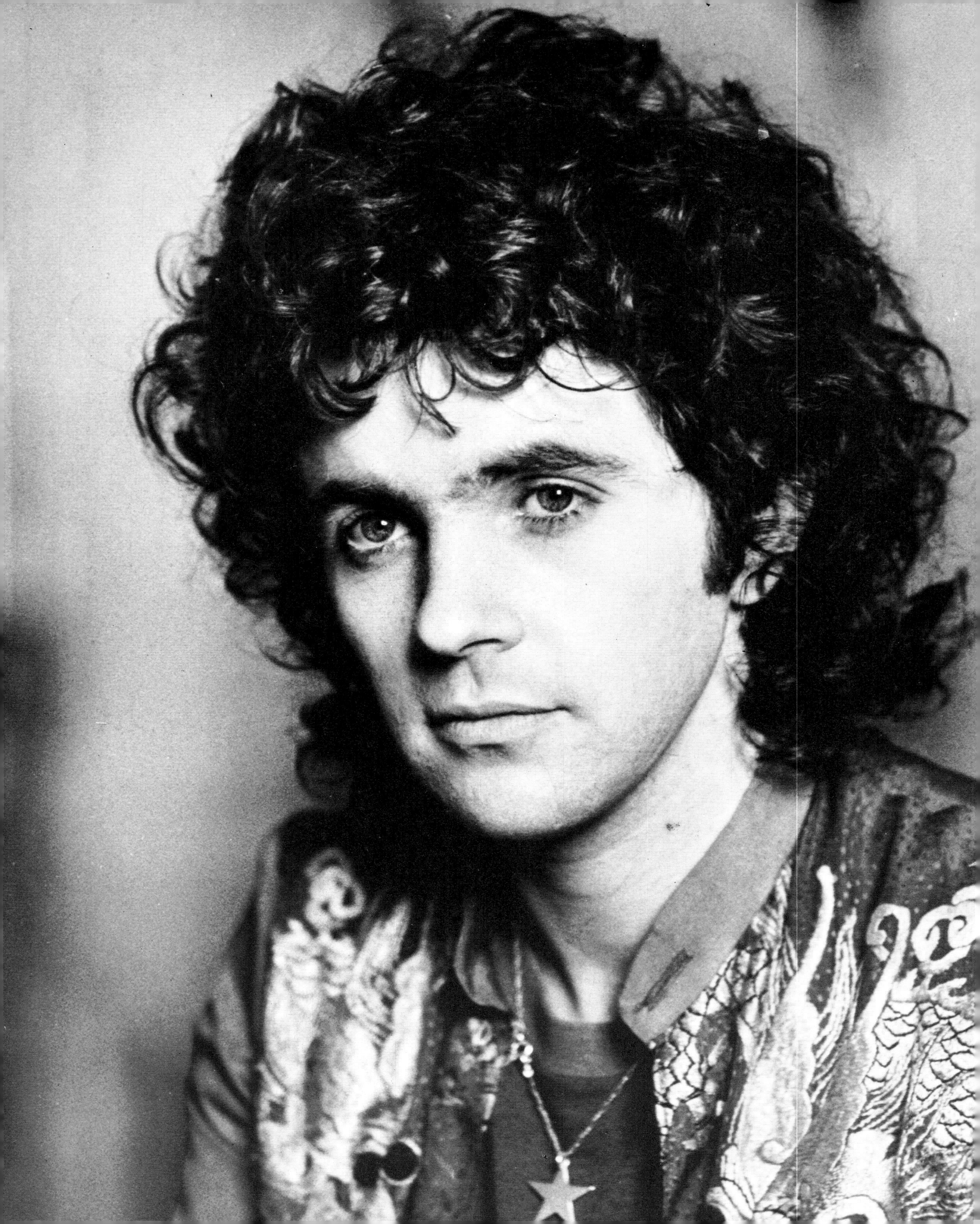

STARDUST

STARDUST 1974
Columbia Pictures, color, 111 minutes

DIRECTOR: Michael Apted
PRODUCERS: David Puttnam, Sandy Lieberson
SCREENPLAY: Ray Connolly
MUSIC PRODUCED BY: Dave Edmunds
CAST: David Essex, Adam Faith, Larry Hagman, Edd Byrnes, Rosalind Ayres, Ines Des Longchamps, Marty Wilde
MUSICAL PERFORMERS: Dave Edmunds, David Essex, the Stray Cats
SONGS PERFORMED: *Stardust, Take It Away, You Kept Me Waiting,* David Essex
SOUNDTRACK SONGS: *House of the Rising Sun,* the Animals; *Gotta Get a Message to You,* the Bee Gees; *The Letter,* the Boxtops; *One Fine Day,* the Chiffons; *A Little Help From My Friends,* Joe Cocker; *Dream Lover,* Bobby Darin; *Layla,* Derek and the Dominoes; *Up On the Roof,* the Drifters; *Da Doo Ron Ron,* Dave Edmunds and the Electricians; *Let It Be Me, Make Me Good, Need a Shot of Rhythm and Blues, Some Other Guy, When Will I Be Loved,* Dave Edmunds and the Stray Cats; *Americana Stray Cat Blues, Dea Sancta,* David Essex; *You've Got Your Troubles,* the Fortunes; *Don't Let the Sun Catch You Crying,* Gerry and the Pacemakers; *All Along the Watchtower,* Jimi Hendrix; *Carrie Ann,* the

UK advertisement for STARDUST.

Closely Now, With One More Look At You, Woman in the Moon
SOUNDTRACK: CBS/Columbia
VIDEO: WEA – US

Not entirely badly done, but way, *way* too much Barbra Streisand. The basic story, of a rising young star who falls in love with a falling one, is in theory perfectly adaptable to a rock'n'roll setting; but you do need stars who can actually sing rock'n'roll. Neither Barbra, who's too pop, nor Kristofferson, who could never actually *sing*, is up to it. The script, or at least those parts of it not all taken up with Streisand, is pretty good, but the songs aren't, and cannot carry the weight of the story.

STARDUST David Essex.

Paul Nicholas (left) and David Essex (right) are the Stray Cats in STARDUST.

Hollies; *White Rabbit*, Jefferson Airplane; *Do You Want To Know a Secret?*, Billy J. Kramer and the Dakotas; *Baby I'm Yours*, Barbara Lewis; *Summer In the City*, the Lovin' Spoonful; *Eve of Destruction*, Barry McGuire; *Monday Monday*, the Mamas and the Papas; *Do Wah Diddy*, Manfred Mann; *Whiter Shade of Pale*, Procol Harum; *Dancin' In the Street*, Martha and the Vandellas; *You've Lost That Lovin' Feeling*, the Righteous Brothers; *Dizzy*, Tommy Roe; *What Becomes of the Broken Hearted?*, Jimmy Ruffin; *Happy Birthday Sweet Sixteen*, Neil Sedaka; *Hats off to Larry*, Del Shannon; *Matthew and Son*, Cat Stevens; *Baby Love*, the Supremes; *My Generation*, the Who; *Uptight*, Stevie Wonder; *She's Not There*, the Zombies
SOUNDTRACK: Arista – US; Ronco – UK
VIDEO: Thorn–EMI – UK

Excellent follow-up to *THAT'LL BE THE DAY*, with Essex as Jim Maclaine, who has finally made it to the top of the music world, only to ruin himself with drugs and general excess. The cast and the performances are superb – Adam Faith steals it again – and the music, compiled and, in part, produced and performed by Dave Edmunds, is brilliant. One of the best.

STAY AWAY JOE   1968
Metro Goldwyn Mayer, color, 102 minutes

DIRECTOR: Peter Tewksbury
PRODUCER: Douglas Lawrence
SCREENPLAY: Michael Hoey
CAST: Elvis Presley, Joan Blondell, Katy Jurado, Burgess Meredith
MUSICAL PERFORMER: Elvis Presley
SONGS PERFORMED: *All I Needed Was the Rain, Dominique, Going Home, Stay Away, Stay Away Joe*

Too bad, because Elvis made a rather convincing Indian, but this is one of his worst features. The good cast is largely wasted, and he seems to sleep-walk through his role as an Indian bronco rider who goes home to sort out the folks on the reservation. Feeble and sparse songs.

STAY AWAY JOE   Joan Blondell and Elvis.

STAYING ALIVE   1983
Paramount Pictures, color, 100 minutes

DIRECTOR: Sylvester Stallone
PRODUCERS: Sylvester Stallone, Robert Stigwood
SCREENPLAY: Sylvester Stallone, Norman Wexler
CAST: John Travolta, Finola Hughes, Cynthia Rhodes, Steve Inwood
SONGS PERFORMED: *I Love You Too Much, Life Goes On, The Woman In You, Staying Alive*, the BeeGees; *Look Out for Number One*, Tommy Fagher; *Far From Over, Moody Girls*; Frank Stallone
VIDEO: CIC – UK; Paramount – US

The usual story of an ambitious dancer battling his way to the top – like *ROCKY*, really, and Sylvester Stallone directs with more verve than is usual in this otherwise typical dance musical. He has a stronger cast to work with, too; but the plot is weak, and the *new*

STAYING ALIVE John Travolta.

music (aside from the BeeGees' songs from the original *SATURDAY NIGHT FEVER*, to which this is a sort of sequel) is also weak. Okay but no more.

STREETS OF FIRE 1984
Universal-RKO, color, 90 minutes

DIRECTOR: Walter Hill
PRODUCERS: Lawrence Gordon, Joel Silver
SCREENPLAY: Larry Gross, Walter Hill
SCORE: Ry Cooder
SPECIAL MUSICAL MATERIAL SUPERVISED BY: Jimmy Iovine
CHOREOGRAPHY: Jeffrey Hornaday
CAST: Michael Paré, Diane Lane, Amy Madigan, Rick Moranis
MUSICAL PERFORMERS: the Blasters, Winston Ford (for the Sorels), Laurie Sargent (for Diane Lane)
SONGS PERFORMED: *Blue Shadows, One Bad Stud*, the Blasters; *Countdown to Love*, Winston Ford; *Never Be You, Sorcerer*, Laurie Sargent
SOUNDTRACK SONGS: *First Love First Tears, Get Out of Denver, Hold That Snake, Rumble, You Got What You Wanted*, the Ry Cooder Band; *I Can Dream About You, Nowhere Fast, Tonight Is What It Means to Be Young*, Fire Inc.; *Deeper and Deeper*, the Fixx
SOUNDTRACK: MCA
VIDEO: CIC – UK; MCA – US

Incredibly stylish but empty street-glamour musical. Walter Hill has a great feel for the city, and this post-decline-of-Western-Civilisation New York looks wonderful photographed by Andrew Laszlo; but there's

STREETS OF FIRE Michael Paré.

MUSICALS

no *there* there. The perfunctory plot has a Pat Benatar-like rock superstar (Lane) kidnapped by the repulsively slimy leader of an all-powerful street gang. Her former boyfriend (Paré) back from the wars (they never say *what* wars) is hired by her nasty manager (Moranis) to rescue her; on the way he picks up a tough woman veteran (Madigan) as a sidekick. Unfortunately, Paré can't act and Lane can't sing; all her overblown performances are dubbed and the 'Special Musical Material' supervised by Jimmy Iovine is strikingly inferior to the background score by Ry Cooder. That said, the total atmosphere *can* be pretty enjoyable, and it's not *supposed* to be Shakespeare.

SUMMER HOLIDAY 1963
Warner Brothers, color, 109 minutes

DIRECTOR: Peter Yates
PRODUCERS: Peter Yates
MUSIC BY: Stanley Black
CAST: Cliff Richard, Laurie Peters, Melvyn Hayes, Una Stubbs, the Shadows (Hank Marvin, Bruce Welch, Jet Harris, Tony Meehan)
MUSICAL PERFORMERS: Cliff and the Shadows, Grazina Frame
SONGS PERFORMED: *All At Once, Bachelor Boy, Big News, Dancing Shoes, The Next Time, Stranger In Town, Summer Holiday*, Cliff and the Shadows; *Swingin' Affair*, Cliff, Grazina Frame; *Foot Tapper, Les Girls, Round and Round*, the Shadows
SOUNDTRACK: Epic – US; Columbia – UK
VIDEO: Thorn–EMI – UK

Kids drive to Greece in a London double-decker bus in this lively musical-travel flick. Cliff and the boys stop to perform about every five minutes, and amazingly enough, they pick up some girls on the way. Some good songs, too. The unquestioning sense of freedom and optimism makes this a classic picture of early Sixties' youth. Everybody has a job.

SUMMER HOLIDAY   Cliff in bus conductor's suit.

Cliff Richard and Laurie Peters in SUMMER HOLIDAY.

SURF PARTY 1964
Twentieth Century Fox, color, 68 minutes

DIRECTOR: Maury Dexter
PRODUCER: Maury Dexter
SCREENPLAY: Harry Spalding
CAST: Bobby Vinton, Jackie De Shannon, Patricia Morrow, Kenny Miller, Lory Patrick

Bobby Vinton guest-starred in SURF PARTY.

MUSICAL PERFORMERS: the Astronauts, Jackie De Shannon, the Routers, Bobby Vinton
SONGS PERFORMED: *Fire Water*, *Surf Party*, the Astronauts; *Glory Wave*, Jackie De Shannon; *Crack Up*, the Routers; *If I Were An Artist*, Bobby Vinton
SOUNDTRACK: Twentieth Century Fox – US; Stateside – UK

Three girls go to Malibu to find a missing brother. Not dire but pretty dull stuff; Bobby Vinton and Jackie De Shannon were a sort of second-string Frankie and Annette, if you can imagine such a thing.

SWINGER'S PARADISE see WONDERFUL LIFE

SWINGIN' ALONG A.K.A DOUBLE TROUBLE 1962
Lippert Films, color, 74 minutes

DIRECTOR: Charles Barton
PRODUCER: Jack Leewood
SCREENPLAY: Arthur Morton
CAST: Tommy Noonan, Peter Marshall, Barbara Eden, Connie Gilchrist
MUSICAL PERFORMERS: Ray Charles, Bobby Vee
SONGS PERFORMED: *What'd I Say*, Ray Charles

This time it's not a talent contest, it's a songwriting contest. Tommy Noonan wins. So much for the plot; but the music isn't much, either, except, naturally, for Ray Charles.

A SWINGIN' SUMMER 1965
United Screen Arts, color, 80 minutes

DIRECTOR: Robert Sparr
PRODUCER: Reno Carell
SCREENPLAY: Leigh Chapman
CAST: William Wellman Jnr., James Stacy, Quinn O'Hara, Martin West, Raquel Welch
MUSICAL PERFORMERS: Donnie Brooks, Gary Lewis and the Playboys, Jody Miller, the Righteous Brothers, the Rip Chords, Raquel Welch
SONGS PERFORMED: *Pennie the Poo*, Donnie Brooks; *Nitro*, *Out to Lunch*, Gary Lewis and the Playboys; *A Swingin' Summer*, Jody Miller; *Justine*, the Righteous Brothers; *Red Hot Roadster*, the Rip Chords; *Ready to Groove*, Raquel Welch
SOUNDTRACK: Hanna-Barbera – US

Teens save a local dance hall from destruction; Raquel doesn't talk about *this* one much now that she's a serious actress. Mixed bag of music, though the Righteous Brothers and (yes) Gary Lewis and the Playboys are worth seeing. But what about *Pennie the Poo*!

MUSICALS

TEENAGE MILLIONAIRE 1961
United Artists, black & white, 90 minutes

DIRECTOR: Lawrence Doheny
PRODUCER: Howard B. Kreitsek
SCREENPLAY: H. B. Cross
CAST: Jimmy Clanton, Rocky Graziano, Zazu Pitts, Jack Larson, Diana Jergens
MUSICAL PERFORMERS: the Bill Black Combo, Chubby Checker, Jimmy Clanton, Dion, Vicki Spencer, Jackie Wilson
SONGS PERFORMED: *Green Light*, Jimmy Clanton; *Let's Twist Again*, Chubby Checker; *Back to School Blue, Happy Times, Hello Mr Dream, I Wait, The Jet, Kissin' Game, Lonely Life, Oh Mary, Possibility, Smokie, Somebody Nobody Wants, Teenage Millionaire, The Way I Am, Yogi*
SOUNDTRACK: Ace – US

Not too bad – rich kid Jimmy Clanton makes a record without revealing his identity. Rocky plays his bodyguard. Clanton was usually quite good, and there are some good guest performances.

THANK GOD IT'S FRIDAY 1978
Columbia Pictures, color, 100 minutes

DIRECTOR: Robert Klane
PRODUCER: Rob Cohen
SCREENPLAY: Barry Armyan Bernstein
CAST: Jeff Goldblum, Valerie Landsburg, Donna Summer, Terri Nunn, Ray Vitte
MUSICAL PERFORMERS: the Commodores, Donna Summer
SONGS PERFORMED: *Easy, Brickhouse, Too Hot To Trot*, the Commodores; *The Last Dance*, Donna Summer
SOUNDTRACK SONGS: *After Dark*, Patti Brooks; *It's Serious*, Cameo; *You're the Reason I Feel Like Dancing*, the Fifth Dimension; *Dance All Night*, Cuba Gooding; *I'm Here Again*, Thelma Houston; *I Wanna Dance*, Marathon; *Down to Lovetown*, the Originals; *Lovin' Livin' and Givin'*, Diana Ross; *Je T'Aime, Love To Love You Baby, Try With Your Love*, Donna Summer; *Let's Make a Deal*, Syreeta and G. C. Cameron; *Hollywood, I Am What I Am*, the Village People; *Leatherman's Theme*, the Wright Brothers Flying Machine
SOUNDTRACK: Casablanca
VIDEO: Columbia – US

One diverting night at a Hollywood disco, with various characters drifting in and out. There is the inevitable dance contest and a young singer trying to get on the radio. A light, fast script, good actors, and a really superior disco soundtrack make this very entertaining.

THANK GOD IT'S FRIDAY The Commodores; Lionel Ritchie (center top).

THAT'LL BE THE DAY 1973
Mayfair Films, color, 91 minutes

DIRECTOR: Claude Whatham
PRODUCERS: Sandy Lieberson, David Puttnam
SCREENPLAY: Ray Connolly
MUSICAL SUPERVISION: Neil Aspinall, Keith Moon
CAST: David Essex, Rosemary Leach, James Booth, Ringo Starr, Rosalind Ayres, Billy Fury, Keith Moon
MUSICAL PERFORMERS: David Essex, Billy Fury
SONGS PERFORMED: *Rock On*, David Essex; *Get Yourself Together*, *Long Live Rock*, *That's All Right*, *A Thousand Stars*, *What'd I Say*, Billy Fury
SOUNDTRACK SONGS: *Chantilly Lace*, the Big Bopper; *Tequila*, the Champs; *At the Hop*, Danny and the Juniors; *Alley Oop*, Dante and the Evergreens; *Little Darling*, the Diamonds; *Runaround Sue*, Dion; *Bye Bye Love*, *Devoted to You*, *Till I Kissed You*, *Wake Up Little Suzie*, the Everly Brothers; *Red River Rock*, Johnny and the Hurricanes; *Sealed With a Kiss*, Brian Hyland; *Raunchy*, Bill Justis; *Party Doll*, Buddy Knox; *Why Do Fools Fall In Love?*, Frankie Lymon and the Teenagers; *Great Balls of Fire*, Jerry Lee Lewis; *Tutti Frutti*, Little Richard; *Book of Love*, the Monotones; *I Love How You Love Me*, the Paris Sisters; *Smoke Gets In Your Eyes*, the Platters; *Born Too Late*, the Ponitails; *Running Bear*, Johnny Preston; *Personality*, Lloyd Price; *Honeycomb*, Jimmie Rodgers; *Runaway*, Del Shannon; *Linda Lou*, Ray Sharp; *Red Leather Jacket*, Viv Stanshall; *What In the World*, Stormy Tempest; *Poetry In Motion*, Johnny Tillotson; *Well All Right*, Bobby Vee; *That'll Be the Day*, Bobby Vee and the Crickets; *Slow Down*, Eugene Wallace; *Boney Moronie*, Larry Williams; *It'll Be Me*, Wishful Thinking
SOUNDTRACK: Ronco – UK
VIDEO: Thorn – US

Excellent drama, not really a musical, but with a great score of oldies – not the usual stuff, but a very well-chosen selection. The plot follows poor, discontented Jim Maclaine, who finds a way up and out through rock; the story is one of the continuous romances of rock'n'roll.

Director Claude Waltham, Ringo Starr and David Essex on the set filming THAT'LL BE THE DAY.

THIS IS SPINAL TAP 1984
Embassy Pictures, color, 79 minutes

DIRECTOR: Rob Reiner
PRODUCER: Karen Murphy
SCREENPLAY: Christopher Guest, Michael McKean, Harry Shearer, Rob Reiner
MUSIC AND LYRICS BY: Christopher Guest, Michael McKean, Harry Shearer, Rob Reiner
CAST: Christopher Guest, Michael McKean, Harry Shearer, June Chadwick, Rob Reiner, Ed Begley Jr., Paul Shaffer, Patrick MacNee, Howard Hessman
MUSICAL PERFORMERS: Christopher Guest, Michael McKean, Harry Shearer, R. J. Parnell, David Kaff, John Sinclair
SONGS PERFORMED: *All the Way Home*, *Big Bottom*, *Cups and Cakes*, *Gimme Some Money*, *Heartbreak Hotel*, *Heavy Duty Rock'n'Roll*, *Hell*

Hole, Jazz Odyssey, Listen to What the Flower People Say, Rock'n'Roll Creation, Sex Farm, Stonehenge, Tonight I'm Gonna Rock You
SOUNDTRACK: Polydor
VIDEO: Embassy

A wonderful satire of heavy metal in particular and rock in general; razor-sharp, knowing, and loving. Spinal Tap are luckless English rockers on a tour of the States; their progress is captured on film by dedicated filmmaker Marty DiBurgi. They're all idiots, and their travels are fraught with personal, musical and professional disasters. Every character is a meticulous and delicately observed parody, but somehow their feelings are still genuine; they become important to you, and you *care* what happens to them; this is a triumph for the writers and actors. One of the best rock movies ever.

TICKLE ME   1965
Allied Artists, color, 90 minutes

DIRECTOR: Norman Taurog
PRODUCER: Ben Schwalb
SCREENPLAY: Edward Bernds, Elwood Ullman
CAST: Elvis Presley, Julie Adams, Merry Andrews, Jocelyn Lane, Jack Mullaney
MUSICAL PERFORMER: Elvis Presley
SONGS PERFORMED: *Dirty Dirty Feeling, I Feel I've Known You Forever, I'm Yours, It Feels So Right, Long Lonely Highway, Night Rider, Put the Blame On Me, Slowly But Surely, Such An Easy Question*
VIDEO: Key – US

With a title like that, you can see that this is going to be one of the sillier Elvis pictures. Here he works on an all-girl dude ranch; naturally, he gets mixed up with more than one female. Quite a lot of music, but not much that's good.

TILT   1978
Barber Dann, color, 111 minutes

DIRECTOR: Rudy Durand
PRODUCER: Ron Joy
CAST: Brooke Shields, Ken Marshall, Charles Durning, Harvey Lewis
MUSICAL PERFORMERS: Randy Bishop and Marty Gwinn, the Bill Wray Band
SONGS PERFORMED: *Don't Let the Rain Get To You, You Really Didn't Have To Do It*, Randy Bishop and Marty Gwinn; *Don't Stop the Music, Friends, Koala Shuffle, Mercedes Morning, Melody Man, My Music, Pinball That's All, Rock'n'Roll Rodeo*
SOUNDTRACK: ABC – US

Imbecilic tale of a girl pinball whiz getting ripped off by a musician. Truly stupid, and the music is awful too.

TIMES SQUARE   1980
Columbia-EMI-Warner, color, 102 minutes

DIRECTOR: Alan Moyle
PRODUCER: Kevin McCormack
SCREENPLAY: Jacob Brackman
ORIGINAL SCORE: Blue Weaver
CAST: Tim Curry, Trini Alvarado, Robin Johnson
MUSICAL PERFORMERS: Robin Johnson, with Trini Alvarado and with David Johansen
SONGS PERFORMED: *Damn Dog*, Robin Johnson; *Your Daughter Is One*, Robin Johnson, Trini Alvarado; *Flowers In the City*, Robin Johnson, David Johansen
SOUNDTRACK SONGS: *Dangerous Type*, the Cars; *Grinding Halt*, the Cure; *The Night Was Not*, Desmond Child and Rouge; *You Can't Hurry Love*, D. L. Byron; *Pretty Boys*, Joe Jackson; *Innocent Not Guilty*, Garland Jeffreys; *Down In the Park*, Gary Numan; *Talk of the Town*, the Pretenders; *Rock Hard*, Suzi Quatro; *Help Me*, Marcy Levy and Robin Gibb; *I Wanna Be Sedated*, the Ramones; *Walk On the Wild Side*, Lou Reed; *Same Old Scene*, Roxy Music; *Babylon's Burning*, the Ruts; *Pissing In the River*, Patti Smith; *Life During Wartime*, Talking Heads; *Take This Town*, XTC
SOUNDTRACK: RSO

VIDEO: Thorn–EMI – UK, US

A view of New York punk, too late and certainly too little – this might as well be a Disney picture for all the superficial sleeze, which amounts to not much more than exaggerated make-up and the wearing of black plastic bags. This hardly amounts to the downfall of western civilization. The plot, such as it is, concerns a middle-class runaway and a young punk who become friends and tear around New York for a while. Only Tim Curry, as a sympathetic DJ (and David Johansen, as his sympathetic self), bring any sincerity to the whole mess. The soundtrack, however, is excellent.

TOMMY 1975
Columbia Pictures, color, 111 minutes

DIRECTOR: Ken Russell
PRODUCERS: Ken Russell, Robert Stigwood
SCREENPLAY: Ken Russell
FROM: the opera by Pete Townshend and the Who
CAST: Roger Daltrey, Ann-Margret, Oliver Reed, Elton John, Keith Moon, Paul Nicholas, Jack Nicholson, Robert Powell, John Entwhistle, Tina Turner
MUSICAL PERFORMERS: Ann-Margret, Eric Clapton, Roger Daltrey, Elton John, Keith Moon, Paul Nicholas, Pete Townshend, Simon Townshend, Tina Turner, the Who (Roger Daltrey, John Entwhistle, Keith Moon, Pete Townshend)
SONGS PERFORMED: *I'm Free, Listening to You, See Me, Feel Me, Sensation, We're Not Gonna Take It*, Roger Daltrey; *Today It Rained Champagne, Mother and Son*, Roger Daltrey, Ann-Margret; *Welcome*, Roger Daltrey, Ann-Margret, Oliver Reed; *Sally Simpson*, Roger Daltrey, Pete Townshend; *Eyesight to the Blind*, Eric Clapton; *Pinball Wizard*, Elton John; *Fiddle About, Tommy's Holiday Camp*, Keith Moon; *Cousin Kevin*, Paul Nicholas; *Amazing Journey, Captain Walker Didn't Come Home/It's a Boy*, Pete

T-51

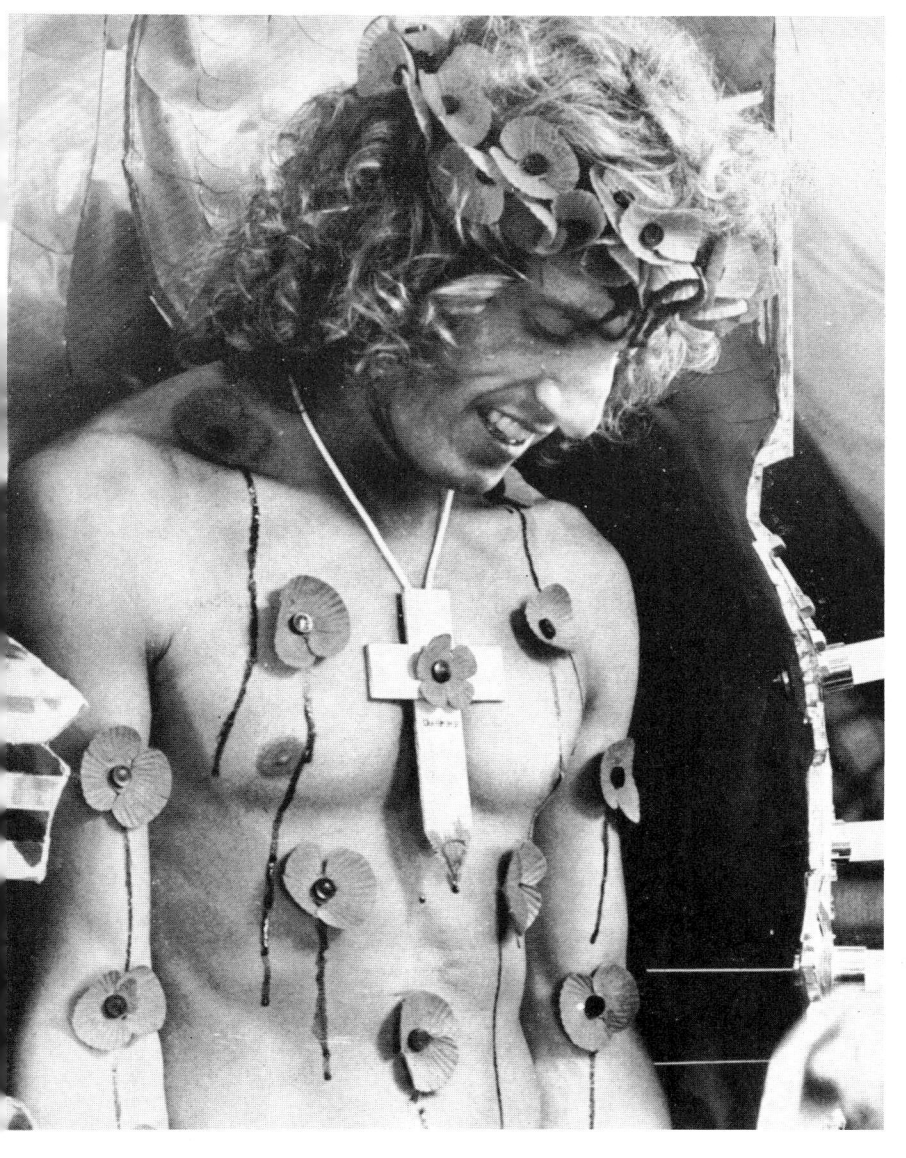

TOMMY Roger Daltrey in the leading role.

Townshend; *Miracle Cure*, Simon Townshend; *Acid Queen*, Tina Turner; *Sparks*, the Who
SOUNDTRACK: MCA – US; Polydor – UK
VIDEO: Thorn–EMI – UK; Columbia – US

Needless to say, Russell's version of Townshend's rock opera is thoroughly over the top. It's also quite likeable, and some of the set pieces – forerunners of videos, really – are superb, as Russell himself has been pointing out recently. The plot, for those who don't know, is about a psychosomatic deaf-mute who becomes a pinball genius and founds a new religion; the effectiveness of this is due to character, symbolism and emotive power, rather than story. Some great performances of some of the Who's best songs by the myriad stars, especially Tina Turner and Elton John.

TOMMY Keith Moon.

THE TOMMY STEELE STORY

THE TOMMY STEELE STORY A.K.A. ROCK AROUND THE WORLD 1957
Anglo-Amalgamated, black & white, 82 minutes

DIRECTOR: Gerard Bryant
PRODUCERS: Peter Rogers, Herbert Smith
SCREENPLAY: Norman Hudis
CAST: Tommy Steele, Hilda Fenemore, Patrick Westwood
MUSICAL PERFORMERS: Humphrey Lyttleton, the Chas McDevitt Skiffle Group with Nancy Whiskey, the Tommy Eytle Calypso Band, Chris O'Brien's Caribbeans, Tommy Steele
SONGS PERFORMED: *Build Up, Butterfingers, Cannibal Pot, Doomsday Rock, Elevator Rock, I Like, A Handful of Songs, Take My Baby Back, Teenage Party, Time to Kill, Two Eyes, Water Water, Will It Be You, You Gotta Go*
SOUNDTRACK: Decca – UK

According to this, he was discovered in a coffee bar. Now there's a novel idea. Anyway, this is banal and fairly witless, though there are lots of songs.

Tommy is discovered in a coffee bar in THE TOMMY STEELE STORY

119

MUSICALS

THE TOMMY STEELE STORY
Cliff Richard and Tommy Steele.

TOP SECRET 1985
Paramount Pictures, color, 90 minutes

DIRECTORS: Jim Abrahams, David Zucker, Jerry Zucker
PRODUCERS: Jon Davison, Hunt Lowry
SCREENPLAY: Jim Abrahams, Martyn Burke, David Zucker, Jerry Zucker
MUSIC COMPOSED AND CONDUCTED BY: Maurice Jarre
ADDITIONAL LYRICS BY: Howard Kaylan, Mark Volman
SONGS PRODUCED BY: Mike Moran
MUSICAL PERFORMER: Val Kilmer
SONGS PERFORMED: *Are You Lonesome Tonight?, Spend This Night With Me, Straighten Out the Rug, Tutti Fruitti*
SOUNDTRACK SONGS: *How Silly Can You Get, Skeet-Surfin'*, Val Kilmer

Sssh TOP SECRET

SOUNDTRACK: Passport Records – US
VIDEO: CIC – UK

An extremely silly and amusing spoof of many genres of film: rock musicals, war movies, spy movies, escape movies, a dash of western, *The Blue Lagoon* and *The Wizard of Oz*. Val Kilmer is excellent (*and* does his own songs) as Nick Rivers, a straight-faced rock hero who gains international stardom exploiting a new teen craze, skeet-surfing ('when we shoot the curl, we *really* shoot the curl'), and gets involved in a ridiculous plot to rescue an absent-minded scientist from neo-Nazis in West Germany. Full of very funny cameos by well-known faces like Peter Cushing and Omar Sharif and terrific over-the-top performances; it also features a white cow with real talent who wears galoshes and smokes a cigarette.

TROUBLE AT 16   see PLATINUM HIGH SCHOOL

THE TROUBLE WITH GIRLS   1969
Metro Goldwyn Mayer, color, 104 minutes

DIRECTOR: Peter Tewksbury
PRODUCER: Lester Welch
SCREENPLAY: Arnold Peyser, Lois Peyser
CAST: Elvis Presley, Sheree North, Joyce Van Patten, Marlyn Mason, Nichole Jaffe, John Carradine, Vincent Price
MUSICAL PERFORMER: Elvis Presley
SONGS PERFORMED: *Almost, Aura Lee, Clean Up Your Own Back Yard, Sign of the Zodiac, Swing Low Sweet Chariot*
SOUNDTRACK: RCA – US

Elvis' last musical is quite nice – none of the excitement of his first films, but a harmlessly mild period story about a travelling tent show (or chautaqua) that runs into trouble in a small town. Few songs, none of them are great.

TWIST ALL NIGHT A.K.A. THE YOUNG AND THE COOL   1962
76 minutes

DIRECTOR: William J. Hole Jnr.
CAST: Louis Prima, June Wilkinson, Gertrude Michael
MUSICAL PERFORMERS: Louis Prima, Sam Butera and the Witnesses
SONGS PERFORMED: *Alright Okay You Win, Better Twist Now Baby, Chantilly Lace, Fool Around, Sam's Boogie, Tag That Twistin' Dolly, When the Saints Go Twistin' In*

Another low-budget try for Louis Prima; here, he and his band have trouble keeping their nightclub afloat. It's just one twist after another, which palls somewhat.

TWIST AROUND THE CLOCK   1961
Columbia Pictures, black & white, 86 minutes

DIRECTOR: Oscar Rudolph
PRODUCER: Sam Katzman
SCREENPLAY: James B. Gordon

TWIST AROUND THE CLOCK – Chubby Checker in action.

CAST: Vicki Spencer, Clay Cole, Chubby Checker, Dion
MUSICAL PERFORMERS: Chubby Checker, Clay Cole, Dion, the Marcels, Vicki Spencer
SONGS PERFORMED: *Don't Twist With Anyone Else But Me, Merry Twistmas, Twist Along, Twistin' USA, Your Lips and Mine*, Chubby Checker; *Twist Around the Clock*, Clay Cole; *The Majestic, Runaround Sue, The Wanderer*, Dion; *Blue Moon*, the Marcels; *He's So Sweet*, Vicki Spencer

Chubby Checker discovers the twist craze. This has some good music; not only Dion, who's rarely seen in films, but the Marcels' *Blue Moon*. I wonder who thought of *Merry Twistmas*?

TWO A PENNY 1967
Worldwide Films, color, 98 minutes

DIRECTOR: James F. Collier
PRODUCER: Frank R. Jacobsen
MUSICAL DIRECTOR: Mike Leander

TWO A PENNY Cliff and Ann Holloway.

CAST: Cliff Richard, Dora Bryan, Avril Angers, Ann Holloway, Billy Graham
MUSICAL PERFORMER: Cliff Richard
SONGS PERFORMED: *And Me (I'm On the Outside Now), I'll Love You Forever Today, Lonely Girl, Questions, Twist and Shout, Two a Penny*
SOUNDTRACK: Columbia – UK; Light – US

Cliff, as a young pop star, gets involved in drugs – now, who's going to believe that? – but eventually finds God and reforms. Not much music.

TWO TICKETS TO PARIS 1962
Columbia, 90 minutes

DIRECTOR: Greg Garrison
PRODUCER: Harry Romm
MUSICAL DIRECTOR: Henry Glover
CAST: Gary Crosby, Jeri Lynne Fraser, Kay Medford, Joey Dee and the Starlighters
MUSICAL PERFORMERS: Joey Dee and the Starlighters, Jeri Lynne Fraser
SONGS PERFORMED: *C'est Si Bon, This Boat, Twistin' On a Liner, What Kind of Love Is This*, Joey Dee and the Starlighters; *Baby Won't You Please Come Home, Teenage Vamp*, Jeri Lynn Fraser; *Willy Willy*, the Starlighters
SOUNDTRACK: Roulette – US

Joey Dee and the Starlighters go to Paris, for some reason. The usual barely-existent story strung with songs, which are not bad; Joey Dee and Company were always worth a listen.

UNTAMED YOUTH 1957
Warner Brothers, black & white, 80 minutes

DIRECTOR: Howard W. Koch
PRODUCER: Aubrey Schenck
SCREENPLAY: John C. Higgens
CAST: Mamie Van Doren, Lori Nelson, John Russell, Don Burnett, Eddie Cochran
MUSICAL PERFORMERS: Eddie Cochran, Mamie Van Doren

SONGS PERFORMED: *Cottonpicker*, Eddie Cochran; *Oobala Baby*, Mamie Van Doren

Two girl singers are arrested and sent to a co-ed prison farm (but at least it's not run by nuns, like *GIRLS' TOWN*). This gives them an opportunity to indulge in a lot of Fifties' sin, sex, and song, including an appearance by Eddie Cochran (as a character called 'Bong'). A real exploitation classic.

VIVA LAS VEGAS A.K.A. LOVE IN LAS VEGAS 1964
Metro Goldwyn Mayer, color, 86 minutes

DIRECTOR: George Sidney
PRODUCERS: Jack Cummings, George Sidney
SCREENPLAY: Sally Benson
CAST: Elvis Presley, Ann-Margret, William Demarest, Cesare Danova, Nicky Blair
MUSICAL PERFORMERS: Ann-Margret, Elvis Presley
SONGS PERFORMED: *I Need Somebody to Lean On, If You Think I Don't Need You, Night Life, Today Tomorrow and Forever, Viva Las Vegas, Yellow Rose of Texas, What'd I Say*, Elvis Presley; *C'mon Everybody, The Lady Loves Me*, Ann-Margret, Elvis Presley
SOUNDTRACK: RCA (EP)
VIDEO: MGM–UA – US

In Ann Margret, Elvis finally met a girl who could keep up with him; the numbers they do together have that old fire. Here he is a race driver (again) who chases Annie all the way to the title city – no big drama, but a good script, good cast and skilful direction make this enjoyable to watch.

VIVA LAS VEGAS   Elvis and Ann-Margret in various scenes.

MUSICALS

WHAT A CRAZY WORLD 1963
Warner Brothers, 88 minutes

DIRECTOR: Michael Carreras
PRODUCER: Michael Carreras
SCREENPLAY: Michael Carreras, Allen Klein
CAST: Joe Brown, Marty Wilde, Susan Maughan, Harry Corbett, Avis Bunnage
MUSICAL PERFORMERS: Joe Brown and the Bruvvers, Freddie and the Dreamers
SONGS PERFORMED: *Alfred Hitchins, Bruvvers, I Sure Know a Lot About Love, Independence, Just You Wait and See, Layabout's Lament, Oh What a Family, Please Give Me a Chance, Sally Ann, Things We Never Said, Wasn't It a Handsome Punch-Up?, What a Crazy World We're Living In*
SOUNDTRACK: Piccadilly – UK

Young man gets a job with a music publisher and writes a hit song. Only interesting, really, because Joe Brown is rarely seen in movies. Unfortunately, this also has Freddie and the Dreamers in it, which is the kiss of death in terms of film quality.

WHEN THE BOYS MEET THE GIRLS 1965
Metro Goldwyn Mayer, color, 97 minutes

DIRECTOR: Alvin Ganzer
PRODUCER: Sam Katzman
SCREENPLAY: Robert E. Kent
FROM: the musical *Girl Crazy*, by George and Ira Gershwin
CAST: Connie Francis, Harve Presnell, Sue Ann Langdon
MUSICAL PERFORMERS: Louis Armstrong, Connie Francis, Herman's Hermits, Liberace, Harve Presnell; Sam the Sham and the Pharaohs
SONGS PERFORMED: *Throw It Out of Your Mind*, Louis Armstrong; *Embraceable You, Mail Call, When the Boys Meet the Girls*, Connie Francis; *But Not For Me, I Got Rhythm*, Connie Francis,

Joe Brown and Susan Maughan in WHAT A CRAZY WORLD.

WHAT A CRAZY WORLD Freddie and the Dreamers in action.

Joe Brown guested in WHAT A CRAZY WORLD.

Harve Presnell: *Biding My Time*, *Listen People*, Herman's Hermits; *Aruba Liberace*, Liberace; *Monkey See Monkey Do*, Sam the Sham and the Pharaohs
SOUNDTRACK: MGM

Weird re-make of the Gershwin brothers' musical *Girl Crazy*, which was first seen in 1930 and last seen as a vehicle for Judy Garland and Mickey Rooney in 1943. The mix of acts is remarkably diverse; how all these characters get to the same dude ranch must remain the scriptwriter's secret. Anyway, the music is worth hearing, and Connie Francis does very creditably with the Gershwin material. (It sounds a little odd cheek by jowl with Sam the Sham, but never mind.)

WILD FOR KICKS see BEAT GIRL

WILD IN THE COUNTRY 1961
Twentieth Century Fox, color, 114 minutes

DIRECTOR: Philip Dunne
PRODUCER: Jerry Wald

WILD IN THE COUNTRY Elvis gets serious.

MUSICALS

SCREENPLAY: Clifford Odets
FROM: the novel *The Lost Country*, by J. R. Salamanca
CAST: Elvis Presley, Tuesday Weld, Hope Lange, Millie Perkins, John Ireland, Gary Lockwood
MUSICAL PERFORMER: Elvis Presley
SONGS PERFORMED: *Forget Me Never, I Slipped I Stumbled I Fell, In My Way, Lonely Man, Wild In the Country*
VIDEO: Key – US

One of the few Elvis films which could have stood on its own as a straight drama, due to a script by Clifford Odets and a professional cast. Elvis is a troubled youth with writing talent (a bit hard to swallow) who is guided away from hell-raising and towards expressing himself by Hope Lange; meanwhile, he's torn between a good girl and a bad girl. The songs are actually not much, but it's a very watchable movie anyway, as Sixties' problem-dramas go.

WILD IN THE STREETS 1968
American International Pictures, color, 96 minutes

DIRECTOR: Barry Shear
PRODUCERS: Samuel Z. Arkoff, James H. Nicholson
SCREENPLAY: Robert Thom
SONGS: Barry Mann, Cynthia Weil
CAST: Christopher Jordan, Diane Varsi, Shelley Winters, Hal Holbrook, Millie Perkins, Richard Pryor
MUSICAL PERFORMERS: the Gurus, Jerry Howard, Second Time, the Senators, 13th Power
SONGS PERFORMED: *Shelley In Camp*, the Gurus; *Wild In the Streets*, Jerry Howard; *Sally Le Roy*, Second Time; *Psychedelic Senate*, the Senators; *Fifty-Two Percent, Fourteen or Fight, Love to Be Your Man, Shape of Things to Come*, 13th Power
SOUNDTRACK: Sidewalk – US; Capitol – UK

The ultimate youth exploitation flick – the voting age is lowered to fourteen, and a ranting pop star is elected president; then he

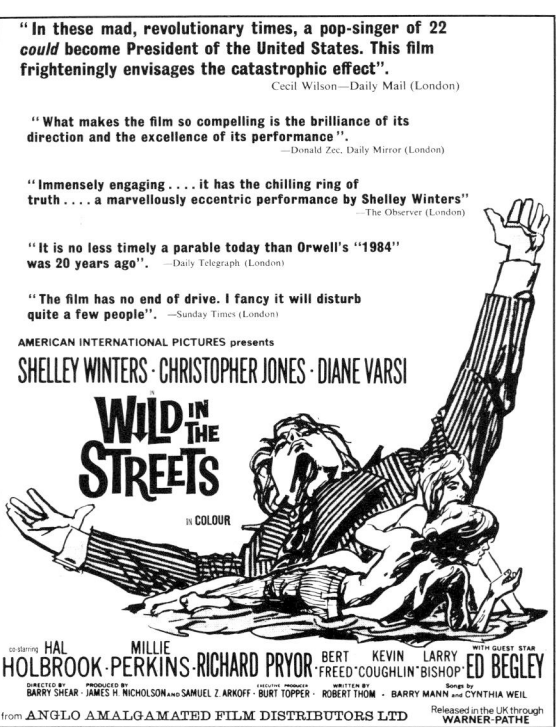

WILD IN THE STREETS Richard Pryor, Christopher Jones, and Shelley Winters.

UK advertisement for WILD IN THE STREETS.

126

effects a plan to dispose of everyone over thirty. Wild is right – no one could possibly take this seriously, but it's lots of fun.

WILD ON THE BEACH   1965
Twentieth Century Fox, black & white, 77 minutes

DIRECTOR: Maury Dexter
PRODUCER: Maury Dexter
SCREENPLAY: Harry Spalding
CAST: Frankie Randall, Sherry Jackson, Russ Bender, Cindy Malone, Sandy Nelson, Sonny and Cher
SONGS PERFORMED: *Little Speedy Gonzales*, *Rock the World*, *Snap It*, the Astronauts; *Tick a Tick a Tick*, Russ Bender; *Winter Nocturne*, Jackie and Gayle; *Run Away From Him*, Cindy Malone; *Drum Dance*, Sandy Nelson; *House on the Beach*, Frankie Randall; *It's Gonna Rain*, Sonny and Cher
SOUNDTRACK: RCA – US

Dim comedy about a boy opening up a girls' boarding house. No one here has been heard of for a long time, except Sonny and Cher, and it's not surprising.

WILD WILD WINTER   1966
Universal International Pictures, color, 80 minutes

DIRECTOR: Lennie Weinrib
PRODUCER: Bart Patton
SCREENPLAY: David Malcolm
SCORE: Frank Wilson
CAST: Gary Clarke, Chris Noel, Suzie Kaye, Don Edmonds, Les Brown Jnr.
MUSICAL PERFORMERS: the Astronauts, the Beau Brummels, Dick and Dee Dee, Jackie and Gayle, Jay and the Americans
SONGS PERFORMED: *A Change of Heart*, the Astronauts; *Just Wait and See*, the Beau

WILD IN THE STREETS   Christopher Jones.

Brummels: *Heartbeats*, Dick and Dee Dee; *Our Love's Gonna Snowball*, Jackie and Gayle; *Two of a Kind*, Jay and the Americans
SOUNDTRACK: Decca – US

Two boys go to a ski resort to pick up girls. What an original plot! Late and lame entry in the mid-Sixties' series of teen pics, with a poor cast and poor songs.

WINTER A GO-GO 1965
Columbia, color, 88 minutes

DIRECTOR: Richard Benedict
PRODUCER: Reno Carell
SCREENPLAY: Bob Kanter
STORY: Reno Carell
CHOREOGRAPHY: Kay Carson
CAST: James Stacy, William Wellman Jnr., Beverly Adams, Julie Parrish
MUSICAL PERFORMERS: the Hondells, Joni Lyman, the Nooney Rickett Four, the Reflections
SONGS PERFORMED: *King of the Mountain*, Joni Lyman; *Do That Ski, Ski City*, the Nooney Rickett Four; *I'm Sweet On You*, the Reflections

Truly awful boy-meets-girl hijinks at a ski resort. Somehow the ski series never became as popular as the beach series. Maybe because the girls wore clothes. Maybe because the music was usually terrible, too, as here.

THE WIZ 1978
Universal International Pictures, color, 134 minutes

DIRECTOR: Sidney Lumet
PRODUCER: Rob Cohen
SCREENPLAY: Joel Schumaker
FROM: the musical by William Brown and Charlie Small
ADDITIONAL MUSIC BY: Quincy Jones, Ashford and Simpson
MUSICAL DIRECTOR: Quincy Jones
CAST: Diana Ross, Michael Jackson, Nipsey Russell, Ted Ross, Mabel King, Richard Pryor, Lena Horne
SONGS PERFORMED: *Be a Lion, Believe In Yourself, Can I Go On?, Don't Nobody Bring Me No Bad News, Ease On Down the Road, Emerald City Ballet, Everybody Rejoice, The Feeling That We Have, He's the Wizard, Is This What Feeling Gets?, Poppy Girls, Slide Some Oil to Me, Soon As I Get Home, What Would I Do If I Could Feel?, You Can't Win*
SOUNDTRACK: MCA
VIDEO: CIC – UK; MCA – US

Ill-conceived re-telling of L. Frank Baum's story of the journey to Oz. The main problem is that Dorothy is presented as an adult, not a child; thus the whole tone of frank and innocent wonder is lost. Diana Ross's thirty-year-old just seems retarded, not innocent. New York as the magical city, however, was a fine idea, and the brilliant sets by Tony Walton are the best things in the film. The other performances are good, but can't make up for the weak central figure; there are some catchy tunes, but too many veer into the goopily sentimental. The wicked, squawking, sarcastic New York crows are great, though.

WONDERFUL LIFE A.K.A. SWINGER'S PARADISE 1964
Warner Brothers, color, 113 minutes

DIRECTOR: Sidney J. Furie
PRODUCER: Kenneth Harper
MUSICAL SUPERVISION: Norrie Paramour
CHOREOGRAPHY: Gillian Lynne
CAST: Cliff Richard, Walter Slezak, Susan Hampshire, the Shadows (Hank Marvin, Bruce Welch, Jet Harris, Tony Meehan), Melvyn Hayes, Una Stubbs
MUSICAL PERFORMERS: Cliff Richard and the Shadows
SONGS PERFORMED: *All Kinds of People, Do You Remember, A Girl In Every Port, Home, In the Stars, A Little Imagination, A Matter of*

Moments, On the Beach, We Love a Movie, Wonderful Life, Youth and Experience, Cliff Richard, the Shadows; *Theme From Young Lovers, Walkin',* the Shadows
SOUNDTRACK: Columbia – UK; Epic – US

Young performers make an independent movie under the nose of their repressive director. Very light but okay Cliff musical, lots of songs.

WONDERFUL TO BE YOUNG   see   THE YOUNG ONES

XANADU   1980
Universal International Pictures, color, 93 minutes

DIRECTOR: Robert Greenwald
PRODUCER: Lawrence Gordon
SCREENPLAY: Richard Christian Danus, Marc Reid Rubel
CAST: Michael Beck, Gene Kelly, Olivia Newton-John
MUSICAL PERFORMERS: Olivia Newton-John, the Tubes
SONGS PERFORMED: *All Over the World, I'm Alive, Magic, Suddenly, Xanadu,* Olivia Newton-John; *Dancin',* the Tubes
SOUNDTRACK: MCA
VIDEO: CIC – UK; MCA – US

Silly and charmless whimsy about a goddess who takes the form of Olivia Newton-John and inspires a young painter and a veteran dancer to open a disco. (Newton-John has a nerve presuming to inspire Gene Kelly – it should have been the other way around). Some good tunes, it must be admitted, but you can hear them on the radio, you don't have to see the film.

YELLOW SUBMARINE   1968
Apple Films, color, 85 minutes

DIRECTOR: George Dunning

YELLOW SUBMARINE   The boys meet the Nowhere Man.

PRODUCER: Al Brodax
SCREENPLAY: Al Brodax, Jack Mendelsohn, Lee Minoff, Erich Segal
ANIMATION DIRECTOR: Bob Balser
ALL MUSIC BY: the Beatles
ADDITIONAL MUSIC: George Martin
CAST (VOICES): John Clive, Geoffrey Hughes, Peter Batten, Paul Angelus
MUSIC WRITTEN AND PERFORMED BY: the Beatles.
SONGS INCLUDED: *A Day In the Life, All Together Now, All You Need Is Love, Eleanor Rigby, Hey Bulldog* (not in US release), *It's All Too Much, Lucy In the Sky With Diamonds, Nowhere Man, Only a Northern Song, Sgt. Pepper's Lonely Hearts Club Band, When I'm Sixty-Four, Yellow Submarine*
SOUNDTRACK: Apple

Delightful animated Beatles; fresh and fun in every way; with terrific songs, some of them written for the movie. The fab four also make a film appearance at the end of the film. The story, if you've been on Mars for the last twenty years, is of musical Pepperland enlisting the boys' help to fight off the music-hating Blue Meanies. Some gorgeous animated illustrations of old and new songs.

THE YOUNG AND THE COOL
see **TWIST ALL NIGHT**

THE YOUNG ONES A.K.A. WONDERFUL TO BE YOUNG 1961
Warner Brothers, color, 108 minutes

DIRECTOR: Sidney J. Furie
PRODUCER: Kenneth Harper
CAST: Cliff Richard, Carole Gray, Robert Morley, Richard O'Sullivan, Melvyn Hayes, Annette Robertson, the Shadows
MUSICAL PERFORMERS: Cliff Richard and the Shadows
SONGS PERFORMED: *Living Doll, The Young Ones, When the Girl In Your Arms*, Cliff Richard; *Peace Pipe, The Savage*, the Shadows; *All For One, Got a Funny Feeling, Lessons In Love, Nothing's Impossible, What Do You Know We've Got a Show*

One of Cliff's best musicals, it *still* uses the same old plot about teens getting together to put on a show. More pop than rock, but entertainingly tuneful.

THE YOUNG SWINGERS 1963
Twentieth Century Fox, black & white, 71 minutes

DIRECTOR: Maury Dexter
PRODUCER: Maury Dexter
SCREENPLAY: Harry Spalding
CAST: Molly Bee, Gene McDaniels, Jack Larson, Rod Lauren

SONGS PERFORMED: *Come A-Running, Come to the Party, Elijah, Greenback Dollar, I Can't Get You Out of My Heart, Mad Mad Mad, Voice On the Mountain, Watusi Surfer, You Pass Me By*

No-star teen exploitation with a remarkable plot – kids get together to put on a show to save their local hang-out. Weak songs, weak film.

ZACHARIAH 1971
ABC Films, color, 93 minutes

DIRECTOR: George Englund
PRODUCER: George Englund
SCREENPLAY: the Firesign Theater (Phil Austin, Peter Bergman, David Ossman, Phil Proctor)
SCORE: James Haskell
CAST: John Rubenstein, Pat Quinn, Don Johnson
MUSICAL PERFORMERS: Country Joe and the Fish, the James Gang, Doug Kershaw, the New York Rock'n'Roll Ensemble, White Lightnin
SONGS PERFORMED: *All I Need, We're the Crackers*, Country Joe and the Fish; *Country Fever, Laguna Salada*, the James Gang; *The Ballad of Job Cain*, Doug Kershaw; *Gravedigger*, the New York Rock'n'Roll Ensemble; *Shy Ann*, White Lightnin
SOUNDTRACK: ABC – US; Probe – UK

Interesting, at least; a satirical rock western. Instigators Firesign Theater disapproved of the final version, as their script had been ripped to shreds. Too bad, as they've come up with successful projects since. The music is interesting, too. Worth seeing.

CONCERTS AND DOCUMENTARIES

ABBA – THE MOVIE 1977
Warner Brothers, color, 95 minutes

DIRECTOR: Lasse Hallstrom
PRODUCERS: Stig Anderson, Reg Grundy
MUSICAL PERFORMERS: Abba (Benny Andersson, Anni-Frid Lyngstad-Frederiksson, Björn Ulvaeus, Agnetha Ulvaeus)
SONGS PERFORMED: *Dancing Queen, Eagle, Fernando, Get On the Carousel, He Is Your Brother, Hole In Your Sole, I'm a Marionette, Intermezzo Nr 1, Johan På Snippen, I've Been Waiting For You, Mamma Mia, Money Money Money, The Name of the Game, Please Change Your Mind, Polken Gar, Ring Ring, Rock Me, SOS, So Long, Stoned, Thank You For the Music, Tiger, Waterloo, When I Kissed the Teacher, Why Did It Have To Be Me*
VIDEO: Monte – US

The title says it all – this is all Abba and nothing but Abba. There are twenty-five songs in a row, many of them international hits (and a couple of them in Swedish, for a change). And that's about it. If you love them, you'll love this.

BAD MANNERS LIVE IN CONCERT 1983
On-TV Productions Ltd., color, 56 minutes

DIRECTOR: Annie Rowe
PRODUCER: Peter D. Abbey
MUSICAL PERFORMERS: Bad Manners (Louis Alfonso, Buster Bloodvessel, Brian Chew-Itt, Dave Farr-In, Chris Kane, Gus Herman, Andy Marson, Martin Stewart), with Jimmy Scott and Jerry Tremaine
SONGS PERFORMED: *Ben E. Wriggle, Can Can, Cheats On You, Echo 4.2, El-Pussycat, Inner London Violence, Ivor the Engine, Just a Feeling, King Ska Far, Lip Up Fatty, Lorraine, The Magnificent Seven, My Girl Lollipop, Ne Ne Na Na Na Nu Nu, Only Funking, Salad Bar, Samson and Delilah, She's So Sharp, Special Brew, Tequila, Walking In the Sunshine, Woolly Bully*

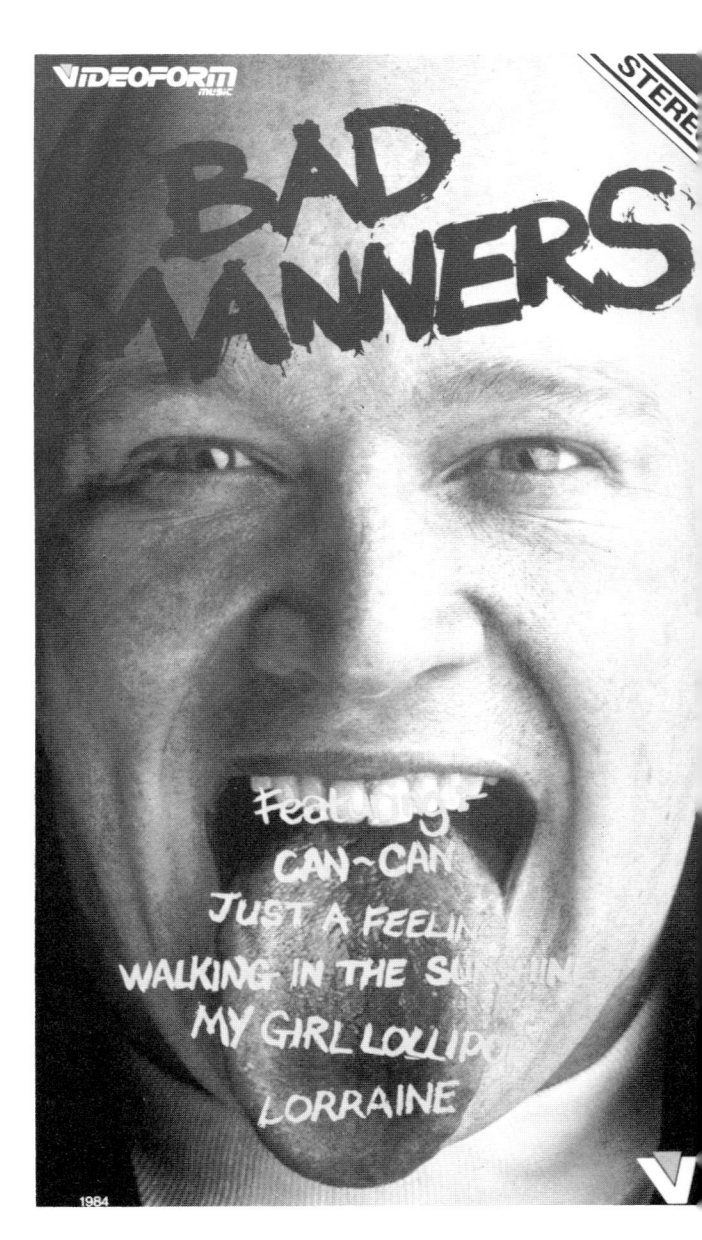

BAD MANNERS

A noisy, friendly and energetic set by the popular ska band, with a light show, dancing girls and an excellent horn section. Rather same-y and loud for an hour-long programme, but it's excellent dance music.

BANJOMAN Earl Scruggs.

BANJOMAN 1977
Blue Pacific Pictures, color, 105 minutes

DIRECTORS: Richard G. Abramson, Michael C. Varhol
PRODUCERS: Richard G. Abramson, Robert French, Michael C. Varhol
MUSICAL PERFORMERS: Joan Baez, David Bromberg, the Byrds, Ramblin' Jack Elliot, Tracy Nelson, the Nitty Gritty Dirt Band, Earl Scruggs Revue, Doc and Merle Watson
SONGS PERFORMED: *Amazing Grace, Blowin' In the Wind, The Night They Drove Old Dixie Down, You Ain't Goin' Nowhere,* Joan Baez; *Billy Fehr, Me and Bobby McGee,* Ramblin' Jack Elliot; *Battle of New Orleans, Diggy Liggy Lo, Honky Tonkin,* the Nitty Gritty Dirt Band; *Black Mountain Rag, Freight Train Boogie, Three Times Seven,* Doc and Merle Watson
SOUNDTRACK: Sire – US

A long list of country and country-rock artists pay tribute to banjo wizard Earl Scruggs in a music-packed but choppy filmed concert. Great sounds but not much to look at.

THE BIG T.N.T. SHOW 1966
American International Pictures, black & white, 93 minutes

DIRECTOR: Larry Peerce
PRODUCER: Phil Spector
MUSICAL DIRECTOR: Phil Spector
MUSICAL PERFORMERS: Joan Baez, the Byrds, Ray Charles, the Ray Charles Orchestra, Bo Diddley, Donovan, the Lovin' Spoonful, Roger Miller, the Ronettes, Ike and Tina Turner

SONGS PERFORMED: *Five Hundred Miles, You've Lost That Lovin' Feeling,* Joan Baez; *The Bells of Rhymney, Turn Turn Turn,* the Byrds; *Georgia On My Mind, Let the Good Times Roll, What'd I Say?,* Ray Charles; *One Two Three, Satisfaction,* the Ray Charles Orchestra; *Bo Diddley, The Break, Road Runner,* Bo Diddley; *My Sweet Joy, Summer Day Reflection, Universal Soldier,* Donovan; *Do You Believe In Magic?, You Didn't Have to Be So Nice,* the Lovin' Spoonful; *Dang Me, Engine No. 9, England Swings, King of the Road,* Roger Miller; *Be My Baby, Shout,* the Ronettes; *It's Gonna Work Out Fine,* Ike and Tina Turner

Big indeed, clumsy, and exciting. David

THE BIG T.N.T. SHOW The Byrds were among the performers; here is Roger McGuinn.

Ike and Tina Turner in THE BIG T.N.T. SHOW.

McCallum incongruously hosts some great performances; special honors go to the Ronettes and Bo Diddley.

BIRD ON A WIRE 1972
EMI, color, 92 minutes

DIRECTOR: Tony Palmer
PRODUCERS: Ron Kass, Martin Machat
MUSICAL PERFORMER: Leonard Cohen
SONGS PERFORMED: *Avalanche, Bird On a Wire, Chelsea Hotel, Famous Blue Raincoat, Marianne, Nancy, One of Us Can't Be Wrong, Sisters of Mercy, You Know Who I Am?*

Bits of several gigs on a world tour by Cohen. Irritating and pretentious, it's true, but included are some damn good songs. Perhaps Cohen is worth another look after all these years.

BLUE SUEDE SHOES 1979
World Northal, color, 97 minutes

DIRECTOR: Curtis Clark
PRODUCER: Penny Clark
MUSICAL PERFORMERS: Crazy Cavan and the Flying Saucers, Eddie Cochran, Bill Haley, Cliff Richard, Tommy Steele, Gene Vincent

A Rock'n'Roll Weekend at a holiday camp in Great Yarmouth is chronicled in this light-minded and light-hearted documentary; clips of classic performers are shown as well as music by recent revival bands. The accent is more on the social aspects of the scene – devoted fans dress, dance, and apparently live in the Fifties.

BLUES ALIVE 1983
Monarch Entertainment, color, 58 minutes

DIRECTOR: Len Dell'Amico
PRODUCERS: Jonathan Stathakis, Pat Weatherford
MUSICAL PERFORMERS: Buddy Guy and Junior Wells, Etta James, Albert King, John Mayall's Original Blues Breakers (Colin Allen, John McVie, Mick Taylor), Sippie Wallace
SONGS PERFORMED: *An Eye For an Eye, Baby What You Want Me to Do, Born Under a Bad Sign, C.C. Rider, Call It Stormy Monday, The Dark Side of Midnight, Don't Start Me Talkin', Messin' With the Kid, My Time After a While, Room to Move, Shorty George, Why Are You So Mean to Me?*
VIDEO: RCA–Columbia – UK

Disappointing reunion of John Mayall's Blues Breakers with some merely okay versions of classic songs and all-too-brief appearances by greats like Etta James, Sippie Wallace and Buddy Guy and Junior Wells. The whole thing takes off, though, when Albert King does a set and sweeps everybody else off the stage, in a display of power, charisma and musical brilliance. Worth seeing for his performance alone.

BOB MARLEY AND THE WAILERS LIVE! 1978
Blue Mountain Films, color, 78 minutes

DIRECTOR: Keith Macmillan
PRODUCER: Scott Millaney
MUSICAL PERFORMERS: Bob Marley and the Wailers
FILMED AT: the Rainbow, London, June 1977
SONGS PERFORMED: *Crazy Baldhead, Exodus, Get Up Stand Up, The Heathen, I Shot the Sheriff, Jammin', Lively Up Yourself, No Woman No Cry, Running Away, Them Bellyful, Trenchtown, Rock, War*
VIDEO: Thorn–EMI – UK & US

None too well-filmed concert footage, but Bob Marley was arguably at his height at the time of this performance, before illness had begun to take a toll. The songs featured are some of his greatest and the sound is generally quite good.

BORN TO BOOGIE 1972
Apple Films, color, 67 minutes

DIRECTOR: Ringo Starr
PRODUCER: Ringo Starr
MUSICAL PERFORMER: Marc Bolan
SONGS PERFORMED: *Baby Strange, Chariot Choogle, Children of the Revolution, Cosmic Dancer, Get It On, Hot Love, Jeepster, Let's Have a Party, Look to the Left, The Slider, Space Ball Picket, Telegram Sam, Tutti Frutti*

Concerts and fantasy sequences just about sum up the remarkably imaginative talent of the late Marc Bolan, the motive force behind T. Rex and an important solo artist. The elaborate productions of the Seventies date somewhat, but these songs don't – they are marvellous.

BROTHERS OF THE ROAD – THE ALLMAN BROTHERS BAND 1982
Monarch Entertainment, color, 59 minutes

DIRECTOR: Len Dell'Amico
PRODUCERS: Len Dell'Amico, Amy Polan, Jonathan Stathakis
MUSICAL PERFORMERS: Allman Brothers Band (Greg Allman, Dickey Betts, David Goldflies, Mike Lawler, Dan Toler, David Toler, Butch Trucks; Keith England, Bonnie Ballie, vocals)
SONGS PERFORMED: *Blue Sky, Jessica, Never Knew How Much (I Needed You), One Way Out, Pony Boy, Ramblin' Man, Statesboro Blues, Southbound, Whippin' Post, You Don't Love Me*
VIDEO: RCA–Columbia – UK

Straightforward concert by the re-formed band, performing a lot of their classic tunes, filmed at a sunny outdoor pavilion at the University of Florida; not wildly exciting, but enjoyable nostalgia for fans.

CARLENE CARTER LIVE IN LONDON 1983
Trilion Pictures Ltd, color, 58 minutes

DIRECTOR: None credited
PRODUCER: Phillip Goodhand-Tait
MUSICAL PERFORMERS: Carlene Carter and band consisting of: Ben Barson, James Eller, Kook Lawry, Mark Saunders, Annie Whitehead
SONGS PERFORMED: *Breathless, Cry, Gotta Love Like a Glove, Heart's In Traction, Heart to Heart, I'm Still Waiting, I'm So Cool, I'm the Kind of Sugar Daddy Likes, In a Heartbeat, Love Is a Four-Letter Verb, Madness, Meant it For a Minute, Never Together But Close Sometimes, One Way Ticket, Open Fire, Working Nine to Five A.M.*

Amiable and competent but not very exciting record of a Carlene Carter gig at the Marquee Club. She sings some good songs backed by capable musicians, including a woman trombone player, but there's not enough variety.

CELEBRATION AT BIG SUR 1971
A.K.A FESTIVAL AT BIG SUR
Twentieth Century Fox, color, 82 minutes

DIRECTORS: Baird Bryant, Joanna Demetrakis
PRODUCER: Carl Gottlieb
MUSICAL PERFORMERS: Joan Baez, the Combs Sisters, Crosby, Stills, Nash and Young, Joni Mitchell, Dorothy Morrison, John Sebastian
SONGS PERFORMED: *All God's Children, I Shall Be Released, Song for David, Sweet Sir Galahad,* Joan Baez; *Get Together, Sea of Madness,* Crosby, Stills, Nash and Young; *Woodstock,* Joni Mitchell; *Everybody Let's Get Together,* Dorothy Morrison; *Daydream,* John Sebastian; *Mobile Line,* John Sebastian and Steven Stills; *Oh Happy Day,* the Combs Sisters, others

Grainy visuals but some fine performances filmed at the Big Sur Folk Festival in 1969. An

FESTIVAL AT BIG SUR (left to right): Graham Nash, Joni Mitchell, John Sebastian, Steven Stills, Joan Baez.

invaluable record of the folk-rock scene of the day; it's demise was not far off.

CHUCK BERRY FEATURING TINA TURNER 1982
Oak Media, color, 60 minutes

DIRECTOR: Scott Sternberg
PRODUCERS: C. D. Haifley, Jack Malstead
MUSICAL PERFORMERS: Chuck Berry, Tina Turner, and band consisting of James R. Horn, James Marsala, Willie Orneals, William D. Smith, Richie Zito
SONGS PERFORMED: *Around and Around, Brown Eyed Handsome Man, Johnny B. Goode, Maria Maria, Nadine, The Promised Land, Reelin' and Rockin', Rock and Roll Music, Roll Over Beethoven, School Days, Sweet Little Sixteen, Too Much Monkey Business*
VIDEO: Heron – UK

A truly awful set; it's tragic that this seems to be the only video available starring the great Chuck Berry. Here he is totally disinterested and backed by a dull, half-hearted pick-up band. Tina Turner appears in one brief number at the end. Really not worth seeing – what a shame.

THE CONCERT FOR BANGLADESH
1972
Twentieth Century Fox, color, 100 minutes

DIRECTOR: Saul Swimmer
PRODUCERS: George Harrison, Allen Klein
RECORDING SUPERVISION: Phil Spector
MUSICAL PERFORMERS: Eric Clapton, Bob Dylan, George Harrison, Billy Preston, Leon Russell, Ravi Shankar, Ringo Starr, Klaus Voorman
SONGS PERFORMED: *Blowin' In the Wind, A Hard Rain's A-Gonna Fall, It Takes a Lot to Laugh It Takes a Train to Cry, Just Like a Woman*, Bob Dylan; *Awaiting On Your All, Bangladesh, Beware of Darkness, Here Comes the Sun, My Sweet Lord, Something, Wah Wah, While My Guitar Gently Weeps*, George Harrison; *That's the Way God Planned It*, Billy Preston; *Jumpin' Jack Flash, Youngblood*, Leon Russell; *Bangla Dhun*, Ravi Shankar; *It Don't Come Easy*, Ringo Starr
SOUNDTRACK: Apple
VIDEO: Thorn–EMI – US

Just what it says – the giant, all-star concert put together by George Harrison in New York City's Madison Square Garden in 1971, during the *first* wave of social consciousness that swept rock'n'roll. An interesting mix of musicians, well worth seeing; and Phil Spector doesn't seem to have actually *done* anything to the music, which is probably a good thing, considering his handling of the *Let It Be* tapes.

D.O.A. – A RIGHT OF PASSAGE 1980
High Times Films, color, 90 minutes

DIRECTOR: Lech Kowalski
PRODUCER: Lech Kowalski
MUSICAL PERFORMERS: Generation X, Rich Kids, the Sex Pistols, Terry and the Idiots, X-Ray Spex
SONGS PERFORMED: *Kiss Me Deadly*, Generation X; *Anarchy in the UK*, *God Save the Queen*, *Pretty Vacant*, the Sex Pistols; *Oh Bondage Up Yours*, X-Ray Spex
SOUNDTRACK SONGS: *Nightclubbing*, Iggy Pop; *Police and Thieves*, the Clash
VIDEO: Light – US

Coverage of a seven-city Sex Pistols tour, with an overview of the contemporary punk scene. This is accomplished by interviews with fans, aspiring bands and, chillingly, the late Sid Vicious and Nancy Spungen. Probably a valuable record of an important time in the development of rock, but hard to watch.

DANCE CRAZE 1981
Playpont Films, color, 89 minutes

DIRECTOR: Joe Massot
PRODUCER: Joe Massot
MUSICAL PERFORMERS: Bad Manners, the Beat (known as the English Beat in the US), the Bodysnatchers, Madness, Selector, the Specials
SONGS PERFORMED: *Inner London Violence*, *Lip Up Fatty*, *Ne Ne Na Na Na Nu Nu*, *Wooly Bully*, Bad Manners; *Mirror In the Bathroom*, *Ranking*

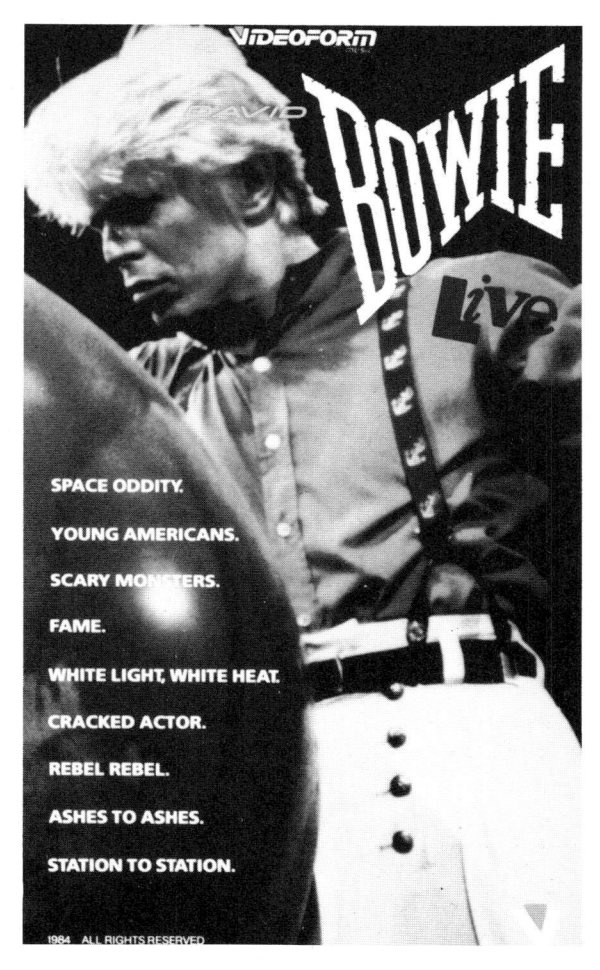

DAVID BOWIE LIVE

Full Stop, *Roughrider*, *Twist'n'Crawl*, the Beat; *Do the Rocksteady*, *Easy Life*, *007*, the Bodysnatchers; *Madness*, *Night Boat to Cairo*, *One Step Beyond*, *The Prince*, *Razor Blade Alley*, *Swan Lake*, Madness; *Missing Words*, *On My Radio*, *Three Minute Hero*, *Too Much Pressure*, Selector; *Concrete Jungle*, *Man at C & A*, *Nite Club*, *Too Much Too Young*, the Specials
SOUNDTRACK: 2-Tone – UK; Chrysalis – US

Concert footage of various ska bands, including Madness, the Beat and the Specials, intercut with some fairly pointless Fifties' and Sixties' newsreels. Lively and enjoyable.

CONCERTS AND DOCUMENTARIES

DAVID BOWIE LIVE 1984
Concert Productions International, color, 51 minutes

DIRECTOR: David Mallet
PRODUCER: Anthony Eaton
PRODUCTION CONCEIVED BY: David Bowie
SOUND RE-MIXED BY: Bob Clearmountain
FILMED AT: PNE Coliseum, Vancouver, Canada
MUSICAL PERFORMERS: David Bowie with band consisting of Carlos Alomar, Steve Elson, Stan Harrison, David Lebolt, Lanny Pickett, Carmine Rojas, Earl Slick and Tony Thompson, with Frank and George Simms on vocals.
SONGS PERFORMED: *Ashes to Ashes, Cracked Actor, Fame, Rebel Rebel, Scary Monsters, Space Oddity, Station to Station, White Light, White Heat, Young Americans*
VIDEO: Heron – UK

Extremely classy (as Bowie's presentations always are), well-produced and original concert video, with music from the Serious Moonlight Tour. This set consists mainly of classics like *Fame* and *Rebel Rebel*, each one introduced by a frame showing the incarnation Bowie was going through at the time the song came out, and the date, an interesting touch. There is also an interview with the star in his dressing room. Another video has been released emphasizing the new material used on the tour, *David Bowie – Serious Moonlight*; great music and well worth watching.

DIVINE MADNESS 1980
Warner Brothers, color, 94 minutes

DIRECTOR: Michael Ritchie
PRODUCER: Michael Ritchie
MUSICAL PERFORMERS: Bette Midler, the Harlettes
SONGS PERFORMED: *Big Noise From Winnetka; Boogie Woogie Bugle Boy; Chapel of Love; Delores Delage; E Street Shuffle; Fire Down Below; I Shall Be Released; Leader of the Pack; The Rose; Shiver Me Timbers; Stay With Me; Summer (The First Time); You Can't Always Get What You Want*
SOUNDTRACK: Atlantic
VIDEO: WEA – US

The Divine Miss M in concert in Pasadena, California. Bette isn't really a rock singer, though she has been working on it, but her stage shows are far more interesting than the average rock concert, with elaborate and witty staging and costumes – more like a mini-musical comedy, really. Here she performs some terrific swing numbers as well as some classic girl-group rock with the multi-talented Harlettes.

DON'T LOOK BACK 1965
Leacock-Pennebaker Films, black & white, 96 minutes

DIRECTOR: D. A. Pennebaker
PRODUCERS: Don Court, Albert Grossman
MUSICAL PERFORMERS: Joan Baez, Donovan, Bob Dylan
SONGS PERFORMED: *Love Is Just a Four Letter Word*, Joan Baez; *To Sing For You*, Donovan; *Don't Think Twice It's All Right, Gates of Eden, It's All Over Now Baby Blue, It's Alright Ma (I'm Only Bleeding), The Lonesome Death of Hattie Carroll, Subterranean Homesick Blues, The Times They Are a Changin'*, Bob Dylan

Absolutely essential viewing – the young, wildly successful, but hardly innocent Dylan on tour in Britain in 1965. Pennebaker's faintly grainy but lucid black-and-white photography gives an unforgettable picture of an extraordinary personality, by turns sulky and professional. Joan Baez, Donovan and Allen Ginsberg appear.

EARTH, WIND AND FIRE IN CONCERT 1982
Crystalite Productions, color, 55 minutes

DIRECTOR: Michael Schultz

PRODUCERS: Gloria Schultz, Michael Schultz, Maurice White
RECORDED LIVE IN: Oakland Coliseum, California; originally shown on Home Box Office
MUSICAL PERFORMERS: Earth, Wind and Fire (Philip Bailey, Roland Bautista, Larry Dunn, Johnny Graham, Ralph Johnson, Beloyd Taylor, Fred White, Maurice White, Verdine White, Andrew Woolfolk) and the Phoenix Horns (Rahmlee Davis, Michael Harris, Don Myrick, and Louis Satterfield)
SONGS PERFORMED: *Fantasy, Gratitude, I've Had Enough, In the Stone, Jupiter, Keep Your Head to the Sky, Let Your Feelings Show, Let's Groove, Reasons, Remember the Children, Shining Star, Sing a Song, That's the Way of the World, Where Have All the Flowers Gone*
SOUNDTRACK: CBS
VIDEO: Heron – UK; Vestron – US

An extravagant and good-humored show from the popular funk group, with glittery costumes, dancers, a horn section and elaborate special lighting effect. Earth, Wind and Fire energetically perform some of their biggest hits (most of them written by Maurice White), including *Sing a Song* and *Shining Star*, in a well-paced and entertaining set.

ELVIS ON TOUR   1972
Metro Goldwyn Mayer, color, 93 minutes

DIRECTORS: Pierre Adidge, Robert Abel
PRODUCERS: Pierre Adidge, Robert Abel
MUSICAL PERFORMERS: Elvis Presley, the Sweet Inspirations, Kathy Westmorland and the Stamps Quartet, and a band consisting of James Burton, Charlie Hodge, Glenn Mardin, Ronnie Tutt, Jerry Scheff and John Wilkinson
SONGS PERFORMED: *Amen, American Trilogy, A Big Hunk of Love, Bridge Over Troubled Water, Burning Love, Can't Help Falling In Love, C.C. Rider, Don't Be Cruel, Funny How Time Slips Away, I Got a Woman, I Saw the Light, Johnny B. Goode, Lawdy Miss Clawdy, Lead Me Guide Me,*

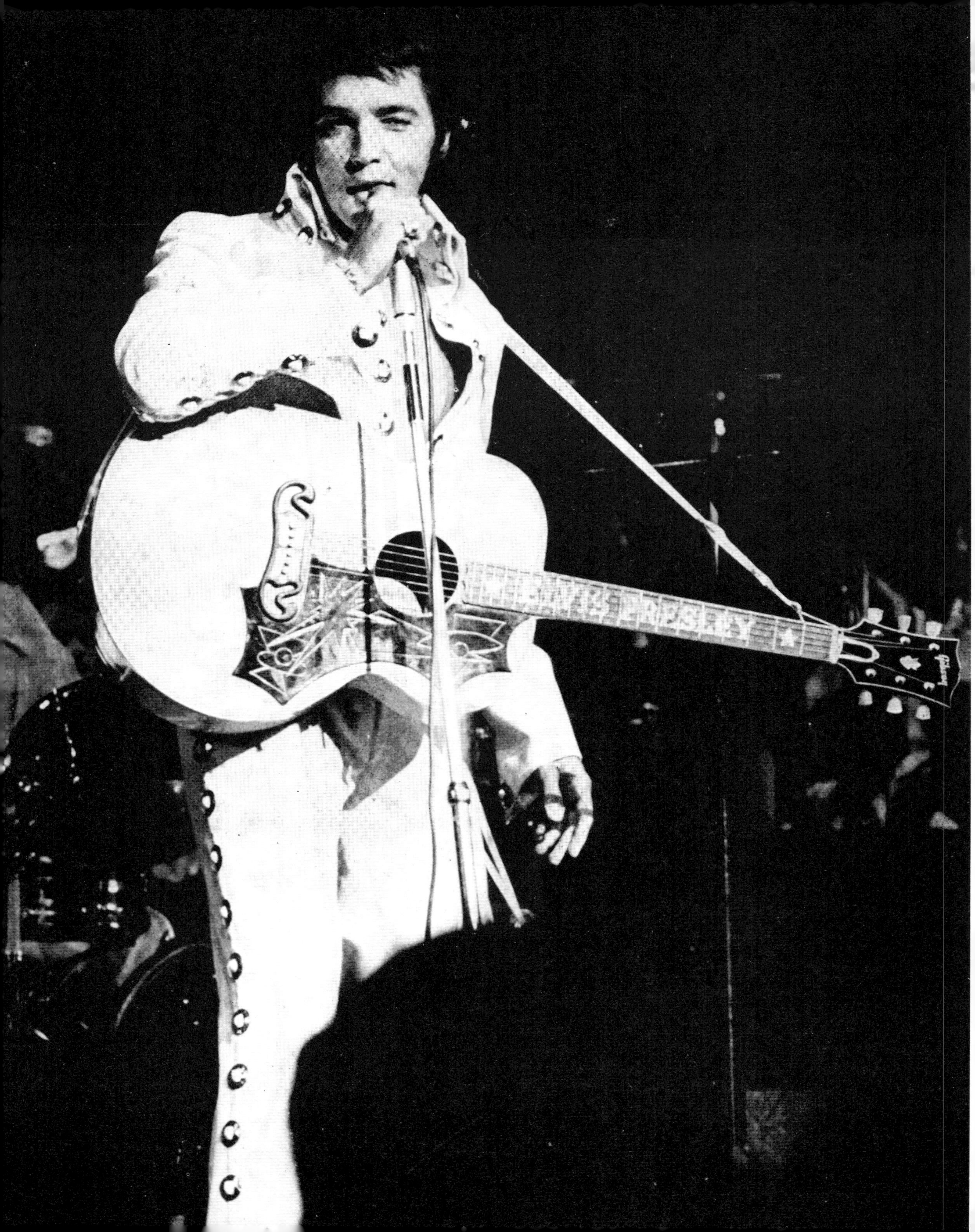
ELVIS PRESLEY

The Light House, Love Me Tender, Memories, Mystery Train, Never Been to Spain, Polk Salad Annie, Proud Mary, Ready Teddy, Rock My Soul, Separate Ways, Suspicious Minds, Sweet Sweet Spirit, That's All Right, Until It's Time For You To Go, You Gave Me a Mountain
SOUNDTRACK: RCA
VIDEO: MGM–UA – US

Elvis seems fairly together in this filming of a cross-country tour of the States in 1971. There is also some historic footage of an early appearance on the Ed Sullivan Show, and a brilliant improvisation-rehearsal with a gospel quartet, which he effortlessly dominates.

ELVIS – THAT'S THE WAY IT IS
1970
Metro Goldwyn Mayer, color, 107 minutes

DIRECTOR: Denis Saunders
PRODUCER: Herbert F. Solow
MUSICAL PERFORMERS: Elvis Presley, the Sweet Inspirations
SONGS PERFORMED: *All Shook Up, Blue Suede Shoes, Bridge Over Troubled Waters, Can't Help Falling In Love, Crying Time, Heartbreak Hotel, How the Web Was Woven, I Just Can't Help Believing, I've Lost You, Little Sister, Love Me, Love Me Tender, Mary In the Morning, Mystery Train, The Next Step Is Love, One Night With You, Patch It Up, Polk Salad Annie, Stranger In the Crowd, Suspicious Minds, Sweet Caroline, That's All Right, Tiger Man, What'd I Say, Words, You Don't Have To Say You Love Me, You've Lost That Lovin' Feeling*
SOUNDTRACK: RCA

Rehearsals and the opening nights of Elvis' first live concert tour since 1957. He proved he still had it in an exciting, varied, and fast-paced nightclub act. It's perhaps over-slick, but that's Las Vegas.

ERIC CLAPTON AND HIS ROLLING HOTEL
1980
Angle Films Ltd, color, 70 minutes

DIRECTOR: Rex Pike
PRODUCER: Rex Pike
MUSICAL PERFORMERS: Eric Clapton, George Harrison, Elton John, Muddy Waters
SONGS PERFORMED: *Cocaine, Lay Down Sally, Layla, Tulsa Time*, Eric Clapton; *Further On Up the Road*, Eric Clapton, George Harrison, Elton John; *Got My Mojo Workin', Mannish Boy*, Muddy Waters

The rolling hotel is a special train built by Hermann Goering, rehabilitated by housing the musicians and crew of Clapton's 1979 tour of Germany. Mostly concert footage and (mercifully) brief interviews; some fine performances.

FESTIVAL
1967
Peppercorn-Wormser Films, color, 98 minutes

DIRECTOR: Murray Lerner
PRODUCER: Murray Lerner
MUSICAL PERFORMERS: Joan Baez, the Paul Butterfield Blues Band, Judy Collins, Donovan, Bob Dylan, Dick and Mimi Farina, Son House, Mississippi John Hurt, Spider John Koerner, Fred McDowall, Peter Paul and Mary, Buffy Sainte-Marie, the Staple Singers, Sonny Terry and Brownie McGhee, Peter Yarrow
SONGS PERFORMED: *All My Trials, Mary Hamilton*, Joan Baez; *Colores*, Joan Baez and Donovan; *Go Tell Aunt Rhody*, Joan Baez, Peter Yarrow; *Born In Chicago*, the Paul Butterfield Blues Band; *Turn Turn Turn*, Judy Collins; *The War Drags On*, Donovan; *All I Really Want To Do*, Bob Dylan; *Maggie's Farm*, Dylan and the Paul Butterfield Blues Band; *Pack Up Your Sorrows*, Dick and Mimi Farina; *Son House Blues*, Son House; *Candy Man*, Mississippi John Hurt; *Blues*, Spider John Koerner; *Highway 61*, Fred McDowall; *Codine*,

CONCERTS AND DOCUMENTARIES

Buffy Sainte-Marie; *Help Me Jesus*, the Staple Singers; *Key to the Highway*, Sonny Terry and Brownie McGhee

Folk and blues in full bloom – film of the Newport Folk Festivals from 1963 to 1966. A remarkably well-chosen and interesting mix of artists, from Jim Kweskin's Jug Band to Mississippi John Hurt to the newly-electric Bob Dylan in 1966. An invaluable documentary.

FESTIVAL AT BIG SUR see **CELEBRATION AT BIG SUR**

FILLMORE 1972
Twentieth Century Fox, color, 105 minutes

DIRECTOR: Richard T. Heffron
PRODUCER: Herbert F. Decker
MUSICAL PERFORMERS: Elvin Bishop, Cold Blood, Grateful Dead, Hot Tuna, It's a Beautiful Day, Jefferson Airplane, Lamb, Quicksilver Messenger Service, Santana, Boz Scaggs
SONGS PERFORMED: *Sky Is Crying*, Elvin Bishop; *Feel To Be Free*, Cold Blood; *Casey Jones*, *Johnny B. Goode*, the Grateful Dead; *Candy Man*, *Uncle Sam's Blues*, Hot Tuna; *White Bird*, It's a Beautiful Day; *We Can Be Together*, Jefferson Airplane; *Hello Friends*, *River Boulevard*, Lamb; *Fresh Air*, *Mojo*, Quicksilver Messenger Service; *In a Silent Way*, *Incident at Neshibur*, Santana; *Hollywood Blues*, *I'll Be Gone Long*, Boz Scaggs
SOUNDTRACK: Fillmore Records – US

Just a documentary then, nostalgic now – the record of the closing of Bill Graham's seminal venue, the Fillmore West in San Francisco. Wonderful music, absolutely typical of the scene. Remember *White Bird*?

GIMME SHELTER Mick Jagger and the audience and then …

… the action starts at Altamont.

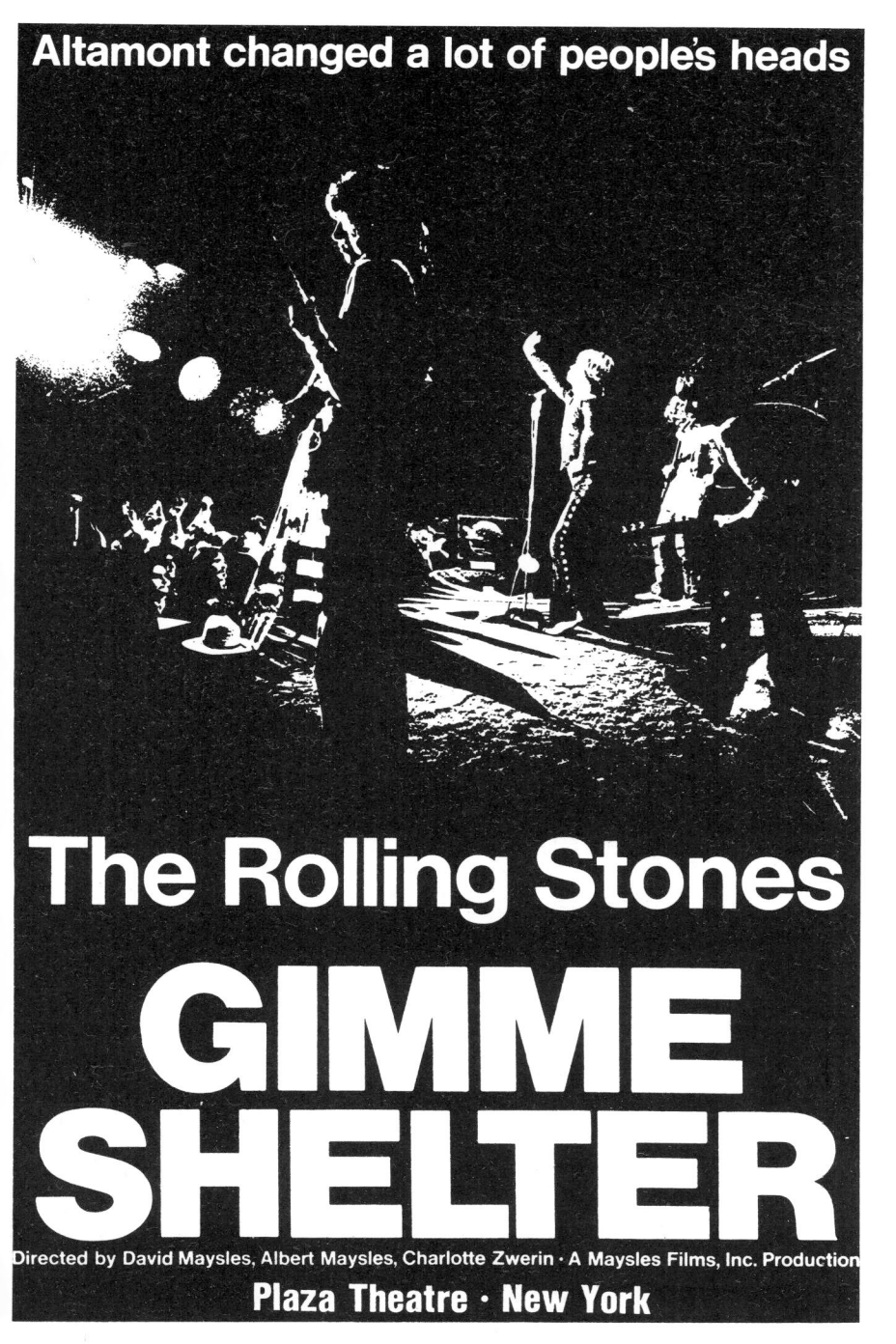

US advertisement for GIMME SHELTER.

GARY NUMAN – THE BERSERKER TOUR 1984
Trilion Pictures Ltd, color, 59 minutes

DIRECTOR: Derek Burbidge
PRODUCER: Phillip Goodhand-Tait
MUSICAL PERFORMERS: Gary Numan
SONGS PERFORMED: *Berserker, Cold War, The Iceman Comes, Music For Chameleons, My Dying Machine, Remind Me to Smile, Sister Surprise, This Is New Love, This Prison Moon, We Are Glass, We Take Mystery to Bed*
VIDEO: Guild – UK

Concise and well-filmed record of Numan's most recent tour. Elaborately staged and lit, with a fine, tight band, this is interesting even for non-fans.

GIMME SHELTER 1970
Cinema 5, color, 90 minutes

DIRECTORS: Albert Maysles, David Maysles, Charlotte Zwerin
PRODUCER: Ronald Schneider
MUSICAL PERFORMERS: the Flying Burrito Brothers, Jefferson Airplane, the Rolling Stones, Ike and Tina Turner
SONGS PERFORMED: *Six Days On the Road*, the Flying Burrito Brothers; *The Other Side of Life*, Jefferson Airplane; *Brown Sugar, Gimme Shelter, Honky Tonk Woman, Jumpin' Jack Flash, Love In Vain, Satisfaction, Street Fighting Man, Sympathy For the Devil, Under My Thumb, Wild Horses, You Gotta Move*, the Rolling Stones; *I've Been Loving You Too Long*, Ike and Tina Turner
VIDEO: Columbia – US

The Altamont Concert in December 1969, where a fan rushing the stage with a gun was killed by the Hell's Angels hired as guards, practically on-screen; obviously more than a concert film, though the sound and camerawork are excellent; this became an examination of what went wrong. The Stones meant this to be a mini-Woodstock, with lots of sunshine and happy hippies. Instead, through ignorance (in hiring the Angels to begin with) and disorganization, it turned into a nightmare and, essentially, the end of the illusion that music could induce peace and love. Extremely important documentary.

GLASTONBURY FAYRE 1973
Colossal Pictures/Goodtime Enterprises, color, 96 minutes

DIRECTOR: Peter Neal

CONCERTS AND DOCUMENTARIES

PRODUCERS: Sanford Lieberson, David Puttnam, David Speechley
MUSICAL PERFORMERS: Daevid Allen and Gong, Arthur Brown and Kingdom Come, Fairport Convention, Family, Linda Lewis, Magic Michael, Melanie, Quintessence, Terry Reid, Traffic

The rock festival held at mid-summer in Glastonbury in 1971. Hippies were running out of steam by this point, and contractual wrangles delayed the release of this film and eliminated several important performances, like David Bowie, Marc Bolan and Pete Townshend. What's here is generally minor but interesting in its way.

GO GO MANIA see **POP GEAR**

THE GRATEFUL DEAD 1977
Monarch-Noteworthy Films, color, 131 minutes

DIRECTOR: Jerry Garcia
PRODUCER: Ron Rakow
MUSICAL PERFORMERS: the Grateful Dead
VIDEO: WEA – US

Five nights for the Deadheads of San Francisco in 1974, opening with an hallucinogenic animated sequence by Gary Guiterez. Many, many *long* numbers, crowd-pleasers every one. Terrific sound; one of the first concert features recorded with the Dolby stereo.

THE GREAT ROCK'N'ROLL SWINDLE 1979
Virgin Films, color/black & white, 105 minutes

DIRECTOR: Julian Temple
PRODUCERS: Don Boyd, Jeremy Thomas
SCREENPLAY: Julian Temple
CAST: Malcolm McLaren, John Lydon, Steve

146

Jones, Paul Cook, Sid Vicious, Ronald Biggs, Jess Conrad, Dave Dee, Irene Handl, Jerizmy, Glen Matlock, Mary Millington, Nancy Spungen, Tenpole Tudor
MUSICAL PERFORMERS: Ronald Biggs, the Black Arabs, Jerizmy, Malcolm McLaren, the Sex Pistols, Tenpole Tudor
SONGS PERFORMED: *Belsen Was a Gas, No One Is Innocent*, Ronald Biggs; *Black Arabs Medley*, the Black Arabs; *Anarchie pour le UK*, Jerizmy; *You Need Hands*, Malcolm McLaren; *Anarchy In the UK, Belsen Was a Gas, Bodies, C'Mon Everybody, Friggin' In the Riggin', God Save the Queen, The Great Rock'n'Roll Swindle, Holidays In the Sun, Johnny B. Goode, Lonely Boy, My Way, No Feelings, No Fun, Pretty Vacant, Silly Thing, Something Else, Watcha Gonna Do About It*, the Sex Pistols; *Rock Around the Clock, Who Killed Bambi?*, Tenpole Tudor
SOUNDTRACK: Virgin

Scrappy and jumbled documentary about Machiavellian manager Malcolm McLaren, the Sex Pistols, and the punk scene in general. It actually tells you something about the importance of the band. The trouble is, as soon as you organize punk enough to point a camera at it, you've destroyed its essentially reactionary fever. This was put together after the deaths of Sid Vicious and Nancy Spungen, by the way. And you might feel that you don't *want* to see a film with a song titled *Belsen Was a Gas*; it's all a matter of taste.

THE GUESS WHO TOGETHER AGAIN 1983
Concert Productions International, color, 85 minutes

DIRECTOR: Michael Watt
FILMED IN: Toronto, Canada
MUSICAL PERFORMERS: the Guess Who (Randy Bachman, Burton Cummings, Jim Kale, Garry Peterson)
SONGS PERFORMED: *Ain't Seen Nothing Yet, Albert Flasher, American Woman, Clap For the Wolfman, Hang On to Your Life, Hand Me Down World, Laughing, Mother Nature, My Own Way to Rock, No Sugar Tonight, No Time, Orly, Runnin' Back to Saskatoon, Shakin' All Over, Sour Suite, Takin' Care of Business, Undone*
VIDEO: Heron – UK

A damn good re-union concert; members of the late Sixties group the Guess Who all went on to bigger and better things, so this is not just a collection of has-beens reminiscing, but a band of really accomplished musicians and performers. They do a tight, fast set of excellent song, from their hit *Shakin' All Over* to *American Woman* and *You Ain't Seen Nothing Yet*. Well worth seeing and hearing; it's too bad there doesn't seem to be a soundtrack album.

HEARTLAND REGGAE 1980
Crawley Films Ltd, color, 87 minutes

DIRECTOR: J. P. Lewis
PRODUCER: J. P. Lewis
MUSICAL PERFORMERS: Althea and Donna, Dennis Brown, the I-Threes, Jacob Miller and Inner Circle, U. Roy, Peter Tosh, Little Junior Tucker
VIDEO: Con – US

A concert celebrating Haile Selassie's visit to Jamaica twelve years before, a very important event to Rastas. Unfortunately, the sound and the filming aren't very good. More a social document than a musical one.

IMAGINE 1972
Apple Films, color, 81 minutes

DIRECTORS: John Lennon, Yoko Ono
PRODUCERS: John Lennon, Yoko Ono
MUSICAL PERFORMERS: John Lennon, Yoko Ono, the Plastic Ono Band with the Flux Fiddlers
SONGS PERFORMED: *Crippled Inside, Gimme Some Truth, How?, How Do You Sleep?, I Don't Want To Be a Soldier, Imagine, It's So Hard, Oh My*

John and Yoko in IMAGINE.

IT'S YOUR THING   The Isley Brothers.

Love, *Oh Yoko*, *Power To the People*, John Lennon; *Midsummer New York*, *Mind Train*, *Mrs Lennon*, Yoko Ono

Performances, home movies, TV clips and set-pieces, with John and Yoko and the Plastic Ono Band. An excellent selection of Lennon's solo work, as a matter of fact, though the pre-video jumble of styles can be disconcerting at first.

IT'S YOUR THING   1970
Medford Films, color, 102 minutes

DIRECTOR: Mike Gariguilo
PRODUCERS: the Isley Brothers
MUSICAL PERFORMERS: Patti Austin, Brooklyn Bridge, the Five Stairsteps, the Edwin Hawkins Singers, the Isley Brothers, Moms Mabley, Ike and Tina Turner, the Clara Ward Singers, Judy White, the Winstons, the Young Gents
SONGS PERFORMED: *Family Tree*, Patti Austin; *Oh Happy Day*, the Edwin Hawkins Singers; *Abraham Martin and John*, Moms Mabley; *Get Back*, *Honky Tonk Woman*, *I Want to Take You Higher*, *Proud Mary*, Ike and Tina Turner

A star-studded soul festival held at Yankee Stadium, produced by the Isley Brothers. Some smoking performances, especially by the Isleys themselves.

JANIS   1974
Universal International Pictures, color, 97 minutes

DIRECTORS: Howard Alk, Seaton Findlay
PRODUCER: Howard Alk
MUSICAL PERFORMERS: Janis Joplin, Big Brother and the Holding Company, the Full Tilt Boogie Band, the Kozmic Blues Band
SONGS PERFORMED: *Ball and Chain*, *Comin' Home*, *Cry Baby*, *The Good Days*, *I Can't Turn You Loose*, *Maybe*, *Me and Bobby McGee*, *Mercedes Benz*, *Move Over*, *Piece of My Heart*, *Summertime*, *Tell Mama*, *Try*
SOUNDTRACK: Columbia – US; CBS – UK

Straightforward authorized biography of the Texas blues singer with, thankfully, little talk and lots of music. The performances say it all.

Jimi Hendrix (top), Noel Redding (left), Mitch Mitchell (right).

JIMI HENDRIX 1973
Warner Brothers, color, 102 minutes

DIRECTORS: Joe Boyd, John Head, Gary Weis
PRODUCER: Joe Boyd
MUSICAL PERFORMERS: Jimi Hendrix, the Band of Gypsies, the Jimi Hendrix Experience
SONGS PERFORMED: *Hear My Train A-Comin', Hey Baby, In From the Storm, Johnny B. Goode, Like a Rolling Stone, Machine Gun, Purple Haze, Red House, Rock Me Baby, The Star Spangled Banner, Wild Thing*
SOUNDTRACK: Reprise
VIDEO: WEA – US

An extensive television interview, clips of family members and friends, and lots of concert sequences make this the best available record of Hendrix's work and influence; one of the best rock documentaries.

JOHNNY CASH – THE MAN, HIS WORLD, HIS MUSIC 1969
Continental Films, color, 94 minutes

DIRECTOR: Robert Elfstrom
PRODUCERS: Arthur Barron, Evelyn Barron
MUSICAL PERFORMERS: Johnny Cash, Bob Dylan, Carl Perkins
SONGS PERFORMED: *Folsom Prison Blues, Ring of Fire*, Johnny Cash; *One Too Many Mornings*, Johnny Cash, Bob Dylan; *Blue Suede Shoes*, Carl Perkins

Cash returns to his home town of Dyess, Arkansas, and performs many of his best known songs in concert scenes; Carl Perkins, who for years was part of Cash's touring act, is given the opportunity to do his *Blue Suede Shoes*.

JOURNEY THROUGH THE PAST 1973
New Line Pictures, color, 96 minutes

DIRECTOR: Bernard Shakey (Neil Young)

CONCERTS AND DOCUMENTARIES

PRODUCER: Frederic Underhill
MUSICAL PERFORMERS: Crosby, Stills, Nash and Young, Buffalo Springfield, Neil Young
SONGS BY: Neil Young including *Find the Cost of Freedom*, *The Needle and the Damage Done*
SOUNDTRACK: Reprise

Young directed this under the name of 'Bernard Shakey', as he has some other films. This is his usual mix of talk, improvisation and concert performances. Most of it is pretty tiresome, but the music is great. The album of the same name is not actually a soundtrack; it contains other material.

THE KIDS ARE ALRIGHT 1979
New World Pictures, color, 96 minutes

DIRECTOR: Jeff Stein
PRODUCERS: Bill Curbishley, Tony Klinger
MUSICAL PERFORMERS: the Who (Roger Daltrey, John Entwhistle, Keith Moon, Pete Townshend)
SONGS PERFORMED: *Anyway Anyhow Anywhere*, *Baba O'Riley*, *Barbara Ann*, *Can't Explain*, *Cobwebs and Strange*, *Happy Jack*, *Heatwave*, *I Can See For Miles*, *I'm a Boy*, *Long Live Rock*, *Magic Bus*, *Pictures of Lily*, *Pinball Wizard*, *A Quick One*, *Roadrunner*, *See Me Feel Me*, *Shout*, *Sparks*, *Substitute*, *Success Story*, *Tommy Can You Hear Me*, *Who Are You*, *Won't Get Fooled Again*, *Young Man Blues*
VIDEO: Vestron – US

The best rock documentary because, through old and new clips and interviews, it really gives an overview of the band's strengths and weaknesses. If you had never heard of the Who, this would tell you how and why they were important, and it does this without pretension. There is at least one sequence never before seen, a brilliant live version of the 'mini-opera' *A Quick One* from the Rolling Stones' unreleased *Rock'n'Roll Circus*, which is actually better than the studio version. All in all, a must-see.

THE KIDS ARE ALRIGHT The Who.

The sullen young Who in THE KIDS ARE ALRIGHT.

LADIES AND GENTLEMEN – THE ROLLING STONES 1974
Dragon Aire Films, color, 83 minutes

DIRECTOR: Rollin Binzer
PRODUCERS: Rollin Binzer, Marshall Chess, Bob Fries, Steve Gebhardt
MUSICAL PERFORMERS: the Rolling Stones

THE KIDS ARE ALRIGHT The Who onstage early in their career: John Entwhistle (left), Roger Daltrey (right).

SONGS PERFORMED: *Bitch, Brown Sugar, Gimme Shelter, Jumpin' Jack Flash, Love In Vain, Midnight Rambler, Street Fightin' Man, Tumblin' Dice*

Just what it says – the Stones' tour of the US in 1972. Excellent sound and a good collection of their best and best-known songs, well photographed in general.

THE LAST WALTZ 1978
United Artists, color, 117 minutes

DIRECTOR: Martin Scorcese
PRODUCER: Robbie Robertson
MUSICAL PERFORMERS: the Band, Eric Clapton, Rick Danko, Neil Diamond, Dr John, Bob Dylan, Emmylou Harris, Ronnie Hawkins, Joni Mitchell, Van Morrison, Ringo Starr, Muddy Waters, Ronnie Wood, Neil Young
SONGS PERFORMED: *Chest Fever, Don't Do It, Genetic Method, It Makes No Difference, Theme From 'The Last Waltz', The Night They Drove Old Dixie Down, Ophelia, Old Time Religion, Shape I'm In, Stagefright*, the Band; *Further On Up the Road*, Eric Clapton; *Sip the Wine*, Rick Danko; *Dry Your Eyes*, Neil Diamond; *Such a Night*, Dr John; *Baby Let Me Follow You Down, Forever Young*, Bob Dylan; *Evangeline*, Emmylou Harris; *Who Do You Love?*, Ronnie Hawkins; *Coyote*, Joni Mitchell; *Caravan*, Van Morrison; *Mannish Boy*, Muddy Waters; *Helpless*, Neil Young; *I Shall Be Released*, all
SOUNDTRACK: Warner Brothers
VIDEO: Twentieth Century Fox – US

The Band's last concert on Thanksgiving Day 1978, at the Winterland Ballroom in San

Francisco. An amazing line-up of great performers – even Van Morrison looks very lively – and Neil Diamond does one of his best songs, reminding us that he does have talent. The concert is interspersed with some interviews with the band and reminiscences, but these are brief. Scorcese's serious-minded questions and Robertson's pretentious answers did, however, provide fertile material for Rob Reiner's brilliant satire, *This Is Spinal Tap* a few years later.

LET IT BE   1970
United Artists, color, 81 minutes

DIRECTOR: Michael Lindsay-Hogg
PRODUCER: Neil Aspinall
MUSICAL PERFORMERS: the Beatles (George Harrison, John Lennon, Paul McCartney, Ringo Starr), Billy Preston
SONGS PERFORMED: *Across the Universe, Dig It, Don't Let Me Down, For You Blue, Get Back, I Dig a Pony, I Me Mine, I've Got a Feeling, Let It Be, The Long and Winding Road, Maxwell's Silver Hammer, Octopus's Garden, Oh Darling, One After 909, Shake Rattle and Roll, Two of Us, You Really Got a Hold On Me*
SOUNDTRACK: Apple
VIDEO: Twentieth Century Fox – US

The Beatles' last sessions together inevitably have undertones of sadness; but, even so, they perform some of their best songs here, despite the obvious interpersonal tensions. The music as heard in the film is actually much better than the album, which was controversially produced by Phil Spector; beautiful tunes like *Across the Universe* and *Two of Us* are unsullied by added choruses, etc. The wonderful concluding rooftop concert (Well, one song – *Get Back*) reminds you just what a good band they were before it breaks up in disarray, which seems an appropriate ending.

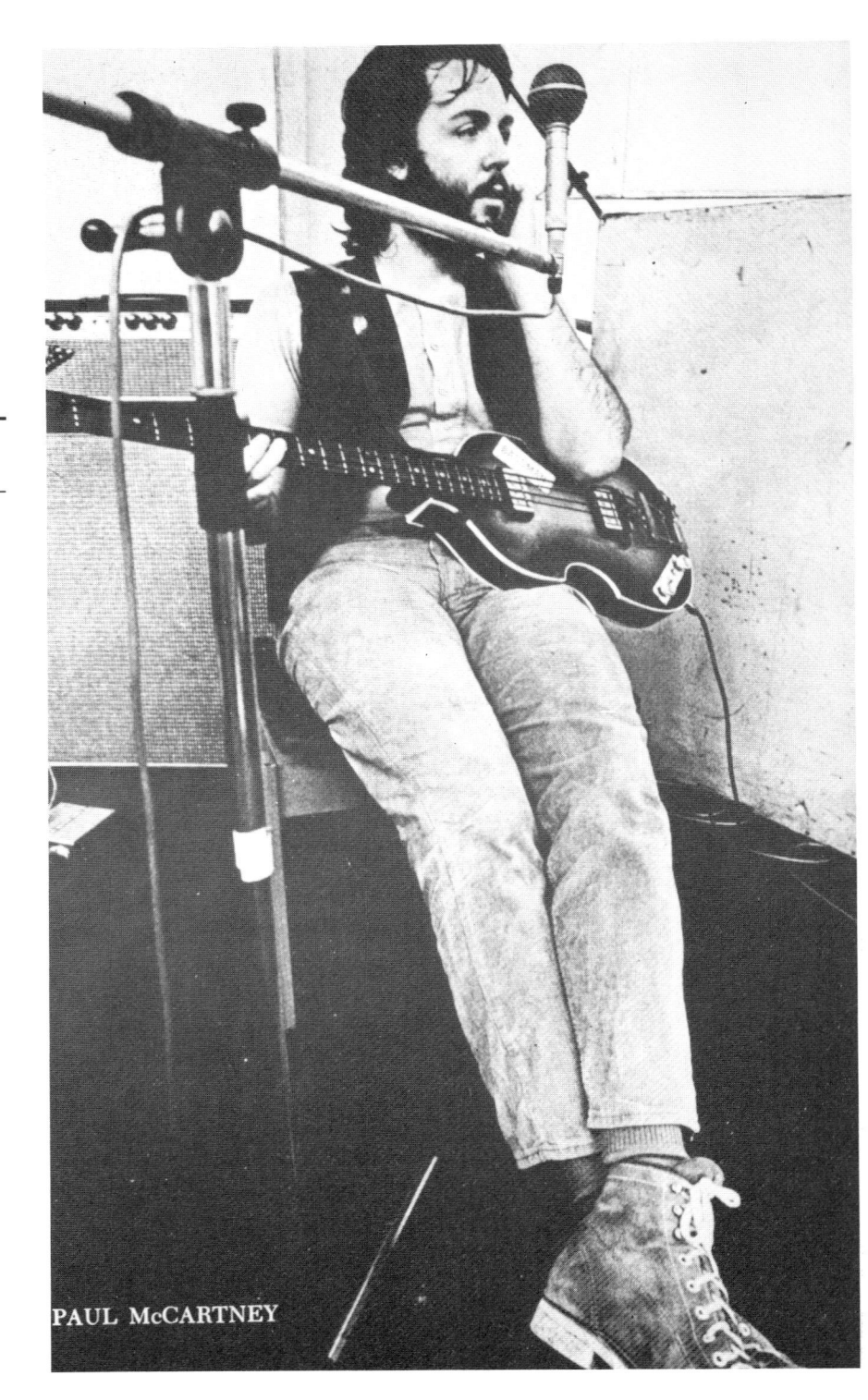

LET IT BE   Paul McCartney.

LET THE GOOD TIMES ROLL   Bo Diddley.

LET THE GOOD TIMES ROLL   1973
Columbia Pictures, color, 99 minutes

DIRECTORS: Robert Abel, Sid Levin
PRODUCER: Gerald I. Isenberg
MUSICAL PERFORMERS: Chuck Berry, Chubby Checker, the Coasters, Danny and the Juniors, Bo Diddley, Fats Domino, the Five Satins, Bill Haley and His Comets, Little Richard, the Shirelles, Shirley and Lee
SONGS PERFORMED: *Reelin' and Rockin'*, *School Days*, *Sweet Little Sixteen*, Chuck Berry; *Let's Twist Again*, *Pony Time*, *The Twist*, Chubby Checker; *Charlie Brown*, *Poison Ivy*, the Coasters; *At the Hop*, Danny and the Juniors; *Hey Bo Diddley*, *I'm a Man*, Bo Diddley; *Blueberry Hill*, *My Blue Heaven*, Fats Domino; *Earth Angel*, *I'll Be Seeing You*, *In the Still of the Night*, *Save the Last Dance For Me*, *Sincerely*, the Five Satins; *Rock Around the Clock*, *Shake Rattle and Roll*, Bill Haley and His Comets; *Good Golly Miss Molly*, *Lucille*, *Rip It Up*, Little Richard; *Everybody Loves a Lover*, *Soldier Boy*, the Shirelles; *Let the Good Times Roll*, Shirley and Lee
SOUNDTRACK: Bell

A documentary of rock'n'roll from the Fifties, interspersed with scenes from an exciting rock revival show at Madison Square Garden. The usual classics are on view, but there are also some artists who are more rarely seen, like the Coasters and, best of all, the great Shirley and Lee, doing their sparkling *Let the Good Times Roll*.

CONCERTS AND DOCUMENTARIES

LET'S SPEND THE NIGHT TOGETHER 1984
Columbia Pictures, color, 90 minutes

DIRECTOR: Hal Ashby
PRODUCER: Ronald L. Schwary
SOUND MIXED BY: Bob Clearmountain
FILMED AT: Sun Devil Stadium in Tempe, Arizona, and the Brendan Byrne Arena in Rutherford, New Jersey, USA
DIRECTOR OF PHOTOGRAPHY: Caleb Deschanel
MUSICAL PERFORMERS: the Rolling Stones (Mick Jagger, Keith Richard, Charlie Watts, Ron Wood, Bill Wyman)
SONGS PERFORMED: *All Down the Line, Beast of Burden, Black Limousine, Brown Sugar, Going to A-Go-Go, Hang Fire, Honky Tonk Woman, Jumpin' Jack Flash, Just My Imagination, Let It Bleed, Let Me Go, Let's Spend the Night Together, Little T and A, Miss You, Neighbors, Satisfaction, Shattered, She's So Cold, Start Me Up, Time Is On My Side, Tumblin' Dice, Twenty Flight Rock, Under My Thumb, Waiting On a Friend, You Can't Always Get What You Want*

Quite a good record of the Stones' gigantic 1984 tour of the USA. Hal Ashby shows the complicated logistics involved in setting up the massive stage (which had to be visible to audiences in the tens of thousands) and this and the aerial views of the crowds are the most interesting features of the film; it's much better than being there. The fact is, these huge stadiums do *not* make for good music and, unfortunately, a band like the Stones can hardly play anywhere else. Here they do their classics well, though not brilliantly, reminding you just how many truly great songs they've recorded, but their covers of elegant Motown numbers like *Just My Imagination* are simply poor. Worth seeing, and historically important, but it's not great music.

LET'S SPEND THE NIGHT TOGETHER   Mick Jagger.

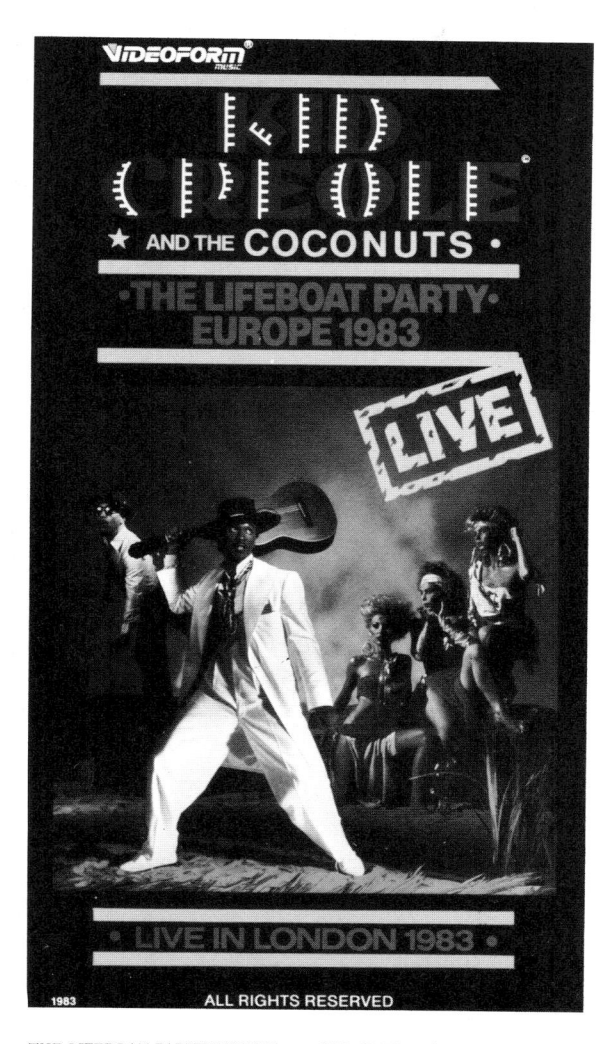

THE LIFEBOAT PARTY EUROPE 1983 KID CREOLE AND THE COCONUTS

LIFEBOAT PARTY – KID CREOLE AND THE COCONUTS LIVE IN LONDON 1983
On-TV Ltd, color, 60 minutes

DIRECTOR: Mike Mansfield
PRODUCER: Peter Abbey
FILMED AT: Hammersmith Odeon, London.
MUSICAL PERFORMERS: Kid Creole and the Coconuts (August Darnell, Andy Hernandez, Taryn Hagey, Adriana Kaegi, Cheryl Poirier; Carol Colman, Ken Fradley, Charles Lagond, Eddie Magic, Mark Mazur, Peter Schott, Dave Spann, Lee Robertson)
SONGS PERFORMED: *Annie I'm Not Your Daddy, Broadway Rhythm, Call Me the Entertainer, Don't Take My Coconuts, Gina Gina, I'm a Wonderful Thing Baby, If You Want to Be Happy, Imitation, Lifeboat Party, Naughty Boy, Stool Pigeon, There's Something Wrong In Paradise*
VIDEO: Heron – UK

A very neat, flashy show of Kid Creole's best material, with an elaborate tropical set, a big band, Coati Mundi and the wonderful Coconuts. August Darnell's snap-brimmed street-wise persona is very effective in several funny exchanges with his fellow performers and the audience. The music is based on fast Latin dance rhythms, but different songs still retain a lot of individuality, and the arrangements are terrific, especially the horns. This is not quite a *must* see, but a *do* see.

THE LONDON ROCK AND ROLL SHOW 1973
Notting Hill Films, color, 84 minutes

DIRECTOR: Peter Clifton
PRODUCER: Peter Clifton
MUSICAL PERFORMERS: Chuck Berry, Bo Diddley, Bill Haley and His Comets, Heinz and the Houseshakers, Jerry Lee Lewis, Little Richard, Screaming Lord Sutch

More interesting for the atmosphere than for most of the music, which is in any case constantly interrupted for interviews and comment, most of it useless. The audience at London's Wembley Arena are amazingly varied, from Fifties' revivalist Teddy Boys to long-haired hippies. The music is not wildly exciting, with the exception of Bill Haley and His Comets, who surprisingly steal the show.

Leon Russell and Joe Cocker (left); Joe Cocker and his band (right) on stage in MAD DOGS AND ENGLISHMEN.

MAD DOGS AND ENGLISHMEN   1971
Metro Goldwyn Mayer, color, 118 minutes

DIRECTOR: Pierre Adidge
PRODUCERS: Robert Abel, Pierre Adidge, Harry Marks
MUSICAL PERFORMERS: Joe Cocker, Claudia Linnear, Leon Russell, band consisting of: Chuck Blackwell, Rita Coolidge, Jim Gordon, Jim Keltner, Bobby Keys, Sandy Komikoff, Don Preston, Jim Price, Carl Radle, Chris Stainton
SONGS PERFORMED: *Change In Louise, Darling Be Home Soon, Delta Lady, Feelin' Alright, Give Peace a Chance, Honky Tonk Women, Lawdy Miss Clawdy, The Letter, A Little Help From My Friends, She Came In Through the Bathroom Window, Something, Space Captain,* Joe Cocker; *Let It Be,* Claudia Linnear; *Bird On a Wire, Mad Dogs and Englishmen Theme,* Leon Russell
SOUNDTRACK: A&M

Cocker's 1970 tour of the US, with a massive entourage of musicians and followers. Impressive for the logistics involved, if nothing else. Some interesting split-screen photography, and very good sound recording of a long list of Cocker classics.

MANHATTAN TRANSFER   1981
Made for Chicago Public TV, color, 60 minutes

DIRECTOR: Dick Carter
PRODUCER: Ken Erlich
MUSICAL DIRECTOR: Yaron Gershovsky
MUSICAL PERFORMERS: Manhattan Transfer (Cheryl Bentyne, Tim Hauser, Alan Paul, Janis Siegel)
SONGS PERFORMED: *Bacon Fat, Birdland, Body and Soul, Four Brothers, Gloria, Jeanine, A Nightingale Sang In Berkeley Square, Operator, Parker's Mood, Trickle Trickle, Turn Me Loose, Twilight Zone, You Can Depend On Me*
VIDEO: Heron – UK

A live concert taped for American public television. The music is excellent, but there's not enough *of* it – there's too much behind-the-scenes footage of none-too-interesting talk and rehearsals. Even so, the set does amply demonstrate the group's incredible musicality and wide command of difficult styles.

MEDICINE BALL CARAVAN   1971
Warner Brothers, color, 88 minutes

DIRECTOR: Francois Reichenbach
PRODUCERS: Tom Donahue, Francois Reichenbach
MUSICAL PERFORMERS: Alice Cooper, Delaney and Bonnie, Doug Kershaw, B. B. King, Stoneground, Sal Valentino, the Youngbloods
SONGS PERFORMED: *Free the People,* Delaney and Bonnie; *Black Juju,* Alice Cooper; *Battle of New Orleans, Louisiana Man, Orange Blossom Special,* Doug Kershaw; *How Blue Can You Get?, Just a*

Little Love, B. B. King; *Freakout, It Takes a Lot To Laugh It Takes a Train To Cry*, Stoneground; *Dreambo*, Sal Valentino; *Act Naturally, Hippy From Olema*, the Youngbloods
SOUNDTRACK: Warner Brothers

An onslaught of hippies sweeping across unsuspecting America, as an enormous group of musicians, crew, and friends (154) travelled from San Francisco towards the East Coast giving concerts along the way. A document of time and place as well as of the music performed. Well worth seeing.

MONTEREY POP   1969
Leacock-Pennebaker Films, color, 79 minutes

DIRECTORS: James Desmond, Barry Feinstein, Albert Maysles, Roger Murphy, Richard Leacock, Nick Proferes, D. A. Pennebaker
PRODUCERS: Richard Leacock, D. A. Pennebaker
MUSICAL PERFORMERS: Big Brother and the Holding Company, Eric Burdon and the Animals, Canned Heat, Country Joe and the Fish, Jimi Hendrix, Jefferson Airplane, Janis Joplin, the Mamas and the Papas, Scott McKenzie, Hugh Masekela, Otis Redding, Ravi Shankar, the Who
SONGS PERFORMED: *Combination of the Two*, Big Brother and the Holding Company; *Paint It Black*, Eric Burdon and the Animals; *Rollin' and Tumblin'*, Canned Heat; *Section 43*, Country Joe and the Fish; *Wild Thing*, Jimi Hendrix; *High Flying Bird, Today*, Jefferson Airplane; *Ball and Chain*, Janis Joplin; *California Dreamin', Creeque Alley, I've Got a Feeling*, the Mamas and the Papas; *San Francisco*, Scott McKenzie; *Bajabula Bonke*, Hugh Masekela; *I've been Loving You Too Long, Shake*, Otis Redding; *Raga Bhimpalasi*, Ravi Shankar; *My Generation*, the Who

Invaluable film of the Monterey Pop Festival of 1967, the first full-length rock-concert movie. Some wonderful music and some great moments – Cass Elliott in the audience, watching Janis do *Ball and Chain*, apparently awestruck; a small, pale Roger Daltrey conversing with a large, dark Otis Redding. Lots of songs and not, thank heavens, much talk.

MONTEREY POP   Otis Redding.

A NIGHT WITH LOU REED   1983
RCA Video Productions, color, 60 minutes

DIRECTOR: Clark Santee
PRODUCERS: Richard Baker, Bill Boggs
MUSICAL PERFORMERS: Lou Reed, Robert Quine, Fernando Saunders, Fred Maher
SONGS PERFORMED: *Don't Talk to Me About*

A night with Lou Reed

Work, I'm Waiting For the Man, Kill Your Sons, Martial Law, New Age, Rock'n'Roll, Satellite of Love, Sweet Jane, Turn Out the Lights, Walk On the Wild Side, Waves of Fear, White Light/White Heat, Women
VIDEO: RCA–Columbia – UK; Columbia – US

This is a real surprise; not just another show, but an absolutely terrific set with an exciting and expert band, taped at New York City's Bottom Line Club. The once corpse-like Reed looks ridiculously healthy, plays some white-hot screeching guitar, and performs new songs plus classics—he'll never be able to get away with *not* doing *Walk On the Wild Side*, and here he gives it a scorching new reading. Altogether an excellent hour of rock'n'roll.

NO NUKES 1980
Warner Brothers, color, 103 minutes

DIRECTORS: Danny Goldberg, Anthony Potenza, Julian Schlossberg
PRODUCERS: Danny Goldberg, Julian Schlossberg
MUSICAL PERFORMERS: Jackson Browne, Crosby, Stills and Nash, the Doobie Brothers, Nicolette Larson, Graham Nash, Bonnie Raitt, Gil Scott-Heron, Bruce Springsteen, James Taylor and Carly Simon, Jesse Colin Young
SONGS PERFORMED: *Before the Deluge, Running On Empty*, Jackson Browne; *Suite Judy Blue Eyes*, Crosby, Stills and Nash; *What a Fool Believes*, the Doobie Brothers; *Takin' It to the Streets*, the Doobie Brothers, Jackson Browne, Nicolette Larson, Graham Nash, Bonnie Raitt, Carly Simon, James Taylor, Phoebe Snow; *Barrels of Pain, Our House*, Graham Nash; *Runaway*, Bonnie Raitt; *We Almost Lost Detroit*, Gil Scott-Heron; *Devil With the Blue Dress On, Quarter To Three, The River, Thunder Road*, Bruce Springsteen; *Stay*, Bruce Springsteen, Jackson Browne; *Stand and Fight, Your Smiling Face*, James Taylor; *Mocking Bird*, James Taylor and Carly Simon; *The Times They Are A-Changin'*, James Taylor, Carly Simon, John Hall, Graham Nash; *Get Together*, Jesse Colin Young, Jackson Browne, Graham Nash, Steven Stills
SOUNDTRACK: Asylum (triple album)
VIDEO: Twentieth Century Fox

Five benefit concerts for MUSE (Musicians United for Safe Energy), in September 1979, at Madison Square Garden. Mostly soft rock, but the occasion drew some unusually fiery performances from people like James Taylor, whose *Stand and Fight* is strong and rousing. Another delightful moment has Graham Nash doing *Our House*, accompanying himself on piano, and finding the entire audience singing along is unison. Bruce Springsteen, of course, blasts everyone else off the stage with an amazingly energetic and varied set, making one wish that more of his performances were available on film for those who can't camp out all night to get concert tickets. Anyway, an enjoyable and worthy entertainment.

ONE PLUS ONE see SYMPATHY FOR THE DEVIL

UK advertisement for PICTURES AT AN EXHIBITION.

CONCERTS AND DOCUMENTARIES

PICTURES AT AN EXHIBITION 1972
Crown-International Pictures, color, 98 minutes

DIRECTOR: Nicholas Ferguson
PRODUCER: Lindsey Clennel
MUSICAL PERFORMERS: Emerson, Lake and Palmer
NUMBERS PERFORMED: *The Barbarian, Knife Edge, Nut Rocker, Pictures at an Exhibition, Take a Pebble*

Classical tunes given a rock interpretation by Emerson, Lake and Palmer. A little of this goes a long way for most people, though it is technically good.

PINK FLOYD AT POMPEII A.K.A. PINK FLOYD 1971
EMI, color, 85 minutes

DIRECTOR: Adrian Maben
PRODUCER: Michel Arnaud
MUSICAL PERFORMERS: Pink Floyd (David Gilmour, Nick Mason, Roger Waters, Richard Wright)
SONGS PERFORMED: *Careful With That Axe Eugene, Dark Side of the Moon, Echoes, Mademoiselle Nobs, One of These Days I'm Gonna Cut You Into Little Pieces, A Saucerful of Secrets, Set the Controls For the Heart of the Sun*
VIDEO: Vestron – US

Probably a must for Pink Floyd maniacs, this is an hour and a half of long songs performed in the Roman amphitheater at Pompeii. Unfortunately there are also interviews and backstage scenes, most of them incredibly pretentious, not too surprisingly. However, well-filmed and the sound is good.

POP GEAR A.K.A. GO GO MANIA 1965
American International Pictures, color, 70 minutes

DIRECTOR: Frederic Goode

POP GEAR – Peter and Gordon ...

... and the Rockin' Berries co-starred.

PRODUCER: Harry Field
MUSICAL PERFORMERS: the Animals, the Beatles, the Four Pennies, the Fourmost, Herman's Hermits, the Honeycombs, Billy J. Kramer and the Dakotas, the Nashville Teens, Peter and Gordon, Tommy Quickly, the Rockin' Berries, Sounds Incorporated

Fairly rotten quickie compilation of all the British Invasion Bands available, and some who never actually made it, introduced by DJ Jimmy Savile. Only the Beatles look like anything, in some performances excerpted from a newsreel. Otherwise, sketchy and with muddy sound.

POPCORN – AN AUDIO-VISUAL THING A.K.A. POPCORN – AN AUDIO-VISUAL EXPERIENCE 1969
Sherpix, color, 85 minutes

DIRECTOR: Peter Clifton
PRODUCER: Peter Ryan
MUSICAL PERFORMERS: the Beach Boys, the Bee Gees, Joe Cocker, Johnny Farnham, the Fifth Dimension, the Groove, Jimi Hendrix, Russell Morris, Otis Redding, the Rolling Stones, the Spencer Davis Group, Vanilla Fudge
SONGS : *Heroes and Villains*, the Beach Boys; *To Love Somebody*, the Bee Gees; *A Little Help From My Friends*, Joe Cocker; *Everybody Ought To Sing a Song*, Johnny Farnham; *Have You Tried Love?*, the Fifth Dimension; *Relax Me*, the Groove; *Hey Joe*, *Wild Thing*, Jimi Hendrix; *The Real Thing*, Russell Morris; *Respect*, *Satisfaction*, Otis Redding; *Jumpin' Jack Flash*, *Two Thousand Light Years From Home*, the Rolling Stones; *Gimme Some Lovin'*, the Spencer Davis Group; *Itchykoo Park*, the Small Faces; *The Beat Goes On*, Vanilla Fudge

Pointless documentary of late Sixties' counter-culture icons, including surfers, Twiggy, a commune in Katmandu and an atom bomb blast, strung together without much thought, apparently. Some quite good concert clips, though, with Hendrix and the Stones doing material less often seen, like *Hey Joe* and *2000 Light Years From Home*.

POPCORN – AN AUDIO-VISUAL EXPERIENCE/THING   The Beach Boys are among the musicians heard in this film.

RAINBOW BRIDGE 1971
Alcyone Films, color, 108 minutes

DIRECTOR: Chuck Wein
PRODUCER: Barry de Prendergast
MUSICAL PERFORMERS: Jimi Hendrix, the Jimi Hendrix Experience, the Ghetto Fighters, Juma Edwards
SONGS: *Dolly Dagger, Earth Blue, Easy Rider, Foxy Lady, Hear My Train A-Comin', Hey Baby, Look Over Yonder, Pali Gap, Purple Haze, Room Full of Mirrors, The Star Spangled Banner, Voodoo Chile*
SOUNDTRACK: Reprise

An occult commune is the *main* subject of this documentary, and that part is dire. But the last half hour or so is a Jimi Hendrix concert given on the island of Maui, which is well worth seeing. It's at the end, though, so you don't have to watch the rest of it.

REGGAE 1970
Contemporary, color, 60 minutes

DIRECTOR: Horace Ove
PRODUCER: Horace Ove
MUSICAL PERFORMERS: Black Faith, Bob and Marcia, Desmond Dekker, John Holt, Junior Lincoln, the Maytals, Prince Buster, the Pyramids

The Caribbean Music festival in 1970; some fine music unfortunately intercut with silly sociology and unsuitable movie clips.

REGGAE SUNSPLASH 1980
International Harmony Films, color, 107 minutes

DIRECTOR: Stefan Paul
PRODUCER: Kino Aresenal Tubingen
MUSICAL PERFORMERS: Burning Spear, Bob Marley and the Wailers, Third World, Peter Tosh
VIDEO: Sony – US (released in two parts)

Pretty badly filmed concert material prefaced by some local color and hilarious interviews in which the serious-minded German film-makers are confronted by some distinctively tongue-in-cheek Rasta philosophizing. The music is brilliant and the ecstatic atmosphere of the concerts is well captured; Marley's set in particular is riveting.

REVOLUTION 1969
United Artists, color, 90 minutes

DIRECTOR: Jack O'Connell
PRODUCER: Jack O'Connell
MUSICAL PERFORMERS: the Steve Miller Band, Mother Earth, Quicksilver Messenger Service
SONGS PERFORMED: *Mercury Blues, Superbyrd, Your Old Lady*, the Steve Miller Band; *Revolution, Stranger In My Home Town, Without Love*, Mother Earth; *Babe I'm Gonna Leave You, Codine*, Quicksilver Messenger Service
SOUNDTRACK: United Artists
VIDEO: Cabal – US

You just *know* what a late Sixties' feature with a title like this will be like, and you'll be right – unreconstructed hippiedom. There are some scenes of San Francisco local color, like a Rama Krishna Temple, a commune (naturally), and a summer solstice party. But there is also some fine music, with some of the top bands of the era. Worth hearing if not seeing.

ROCK AND ROLL – THE EARLY DAYS 1984
Archive Films, color/black & white, 59 minutes

DIRECTORS: Patrick Montgomery, Pamela Page
PRODUCER: Patrick Montgomery
NARRATOR: John Heard
MUSICAL PERFORMERS: Chuck Berry, Bo Diddley, Fats Domino, the Everly Brothers, Bill Haley and His Comets, Buddy Holly, Elvis Presley, Gale Storm, Joe Turner
SONGS: *Well All Right*, Len Amato; *Maybelline*,

Chuck Berry; *Sh-Boom*, the Chords; *Summertime Blues*, Eddie Cochran; *Bo Diddley*, Bo Diddley; *Ain't That a Shame*, Fats Domino; *Rock Around the Clock*, Bill Haley and His Comets; *Mystery Train, That's All Right Mama*, Elvis Presley; *Hound Dog*, Big Mama Thornton; *Shake Rattle and Roll, Good Rockin' Tonight*, Joe Turner; *La Bamba*, Ritchie Valens; *Hootchie Cootchie Man*, Muddy Waters
VIDEO: RCA-Columbia – UK

An entertaining musical documentary with an exciting array of authentic film clips of rock's original stars, some very rare. John Heard's narration is warm and lively, and the music is excellent. Some greats, like Gene Vincent, are heard but not seen, which is a shame, and some performers peripheral to rock appear, like Pat Boone (making an absolute fool of himself when interviewed about the meaning of *Tutti Fruitti*) and Ernest Tubb. The history is sketchy and ill-informed; just ignore it, and look and listen.

ROCK AND SOUL LIVE – DARYL HALL AND JOHN OATES 1983
M-1 Musical Enterprises, color, 91 minutes

DIRECTOR: Marty Callner
PRODUCER: Danny O'Donovan
SOUND MIXED BY: Bob Clearmountain
RECORDED LIVE AT: Montreal Forum, March 10–11, 1983
MUSICAL PERFORMERS: Daryl Hall, John Oates, and band consisting of Mickey Curry, Charlie DeChant, G. E. Smith, Tom T-Bone Wolk
SONGS PERFORMED: *Art of Heartbreak, Diddy Doo Wop, Family Man, I Can't Go For That, Italian Girls, Kiss On My List, Maneater, One On One, Open All Night, Room to Breathe, Sara Smile, She's Gone, Wait For Me, You Make My Dreams Come True, You've Lost That Loving Feeling*
VIDEO: RCA–Columbia – UK

ROCK AND ROLL – THE EARLY DAYS

CONCERTS AND DOCUMENTARIES

Well-done feature length concert by Philadelphia duo Hall and Oates. The production is very good, though their voices obviously suffered a bit from extensive touring; here they're not quite up to *You've Lost That Loving Feeling*. All of their big hits are performed, but the emphasis is on the newer songs and real classics, like *I Can't Go For That* and *She's Gone* are relegated to medleys. All in all, though, an hour and a half of good music.

ROCKSHOW   1979
MPL Communications, color, 106 minutes

DIRECTOR: None credited
MUSICAL PERFORMERS: Paul McCartney and Wings
SONGS PERFORMED: *Band On The Run, Beware My Love, Bluebird, Go Now, Hi Hi Hi, I've Just Seen a Face, Jet, Let 'Em In, Let Me Roll It, Letting Go, Listen To What the Man Said, Live and Let Die, Magneto and Titanium Man, Maybe I'm Amazed, Medicine Jar, Silly Love Songs, Soily, Spirits of Ancient Egypt, Time To Hide, Venus and Mars, Yesterday, You Gave Me the Answer*
VIDEO: Thorn–EMI – US, UK

Straightforward concert film of Wings in Seattle, Washington, in 1976. Not very skilfully photographed, but the material is well performed and reminds you just what a gigantically talented songwriter McCartney is. Also, Denny Laine leads the band for a version of his *old* band's, the Moody Blues, lovely *Go Now*, a highlight of the show.

ROOTS ROCK AND REGGAE   1978
Harcourt Films, color, 55 minutes

DIRECTOR: Jeremy Marre
PRODUCER: Jeremy Marre

ROCKSHOW   Paul McCartney and Wings' concert.

MUSICAL PERFORMERS: the Abyssinians, Jimmy Cliff, the Gladiators, Inner Circle, Bob Marley and the Wailers, the Mighty Diamonds, Junior Murvin, Toots and the Maytals
SONGS PERFORMED: *Satta Massagana*, the Abyssinians; *From the Beginning, I'm a Wanted Man*, Jimmy Cliff; *Hearsay, Jah Works*, the Gladiators; *All Night, Forward Ever, I Found Myself, Love Is a Drug*, Inner Circle; *Lively Up Yourself, Trenchtown Rock, Want More*, Bob Marley and the Wailers; *When the Right Time Comes*, the Mighty Diamonds; *The Longest River, Tell Me, This World*, Toots and the Maytals

Interesting and informative documentary of reggae and its origins. One minor quibble is that the excellent performances are too often broken up by voice-over commentaries; otherwise very effective.

THE ROYAL ALBERT HALL CONCERT FOR ARMS   1983
Color, 120 minutes

DIRECTOR: Stanley Dorfman
PRODUCER: Glyn Johns
MUSICAL PERFORMERS: Jeff Beck, Eric Clapton, Ray Cooper, Andy Fairweather Low, James Hooker, Kenny Jones, Ronnie Lane, Jimmy Page, Simon Phillips, Fernando Saunders, Chris Stainton, Charlie Watts, Steve Winwood, Bill Wyman
SONGS PERFORMED: *City Sirens, Cocaine, Everybody Ought To Make a Change, Gimme Some Lovin', Goodbye Porkpie Hat, Goodnight Irene, Hi Ho Silver lining, Lay Down Sally, Layla, Led Boots, Man Smart Woman Smarter, Prelude, Pump (the Pump), Rambling On My Mind, Rita Mae, Road Runner, Slowdown Sundown, Stairway to Heaven, Star Cycle, Take Me To the River, Tulsa Time, Who's to Blame*
VIDEO: Heron – UK

This all-star concert was organized to raise money for the Ronnie Lane Appeal for Action into Research for Multiple Sclerosis in 1983, when the rock music world became aware of well-known bassist Lane's struggle with the disease. Benefits often turn out to be more good intentions than good music, but fortunately this one is very good indeed. This is in large part due to the greatly under-rated Andy Fairweather Low, who acted as a sort of ringmaster, easing the line-up of superstars and guitar heroes on and off the stage with unobtrusive graciousness and generally keeping things moving. The songs are good, blues-based rock, with a selection of classics by Clapton and some Led Zeppelin numbers – including, naturally, *Stairway to Heaven* – by Jimmy Page. Altogether a fine show, and a good cause.

RUST NEVER SLEEPS   1979
International Harmony Pictures, color, 103 minutes

DIRECTOR: Bernard Shakey
PRODUCER: L. A. Johnson
MUSICAL PERFORMER: Neil Young
SONGS PERFORMED: *My My Hey Hey, Ride My Llama, Welfare Mother*
SOUNDTRACK: Reprise

Another Epic from Neil Young, disguised ineffectively as Bernard Shakey. This one has the usual nonsense – strange props, roadies dressed as Jawas from *STAR WARS* – but the songs and Young's performance are very good, as always. The guy *never* does a bad job, actually; it's hard to see why he needs to dress up his music in this distracting way.

SAVE THE CHILDREN   1973
Paramount Pictures, color, 123 minutes

DIRECTOR: Stan Lathan
PRODUCER: Matt Robinson
MUSICAL PERFORMERS: Cannonball Adderley, Jerry Butler and Brenda Lee Eager, Sammy Davis Jr., Roberta Flack, Marvin Gaye,

CONCERTS AND DOCUMENTARIES

Gladys Knight and the Pips, Main Ingredient, Curtis Mayfield, The Ramsey Lewis Trio, the O'Jays, the PUSH Choir, the Temptations, Nancy Wilson, Bill Withers, Zulema

SONGS PERFORMED: *Country Preacher*, Cannonball Adderley; *Close to You*, Jerry Butler and Brenda Lee Eager; *I've Gotta Be Me*, Sammy Davis Jr.; *On a Clear Day*, Roberta Flack, Quincy Jones;

THE ROYAL ALBERT HALL CONCERT THE RONNIE LANE APPEAL FOR A.R.M.S.

Save the Children, What's Goin' On, Marvin Gaye; *I Heard It Through the Grapevine*, Gladys Knight and the Pips; *Everybody Plays the Fool*, Main Ingredient; *Give Me Your Love*, Curtis Mayfield; *People Make the World Go Round*, the Ramsey Lewis Trio; *Sunshine*, the O'Jays; *I'm Too Close to Heaven to Turn Around*, the PUSH Choir; *Papa Was a Rollin' Stone*, the Temptations; *The Greatest Performance of My Life*, Nancy Wilson; *Lean On Me*, Bill Withers; *This Child of Mine*, Zulema
SOUNDTRACK: Motown

An excellent, vital soul-oriented benefit for Jesse Jackson's PUSH (People United to Save Humanity) organization in 1972. Besides the deeply felt and often gospel-tinged performances, there are news clips of the plight of children around the world.

THE SECRET POLICEMAN'S BALL
1979
Amnesty International Pictures, color, 95 minutes

DIRECTOR: Roger Graef
PRODUCERS: Roger Graef, Thomas Schwalm
MUSICAL PERFORMERS: Tom Robinson, Pete Townshend, John Williams
SONGS PERFORMED: *Glad to Be Gay, 1967 (So Long Ago)*, Tom Robinson; *Drowned, Pinball Wizard*, Pete Townshend; *Won't Get Fooled Again*, Pete Townshend, John Williams
SOUNDTRACK: Island

Hugely enjoyable mostly comic benefit for Amnesty International in London in 1979. The few musical numbers are admirable, especially Townshend and Williams' brilliant acoustic duet on *Won't Get Fooled Again*, but the main body of the film is necessarily humorous, with an enormous cast of stars from *Beyond the Fringe*, Monty Python and the Goodies, including Peter Cook, John Cleese, Michael Palin, Jonathan Miller, Alan Bennett and Terry Jones. The highlight is perhaps the Shakespeare parody *So That's the Way You Like It*, closely followed by Eleanor Bron's fund-raising speech and, of course, the dead parrot. And one important musical credit was left out of the above listing – Michael Palin does the inimitable *Lumberjack Song*, supported by the whole cast.

SING SING THANKSGIVING   1974
Varied Directions Pictures, color, 78 minutes

DIRECTORS: David Hoffman, Harry Willard
PRODUCER: Harry Willard
MUSICAL PERFORMERS: Joan Baez, Mimi Farina, B. B. King, the Voices of East Harlem, Joe Williams
SONGS PERFORMED: *Right On Be Free, To Be Young Gifted and Black*

Slightly over-earnest filming of a Thanksgiving Day concert at the New York State Prison in 1974. Interviews and scenes of prison life complement the music.

THE SONG REMAINS THE SAME   Led Zeppelin (left to right): John Bonham, John Paul Jones, Robert Plant, Jimmy Page.

CONCERTS AND DOCUMENTARIES

THE SONG REMAINS THE SAME
1974
Columbia Pictures, color, 136 minutes

DIRECTORS: Peter Clifton, Joe Massot
PRODUCER: Peter Grant
MUSICAL PERFORMERS: Led Zeppelin (John Bonham, John Paul Jones, Jimmy Page, Robert Plant)
SONGS PERFORMED: *Autumn Lake, Black Dog, Bron-Y-Aur, Dazed and Confused, Heart Breaker, Moby Dick, No Quarter, Rain Song, Rock and Roll, Since I've Been Loving You, The Song Remains the Same, Stairway to Heaven, Whole Lotta Love*
SOUNDTRACK: Swansong
VIDEO: WEA – US

What can one say – the definitive document of Led Zeppelin in action, including their most typical songs, filmed at Madison Square Garden in 1973. Some talk and backstage antics, but mostly song after song, and they certainly do remain the same, you have to say that for them.

SOUL TO SOUL 1971
Cinerama, color, 95 minutes

DIRECTOR: Denis Saunders
PRODUCERS: Richard Bock, Tom Mosk
MUSICAL PERFORMERS: Willie Bobo, Roberta Flack, Eddie Harris, Les McCann and Amoa Azongio, Wilson Pickett, Santana, the Staple Singers, Ike and Tina Turner, Voices of East Harlem
SONGS PERFORMED: *Freedom Song, Trying Times*, Roberta Flack; *Heyjorter*, Les McCann, Eddie Harris and Amoa Azongio; *Funky Broadway, Land of a Thousand Dances*, Wilson Pickett; *Are You Sure?, He's Alright*, the Staple Singers; *I Smell Trouble, Soul to Soul, You Are Gone*, Ike and Tina Turner; *Run Shaker Run, Soul to Soul*, the Voices of East Harlem
SOUNDTRACK: Stax

SOUL TO SOUL   Wilson Pickett wows the audience in Ghana.

QUO – END OF THE ROAD '84

Ghana celebrated its fourteenth anniversary as an independent state by putting on a huge music festival, some of which is depicted here. This documentary displays, as the title indicates, the interface between the traditional African performers and black American soul stars, a combination of love, admiration and slight incomprehension. Very exciting atmosphere and fine music.

STATUS QUO – END OF THE ROAD
1984
Tahuna Ltd, color, 59 minutes

DIRECTOR: Keef
PRODUCER: Keef
FILMED IN: Milton Keynes Bowl
MUSICAL PERFORMERS: Status Quo (Andy Bown, Peter Kircher, Alan Lancaster, Rick Parfitt, Francis Rossi) with Bob Young, harmonica
SONGS PERFORMED: *Bye Bye Johnny, Caroline, Dirty Water, Down Down, Most of the Time, Mystery Song, Railroad, Roadhouse Blues, Rockin' All Over the World, Roll Over Lay Down, Slow Train, What You're Proposing, Whatever You Want, The Wild Side of Life*
VIDEO: Heron – UK

Stadium concert by the UK's leading exponents of what might be called 'heavy boogie' music, Status Quo, beginning with a light show and ending with fireworks. It was probably more fun to be there than to see this on the small screen; a large and devoted audience of headbangers certainly seems to think so, and they sing along en masse to most of the numbers. The video is quite good, but an hour of Quo goes a long way; best for fans.

STOP MAKING SENSE 1984
Talking Heads Films, color, 90 minutes

DIRECTOR: Jonathan Demme
PRODUCER: Gary Goetzman
DIRECTOR OF PHOTOGRAPHY: Jordan Cronenweth

CONCERTS AND DOCUMENTARIES

David Byrne makes a point in STOP MAKING SENSE

Simple effective lighting and superb photography make STOP MAKING SENSE one of the best concert films ever.

STOP MAKING SENSE A great concert performance by David Byrne and the Talking Heads.

CONCEIVED FOR THE STAGE BY: David Byrne
MR BYRNE'S BIG SUIT BUILT BY: Gail Blacker.
MUSICAL PERFORMERS: the Talking Heads (David Byrne, Chris Frantz, Jerry Harrison, Steve Scales, Alex Weir, Tina Weymouth, Bernie Worrell; backing vocals, Ednah Holt and Lynn Mabry)
SONGS PERFORMED: *Burning Down the House, Girlfriend Is Better, Life During Wartime, Once In a Lifetime, Psycho Killer, Slippery People, Swamp, Take Me To the River, What a Day That Was*
SOUNDTRACK: Sire Records – US

Probably *the* most brilliant concert film ever, from start to finish the brainchild of head Head, David Byrne. A stark stage setting is made versatile by use of strikingly original lighting effects (designed by Byrne and Beverly Emmons); the only other prop is Byrne's Big Suit, which grows as the set progresses and receives it's own screen credit. The songs are a powerful collection of the Heads' best, and most of them are even better in these live versions. It's hard to choose, but standouts are *Psycho Killer*, performed solo by David Byrne, and the finale, *Take Me To the River*. This is one of the very few concert films that you wish was longer. Terrific.

SYMPATHY FOR THE DEVIL A.K.A. ONE PLUS ONE 1969
New Line Pictures, color, 99 minutes

DIRECTOR: Jean-Luc Godard
PRODUCERS: Michael Pearson, Ian Quarrier
MUSICAL PERFORMERS: the Rolling Stones (Mick Jagger, Keith Richard, Charlie Watts, Ron Wood, Bill Wyman)

CONCERTS AND DOCUMENTARIES

Brian Jones with Jean-Luc Godard filming SYMPATHY FOR THE DEVIL.

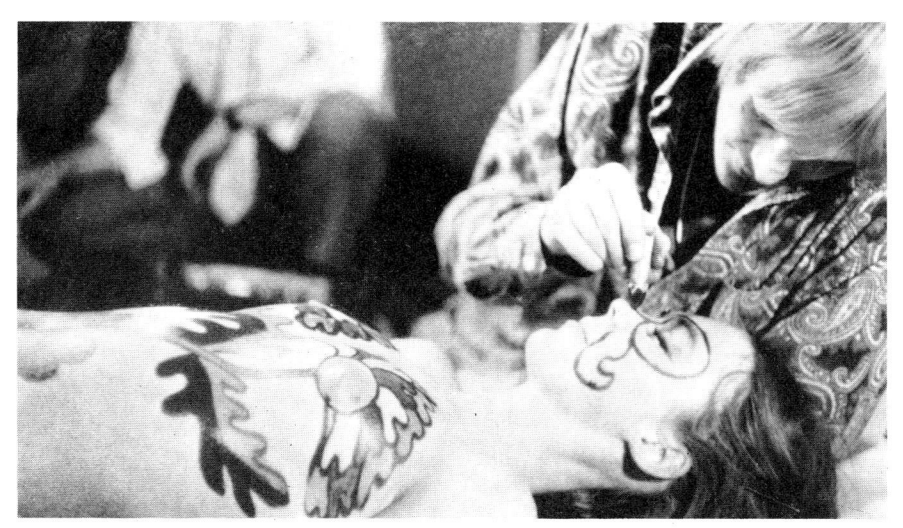

Hippies do weird and wonderful things in TONITE LET'S ALL MAKE LOVE IN LONDON.

SYMPATHY FOR THE DEVIL   Mick Jagger in the studio.

SONGS PERFORMED: *Sympathy For the Devil*

From the music lover's point of view, this is absolutely maddening – Godard took straightforward film of the Stones putting together their song *Sympathy For the Devil* in the studio and intercut it with hugely annoying and pretentious fictional scenes of various revolutionaries, black militants and other dead-serious types. But the shots of the band are so good, so revealing of their expertise and talent, that you watch, just waiting for the next bit. A really incomprehensible idea to anyone but the most fanatical Godard fan, of whom there must be some, I suppose.

TAKE IT OR LEAVE IT   1981
Nutty Stiff Productions, color/black & white, 60 minutes

DIRECTOR: Dave Robinson
PRODUCER: Dave Robinson
SCREENPLAY: Philip MacDonald, Madness, Dave Robinson
MUSICAL PERFORMERS: Madness (Mike Barson, Mark Bedford, Chris Foreman, Chas Smash, Suggs, Lee Thompson)
CAST: Madness
SONGS PERFORMED: *Bed and Breakfast Man, Come On, Don't Quote Me On That, Jailhouse Rock, Madness, One Step Beyond, Rough Kids, See You Later Alligator, Welcome to the House of Fun*
VIDEO: Stiff Films

Cinema-verité style docu-drama of the formation of the popular band Madness. Actually, it's a good look at the hopeful but grubby life *before* success, with the group searching Islington for suitable musicians. But their good-humored charm is unfortunately under-used; this could really be about *any* band.

TONITE LET'S ALL MAKE LOVE IN LONDON   1967
Lorrimer Films, color, 72 minutes

DIRECTOR: Peter Whitehead
PRODUCER: Peter Whitehead
MUSICAL PERFORMERS: Pink Floyd, Twice As Much, Vashti
SONGS PERFORMED: *Interstellar Overdrive*, Pink Floyd; *Night Time Girl*, Twice As Much; *Winter Is Blue*, Vashti
SOUNDTRACK SONGS: Eric Burdon and the New Animals; *Out of Time, Paint It Black*, Chris Farlowe, the Rolling Stones; *Here Comes the Nice*, the Small Faces
SOUNDTRACK: Instant – UK

Silly analysis of swinging London, with some superficial interviews, commentary and film clips, but some interesting music, though some of it is on the soundtrack only.

WATTSTAX   1973
Columbia Pictures, color, 98 minutes

DIRECTOR: Mel Stuart
PRODUCERS: Larry Shaw, Mel Stuart
MUSICAL PERFORMERS: Rance Allen, the Bar-Kays, the Dramatics, the Emotions, Isaac Hayes, Luther Ingram, Jimmy Jones, Albert King, Little Milton, Mel and Tim, the Staple Singers, Johnny Taylor, Carla Thomas, Rufus Thomas, Kim Weston
SONGS PERFORMED: *Lyin' On the Truth*, Rance Allen; *Son of Shaft*, the Bar-Kays; *What You See Is What You Get*, the Dramatics; *Peace Be Still*, the Emotions; *Shaft, Soulsville*, Isaac Hayes; *If Loving You Is Wrong*, Luther Ingram; *Someone Greater Than You and I*, Jimmy Jones; *I'll Play the Blues For You*, Albert King; *Walking the Backstreets and Crying*, Little Milton; *I May Not Be What You Want*, Mel and Tim; *Ol La Le Da, Respect Yourself, We the People*, the Staple Singers; *Jody's Got Your Girl*, Johnny Taylor; *Pick Up the Pieces*, Carla Thomas; *Breakdown, Funky Chicken*, Rufus Thomas; *Lift Every Voice and Sing, The Star Spangled Banner*, Kim Weston
SOUNDTRACK: Stax

Dynamic benefit concert for the Los Angeles neighborhood of Watts, devastated by riots in the late Sixties. Richard Pryor hosts the extensive line-up of soul and blues stars, and documentary coverage of the area is included.

WOODSTOCK   1970
Warner Brothers, color, 184 minutes

DIRECTOR: Michael Wadleigh
PRODUCER: Bob Maurice
MUSICAL PERFORMERS: Joan Baez, Canned Heat,

Isaac Hayes in WATTSTAX.

CONCERTS AND DOCUMENTARIES

WOODSTOCK Sly Stone takes the crowd higher.

Joe Cocker, Country Joe and the Fish, Crosby, Stills, Nash and Young, Richie Havens, Jimi Hendrix, Santana, John Sebastian, Sha Na Na, Sly and the Family Stone, Ten Years After, the Who
SONGS PERFORMED: *Joe Hill, Swing Low Sweet Chariot*, Joan Baez; *Goin' Up the Country*, Canned Heat; *Feel Like I'm Fixin' To Die Rag*, Country Joe and the Fish; *Suite Judy Blue Eyes, Wooden Ships*, Crosby, Stills, Nash and Young; *Freedom*, Richie Havens; *Purple Haze, The Star Spangled Banner*, Jimi Hendrix; *Soul Sacrifice*, Santana; *Younger Generation*, John Sebastian; *At the Hop*, Sha Na Na; *Dance to the Music, Higher, Music Lover*, Sly and the Family Stone; *I'm Goin' Home*, Ten Years After; *Summertime Blues, We're Not Going to Take It*, the Who
SOUNDTRACK SONGS: *Long Time Gone, Woodstock*, Crosby, Stills, Nash and Young

SOUNDTRACK: Atlantic
VIDEO: WEA – US (released in two parts)

Long documentary of the Woodstock Music and Art Festival in August 1969 that really captures the spirit of the event. The amazing performances are alternated with various crowd scenes and interviews with terribly youthful hippies, local townspeople, some angry and some surprisingly supportive, and with the police and medical staffs. But the music is the thing, from Sly and the Family Stone's ecstatic *Higher* to Crosby, Stills, Nash and Young's first performance of *Suite Judy Blue Eyes*, their masterpiece (and they forget some of the lyrics). The next best thing to being there.

YESSONGS 1973
Fair Enterprises, color, 75 minutes

DIRECTOR: Peter Neal
PRODUCER: Brian Lane
MUSICAL PERFORMERS: Yes (Jon Anderson, Steve Howe, Chris Squire, Rick Wakeman, Alan White)
SONGS PERFORMED: *All Good People, The Clap, Close to the Edge, Roundabout, Starship Trooper, Yours Is No Disgrace*
VIDEO: Light – US

Filmed at the Rainbow in London in 1972, this is just what it says – an unadorned view of the then Yes in action, doing some long – even interminable – improvisations. Appealing to their fans, I presume.

YOKO ONO THEN AND NOW 1984
Polygram Music Video, color/black & white, 56 minutes

DIRECTOR: Barbara Graustark
PRODUCER: Barbara Graustark
WRITTEN AND NARRATED BY: Barbara Graustark
MUSICAL PERFORMERS: John Lennon, Yoko Ono
SONGS: *Beautiful Boy, Don't Worry Kyoko, Give Peace a Chance, Goodbye Sadness, Starting Over, Watching the Wheels, Walking On Thin Ice*
VIDEO: Heron – UK

A musical documentary exploring the life of John Lennon's widow. From the time of the Beatles' break up, Yoko Ono has been a target of much personal hostility and misunderstanding; with Lennon's death, this turned abruptly to a kind of dependent devotion from fans that is perhaps more demanding. Few know much about her upbringing as a very wealthy banker's daughter or her solo career as an independent conceptual artist. With interviews, family photos and rare home movies of her life with Lennon, television reporter Barbara Graustark fashions a fascinating picture of a most remarkable person.

CONCERTS AND DOCUMENTARIES

YOU ARE WHAT YOU EAT   Tiny Tim.

YOU ARE WHAT YOU EAT   1968
Commonwealth-United Pictures, color, 75 minutes

DIRECTOR: Barry Feinstein
PRODUCERS: Barry Feinstein, Peter Yarrow
MUSICAL PERFORMERS: Paul Butterfield, David Crosby, Dave Dixon, Electric Flag, Harper's Bizarre, John Herald, Barry McGuire, Rosco, John Simon, Tiny Tim, Peter Yarrow
SONGS PERFORMED: *Teenage Fair*, Paul Butterfield, David Crosby, Dave Dixon, Barry McGuire, Rosko; *Freakout*, Electric Flag, John Simon; *Come To the Sunshine*, Harper's Bizarre; *Family Dog*, John Herald; *My Name Is Jack*, John Simon; *Be My Baby, I Got You Babe, Memphis Tennessee, Sonny Boy*, Tiny Tim; *Don't Remind Me Now of Time, Silly Girl*, Peter Yarrow; *The Wabe, You Are What You Eat*, Peter Yarrow, John Simon
SOUNDTRACK: Columbia – US; CBS – UK

Silly chronicling of teenage hippies, including the usual love-ins, concerts, surfing, and flower-power in general, but with some excellent songs and performances. Anyway, everyone should see Tiny Tim do *Memphis Tennessee* at least once.

SOUNDTRACKS

ALFIE DARLING 1975
EMI, color, 102 minutes

DIRECTOR: Ken Hughes
PRODUCER: Dugald Rankin
STAGE PLAY: Bill Naughton
SCORE: Alan Price
MUSICAL DIRECTOR: Derek Wadsworth
CAST: Alan Price, Jill Townsend, Joan Collins, Hannah Gordon, Rula Lenska

ALL THIS AND WORLD WAR II 1976
Twentieth Century Fox, color/black & white, 88 minutes

DIRECTOR: Susan Winslow
PRODUCERS: Sandy Lieberson, Martin J. Machat
MUSICAL DIRECTOR: Lou Reizner
SOUNDTRACK SONGS: *Magical Mystery Tour*, Ambrosia; *Carry That Weight, Golden Slumbers, She Came In Through the Bathroom Window, Sun King*, the Bee Gees; *Hey Jude*, the Brothers Johnson; *Yesterday*, David Essex; *She's Leaving Home*, Bryan Ferry; *We Can Work It Out*, the Four Seasons; *Because*, Lynsey De Paul; *Strawberry Fields Forever*, Peter Gabriel; *Help*, Henry Gross; *Lucy In the Sky With Diamonds*, Elton John; *Nowhere Man*, Jeff Lynne; *When I'm Sixty-Four*, Keith Moon; *I Am the Walrus, Let it Be, The Long and Winding Road*, Leo Sayer; *Gettin Better*, Status Quo; *Get Back*, Rod Stewart; *Come Together*, Tina Turner; *Lovely Rita, Polythene Pam*, Roy Wood; the London Symphony Orchestra, the Royal Philharmonic Orchestra
SOUNDTRACK: Twentieth Century Fox

ALMOST SUMMER 1977
Universal International Pictures, 89 minutes

DIRECTOR: Martin Davidson
PRODUCER: Rob Cohen
MUSIC: Ron Altbach, Charles Lloyd; Mike Love, Al Jardine, Brian Wilson
CAST: Bruno Kirby, Lee Purcell, John Fredrich, Didi Conn
SOUNDTRACK SONGS: *She Was a Lady, Summertime, Fresh; We Are the Future, High Energy; Almost Summer, Cruisin', Lady Linda, Looking Good, Sad Sad Summer*, Mike Love
SOUNDTRACK: MCA

AMERICAN GRAFFITI 1973
Universal International Pictures, color, 110 minutes

DIRECTOR: George Lucas
PRODUCERS: Francis Ford Coppola, Gary Kurtz
CAST: Richard Dreyfuss, Ronny Howard, Charles Martin Smith, Paul LeMat
SOUNDTRACK SONGS: *All Summer Long*, the Beach Boys; *Almost Grown, Johnny B. Goode*, Chuck Berry; *Chantilly Lace*, the Big Bopper; *Fanny Mae*, Buster Brown; *You're Sixteen*, Johnny Burnette; *Heart and Soul*, the Cleftones; *Love Potion Number 9*, the Clovers; *Sixteen Candles*, the Crests; *Gee*, the Crows; *Peppermint Twist*, Joey Dee; *Come Go With Me*, the Del-Vikings; *Little Darling, The Stroll*, the Diamonds; *Ain't That a Shame*, Fats Domino; *Teen Angel*, Mark Dinning; *Ya Ya*, Lee Dorsey; *To the Aisle*, the Five Satins; *I Only Have Eyes For You*, the Flamingos; *The Great Imposter*, the Fleetwoods; *Do You Wanna Dance?*, Bobby Freeman; *Rock Around the Clock*, Bill Haley and His Comets; *A Thousand Miles Away*, the Heartbeats; *Maybe Baby, That'll Be the Day*, Buddy Holly; *Party Knox*, Buddy Knox; *Book of Love*, the Monotones; *Crying In the Chapel*, Sonny Till and the Orioles; *The Great Pretender, Smoke Gets In Your Eyes*, the Platters; *Runaway*, Del Shannon; *Get a Job*, the Silhouettes; *Since I Don't Have You*, the Skyliners; *Goodnight, Well It's Time to Go*, the Spaniels; *Why Do Fools Fall In Love*, Frankie Lymon and the Teenagers; *See You In September*, the Tempos; *Green Onions*, Booker T. and the MG's
SOUNDTRACK: MCA

SOUNDTRACKS

ANDY WARHOL'S BAD 1976
New World Pictures, color, 94 minutes

DIRECTOR: Jed Johnson
PRODUCERS: Fred Hughes, Andy Warhol
MUSIC: Mike Bloomfield
CAST: Carroll Baker, Perry King, Susan Tyrell, Stefania Casini

ANIMAL HOUSE 1978
Color, 109 minutes

DIRECTOR: John Landis
CAST: John Belushi, Tim Matheson, John Vernon, Thomas Hulce, Peter Riegert
SOUNDTRACK SONGS: *Money*, John Belushi; *Animal House*, *Dream Girl*, Steven Bishop; *Twistin' the Night Away*, *Wonderful World*, Sam Cooke; *Who's Sorry Now*, Connie Francis; *Shama Lang Ding Dong*, *Shout*, DeWayne Jessie; *Louie Louie*, the Kingsmen; *Tossin' and Turnin'*, Bobby Lewis; *Let's Dance*, Chris Montez; *Hey Paula*, Paul and Paula
SOUNDTRACK: MCA

BABYLON 1980
Osiris, color, 95 minutes

DIRECTOR: Franco Rosso
PRODUCER: Gavrik Losey
SCREENPLAY: Martin Stellman, Franco Rosso
SCORE: Dennis Bovell
CAST: Brinsley Forde, Brian Bovell, Karl Howard, Trevor Laird
SOUNDTRACK SONGS: *Hey Jah Children*, *Warrior Charge*, Aswad; *Thank You For the Many Things You've Done*, Cassandra; *Babylon*, Johnny Clark; *Whap'n'Bap'n*, I-Roy; *Can't Give It Up*, Janet Kay; *Turn Me Loose*, Michael Prophet; *LBC Theme*, Jeff Wayne; *Deliver Me From My Enemies*, Yabby U
SOUNDTRACK: Chrysalis – UK

BETWEEN THE LINES 1976
Midwest Film Productions, color, 101 minutes

DIRECTOR: Joan Micklin Silver
PRODUCER: Raphael D. Silver
CAST: John Heard, Jeff Goldblum, Lindsay Crouse, Jill Eikenberry
SOUNDTRACK SONGS: *You To Me Are Everything*, Eric Mercury; *Heat Treatment*, Graham Parker; *Fanny Mae*, *I Don't Want to Go Home*, *Having a Party*, *Love Is On Our Side*, Southside Johnny and the Asbury Jukes

THE BIG CHILL 1982
Columbia Pictures, color, 97 minutes

DIRECTOR: Lawrence Kasdan
PRODUCER: Michael Shamberg
CAST: William Hurt, Kevin Kline, Glenn Close, Mary Kay Place, Tom Berenger, Jeff Goldblum
SOUNDTRACK SONGS: *Tell Him*, the Exciters; *You Make Me Feel Like a Natural Woman*, Aretha Franklin; *I Heard It Through the Grapevine*, Marvin Gaye; *I Second That Emotion*, *The Tracks of My Tears*, Smokey Robinson and the Miracles; *Ain't Too Proud to Beg*, *My Girl*, the Temptations; *Joy to the World*, Three Dog Night; *Good Lovin'*, the Young Rascals

BIG WEDNESDAY 1978
Warner Brothers, color, 119 minutes

DIRECTOR: John Milius
PRODUCERS: Tamara Asseyev, Alex Rose
CAST: Gary Busey, Jan-Michael Vincent, William Katt, Patti d'Arbanville
SOUNDTRACK SONGS: *Green Onions*, Booker T. and the MG's; *The Twist*, Chubby Checker; *He's a Rebel*, the Crystals; *Sherry*, the Four Seasons; *Do You Wanna Dance*, Bobby Freeman; *Will You Still Love Me Tomorrow?*, Carole King; *The Locomotion*, Little Eva; *La Bamba*, Trini Lopez; *Money*, Barrett Strong

BLACK CAESAR A.K.A. THE GODFATHER OF HARLEM 1973
Color, 96 minutes

DIRECTOR: Larry Cohen
PRODUCER: Larry Cohen
SCORE: James Brown, Fred Wesley, Lyn Collins and the JB's
CAST: Fred Williamson, Minnie Gentry, Julius W. Harris
TITLE SONG: *Down and Out in New York City*
SOUNDTRACK: Polydor

THE BLACKBOARD JUNGLE 1955
Metro Goldwyn Mayer, black & white, 101 minutes

DIRECTOR: Richard Brooks
PRODUCER: Pandro S. Berman
CAST: Glenn Ford, Anne Francis, Louis Calhern, Sidney Poitier, Vic Morrow, Paul Mazursky
SOUNDTRACK SONGS: *Rock Around the Clock*, Bill Haley and His Comets

BLUE COLLAR 1978
Universal International Pictures, color, 114 minutes

DIRECTOR: Paul Schrader
PRODUCER: Don Guest
SCORE: Jack Nitzsche
SPECIAL MUSICAL ARRANGEMENTS: Ry Cooder
CAST: Richard Pryor, Harvey Keitel, Yaphet Kotto
SOUNDTRACK SONGS: *Hard Workin' Man*, Captain Beefheart; *Wang Dang Doodle*, Howlin' Wolf; *Saturday Night Special*, Lynyrd Skynyrd; *Goodbye So Long*, Ike and Tina Turner
SOUNDTRACK: MCA

BROTHERS 1977
Color, 104 minutes

DIRECTOR: Arthur Barron
SCORE: Taj Mahal
CAST: Bernie Casey, Vonetta McGee, Ron O'Neal
SOUNDTRACK SONGS: *Brothers Doin' Time, Free the Brothers, Love Theme in the Key of D, Love Theme Number One, Nightride*
SOUNDTRACK: Warner Brothers – US

CALIFORNIA DREAMING 1978
Color, 92 minutes

DIRECTOR: John Hancock
CAST: Glynnis O'Connor, Seymour Cassel, Dorothy Tristan
SOUNDTRACK SONGS: *California Dreamin'*, America; *Among the Yesterdays, Keep It In the Family*, Burton Cummings; *Pass You By*, Flo and Eddie; *Forever*, Michele Phillips; *Come On and Get Ready, Everybody's Dancin'*, Henry Small
SOUNDTRACK: American International

CAPTAIN MILKSHAKE 1970
Color, 89 minutes

DIRECTOR: Richard Crawford
CAST: Geoff Gage, David Korn, Andrea Cagan
SOUNDTRACK SONGS: *Ballad of Tommy Udo, Lie to Me, Oh Death, Tanya*, Kaleidoscope; *Who Do You Love?*, Quicksilver Messenger Service; *Children of the Future*, the Steve Miller Band

CAR WASH 1976
Universal International Pictures, color, 97 minutes

DIRECTOR: Michael Schultz
PRODUCERS: Art Linson, Gary Stromberg
SCORE: Norman Whitfield
CAST: Richard Pryor, Franklin Ajaye, Garrett Morris, Antonio Fargas
SOUNDTRACK SONGS: *Born To Love You, Car Wash, Daddy Rich, I Wanna Get Next to You, Keep On Keepin' On, Put Your Money Where Your Mouth Is, Yo Yo, You Gotta Believe, You're On My Mind,*

Zig Zag, Rose Royce, the Pointer Sisters
SOUNDTRACK: MCA

CARNY 1980
United Artists, color, 105 minutes

DIRECTOR: Robert Kaylor
PRODUCER: Robbie Robertson
SCORE: Alex North, Robbie Robertson
CAST: Jodie Foster, Gary Busey, Robbie Robertson
SOUNDTRACK SONGS: *The Fat Man, Freak's Lament, Garden of Earthly Delights, Pagan Knights, Sawdust and G-Strings, Rained Out,* Robbie Robertson
SOUNDTRACK: Warner Brothers

CATCH US IF YOU CAN A.K.A. HAVING A WILD WEEKEND 1965
Warner Brothers, black & white, 91 minutes

DIRECTOR: John Boorman
PRODUCER: David Deutsch
SCREENPLAY: Peter Nichols
CAST: The Dave Clark Five (Dave Clark, Mike Smith, Lenny Davidson, Dennis Payton, Rick Huxley), Barbera Ferris, Robin Bailey, Yootha Joyce, David Lodge
SOUNDTRACK SONGS: *Catch Us If You Can, Having a Wild Weekend, I Can't Stand It, Move On, Ol Sol, On the Move, Sweet Memories, When*
SOUNDTRACK: Epic – US

CHASTITY 1969
American International Pictures, color, 98 minutes

DIRECTOR: Alessio De Paola
PRODUCER: Sonny Bono
SCORE: Sonny Bono
CAST: Cher, Barbera London, Tom Nolan
SOUNDTRACK SONG: *Band of Thieves*, Cher
SOUNDTRACK: Atco – US

THE CHICKEN CHRONICLES 1977
Color, 92 minutes

DIRECTOR: Francis Simon
MUSICAL DIRECTOR: Ken Lauber
CAST: Steve Guttenberg, Phil Silvers, Ed Lauber
SOUNDTRACK SONGS: *Sea's Getting Rough*, Boffalong; *On the Road Again*, Canned Heat; *Put a Little Love In Your Heart*, Jackie De Shannon; *Everyday With Your Girl, Spooky, Stormy*, Classics IV; *Buy For Me the Rain*, the Nitty Gritty Dirt Band
SOUNDTRACK: United Artists – US

CISCO PIKE 1972
Columbia Pictures, color, 94 minutes

DIRECTOR: Bill L. Norton
PRODUCER: Gerald Ayres
MUSICAL SUPERVISOR: Bob Johnston
CAST: Kris Kristofferson, Gene Hackman, Karen Black, Harry Dean Stanton
SOUNDTRACK SONGS: *Breakdown, Chapter 33, I'd Rather Be Sorry, Lovin' Her Was Easy*, Kris Kristofferson; *Wailin' and Whoopin'*, Sonny Terry

CLAUDINE 1974
Twentieth Century-Fox, color, 92 minutes

DIRECTOR: John Berry
SCORE: Curtis Mayfield
CAST: Diahann Carroll, James Earl Jones, Tamu
SOUNDTRACK SONGS: *Hold On, Make Yours a Happy Home, The Makings of You, Mr Welfare Man, On and On, To Be Invisible*, Gladys Knight and the Pips
SOUNDTRACK: Buddah

COAST TO COAST 1980
Paramount Pictures, color, 95 minutes

DIRECTOR: Joseph Sargent

PRODUCER: John Avnet, Steve Tisch
CAST: Robert Blake, Dyan Cannon, Michael Lerner
SOUNDTRACK SONGS: *Feels So Good to Win*, Ambrosia; *Fool That I Am*, Rita Coolidge; *I Can Tell By the Way You Dance*, *Picking Up Strangers*, Johnny Lee; *Once In a Lifetime*, Bonnie Raitt; *Swayin' to the Music*, Johnny Rivers; *You're Only Lonely*, J. D. Souther
SOUNDTRACK: Full Moon – US

COMING HOME   1978
United Artists, color, 128 minutes

DIRECTOR: Hal Ashby
PRODUCER: Jerome Hellman, Bruce Gilbert
CAST: Jane Fonda, Jon Voight, Bruce Dern, Robert Carradine
SOUNDTRACK SONGS: *Hey Jude*, *Strawberry Fields*, the Beatles; *Once I Was*, Tim Buckley; *For What It's Worth*, Buffalo Springfield; *Time Has Come Today*, the Chambers Brothers; *Just Like a Woman*, Bob Dylan; *Save Me*, Aretha Franklin; *Follow*, Richie Havens; *Manic Depression*, Jimi Hendrix; *White Rabbit*, Jefferson Airplane; *Call On Me*, Janis Joplin; *Jumpin' Jack Flash*, *My Girl*, *No Expectations*, *Out of Time*, *Ruby Tuesday*, *Sympathy for the Devil*, the Rolling Stones; *Born to Be Wild*, Steppenwolf; *Bookends*, Simon and Garfunkel

COOLEY HIGH   1975
American International, color, 101 minutes

DIRECTOR: Michael Schultz
PRODUCER: Steve Kranz
ORIGINAL MUSIC: Freddie Perren
CAST: Lawrence Hilton-Jacobs, Garrett Morris, Glynn Turman
SOUNDTRACK SONGS: *Luther's Blues*, Luther Allison; *So Hard To Say Goodbye to Yesterday*, G. C. Cameron; *I Can't Help Myself*, *Reach Out I'll Be There*, the Four Tops; *Dancing In the Streets*, Martha and the Vandellas; *Beechwood 4-5789*, the Marvellettes; *Mickey's Monkey*, *Ooh Baby Baby*, Smokey Robinson and the Miracles; *Baby Love*, *Stop In the Name of Love*, the Supremes; *My Girl*, the Temptations; *Money*, Barrett Strong; *Roadrunner*, Jr. Walker and the All Stars; *Fingertips*, Little Stevie Wonder
SOUNDTRACK: Motown

ELECTRA GLIDE IN BLUE   1973
United Artists, color, 113 minutes

DIRECTOR: James William Guercio
PRODUCER: James William Guercio
SCORE: James William Guercio
CAST: Robert Blake, Mitchell Ryan, Elisha Cook Jr., Jeannine Riley
SOUNDTRACK SONGS: *Tell Me*, Terry Kath; *Free From the Devil*, Madura; *Most of All*, the Marcels; *Meadow Mountain Top*, *Song of Sad Bottles*, Mark Spoelstra
SOUNDTRACK: United Artists

THE ENDLESS SUMMER   1966
Color, 95 minutes

DIRECTOR: Bruce Brown
PRODUCER:
SCORE: the Sandals
SOUNDTRACK: World Pacific – US

FM   1978
Universal International Pictures, color, 105 minutes

DIRECTOR: John A. Alonzo
PRODUCER: Rand Holston
SCREENPLAY: Ezra Sacks
CAST: Martin Mull, Eileen Brennan, Michael Brandon, Alex Carras, Cleavon Little
MUSICAL PERFORMERS: Linda Ronstadt, Tom Petty and the Heartbreakers, Reo Speedwagon, Jimmy Buffet
SONGS PERFORMED: *Livingston Saturday Night*, Jimmy Buffet; *Breakdown*, *American Girl*, Tom Petty and the Heartbreakers; *Ridin' the Storm Out*, Reo Speedwagon; *Love Me Tender*,

Poor Poor Pitiful Me, Tumbling Dice, Linda Ronstadt
SOUNDTRACK SONGS: *More Than a Feeling*, Boston; *If It Stops You Runnin'*, the Doobie Bros.; *Life In the Fast Lane*, the Eagles; *Don't Stop*, Fleetwood Mac; *There's a Place In the World For a Gambler*, Dan Fogelburg; *Slow Ride*, Foghat; *Feels Like the First Time*, Foreigner; *Just the Way You Are*, Billy Joel; *The Key to My Kingdom*, B. B. King; *Bad Man*, Randy Meisner; *Fly Like An Eagle*, Steve Miller; *Green Grass and High Times*, the Outlaws; *Baby Come Back*, Player; *We Will Rock You*, Queen; *Night Moves*, Bob Seger; *Hollywood, Lido Shuffle*, Boz Scaggs; *Do It Again, FM*, Steely Dan; *Your Smiling Face*, James Taylor; *Life's Been Good*, Joe Walsh; *Sentimental Lady*, Bob Welch; *Southern Man*, Neil Young
SOUNDTRACK: MCA

THE FAMILY WAY   1966
Warner Brothers, color, 115 minutes

DIRECTOR: Roy Boulting
PRODUCERS: John Boulting, Roy Boulting
CAST: Hayley Mills, Hywel Bennett, John Mills, Marjorie Rhodes
SCORE: Paul McCartney
SOUNDTRACK: Decca – UK; London – US

FAST BREAK   1979
Columbia Pictures, color, 107 minutes

DIRECTOR: Jack Smight
PRODUCER: Stephen Friedman
SONGS: Carol Connors, James Di Pasquale, David Shire
CAST: Gabe Kaplan, Harold Sylvester, Mike Warren, Bernard King
SOUNDTRACK SONGS: *More Than Just a Friend*, Billy Preston; *Go For It, With You I'm Born Again*, Billy Preston, Syreeta; *He Didn't Stay*, Syreeta
SOUNDTRACK: Motown

THE FISH THAT SAVED PITTSBURGH   1979
Color, 104 minutes

DIRECTOR: Gilbert Moses
SCORE: Tom Bell
CAST: Juliul Erving, Meadowlark Lemon, Kareem Abdul-Jabbar, Jonathan Winters, Stockard Channing
SOUNDTRACK SONGS: *Ragtime*, Thom Bell, Eubie Blake; *The Fish That Saved Pittsburgh*, Bell and James; *No One Does It Better*, the Detroit Spinners; *Chance of a Lifetime*, the Four Tops; *Magic Mona*, Phyllis Hyman; *Mighty Mighty Pisces*, the Sylvers
SOUNDTRACK: Lorimar – US

FLASH GORDON   1980
Universal International Pictures, color, 110 minutes

DIRECTOR: Michael Hodges
PRODUCER: Dino Di Laurentiis
SCORE: Queen, Howard Blake
CAST: Sam Jones, Melody Anderson, Max Von Sydow
SOUNDTRACK: Elektra – US; EMI – UK

FOXES   1979
United Artists, color, 108 minutes

DIRECTOR: Adrian Lynes
PRODUCERS: Gerald Ayres, David Puttnam
CAST: Jodie Foster, Sally Kellerman, Scott Baio, Randy Quaid, Adam Faith
SOUNDTRACK SONGS: *Virginia*, Angel; *Rock'n'Roll Dancing, That's What I Like About My Baby*, the Beckmeier Brothers; *More Than a Feeling*, Boston; *Shake It*, Brooklyn Dreams; *Bad Love*, Cher; *Fly Too High*, Janis Ian; *Greedy Man*, Munich Machine; *Ship of Fools*, Bob Seger; *On the Radio*, Donna Summer
SOUNDTRACK: Casablanca – US

FRATERNITY ROW 1977
Color, 101 minutes

DIRECTOR: Thomas J. Tobin
SCORE: Don McLean
CAST: Gregory Harrison, Scott Newman, Peter Fox
SOUNDTRACK SONGS: *If You Can Dream, The Pattern Is Broken*, Don McLean

FRIENDS 1971
Paramount Pictures, color, 102 minutes

DIRECTOR: Lewis Gilbert
PRODUCER: Lewis Gilbert
SCORE: Elton John, Bernie Taupin
CAST: Sean Bury, Anicee Alvina, Tony Robbins
SOUNDTRACK SONGS: *Can I Put You On, Friends, Honey Roll, I Meant To Do My Work Today, Michelle's Song*, Elton John
SOUNDTRACK: Paramount – US; ABC – UK

GETTING STRAIGHT 1970
Columbia Pictures, color, 125 minutes

DIRECTOR: Richard Rush
PRODUCER: Paul Lewis
CAST: Elliot Gould, Candice Bergen, Jeff Corey
SOUNDTRACK SONGS: *I'll Build a Bridge*, New Establishment; *Getting Straight, Moon Rock, Shades of Gray, Talk*, P. K. Limited
SOUNDTRACK: Colgems – US; RCA – UK

THE GODFATHER OF HARLEM see BLACK CAESAR

GOLD 1972
Caroline International, color, 92 minutes

DIRECTORS: Bill Desloge, Bob Levis
PRODUCER: Ronan O'Rahilly
CAST: Gary Goodrow, Sam Ridge
SOUNDTRACK SONGS: *Mud People, Organ Music*, Warner Jepson; *They're Gonna Step On You*, John Kongas; *Go On Back to Mama, Gold, Move Over Gabriel*, David McWilliams; *Money Man*, Barry St. John; *I Is De Daw*, Sailcat
SOUNDTRACK: Mother – UK; ABC – US

THE GRADUATE 1967
Avco-Embassy, color, 105 minutes

DIRECTOR: Mike Nichols
PRODUCER: Lawrence Turman
CAST: Dustin Hoffman, Anne Bancroft, Katherine Ross
SOUNDTRACK SONGS: *April Come She Will, The Bright Green Pleasure Machine, Scarborough Fair, Sound of Silence, Mrs Robinson*, Simon and Garfunkel
SOUNDTRACK: Columbia – US

GREEN ICE 1981
ITC, color, 116 minutes

DIRECTOR: Ernest Day
PRODUCER: Colin M. Brewer
SONGS BY: Bill Wyman
SCORE: Bill Wyman
CAST: Ryan O'Neal, Omar Sharif
SONGS PERFORMED: *Floating (Cloudhopper) Theme, Tenderness*, Maria Muldaur
SOUNDTRACK: Polydor – UK

HAMMER 1973
United Artists, color, 92 minutes

DIRECTOR: Bruce Clark
PRODUCER: Al Adamson
SCORE: Solomon Burke
CAST: Fred Williamson, Vonetta McGee, Bernie Hamilton

HAROLD AND MAUDE   1971
Paramount Pictures, color, 91 minutes

DIRECTOR: Hal Ashby
PRODUCER: Colin Higgins
SCORE: Cat Stevens
CAST: Ruth Gordon, Bud Cort, Vivian Pickles, Ellen Geer

HAVING A WILD WEEKEND   see CATCH US IF YOU CAN

HERE WE GO ROUND THE MULBERRY BUSH   1967
Lopert Pictures, color, 96 minutes

DIRECTOR: Clive Donner
PRODUCER: Larry Kramer
CAST: Barry Evans, Judy Geeson, Adrienne Posta, Angela Scoular
MUSICAL PERFORMERS: The Spencer Davis Group, Andy Ellison, Traffic
SOUNDTRACK SONGS: *Every Little Thing, Just Like Me, Picture of Her, Possession, Taking Out Time, Virgin's Dream, Waltz for Caroline*, the Spencer Davis Group; *It's Been a Long Time*, Andy Ellison; *Am I What I Was or Was I What I Am?, Here We Go Round the Mulberry Bush, Utterly Simple*, Traffic
SOUNDTRACK: United Artists

THE HOLLYWOOD KNIGHTS   1980
Columbia Pictures, color, 91 minutes

DIRECTOR: Floyd Mutrux
PRODUCER: Richard Lederer
CAST: Tony Danza, Fran Drescher, Randy Gormel
SOUNDTRACK SONGS: *Pipeline*, the Chantays; *What'd I Say*, Ray Charles; *One Fine Day*, the Chiffons; *Big Girls Don't Cry*, the Four Seasons; *Heatwave*, Martha and the Vandellas; *The Midnight Hour*, Wilson Pickett; *Wipe Out*, the Surfaris
SOUNDTRACK: Casablanca – US

HOMER   1970
Color, 91 minutes

DIRECTOR: John Trent
SCORE: Don Scardino
CAST: Don Scardino, Tisa Farrow, Alex Nichol
SOUNDTRACK SONGS: *Bluebird, For What It's Worth, Rock'n'Roll Woman*, Buffalo Springfield; *Turn Turn Turn*, the Byrds; *Spoonful*, Cream; *How Many More Times*, Led Zeppelin; *Nashville Cats*, the Lovin' Spoonful; *Man of Music*, Don Scardino; *Brave New World*, the Steve Miller Band
SOUNDTRACK: Warner Brothers

I LOVE YOU ALICE B. TOKLAS   1968
Warner Brothers, color, 93 minutes

DIRECTGR: Hy Averback
PRODUCER: Charles Maguire
MUSIC: Harper's Bizarre, Strawberry Alarm Clock
CAST: Peter Sellers, Jo Van Fleet, Joyce Van Patten
SOUNDTRACK: Warner Brothers – US

I WANNA HOLD YOUR HAND   1978
Universal International Pictures, color, 104 minutes

DIRECTOR: Robert Zemeckis
PRODUCERS: Tamara Asseyev, Alex Rose, Steven Spielberg
MUSIC: the Beatles
CAST: Nancy Allen, Susan Kendell Newman, Bobby Di Cicco, Marc McClure
SOUNDTRACK SONGS: Original recordings by the Beatles

JAMES DEAN – THE FIRST AMERICAN TEENAGER 1975
Visual Programme Systems, color, 80 minutes

DIRECTOR: Ray Connolly
PRODUCERS: David Puttnam, Sandy Lieberson
NARRATION: Stacy Keach
SOUNDTRACK SONGS: *Movin' On*, Bad Company; *Rebel Rebel*, David Bowie; *James Dean*, the Eagles; *Funeral For a Friend*, Elton John; *Walk On the Wild Side*, Lou Reed; *The Immigrant*, Neil Sedaka; *Words*, Neil Young

JONATHAN LIVINGSTON SEAGULL 1973
CIC, animated, color, 120 minutes

DIRECTOR: Hall Bartlett
PRODUCER: Hall Bartlett
SCORE: Neil Diamond
SOUNDTRACK SONGS: *Anthem, Be, Dear Father, Lonely Looking Sky, Skybird*
SOUNDTRACK: Columbia – US; CBS – UK

JOYRIDE 1977
Color, 92 minutes

DIRECTOR: Joseph Roben
MUSICAL DIRECTOR: Jimmy Haskell
CAST: Desi Arnaz Jr, Robert Carradine, Melanie Griffith, Anne Lockhart
SOUNDTRACK SONGS: *Boy Blue, Can't Get It Out of My Head, Rockaria, So Find, Telephone Line, Tightrope*, Electric Light Orchestra; *The Best That I Know How*, Barry Mann
SOUNDTRACK: Jet – US

THE LANDLORD 1970
United Artists, color, 110 minutes

DIRECTOR: Hal Ashby
PRODUCER: Norman Jewison
CAST: Beau Bridges, Diana Sands, Lou Gossett, Lee Grant, Pearl Bailey
SOUNDTRACK SONGS: *Doin' Me Dirty, Let Me Love You*, Lorraine Elliman; *Brand New Day, God Bless the Children*, the Staple Singers
SOUNDTRACK: United Artists

LAST SUMMER 1969
Twentieth Century Fox, color, 97 minutes

DIRECTOR: Frank Perry
PRODUCERS: Sidney Beckerman, Alfred Crown
SCORE: John Simon
CAST: Richard Thomas, Barbara Hershey, Bruce Davison, Cathy Burns
SOUNDTRACK SONGS: *Temptation Lust and Laziness*, Aunt Mary's Transcendental Slip and Lurch Band; *Firehouse Blues*, Bad Karma Dan; *Cordelia, Sonuvagun*, Buddy Bruno; *Safari Mary*, Henry Diltz; *Magnetic Mama*, Electric Meatball; *Drivin' Daisy*, Cyrus Farryar
SOUNDTRACK: Warner Brothers – US

McVICAR 1980
Crown International Pictures, color, 112 minutes

DIRECTOR: Tom Clegg
PRODUCERS: Roy Baird, Bill Curbishley, Roger Daltrey
MUSICAL DIRECTOR: Jeff Wayne
CAST: Roger Daltrey, Adam Faith, Cheryl Campbell
SOUNDTRACK SONGS: *Free Me, I'm Not Going Home, Just a Dream Away, McVicar, Waiting For a Friend, White City Lights, Without Your Love*, Roger Daltrey
SOUNDTRACK: Polydor

THE MAGIC CHRISTIAN 1970
Commonwealth-United Films, color, 93 minutes

DIRECTOR: Joseph McGrath
PRODUCER: Denis O'Dell
SCORE: Badfinger (Peter Ham, Ron Ivey, Micky Gibbons, Tommy Evans)

CAST: Peter Sellers, Ringo Starr, Spike Milligan, Raquel Welch, Christopher Lee
SOUNDTRACK SONGS: *Carry On to Tomorrow, Come and Get It, Rock of Ages,* Badfinger; *Mad About the Boy,* Yul Brynner; *Something In the Air,* Thunderclap Newman
SOUNDTRACK: Pye – UK; Commonwealth-United – US

MAHONEY'S LAST STAND 1975
Color, 108 minutes

DIRECTOR: Harvey Hart
SCORE: Ronnie Lane, Ron Wood
CAST: Alexis Kanner, Sam Waterson, Maude Adams
MUSIC PRODUCED BY: Glyn Johns
SPECIAL EFFECTS: Pete Townshend
SOUNDTRACK: Atlantic

MEAN STREETS 1973
Warner Brothers, color, 110 minutes

DIRECTOR: Martin Scorcese
PRODUCER: Jonathan Taplin
CAST: Robert DeNiro, Harvey Keitel
SOUNDTRACK SONGS: *Pledging My Love,* Johnny Ace; *You,* the Aquatones; *Desiree,* the Chants; *I Love You So,* the Chantells; *Rubber Biscuit,* the Chips; *Hideaway, I Look Away,* Eric Clapton; *Those Oldies But Goodies,* Little Caesar and the Romans; *Please Mr Postman,* the Marvellettes; *Ship of Love,* the Nutmegs; *Jumpin' Jack Flash, Tell Me,* the Rolling Stones; *Be My Baby,* the Ronettes; *Mickey's Monkey,* Smokey Robinson and the Miracles

MEDIUM COOL 1970
Paramount Pictures, color, 111 minutes

DIRECTOR: Haskell Wexler
PRODUCERS: Tully Friedman, Haskell Wexler
SCORE: Mike Bloomfield

CAST: Robert Forster, Peter Bonerz, Verna Bloom, Marianna Hill
SOUNDTRACK SONGS: *Merry Go Round,* the Mothers of Invention

MELODY 1971
British Lion, color, 106 minutes

DIRECTOR: Waris Hussein
PRODUCER: David Puttnam
SCREENPLAY: Alan Parker
MUSIC: The Bee Gees
SCORE: Richard Hewson
CAST: Jack Wild, Mark Lester
SOUNDTRACK SONGS: *The First of May, Give Your Best, In the Morning, Melody Fair, To Love Somebody, Working On It Night and Day,* the Bee Gees; *Spicks and Specks,* Barry Gibb; *Teach Your Children,* Crosby, Stills, Nash and Young
SOUNDTRACK: Polydor – UK; Atco – US

MOMENT BY MOMENT 1978
Universal Pictures, color, 94 minutes

DIRECTOR: Jane Wagner
PRODUCER: Robert Stigwood
CAST: John Travolta, Lily Tomlin, Andra Akers, Debra Feuer
SOUNDTRACK SONGS: *Moment by Moment,* Yvonne Elliman; *Shimme Do Wah Say,* Andy Fairweather Low; *The Lady Wants to Know,* Michael Franks; *Sometimes When We Touch,* Dan Hill; *You Know I Love You, Your Heart Never Lies,* Charles Lloyd; *Hollywood Boulevard,* Ray Parker Jr.; *Strangered In the Night,* Tom Petty and the Heartbreakers; *For You and I,* 10 CC
SOUNDTRACK: RSO

MONDO DAYTONA A.K.A. WEEKEND REBELLION 1968
Documentary, color, 80 minutes

DIRECTOR: Frank Willard
SOUNDTRACK SONGS: *Down In the Boondocks, Hush,*

These Are Not My People, Billy Joe Royal; *Breakthrough, Spooky*, Mike Sharp; *Double Shot of My Baby's Love, She Drives Me Out of My Mind*, the Swinging Medallions; *Laugh It Off, What Kind of Fool*, the Tams

MORE AMERICAN GRAFFITI 1979
Universal International Pictures, color, 111 minutes

DIRECTOR: W. B. L. Norton
PRODUCER: George Lucas
CAST: Ron Howard, Cindy Williams, Mackenzie Phillips, Paul Le Mat
SOUNDTRACK SONGS: *My Boyfriend's Back*, the Angels; *Turn Turn Turn*, the Byrds; *Cool Jerk*, the Capitols; *Pipeline*, the Chantays; *Feel Like I'm Fixin' to Die Rag*, Country Joe and the Fish; *Strange Brew, Season of the Witch*, Donovan; *Light My Fire*, the Doors; *Just Like a Woman, Like a Rolling Stone*, Bob Dylan; *Respect*, Aretha Franklin; *Your Precious Love*, Marvin Gaye and Tammi Terrell; *Cream Puff War*, the Grateful Dead; *Dead Man's Curve*, Jan and Dean; *Heat Wave*, Martha and the Vandellas; *Beechwood 4-5789*, the Marvellettes; *Hang On Sloopy*, the McCoys; *96 Tears*, ? and the Mysterians; *Our Day Will Come*, Ruby and the Romantics; *Ballad of the Green Berets*, Barry Sadler; *I'm a Man, The Race Is On*, Doug Sahm; *Wooly Bully*, Sam the Sham and the Pharaohs; *Sounds of Silence*, Simon and Garfunkel; *When a Man Loves a Woman*, Percy Sledge; *You Really Got a Hold On Me*, Smokey Robinson and the Miracles; *Tighten Up Your Wig*, Steppenwolf; *Incense and Peppermints*, Strawberry Alarm Clock; *Reflection, Stop In the Name of Love, Where Did Our Love Go?*, the Supremes; *What Kind of Fool Do You Think I Am?*, the Tams; *Mr Lonely*, Bobby Vinton; *You Were On My Mind*, the We Five; *Since I Fell For You*, Lenny Welch; *My Guy*, Mary Wells; *Fingertips*, Little Stevie Wonder; *Good Lovin*, the Young Rascals; *Lumpy Gravy*, Frank Zappa; *She's Not There*, the Zombies
SOUNDTRACK: MCA

MOTHER, JUGS AND SPEED 1975
Twentieth Century Fox, color, 95 minutes

DIRECTOR: Peter Yates
PRODUCERS: Peter Yates, Tom Mankiewicz
CAST: Bill Cosby, Raquel Welch, Larry Hagman, Harvey Keitel, Allen Garfield, Bruce Davison
SOUNDTRACK SONGS: *Get The Funk Out Ma Face, Thunder Thumbs and Lightning Licks*, the Brothers Johnson; *Mellow Out*, the Crusaders; *Show Me the Way*, Peter Frampton; *Dance*, Paul Jabara; *Star In My Life*, Steve Marriott; *No Love Today*, Michelle Phillips; *My Soul Is a Witness*, Billy Preston
SOUNDTRACK: A&M

NOTHING BUT A MAN 1963
Color, 95 minutes

DIRECTOR: Michael Roemer
CAST: Ivan Dixon, Abbey Lincoln, Gloria Foster
SOUNDTRACK SONGS: *Heatwave, This Is When I Need You Most*, Martha and the Vandellas; *I'll Try Something New, Mickey's Monkey, Way Over There, You've Really Got a Hold On Me*, Smokey Robinson and the Miracles; *Bye Bye Baby*, Mary Wells; *Fingertips*, Little Stevie Wonder

O LUCKY MAN 1973
Warner Brothers, color, 174 minutes

DIRECTOR: Lindsay Anderson
PRODUCERS: Lindsay Anderson, Michael Medwin
SCORE: Alan Price
CAST: Malcolm McDowell, Arthur Lowe, Ralph Richardson, Rachel Roberts
SOUNDTRACK SONGS: *Changes, Justice, Look Over Your Shoulder, My Home Town, O Lucky Man, Poor People, Sell Sell*, Alan Price
SOUNDTRACK: Warner Brothers

OUTLAW RIDERS 1971
Color

DIRECTOR: Tony Houston
SCORE: Simon Stokes and the Nighthawks
CAST: Bryan West, Bambi Allen, Darlene Duralia
SOUNDTRACK SONGS: *Big City Blues, Where Are You Going?, Which Way?, You've Been In*

OVER THE EDGE 1979
Warner Brothers, color, 95 minutes

DIRECTOR: Jonathan Kaplan
PRODUCER: George Litto
CAST: Matt Dillon, Michael Kramer, Vincent Spano
SOUNDTRACK SONGS: *Just What I Needed, My Best Friend's Girl*, the Cars; *Ooh Child*, Valerie Carter; *Downed, Hello There, Speak Now Or Forever Hold Your Peace*, Cheap Trick; *Come On*, Jimi Hendrix; *All That You Dream*, Little Feat; *Teenage Lobotomy*, the Ramones; *You Really Got Me*, Van Halen
SOUNDTRACK: Warner Brothers – US

PACIFIC VIBRATIONS 1970
Documentary, color, 92 minutes

DIRECTOR: John Severson
SOUNDTRACK: Beaver and Krauss, Ry Cooder, Colorado Purple Gang, Cream, Crosby, Stills, Nash and Young, the Steve Miller Band, Sky Oats, Wolfgang

A PIECE OF THE ACTION 1977
Verdon Productions/First Artists for Warner Bros, color, 135 minutes

DIRECTOR: Sidney Poitier
PRODUCER: Melville Tucker
SCORE: Gil Askey, Curtis Mayfield
CAST: Bill Cosby, Sidney Poitier, James Earl Jones, Denise Nicholas
SOUNDTRACK SONGS: *Chocolate City, Good Lovin' Daddy, Koochie Koochie Koochie, Of Whom Should I Be Afraid?, Orientation, A Piece of the Action, Till Blossoms Bloom*, Mavis Staples
SOUNDTRACK: Curtom – US

THE POINT 1970
Animated, color, 75 minutes

DIRECTOR: Fred Wolf
NARRATION: Alan Barzman
SCORE: Harry Nilsson
SOUNDTRACK SONGS: *Are You Sleeping?, Everybody's Got 'Em, Life Line, Me and My Arrow, P.O.V. Waltz, Poli High, Think About Your Troubles*
SOUNDTRACK: RCA

POOR COW 1967
National-General Films, color, 101 minutes

DIRECTOR: Ken Loach
PRODUCER: Joseph Janni
SCORE: Donovan
CAST: Carol White, Terence Stamp, Kate Williams, Malcolm McDowell
SOUNDTRACK SONGS: *Colours, Be Not Too Hard, Poor Love*

POPEYE 1981
Paramount Pictures, color, 118 minutes

DIRECTOR: Robert Altman
PRODUCER: Robert Evans
SCORE: Harry Nilsson
CAST: Robin Williams, Shelley Duvall, Wesley Ivan Hurt, Ray Walston
SOUNDTRACK: Boardwalk – US; Epic – UK

QUADROPHENIA 1979
World-Northall Films, color, 120 minutes

DIRECTOR: Franc Roddam

QUADROPHENIA

PRODUCERS: Roy Baird, Bill Curbishley
SCORE: the Who (Roger Daltrey, John Entwhistle, Keith Moon, Pete Townshend)
CAST: Phil Daniels, Lesley Ash, Mark Wingett, Sting, Philip Davis, Raymond Winstone, Toyah Wilcox
SOUNDTRACK SONGS: *Bell Boy, Doctor Jimmy, 5.15, Four Faces, Get Out and Stay Out, Helpless Dancer, I Am the Sea, I'm One, I've Had Enough, Joker James, Love Reign O'er Me, The Punk and the Godfather, The Real Me, Zoot Suit,* the Who; *Green Onions,* Booker T and the MG's; *Night Train,* James Brown; *Rhythm of the Rain,* the Cascades; *He's So Fine,* the Chiffons; *Da Doo Ron Ron,* the Crystals; *Baby Don't You Do It,* Marvin Gaye; *5-4-3-2-1,* Manfred Mann; *Wishin' and Hopin',* the Merseybeats; *Wah Watusi,* the Orlons; *Blazing Fire,* Patrick Morgan; *Be My Baby,* the Ronettes; *Baby Love,* the Supremes
SOUNDTRACK: Polydor

R.P.M. 1970
Color, 92 minutes

DIRECTOR: Stanley J. Kramer
SCORE: Melanie
CAST: Anthony Quinn, Ann-Margret, Gary Lockwood, Paul Winfield
SOUNDTRACK: Bell – US; Polydor – UK

RADIO ON 1979
British Film Institute, black & white, 101 minutes

DIRECTOR: Chris Petit
PRODUCER: Keith Griffiths
SOUNDTRACK SONGS: *Always Crashing the Same Car, Heroes,* David Bowie; *Satisfaction,* Devo; *Sweet Gene Vincent,* Ian Dury; *Urban Landscape,* Robert Fripp; *Ohm Sweet Ohm, Radioactivity, Trans-Europe Express,* Kraftwerk; *Lucky Number,* Lene Lovich; *Frozen Years,* Rumour; *Three Steps to Heaven,* Sting; *Veronica,* Wreckless Eric

RIOT ON SUNSET STRIP 1967
American International Pictures, color, 85 minutes

DIRECTOR: Arthur Dreifuss
PRODUCER: Sam Katzman
MUSIC: Mike Curb
CAST: Aldo Ray, Mimsey Farmer, Michael Evans
SOUNDTRACK SONGS: *Don't Need Your Loving, Sitting There Standing,* Chocolate Watch Band; *Get Away From Here, Riot On Sunset Strip,* the Standells
SOUNDTRACK: Tower – US

THE RIVER NIGER 1976
Color, 105 minutes

DIRECTOR: Krishna Shah

SCORE: War
CAST: Cicely Tyson, James Earl Jones, Lou Gossett, Glynn Turman

ROOMMATES 1971
Color, 97 minutes

DIRECTOR: Jack Barra
SCORE: Earth Opera
CAST: Dan Mason, Allen Garfield, Harvey Marks

RUMBLEFISH 1984
Universal International Pictures, black & white, 102 minutes

DIRECTOR: Francis Ford Coppola
PRODUCER: Francis Ford Coppola
SCORE: Stewart Copeland
MUSIC PERFORMED BY: Stewart Copeland
CAST: Matt Dillon, Mickey Roarke, Dennis Hopper, Vincent Spano, Diane Scarwid

RUN HOME SLOW 1965
75 minutes

DIRECTOR: Tim Sullivan
SCORE: Frank Zappa
CAST: Mercedes McCambridge, Linda Gaye Scott, Allen Richards

SATAN'S SADISTS 1971
Color, 86 minutes

DIRECTOR: Al Adamson
SCORE: Harley Hatcher
CAST: Russ Tamblyn, Scott Brady, Kent Taylor
SOUNDTRACK SONGS: *Baby How I Fell For You, Gotta Stop That Feeling, I Like the Way You Work, I'm On My Way Out, Is It Better to Have Loved and Lost?, Satan*, the Nightriders
SOUNDTRACK: Smash – US

SATURDAY NIGHT FEVER 1977
Paramount Pictures, color, 118 minutes

DIRECTOR: John Badham
PRODUCER: Robert Stigwood
MUSICAL DIRECTOR: David Shire
CAST: John Travolta, Karen Lynn Gorney, Barry Miller, Paul Pape
SOUNDTRACK SONGS: *How Deep Is Your Love, More Than a Woman, Night Fever, Staying Alive, You Should Be Dancing*, the Bee Gees; *Disco Duck*, Rick Dees; *If I Can't Have You*, Yvonne Elliman; *Boogie Shoes*, K.C. and the Sunshine Band; *Open Sesame*, Kool and the Gang; *K-Jee*, MFSB; *A Fifth of Beethoven*, Walter Murphy; *More Than a Woman*, Tavares; *Disco Inferno*, the Trammps
SOUNDTRACK: RSO

THE SAVAGE SEVEN 1969
American International Pictures, color, 96 minutes

DIRECTOR: Michael Fisher
PRODUCER: Dick Clark
SCORE: Mike Curb
CAST: Robert Walker Jr., Larry Bishop, Adam Roarke
SOUNDTRACK SONGS: *Ballad of the Savage Seven*, American Revolution; *Anyone for Tennis*, Cream
SOUNDTRACK: Atco – US

THE SECRET LIFE OF PLANTS 1978
Paramount Pictures, documentary, color, 89 minutes

DIRECTOR: Wolon Green
PRODUCER: Michael Braun
SCORE: Stevie Wonder
SOUNDTRACK: Tamla – US

SHAFT 1971
Metro Goldwyn Mayer, color, 100 minutes

DIRECTOR: Gordon Parks

PRODUCER: Joel Freeman
SCORE: Isaac Hayes
CAST: Richard Roundtree, Moses Gunn, Lawrence Pressman
SOUNDTRACK: Enterprise – US; Stax – UK

SHAFT IN AFRICA 1973
Metro Goldwyn Mayer, color, 112 minutes

DIRECTOR: John Guillerman
PRODUCER: Roger Lewis
SCORE: Johnny Pate
CAST: Richard Roundtree, Vonetta McGee, Frank Finlay
SOUNDTRACK: ABC – US; Probe – UK

SHAFT'S BIG SCORE! 1972
Metro Goldwyn Mayer, color, 112 minutes

DIRECTOR: Gordon Parks
PRODUCERS: Roger Lewis, Ernest Tidyman
SCORE: Gordon Parks
CAST: Richard Roundtree, Moses Gunn, Drew Bundini Brown
SOUNDTRACK SONGS: *Type Thang*, Isaac Hayes; *Blowin' Your Mind*, *Don't Misunderstand*, O. C. Smith
SOUNDTRACK: MGM

SHINING STAR A.K.A. THAT'S THE WAY OF THE WORLD 1975
Marvin Films, color, 99 minutes

DIRECTOR: Sig Shore
PRODUCER: Sig Shore
SCORE: Earth, Wind and Fire
SOUNDTRACK SONGS: *Shining Star*, *That's the Way of the World*

SHORT EYES 1977
Success, color, 99 minutes

DIRECTOR: Robert M. Young

PRODUCER: Lewis Harris
SCORE: Curtis Mayfield
SONG: *Break It Down*, Freddie Fender
CAST: Bruce Davison, Jose Perez, Nathan George
SOUNDTRACK: Curtom

SILVER DREAM RACER 1980
Rank, color, 111 minutes

DIRECTOR: David Wickes
PRODUCER: René Dupont
SCORE: David Essex, John Cameron
CAST: David Essex, Beau Bridges, Cristina Raines
SOUNDTRACK SONGS: *Looking For Someone*, *Silver Dream Racer*, David Essex; *I Think I'll Always Love You*, Victy Silva
SOUNDTRACK: Mercury

SKATETOWN 1979
Color, 98 minutes

DIRECTOR: William A. Levey
CAST: Scott Baio, Ron Palillo, Flip Wilson, Dave Mason
SOUNDTRACK SONGS: *Boogie Wonderland*, Earth, Wind and Fire with the Emotions; *Boogie Nights*, Heatwave; *Born to Be Alive*, Patrick Hernandez; *Under My Thumb*, Hounds; *Shake Your Body*, the Jacksons; *Feelin' Alright*, *I Fell In Love*, *Skatetown USA*, Dave Mason; *Perfect Dancer*, Marilyn McCoo and Billy Davis; *Roller Girl*, John Sebastian
SOUNDTRACK: Columbia – US

SKIDOO 1968
Paramount Pictures, color, 98 minutes

DIRECTOR: Otto Preminger
PRODUCER: Otto Preminger
SCREENPLAY: Doran William Cannon
MUSIC AND LYRICS BY: Harry Nilsson
CAST: Jackie Gleason, Carol Channing,

Groucho Marx, John Phillip Law, Frankie Avalon, Burgess Meredith, Fred Clark, Michael Constantine
SOUNDTRACK: RCA

SLAP SHOT   1977
Universal International Pictures, color, 122 minutes

DIRECTOR: George Roy Hill
PRODUCERS: Stephen Friedman, Robert J. Wunsch
CAST: Paul Newman, Michael Ontkean, Lindsay Crouse, Strother Martin
SOUNDTRACK SONGS: *Rhiannon, Say That You Love Me*, Fleetwood Mac; *Sorry Seems to Be the Hardest Word*, Elton John; *Right Back Where We Started From*, Maxine Nightingale; *You Make Me Feel Like Dancin'*, Leo Sayer

SLAUGHTER'S BIG RIP-OFF   1973
American International Pictures, color, 93 minutes

DIRECTOR: Gordon Douglas
PRODUCER: Monroe Sachson
SCORE: James Brown, Fred Wesley
CAST: Jim Brown, Brock Peters, Don Stroud
SOUNDTRACK SONGS: *People Get Up and Drive Your Funky Soul, Sexy Sexy Sexy*, James Brown and the JB's; *How Long Can I Keep It Up?*, Lyn Collins
SOUNDTRACK: Polydor

SLUMBER PARTY '57   1976
Cannon-Happy, color, 89 minutes

DIRECTOR: William A. Levey
PRODUCER: John A. Ireland Jr.
CAST: Deborah Winger, Bridget Hollman
SOUNDTRACK SONGS: *Chantilly Lace*, the Big Bopper; *Hey Baby*, Bruce Channel; *Sh-Boom*, the Crew Cuts; *One Summer Night*, the Danieers; *Breakin' Up Is Hard to Do*, Jivin' Gene; *Great Balls of Fire*, Jerry Lee Lewis; *Hey Paula*, Paul and Paula; *Sea of Love*, Phil Phillips; *The Great Pretender*, the Platters; *Running Bear*, Johnny Preston; *What a Difference a Day Makes*, Dinah Washington
SOUNDTRACK: Polydor

SMASHING TIME   1967
Paramount Pictures, color, 96 minutes

DIRECTOR: Desmond Davis
PRODUCERS: Carlo Ponti, Roy Millichap
SONGS: Skip Bifferty, John Addison, George Melly
MUSIC: Victor Smith
MUSICAL DIRECTOR: John Addison
CAST: Rita Tushingham, Lynn Redgrave, Michael York
SOUNDTRACK SONGS: *Baby Don't Go, Carnaby Street, Day Out, It's Always Your Fault, New Clothes, Smashing Time, Trouble, Waiting For My Friend, While I'm Still Young*, Keith West and Tomorrow
SOUNDTRACK: Stateside – UK; ABC – US

SORCERER A.K.A. WAGES OF FEAR   1977
CIC, color, 122 minutes

DIRECTOR: William Friedkin
PRODUCER: William Friedkin
SCORE: Tangerine Dream
CAST: Roy Scheider, Bruno Cremer, Francisco Rabal
SOUNDTRACK: MCA

SOUNDER   1972
Fox-Rank, color, 105 minutes

DIRECTOR: Martin Ritt
PRODUCER: Robert B. Radnitz
SCORE: Taj Mahal
CAST: Paul Winfield, Cicely Tyson, Kevin Hooks

SOUNDTRACK SONGS: *Needed Time*, Lightnin' Hopkins
SOUNDTRACK: Columbia – US; CBS – UK

STEELYARD BLUES   1973
Columbia-Warner, color, 92 minutes

DIRECTOR: Alan Meyerson
PRODUCER: Donald Sutherland
SCORE: Mike Bloomfield, Nick Gravenites
CAST: Donald Sutherland, Jane Fonda, Peter Boyle, John Savage
SOUNDTRACK SONGS: *Being Different Has Never Been a Crime, Brand New Family, Common Ground, Here I Come There She Goes, Make The Headlines, Poachin', Swing With It, They're Letting Me Drive Again, Woman's Love*, Paul Butterfield, Mike Bloomfield, Nick Gravenites, John Kahn, Maria Muldaur, Chris Parker, Merle Saunders, Annie Sampson
SOUNDTRACK: Warner Brothers

THE STRAWBERRY STATEMENT   1970
Metro Goldwyn Mayer, color, 103 minutes

DIRECTOR: Stuart Hagmann
PRODUCER: Irwin Winkler
CAST: Bruce Davison, Kim Darby, James Coco
SOUNDTRACK SONGS: *Long Time Gone*, Crosby, Stills and Nash; *Helpness, Our House*, Crosby, Stills, Nash and Young; *Fishin' Blues*, the Red Mountain Jug Band; *The Circle Game*, Buffy Sainte-Marie; *Something In the Air*, Thunderclap Newman; *Down By the River, The Loner*, Neil Young
SOUNDTRACK: Reprise

SUNNYSIDE   1979
Color, 100 minutes

DIRECTOR: Timothy Galfas
CAST: Joey Travolta, John Lansing, Andrew Rubin
SOUNDTRACK SONGS: *Bo Diddley, Got to Have Your Body, Loving You, New York City Band, Ride That Wave, Sunnyside*, the New York City Band
SOUNDTRACK: Casablanca – US

SUPERFLY   1972
Warner Brothers, color, 96 minutes

DIRECTOR: Gordon Parks
PRODUCER: Sig Shore
SCORE: Curtis Mayfield
CAST: Ron O'Neal, Carl Lee, Sheila Frazier, Julius W. Harris
SOUNDTRACK SONGS: *Freddie's Dead, Superfly*
SOUNDTRACK: Curtom

SUPERFLY T.N.T.   1973
Color, 87 minutes

DIRECTOR: Ron O'Neal
SCORE: Osibisa
CAST: Ron O'Neal, Roscoe Lee Browne, Sheila Frazier
SOUNDTRACK SONGS: *Brotherhood, Come Closer (If You're a Man), Kelele, La Ila I La La, Oye Mama, Prophets, Superfly Man, T.N.T., The Vicarage*
SOUNDTRACK: Buddah

TAKE ME HIGH   1973
Metro Goldwyn Mayer, color, 90 minutes

DIRECTOR: David Askey
PRODUCER: Kenneth Harper
CAST: Cliff Richard, George Cole, Hugh Griffith, Debbie Watling
SOUNDTRACK SONGS: *The Anti-Brotherhood of Man, The Brumberger Duet, Driving, The Game, It's Only Money, Join the Band, Life, Midnight Blue, Take Me High, Why, Winning, The Word Is Love*
SOUNDTRACK: EMI – UK

THAT SUMMER 1979
Columbia-Warner-EMI, color, 93 minutes

DIRECTOR: Harley Cokliss
PRODUCERS: Davina Belling, Clive Parsons
CAST: Ray Winstone, Tony London, Julie Shipley
SOUNDTRACK SONGS: *Kicks, She's So Modern*, the Boomtown Rats; *I Don't Want to Go to Chelsea*, Elvis Costello; *Sex and Drugs and Rock and Roll, What a Waste*, Ian Dury; *Do Anything You Wanna Do*, Eddie and the Hot Rods; *Blank Generation*, Richard Hell and the Voidoids; *Breaking Glass*, Nick Lowe; *Spanish Stroll*, Mink DeVille; *Another Girl Another Planet*, the Only Ones; *Rockaway Beach*, the Ramones; *Because the Night*, Patti Smith; *Whole Wide World*, Wreckless Eric; *New Life*, the Zones
SOUNDTRACK: Arista

THAT'S THE WAY OF THE WORLD
see **SHINING STAR**

TOGETHER BROTHERS 1974
Color, 94 minutes

DIRECTOR: William A. Graham
SCORE: Gene Page, Barry White
CAST: Ahmad Nurradin, Anthony Wilson, Kenneth Bell, Nelson Sims
SOUNDTRACK SONGS: *People of Tomorrow Are the Children of Today*, Love Unlimited; *Honey Can't Ya See, Somebody Gonna Off the Man*, Barry White
SOUNDTRACK: Twentieth Century Fox

THE TOUCHABLES 1968
Twentieth Century Fox, color, 94 minutes

DIRECTOR: Robert Freeman
PRODUCER: John Bryan
CAST: Esther Anderson, Judy Huxtable, Kathy Simonds, Marilyn Richard
SOUNDTRACK SONGS: *Respect*, Ferris Wheel; *All of Us*, Nirvana; *Good Day Sunshine*, Roy Redman; *Blues For a Frog, Dancing Frog*, Mick Weaver (Wynder K. Frogg)
SOUNDTRACK: Stateside – UK; Twentieth Century Fox – US

TRAIN RIDE TO HOLLYWOOD 1975
Color

DIRECTOR: Charles Rondeau
CAST: Guy Marks, Jay Robinson, Roberta Collins
SOUNDTRACK SONGS: *As Time Goes By, Go To Sleep, Hooray For Romance, I'm In Shape, Money, Toot Toot Tootsie Goodbye, Rock'n'Roll Choo Choo, Sh-Boom, Train Ride, What Do I Have To Do?, Yakety Yak*
SOUNDTRACK: London – US

THE TRIP 1967
American International Pictures, color, 85 minutes

DIRECTOR: Roger Corman
PRODUCER: Roger Corman
SCORE: Electric Flag (Mike Bloomfield, Barry Goldberg, Nick Gravenites, Buddy Miles)
CAST: Bruce Dern, Peter Fonda, Susan Strasberg, Dennis Hopper
SOUNDTRACK: Sidewalk – US

TROUBLE MAN 1972
Twentieth Century Fox, color, 99 minutes

DIRECTOR: Ivan Dixon
PRODUCER: Joel D. Freeman
SCORE: Marvin Gaye
CAST: Robert Hooks, Paul Winfield, Ralph Waite, Paula Kelly, Julius W. Harris
SOUNDTRACK: Tamla – US; Motown – UK

TRUCK TURNER 1974
American International Pictures, color, 91 minutes

DIRECTOR: Jonathan Kaplan
PRODUCERS: Paul Heller, Fred Weintraub
SCORE: Isaac Hayes
CAST: Isaac Hayes, Yaphet Kotto, Nichelle Nichols
SOUNDTRACK: Enterprise – US; Stax – UK

UNION CITY 1980
Kinesis Ltd, color, 87 minutes

DIRECTOR: Mark Reichert
PRODUCER: Graham Belin
SCORE: Chris Stein
CAST: Deborah Harry, Dennis Lipscomb, Irina Maleeva

UP IN SMOKE 1978
Paramount Pictures, color, 86 minutes

DIRECTOR: Lou Adler
PRODUCERS: Lou Adler, Lou Lombardo
SCORE: Danny Kortchmar, Waddy Wachtel
CAST: Cheech Marin, Tommy Chong, Strother Martin, Stacy Keach
SOUNDTRACK: Warner Brothers – US

UP THE ACADEMY 1980
Color, 96 minutes

DIRECTOR: Robert Downey
CAST: Ron Liebman, Wendell Brown, J. Hutchinson
SOUNDTRACK SONGS: *Midnight Rendezvous*, the Babys; *We Live For Love*, Pat Benatar; *X Offender*, Blondie; *Beat the Devil, Kicking Up a Fuss*, Blow Up; *Coquette*, Cheeks; *Bad Reputation*, Sammy Hagar; *We Gotta Get Out of Here*, Ian Hunter; *Roadrunner*, Jonathan Richman and the Modern Lovers
SOUNDTRACK: Capitol

UP THE JUNCTION 1967
Paramount Pictures, color, 119 minutes

DIRECTOR: Peter Collinson
PRODUCERS: John Barbourne, Anthony Havelock-Allen
SCORE: Manfred Mann
CAST: Suzy Kendall, Dennis Waterman, Maureen Lipman, Liz Fraser
SOUNDTRACK: Fontana – UK; Mercury – US

UP TIGHT 1968
Paramount Pictures, color, 104 minutes

DIRECTOR: Jules Dassin
PRODUCER: Jules Dassin
CAST: Raymond St Jacques, Ruby Dee, Roscoe Lee Browne
SCORE: Booker T Jones and the MG's
SOUNDTRACK: Stax

VANISHING POINT 1971
Twentieth Century Fox, color, 107 minutes

DIRECTOR: Richard C. Sarafian
PRODUCER: Norman Spencer
SCORE: Jimmy Bowen
CAST: Barry Newman, Cleavon Little, Dean Jagger, Severn Darden
SOUNDTRACK SONGS: *Nobody Knows*, Kim Carnes; *You Got to Believe*, Delaney, Bonnie and Friends; *Runaway Country*, the Doug Dillard Expedition; *Get It Together*, Jimmy Doyle; *So Tired*, Eve; *Freedom of Expression, Super Soul Theme*, the JB Pickers; *I Can't Believe*, Longbranch Pennywhistle; *Mississippi Queen*, Mountain; *Welcome to Nevada*, Jerry Reed; *Dear Jesus God, Over Me*, Segarini and Bishop; *Sweet Jesus*, Red Steagall; *Sing Out For Jesus*, Big Mama Thornton; *Where Do We Go From Here*, Jimmy Walker
SOUNDTRACK: Amos – US; London – UK

VILLAGE OF THE GIANTS 1965
Embassy Pictures, color, 80 minutes

DIRECTOR: Bert I. Gordon
PRODUCER: Bert I. Gordon
SCORE: Jack Nitzsche
CAST: Tommy Kirk, Ronny Howard, Johnny Crawford, Beau Bridges
SOUNDTRACK SONGS: *When It Comes to Your Love, Woman*, the Beau Brummels; *Little Bitty Corrine*, Freddy Cannon; *Nothing Can Stand In My Way*, Mike Clifford

WAGES OF FEAR see SORCERER

THE WANDERERS 1979
Warner Brothers, color, 117 minutes

DIRECTOR: Philip Kaufman
PRODUCER: Martin Ransohoff
CAST: Karen Allen, Ken Wahl, John Friedrich, Toni Kalem
SOUNDTRACK SONGS: *My Boyfriend's Back*, the Angels; *Tequila*, the Champs; *Pipeline, Do You Love Me?*, the Contours; *The Times They Are A-Changin'*, Bob Dylan; *Ya Ya*, Lee Dorsey; *Big Girls Don't Cry, Sherry, Walk Like a Man*, the Four Seasons; *Shout*, the Isley Brothers; *Stand By Me*, Ben E. King; *Soldier Boy*, the Shirelles; *You Really Got a Hold On Me*, Smokey Robinson and the Miracles; *Wipe Out*, the Surfaris; *Stranger Girl*, Ken Wahl; *I Love You*, the Volumes
SOUNDTRACK: Warner Brothers – US; GTO – UK

THE WARRIORS 1978
Paramount Pictures, color, 94 minutes

DIRECTOR: Walter Hill
PRODUCER: Lawrence Gordon
MUSICAL DIRECTOR: Barry De Vorzon
CAST: Michael Beck, James Remar, Thomas Waites
SOUNDTRACK SONGS: *Last of an Ancient Breed*, Desmond Child and Rouge; *In Havana*, Frederick La Plano; *Nowhere to Run*, Arnold McCuller; *Echoes In My Mind*, Mandrill; *Night Run*, the Mersh Brothers; *Love Is a Fire*, Genya Raven; *You're Movin' Too Slow*, Johnny Vastano; *In the City*, Joe Walsh
SOUNDTRACK: A&M

WEEKEND REBELLION see MONDO DAYTONA

WELCOME TO L.A. 1976
United Artists, color, 106 minutes

DIRECTOR: Alan Rudolph
PRODUCER: Robert Altman
SCORE: Richard Baskin
CAST: Keith Carradine, Sally Kellerman, Harvey Keitel, Viveca Lindfors
SOUNDTRACK SONGS: *After the End, When the Arrow Flies*, Richard Baskin; *The Best Temptation of All*, Richard Baskin and Keith Carradine
SOUNDTRACK: Arista

WHAT'S UP' TIGER LILY? 1966
American International Pictures, color, 80 minutes

DIRECTORS: Woody Allen, Senkichi Tanaguchi
PRODUCER: Henry G. Saperstein
SCORE: the Lovin' Spoonful
CAST: Tatsuta Mihasi, Miyi Hana
SOUNDTRACK SONGS: *A Cool Million, Fishin' Blues, Gray Prison Blues, Lookin' to Spy, Phil's Love Theme, Pow, Respoken, Speakin' of Spoken, Unconscious Minuet*
SOUNDTRACK: Kama Sutra – US

WHERE THE BUFFALO ROAM 1980
Universal International Pictures, color, 96 minutes

DIRECTOR: Art Linson
PRODUCER: Art Linson
MUSICAL DIRECTOR: Neil Young
CAST: Bill Murray, Peter Boyle, Rene Auberjonois
SOUNDTRACK SONGS: *Keep On Chooglin'*, Creedence Clearwater Revival; *Highway 61*, Bob Dylan; *I Can't Help Myself*, the Four Tops; *Purple Haze*, Jimi Hendrix; *Buffalo Stomp, Home On the Range, Ode to Wild Bill*, Neil Young
SOUNDTRACK: Backstreet

WHITE ROCK 1976
EMI, documentary, color, 76 minutes

DIRECTOR: Tony Maylam
PRODUCER: Drummond Challis
NARRATED BY: James Coburn
SCORE: Rick Wakeman
SOUNDTRACK: A&M

THE WILD ANGELS 1968
American International Pictures, color, 82 minutes

DIRECTOR: Roger Corman
PRODUCER: Roger Corman
CAST: Peter Fonda, Bruce Dern, Nancy Sinatra, Diane Ladd
SOUNDTRACK SONGS: *Bongo Party, Blue's Theme, The Chase, The Lonely Rider, Rockin' Angel, The Unknown Rider, Wild Angels Ballad, Wild Angels Theme*, Davie Allen and the Arrows; *Lonely In the Chapel, Midnight Rider*, the Hands of Time; *Wild Angels Theme*, the Visitors
SOUNDTRACK: Tower – US

WONDERWALL 1968
Cinecenta, color, 92 minutes

DIRECTOR: Joe Massot
PRODUCER: Andrew Braunsberg
SCORE: George Harrison
CAST: Jack MacGowran, Jane Birkin, Irene Handl
SOUNDTRACK: Apple

THE WORLD IS FULL OF MARRIED MEN 1979
New Realm, color, 106 minutes

DIRECTOR: Robert Young
PRODUCERS: Malcolm Fancey, Oscar Lerman
CAST: Anthony Franciosa, Carroll Baker, Paul Nicholas
SOUNDTRACK SONGS: *Get Down*, Gene Chandler; *Best of My Love*, the Emotions; *The World Is Full of Married Men*, Mick Jackson; *Shame*, Evelyn King; *We Don't Make Each Other Laugh Anymore*, Gladys Knight; *Loveliness*, Paul Nicholas; *Contact*, Edwin Starr; *Heaven Must Be Missing An Angel*, Tavares; *Now That We've Found Love*, Third World; *Woman In Love*, the Three Degrees; *The World Is Full of Married Men*, Bonnie Tyler; *Lovely Day*, Bill Withers
SOUNDTRACK: Ronco – UK

THE WORLD'S GREATEST SINNER 1962
82 minutes

DIRECTOR: Timothy Carey
SCORE: Frank Zappa
CAST: Timothy Carey, Gil Baretto, Betty Rowland

YOU GOT TO WALK IT LIKE YOU TALK IT 1971
Color, 85 minutes

DIRECTOR: Peter Locke
MUSIC PRODUCER: Kenny Vance
SCORE: Walter Becker, Donald Fagen
CAST: Zalman King, Allen Garfield, Richard

Pryor, Liz Torres
SOUNDTRACK: Visa – US; Spark – UK

YOU'RE A BIG BOY NOW 1967
Warner Brothers, color, 96 minutes

DIRECTOR: Francis Ford Coppola
PRODUCER: Phil Feldman
SCORE: John Sebastian
CAST: Peter Kastner, Rip Torn, Julie Harris, Geraldine Page, Michael Dunn
SOUNDTRACK SONGS: *Darling Be Home Soon*, *You're a Big Boy Now*, the Lovin' Spoonful
SOUNDTRACK: Kama Sutra

YOUNGBLOOD 1978
American International Pictures, color, 90 minutes

DIRECTOR: Noel Nosseck
PRODUCERS: Nick Grillo, Alan Riche
SCORE: War
CAST: Lawrence Hilton-Jacobs, Bryan O'Dell, Ren Woods
SOUNDTRACK: MCA

ZABRISKIE POINT 1970
Metro Goldwyn Mayer, color, 112 minutes

DIRECTOR: Michelangelo Antonioni
PRODUCER: Carlo Ponti
SCORE: Pink Floyd
SOUNDTRACK SONGS: *Dance of Death*, John Fahey; *Love Scene*, Jerry Garcia; *Dark Star*, the Grateful Dead; *Brother Mary*, *Mickey's Tune*, Kaleidoscope; *Careful With That Axe Eugene*, *Crumbling Land*, *Heart Beat Pig Meat*, Pink Floyd
SOUNDTRACK: MGM

Index of Film Titles

Abba – The Movie   133
Alfie Darling   179
Alice's Restaurant   11
All This and World War II   179
Almost Summer   179
American Graffiti   179
American Hot Wax   11
American Pop   14
Americathon   14
Andy Warhol's Bad   180
Animal House   180
Attack of the Phantoms   14

Babylon   180
Bad Manners Live In Concert   133
Ballad in Blue   14
Banjoman   134
Be My Guest   14
Beach Ball   14
Beach Blanket Bingo   15
Beach Party   16
Beat Girl   17
Because They're Young   17
Between the Lines   180
Big Beat, The   18
Big Chill, The   180
Big T.N.T. Show, The   135
Big Wednesday   180
Bikini Beach   18
Bird On a Wire   136
Birth of the Beatles   19
Black Caesar   181
Blackboard Jungle, The   181
Blue Collar   181
Blue Hawaii   19
Blue Suede Shoes   136
Blues Alive   136
Blues Brothers, The   21
Blues For Lovers   23

Bob Marley and the Wailers Live!   136
Body Rock   23
Born to Boogie   137
Breakdance – The Movie   23
Breaking Glass   25
Brothers   181
Brothers of the Road – The Allman Brothers Band   137
Buddy Holly Story, The   27

California Dreaming   181
Can't Stop the Music   27
Captain Milkshake   181
Car Wash   181
Carlene Carter Live In London   137
Carnival Rock   28
Carny   182
Catalina Caper   28
Catch My Soul   29
Catch Us If You Can   182
Celebration at Big Sur   137
Change of Habit   29
Chastity   182
Chicken Chronicles, The   182
Chuck Berry Featuring Tina Turner   138
Cisco Pike   182
Clambake   30
Claudine   182
C'mon Let's Live a Little   30
Coast to Coast   182
College Confidential   30
Coming Home   183
Concert for Bangladesh, The   138
Cool Ones, The   30
Cooley High   183
Cukoo Patrol   31

D.O.A. – A Right of Passage   139
Dance Craze   139

Dateline Diamonds   33
David Bowie Live   140
Disc Jockey Jamboree   33
Divine Madness   140
Don't Knock the Rock   33
Don't Knock the Twist   33
Don't Look Back   140
Double Trouble (1962)   34
Double Trouble (1968)   34
Dr Goldfoot and the Girl Bombs   34

Earth, Wind and Fire in Concert   140
Easy Come Easy Go   34
Electra Glide In Blue   183
Elvis On Tour   141
Elvis – That's the Way It Is   143
Elvis – The Movie   34
Endless Summer   183
Eric Clapton and His Rolling Hotel   143
Every Day's a Holiday   36
Expresso Bongo   36

Fame   38
Family Way, The   184
Fast Break   184
Fast Forward   39
Fastest Guitar Alive, The   39
Ferry Cross the Mersey   39
Festival   143
Festival At Big Sur   144
Fillmore   144
Finders Keepers   40
Fish That Saved Pittsburgh, The   184
Flame   41
Flaming Star   41
Flash Gordon   184
Flashdance   42
FM   183
Follow That Dream   42

INDEX OF FILM TITLES

Follow the Boys 43
Footloose 43
Forever Young 45
Foxes 184
Frankie and Johnny 45
Fraternity Row 185
Friends 185
Fun in Acapulco 46
Fury Unleashed 47

G.I. Blues 47
Gary Numan – The Berserker Tour 145
Gas! Or It Became Necessary... 48
Get Yourself a College Girl 48
Getting Straight 185
Ghost in the Invisible Bikini, The 49
Ghost of Dragstrip Hollow, The 49
Gimme Shelter 145
Girl Can't Help It, The 50
Girl Happy 51
Girls Girls Girls 52
Girls on the Beach 52
Girls' Town 51
Give My Regards to Broad Street 53
Glastonbury Fayre 145
Go Go Mania 146
Go Johnny Go 53
Godfather of Harlem, The 185
Godspell 54
Gold 185
Golden Disc, The 55
Gonks Go Beat 56
Good Times 56
Graduate, The 185
Grateful Dead, The 146
Grease 56
Great Rock'n'Roll Swindle 146
Green Ice 185
Groove Tube, The 58
Guess Who Together Again, The 147

Hair 58
Hammer 185
Hard Day's Night, A 59
Harder They Come, The 59
Harem Holiday 60
Harold and Maude 186
Harum Scarum 60
Having a Wild Weekend 186
Head 61
Heartland Reggae 147
Hedy 62
Help! 62
Here We Go Round the Mulberry Bush 186
Hey Let's Twist 64
Hold On 64
Hollywood Knights, The 186
Homer 186
Horror of Party Beach, The 64
Hot Rod Gang 65
Hound Dog Man 65
How to Stuff a Wild Bikini 66

I Love You Alice B. Toklas 186
I Wanna Hold Your Hand 186
Idle On Parade 66
Idolmaker, The 66
Imagine 147
Innocent and the Damned, The 67
It Happened at the World's Fair 67
It's a Bikini World 67
It's All Happening 67
It's All Over Town 67
It's Trad, Dad 68
It's Your Thing 148
I've Gotta Horse 69

Jailhouse Rock 69
Jamboree 71
James Dean – The First American Teenager 187
Janis 148
Jazz Singer, The 71
Jesus Christ Superstar 72
Jimi Hendrix 149
Johnny Cash – the Man, His World, His Music 149
Jonathan Livingston Seagull 187
Journey Through the Past 149
Joyride 187
Jubilee 72
Juke Box Rhythm 73
Just For Fun 73

Keep It Cool 75
Kid Galahad 75
Kids Are Alright, The 150
King Creole 75
Kiss Meets the Phantom 76
Kissin' Cousins 76

Ladies and Gentlemen – The Rolling Stones 150
Landlord, The 187
Last Summer 187
Last Waltz, The 151
Let It Be 152
Let's Rock 76
Let's Spend the Night Together 154
Let the Good Times Roll 153
Lifeboat Party – Kid Creole and the Coconuts Live in London 155
Lisztomania 77
Live a Little, Love a Little 78
Live It Up 78
Lively Set, The 78
London Rock and Roll Show, The 155
Love in Las Vegas 79
Love Me Tender 79
Loving You 80

Mad Dogs and Englishmen 156
Magic Christian, The 187
Magical Mystery Tour 80
Mahoney's Last Stand 188
Manhattan Transfer 156
McVicar 187
Mean Streets 188

Medicine Ball Caravan 156
Medium Cool 188
Melody 188
Mister Rock and Roll 80
Moment by Moment 188
Mondo Daytona 188
Monster Club, The 81
Monterey Pop 157
More American Graffiti 189
Mother, Jugs and Speed 189
Mrs Brown You've Got a Lovely Daughter 81
Muscle Beach Party 82

Never Too Young to Rock 82
Night With Lou Reed, A 157
No Nukes 159
Nothing But a Man 189

O Lucky Man 189
One Plus One 159
One Trick Pony 83
Out of Sight 83
Outlaw Riders 190
Over the Edge 190

Pacific Vibrations 190
Pajama Party 83
Paradise – Hawaiian Style 84
Phantom of the Paradise 84
Pictures at an Exhibition 159
Piece of the Action, A 190
Pied Piper, The 86
Pink Floyd 160
Pink Floyd At Pompeii 160
Pipe Dreams 86
Platinum High School 86
Play It Cool 87
Point, The 190
Poor Cow 190
Pop Gear 160
Popcorn – An Audio-Visual Experience 161
Popcorn – An Audio-Visual Thing 161
Popeye 190
Privilege 87
Psych-Out 88
Purple Rain 91

Quadrophenia 190

R.P.M. 191
Radio On 191
Rainbow Bridge 162
Reggae 162
Reggae Sunsplash 162
Renaldo and Clara 91
Revolution 162
Rich Young and Deadly 93
Ring-a-Ding Rhythm 93
Riot on Sunset Strip 191
River Niger, The 191
Roadie 93
Rock All Night 93
Rock and Roll – The Early Days 162

INDEX OF FILM TITLES

Rock and Soul Live–Daryl Hall and John Oates 163
Rock Around the Clock 94
Rock Around the World 94
Rock, Baby, Rock It 94
Rock'n'Roll High School 94
Rock Pretty Baby 95
Rock Rock Rock 95
Rockers 96
Rockshow 164
Rocky Horror Picture Show, The 96
Roommates 192
Roots Rock and Reggae 164
Rose, The 97
Roustabout 99
Royal Albert Hall Concert for Arms, The 165
Rude Boy 99
Rumblefish 192
Run Home Slow 192
Rust Never Sleeps 165

Satan's Sadists 192
Saturday Night Fever 192
Savage Seven, The 192
Save the Children 165
Seaside Swingers 101
Secret Life of Plants, The 192
Secret Policeman's Ball, The 167
Serious Charge 101
Sgt. Pepper's Lonely Hearts Club Band 101
Shaft 192
Shaft In Africa 193
Shaft's Big Score 193
Shake Rattle and Rock 103
Shining Star 193
Short Eyes 193
Silver Dream Racer 193
Sing Boy Sing 103
Sing Sing Thanksgiving 167
Skatetown 193
Ski Party 104
Skidoo 193
Slap Shot 194
Slaughter's Big Rip-Off 194
Slumber Party '57 194
Smashing Time 194
Some People 105
Son of Dracula 105
Song Remains the Same, The 168
Sorcerer 194
Soul to Soul 168
Sounder 194

Sparkle 106
Speedway 106
Spinout 107
Star Is Born, A 107
Stardust 109
Status Quo – End of the Road 169
Stay Away Joe 110
Staying Alive 110
Steelyard Blues 195
Stop Making Sense 169
Strawberry Statement, The 195
Streets of Fire 111
Summer Holiday 112
Sunnyside 195
Superfly 195
Superfly T.N.T. 195
Surf Party 112
Swinger's Paradise 113
Swingin' Along 113
Swingin' Summer, A 113
Sympathy For the Devil 171

Take It Or Leave It 172
Take Me High 195
Teenage Millionaire 114
Thank God It's Friday 114
That Summer 196
That'll Be the Day 115
That's the Way of the World 196
This Is Spinal Tap 115
Tickle Me 116
Tilt 116
Times Square 116
Together Brothers 196
Tommy 117
Tommy Steele Story, The 119
Tonite Let's All Make Love in London 173
Top Secret 120
Touchables, The 196
Train Ride to Hollywood 196
Trip, The 196
Trouble at 16 121
Trouble Man 196
Trouble With Girls, The 121
Truck Turner 197
Twist All Night 121
Twist Around the Clock 121
Two a Penny 122
Two Tickets to Paris 122

Union City 197

Untamed Youth 122
Up In Smoke 197
Up the Academy 197
Up the Junction 197
Up Tight 197

Vanishing Point 197
Village of the Giants 198
Viva Las Vegas 123

Wages of Fear 198
Wanderers, The 198
Warriors, The 198
Wattstax 173
Weekend Rebellion 198
Welcome to L.A. 198
What a Crazy World 124
What's Up Tiger Lily? 198
When the Boys Meet the Girls 124
Where the Buffalo Roam 199
White Rock 199
Wild Angels, The 199
Wild for Kicks 125
Wild in the Country 125
Wild in the Streets 126
Wild on the Beach 127
Wild Wild Winter 127
Winter a Go-Go 128
Wiz, The 128
Wonderful Life 128
Wonderful to be Young 129
Wonderwall 199
Woodstock 173
World Is Full of Married Men, The 199
World's Greatest Sinner 199

Xanadu 129

Yellow Submarine 129
Yessongs 174
Yoko Ono Then and Now 175
You Are What You Eat 176
You Got To Walk It Like You Talk It 199
You're a Big Boy Now 200
Young and the Cool, The 130
Young Ones, The 130
Young Swingers, The 130
Youngblood 200

Zabriskie Point 200
Zachariah 130

Index of Names

Abba 133
Abbey, Peter D. 133, 155
Abdul-Jabbar, Kareem 184
Abel, Robert 141, 156
Abey, Dennis 82
Abrahams, Jim 120
Abramson, Richard G. 134
Abyssinians, The 165
Ace, Johnny 188
Ackroyd, Dan 21, 23
Adam, Noelle 17
Adams, Beverly 128
Adams, Catlin 71
Adams, Gerald 76
Adams, Jonathan 96
Adams, Julie 116
Adams, Maude 188
Adams, Nick 103
Adamson, Al 185, 192
Addams, Dawn 23
Adderley, Cannonball 165
Adidge, Pierre 141, 156
Adler, Lou 96
Aerosmith 101, 102
Aiello, Josie 23
Ajaye, Franklin 181
Akers, Andra 188
Albright, Lola 75
Alden, Norman 56
Alexander, Gary 53
Alexander, Jeff 69
Alfonso, Louis 133
Alice Cooper 93, 94, 102, 156
Alk, Howard 148
Alland, William 78
Allen, Bambi 190
Allen, Colin 136
Allen, Daevid and Gong 146

Allen, Davie and the Arrows 199
Allen, R.S. 51
Allen, Karen 198
Allen, Nancy 186
Allen, Rance 173
Allen, Steve 30
Allen, Woody 198
Allison, Luther 183
Allman Brothers Band 137
Allman, Greg 137
Alomar, Carlos 140
Alonzo, John A. 183
Altbach, Ron 179
Althea and Donna 147
Altman, John 19
Altman, Robert 190, 198
Alvarado, Trini 116
Alvina, Anicee 185
Amato, Len 162
Ambler, Dail 17
Ambrosia 183
America 181
American Revolution 192
Amilcar 73
Amsterdam, Morey 82
Anderson, Carl 72
Anderson, Esther 196
Anderson, Jon 174
Anderson, Lindsay 189
Anderson, Melody 184
Anderson, Michael Jr. 87
Anderson, Stig 133
Andersson, Benny 133
Andress, Ursula 46
Andrews, Merry 116
Angel 184
Angels, The 189, 198
Angelus, Paul 129

Angers, Avril 14, 122
Animals, The 48, 67, 109, 160
Anka, Paul 51, 77
Ann-Margret 117, 123
Ansara, Michael 60
Anthony, Ray 50
Antonelli, Laura 34
Antonioni, Michelangelo 200
Apted, Michael 109
Aquatones, The 188
Archer, John 94
Archer, Karen 45
Arkoff, Samuel Z. 15, 16, 18, 49, 66, 83, 126
Arkush, Allan 94
Armitage, George 47
Armstrong, Louis 124
Arnaud, Michael 160
Arnaz, Desi Jr 187
Arnaz, Lucy 71
Arnold, Jack 78
Art of Noise, The 24
Ash, Lesley 191
Ashby, Hal 154, 183, 186, 187
Ashcroft, Ray 19
Asher, William 15, 16, 18, 66, 82
Ashford and Simpson 23, 128
Ashley, John 65
Askey, David 195
Askey, Gil 190
Asleep at the Wheel 93
Asner, Edward 29
Aspinall, Neil 115, 152
Asseyev, Tamara 180, 186
Astronauts, The 83, 113, 127
Aswad 180
Atwell, Rick 39
Auberjonois, Rene 199
Aubrey, Anne 66

204

INDEX OF NAMES

Aubrey, James 45
Aucoin, William M. 76
Aunt Mary's Transcendental Slip and Lurch Band 187
Austin, Patti 148
Austin, Phil 130
Avalon, Frankie 16, 18, 56, 66, 71, 82, 104, 194
Averback, Hy 186
Ayres, Gerald 182, 184
Ayres, Rosalind 109, 115
Azongio, Amoa 168

B52's, The 83
Babys, The 197
Bach, Barbara 53
Bachelors, The 68
Bachman, Randy 147
Bacon, Kevin 43
Bacon, Max 87
Bad Company 187
Bad Karma Dan 187
Bad Manners 133, 139
Badfinger 187, 188
Badham, John 192
Baez, Joan 91, 134, 135, 137, 140, 143, 167, 173
Bafoloukas, Theodoras 96
Baier, Richard 58
Bailey, Pearl 187
Bailey, Philip 141
Bailey, Robin 182
Bain, Sherry 86
Baio, Scott 184, 193
Baird, Roy 77, 187, 190, 191
Baker, Barry 99
Baker, Carroll 180, 199
Baker, Herbert 50, 75, 80
Baker, LaVerne 80, 95
Baker, Richard 157
Baker, Roy Ward 81
Bakshi, Ralph 14
Baldwin, Earl 73
Ballie, Bonnie 137
Bancroft, Anne 185
Band, The 151
Band of Gypsies, The 149
Bantams, The 30
Bar-Kays, The 24, 173
Baran, Jack 91
Barbera, Joseph 76
Barbourne, John 197
Baretto, Gil 199
Barkley, Janet 59
Barlett, Richard 95
Barnet, Charlie 18
Barra, Jack 192
Barrett, Tony 56
Barrie, Amanda 69
Barron, Arthur 149, 181
Barron, Evelyn 149
Barry, Jeff 66
Barry, John 17, 67
Barson, Ben 137
Barson, Mike 172

Bart, Lionel 101
Bartel, Paul 94
Bartlett, Hall 187
Bartlett, Jack 28
Barton, Charles 113
Barton, Earl 99
Barzman, Alan 190
Basie, Count 18, 71
Basil, Toni 30, 61
Baskin, Richard 198
Bates, Alan 97
Batten, Peter 129
Bauer, Freddy 27
Bautista, Roland 141
Bava, Mario 34
Baxter, Les 49
Beach Boys, The 52, 161, 179
Beals, Jennifer 42
Beat, The 139
Beatles, The 59, 62, 80, 129, 152, 160, 183, 186
Beau Brummels, The 127, 198
Beaver and Krauss 190
Beck, Jeff 165
Beck, Michael 129, 198
Becker, Walter 199
Beckerman, Sidney 187
Beckmeier Brothers, The 184
Beckwith, Reginald 75
Bee Gees, The 101, 102, 109, 110, 161, 179, 188
Bee, Molly 130
Bedford, Mark 172
Beefheart, Captain 181
Begley, Ed Jr 115
Behm, Marc 62
Belan, Edmund 47
Belew Twins, The 94
Belfer, Hal 48, 73
Belin, Graham 197
Bell and James 184
Bell, Freddy and the Bellboys 48, 94
Bell, Kenneth 196
Bell, Tom 23, 184
Belling, Davina 25, 196
Belsar, Bob 129
Belushi, John 21, 23, 180
Belzer, Richard 58
Benatar, Pat 14, 93, 197
Bender, Russ 50, 127
Bendix, William 66
Benedict, Richard 128
Benn, Harry 33
Bennett, Hywel 184
Benson, Ray 93
Benson, Sally 123
Bent Fabric 94
Benton, Brook 80
Benton, Jerome 91
Bentyne, Cheryl 156
Bercovici, Eric 29
Berenger, Tom 180
Bergen, Candice 185
Bergman, Peter 130
Berline, Byron 97

Berlinger, Warren 17
Berman, Pandro S. 69, 181
Bernard, Judd 34
Bernds, Edward 116
Bernstein, Barry Armyan 114
Berry, Chuck 12, 53, 80, 94, 95, 138, 153, 155, 162, 163, 179
Berry, John 182
Betts, Dickey 137
Bifferty, Skip 194
Big Bopper, The 115, 179, 194
Big Brother & the Holding Co 14, 148, 157
Big Youth 96
Biggs, Ronald 147
Bilk, Acker 67, 68
Bill Black Combo, The 114
Bill Doggett Trio, The 12
Bill Wray Band, The 116
Billy Ray Band, The 97
Bingham, Bob 72
Binyon, Claude 103
Binzer, Rollin 150
Birch, Patricia 56
Birkin, Andrew 86
Birkin, Jane 199
Birrell, Pete 36
Bishop, Elvin 144
Bishop, Larry 192
Bishop, Randy 116
Bishop, Steven 93, 180
Bishop, Tony 19
Bixby, Bill 30, 106
Black Arabs, The 147
Black Faith 162
Black, Karen 182
Black, Stanley 112
Black Knights, The 40
Black, Cilla 40
Blacker, Gail 171
Blackman, Bond 28
Blackman, Joan 19, 75
Blackwell, Chuck 156
Blackwells, The 40
Blair, Joyce 14
Blair, Nicky 123
Blake, Eubie 184
Blake, Howard 184
Blake, Robert 183
Blakely, Ronee 91
Blanchard, Mari 33
Blaser, Herman 23
Blasters, The 111
Blinn, William 91
Blockbusters, The 28, 93
Blondell, Joan 110
Blondie 93, 197
Bloodvessel, Buster 133
Bloom, Verna 188
Bloomfield, Mike 180, 188, 195, 196
Blow Up 197
Blue, David 91
Blues Brothers Band, The 21
Blumgarten, James 80

INDEX OF NAMES

Bob and Marcia 162
Bobby Fuller Four, The 49
Bobo, Willie 168
Bock, Richard 168
Bodysnatchers, The 139
Boenzee Cryque 89
Boffalong 182
Boggs, Bill 157
Bogner, Norman 87
Bolan, Marc 137
Bonds, Gary 'U.S.' 68
Bonerz, Peter 188
Bonham, John 168
Bono, Cher 56, 182
Bono, Sonny 56, 182
Bonoff, Karla 43
Boogaloo Shrimp 24
Booker T. and the MG's 179, 180, 191, 197
Boomtown Rats, The 196
Boorman, John 182
Booth, James 115
Boston 184
Bostwick, Barry 96
Boulting, John 184
Boulting, Roy 184
Bovell, Brian 180
Bovell, Dennis 180
Bowen, Jimmy 71, 197
Bowie, David 140, 187, 191
Bown, Andy 169
Bowties, The 95
Boxtops, The 109
Boyd, Don 146
Boyd, Joe 149
Boyle, Peter 195, 199
Brackman, Jacob 116
Bradshaw, Carl 59
Brady, Scott 192
Brambell, Wilfrid 59
Bramlett, Bonnie 29
Bramlett, Delaney 29
Brandon, Michael 183
Branigan, Laura 23, 42
Braun, Michael 192
Braunsberg, Andrew 199
Brennan, Eileen 183
Bresler, Jerry 17
Bridges, Beau 187, 193, 198
Briggs, David 35
Briley, Martin 23
Brim 23
Broccoli, Albert R. 66
Brodax, Al 129
Broderick, James 11
Bromberg, David 134
Bron, Eleanor 62
Bronner, Robert 71
Bronson, Charles 75
Brook Brothers, The 68
Brooklyn Bridge 148
Brooklyn Dreams 184
Brooks, Donnie 48, 113
Brooks, Patti 114

Brooks, Peter 52
Brooks, Ray 105
Brooks, Richard 181
Brothers Johnson, The 179, 189
Brown, Arthur 146
Brown, Barbara 56
Brown, Blair 83
Brown, Bruce 183
Brown, Bryan 53
Brown, Buster 179
Brown, Dennis 147
Brown, Drew Bundini 193
Brown, Errol 96
Brown, James 21, 23, 104, 181, 191, 194
Brown, Jim 194
Brown, Joe 124
Brown, Joe and the Breakaways 75
Brown, Joe and the Bruvvers 124
Brown, Les Jnr. 127
Brown, Wendell 197
Brown, William 128
Browne, Arthur Jr 30
Browne, Irene 101
Browne, Jackson 159
Browne, Roscoe Lee 195, 197
Brownsville Station 94
Bruckheimer, Jerry 42
Bruno, Buddy 187
Bruton, Stephen 107
Bryan, Dora 122
Bryan, John 196
Bryant, Baird 137
Bryant, Gerard 119
Brynner, Yul 188
Buchanan, Robbie 97
Buckley, Tim 183
Buckner, Robert 79
Buffalo, Norton 97
Buffet, Jimmy 183
Bullock, Harvey 51
Bunnage, Avis 124
Burbidge, Derek 145
Burdon, Eric and the Animals 157
Burdon, Eric and the New Animals 173
Burke, Martyn 120
Burke, Solomon 185
Burnett, Don 122
Burnette, Johnny & the Rock'n'Roll Trio 95, 179
Burning Spear 96, 162
Burns, Cathy 187
Burns, George 101, 102
Burt, Heinz 78
Burton, James 141
Bury, Sean 185
Busey, Gary 27, 107, 108, 182
Bushman, Francis X. 49
Buster, Prince 162
Butera, Sam and the Witnesses 121
Butler, David 30
Butler, Jerry 165
Butler, Michael 58
Butterfield, Paul 176, 195
Butterworth, Donna 84

Byles, Junior 96
Byrds, The 134, 135, 186, 189
Byrne, David 171
Byrnes, Edd 15, 56, 109
Byron, D.L. 116

Cabot, Susan 28
Cadillacs, The 12, 53
Cagan, Andrea 181
Cahn, Edward L. 103
Calhern, Louis 181
Callan, Michael 17
Callner, Marty 163
Calloway, Cab 21, 23
Cameo 114
Cameron, G.C. 114, 183
Cameron, John 193
Campbell, Cheryl 187
Campbell, Glen 30
Campbell, Jo-Ann 53, 64
Campbell, William 18
Candles, The 34
Canned Heat 157, 173, 182
Cannon, Doran William 193
Cannon, Dyan 183
Cannon, Freddie 75, 198
Capitols, The 189
Cara, Irene 38, 42, 106
Cardenas, Elsa 46
Carell, Reno 113, 128
Carey, Michael 78
Carey, Timothy 61, 199
Cargill, Patrick 62
Carnes, Kim 42, 197
Carney, Art 93
Carpenter, John 34
Carr, Allen 27, 56
Carr, Paul 71
Carradine, John 121
Carradine, Keith 198
Carradine, Robert 183, 187
Carras, Alex 183
Carreras, Michael 124
Carroll Brothers, The 33
Carroll, Diahann 182
Carroll, Johnny & His Hot Rocks 94
Cars, The 116
Carson, Robert 107
Carter, Carlene 137
Carter, Dick 156
Carter, Jason 45
Carter, Valerie 190
Cascades, The 28, 191
Casey, Bernie 181
Casey, Warren 56
Cash, Johnny 149
Casini, Stefania 180
Castaways, The 67
Cassandra 180
Cassel, Seymour 181
Cavallo, Jimmy and His Houserockers 95
Cavallo, Robert 91
Cavett, Andy and the Saints 78

INDEX OF NAMES

Cell Block Seven, The 94
Chadwick, June 115
Chaka Khan 24
Challis, Drummond 199
Chambers Brothers, The 183
Chambers, Michael 24
Champs, The 115, 198
Chandler, Chas 41
Chandler, Gene 33, 199
Channel, Bruce 194
Channing, Carol 193
Channing, Stockard 56, 184
Chantays, The 186, 189
Chantelles, The 33, 188
Chants, The 188
Chapman, Leigh 113
Charles, Ray 21, 23, 123, 135, 186
Charles, Tommy 103
Charleson, Ian 73
Charlton, Bobby 59
Chas McDevitt Skiffle Group, The 119
Chase, Chevy 58
Cheap Trick 93, 190
Checker, Chubby 33, 68, 114, 122, 153, 180
Cheeks 197
Chelsea 73
Cher 184
Chess, Marshall 150
Chesterfields, The 12
Chevis, Edmond 95
Chew-Itt, Brian 133
Chiffons, The 109, 186, 191
Child, Desmond and Rouge 116
Chips, The 188
Chocolate Watch Band 191
Chong, Tommy 197
Chords, The 163
Christian, Roger 16
Chuckles, The 50
Churchill, Sarah 101
Ciccio, Carlo 34
Clanton, Jimmy 53, 114
Clapton, Eric 117, 138, 143, 151, 165, 188
Clara Ward Singers, The 148
Clark, Bruce 185
Clark, Curtis 136
Clark, Dave 182
Clark, Dick 17, 34, 88, 192
Clark, Fred 194
Clark, Johnny 180
Clark, Marilyn 64
Clark, Oliver 107
Clark, Penny 136
Clark, Petula 103, 104
Clarke, Gary 127
Clash, The 99, 139
Classics IV 182
Clearmountain, Bob 140, 154, 163
Cleftones, The 179
Clegg, Tom 187
Clennel, Lindsey 160
Cliff, Jimmy 59, 60, 165
Clifford, Linda 38

Clifford, Mike 198
Clifton, Peter 155, 161, 168
Clive, John 82, 129
Close, Glenn 180
Clough, John Scott 39
Clovers, The 179
Club 77 Band, The 97
Coasters, The 12, 153
Coats, Don 94
Coburn, James 199
Cochran, Eddie 12, 50, 53, 122, 123, 136, 163
Cocker, Joe 109, 156, 161, 174
Coco, James 195
Cogan, Shayle 80
Cohen, Larry 181
Cohen, Leonard 136
Cohen, Rob 114, 128, 179
Cokliss, Harley 196
Cold Blood 144
Cole, Clay 122
Cole, George 195
Colley, Kenneth 41
Collier, James F. 122
Collins, Joan 179
Collins, Judy 143
Collins, Lyn and the JB's 181, 194
Collins, Roberta 196
Collinson, Peter 197
Colman, Carol 155
Colorado Purple Gang 190
Columbier, Michel 91
Combs Sisters, The 137
Comfort, Lance 14, 78
Commodores, The 114
Conaway, Jeff 56
Conn, Didi 179
Connelly, Joe 29
Connolly, Ray 45, 109, 115, 187
Connor, Kenneth 31, 56
Connors, Carol 28, 184
Connors, Touch (Mike) 103
Conrad, Jess 147
Conrad, William 30
Conreid, Hans 73
Constantine, Michael 194
Conti, Tom 41
Contours, The 198
Cooder, Ry 111, 181, 190
Cook, Elisha Jr. 183
Cook, Paul 147
Cooke, Sam 180
Coolidge, Rita 156, 183
Cooper, George A. 40
Cooper, Ray 165
Coote, Robert 30
Cope, Kenneth 33
Copeland, Stewart 192
Coppola, Francis Ford 179, 192, 200
Coppola (Shire), Talia 48
Corbett, Harry 124
Corcoran, Noreen 52
Corey, Jeff 185
Corey, Wendell 80

Corff, Robert 48
Corman, Gene 104
Corman, Roger 28, 48, 93, 196, 199
Cort, Bud 48, 186
Cosby, Bill 189, 190
Costello, Elvis 14, 196
Cougar, John 43
Country Joe and the Fish 48, 130, 157, 174, 189
County, Wayne and the Electric Chairs 73
Court, Don 140
Cowan, Will 18
Craig, Monica 96
Craig, Yvonne 76, 104
Crawford, Jimmy 87
Crawford, Johnny 198
Crawford, Richard 181
Cray, Carole 130
Crazy Cavan and the Flying Saucers 136
Cream 186, 190, 192
Creason, Sammy 107
Creedence Clearwater Revival 199
Cremer, Bruno 194
Crests, The 179
Crew Cuts, The 194
Crewsdon, Roy 36
Crickets, The 52, 75, 115
Criss, Peter 76
Cronenweth, Jordan 169
Cropper, Steve 21
Crosby, Cathy 30
Crosby, David 179
Crosby, Gary 51, 122
Crosby, Stills and Nash 159, 195
Crosby, Stills, Nash and Young 137, 150, 174, 188, 190, 195
Cross, H.B. 114
Crouse, Lindsay 180, 194
Crow, Alvin and the Pleasant Valley Boys 93
Crown, Alfred 187
Crows, The 179
Crusaders, The 189
Crystals, The 180, 191
Culbertson, Rod 19
Cummings, Bob 16
Cummings, Burton 147, 181
Cummings, Jack 123
Curb, Mike 34, 191, 192
Curbishley, Bill 150, 187, 191
Cure, The 116
Curreri, Lee 38
Curry, Mickey 163
Curry, Tim 96, 116
Curtiz, Michael 75
Cushing, Peter 121
Cycle V 42

D'Angelo, Beverly 58
d'Arbanville, Patti 180
Dacus, Donnie 58
Dale, Alan 33, 94
Dale, Dick and the Deltones 16, 82
Dale, Jim 103, 104
Dalton, Abby 93

207

INDEX OF NAMES

Daltrey, Roger 77, 117, 150, 187, 191
Daly, Jonathan 83
Daly, Peter-Hugo 25
Dana, Vic 33
Danieers, The 194
Daniels, Phil 25, 191
Danko, Rick 151
Dankworth, Johnny 103
Danny and the Juniors 77, 115, 153
Danova, Cesare 123
Dante and the Evergreens 115
Danus, Richard Christian 129
Danza, Tony 186
Darby, Kim 195
Darden, Severn 197
Darin, Bobby 12, 79, 109
Darnell, August 155
Darren, James 17
Dassin, Jules 197
Dave Clark Five, The 48, 182
David, Alan 56
Davidson, Lenny 182
Davidson, Martin 179
Davis, Billy 193
Davis, Carl 19
Davis, Desmond 194
Davis, Philip 191
Davis, Rahmlee 141
Davis, Sammy Jr 165
Davison, Bruce 187, 189, 193, 195
Davison, Jon 120
Day, Annette 34
Day, Ernest 185
Day, Morris 91
De Bevoise, Allen 23
de Cordova, Frederick 45
De Palma, Brian 84
De Paola, Alessio 182
De Paul, Lynsey 179
de Prendergast, Barry 162
De Shannon, Jackie 30, 112, 113, 182
de Silva, David 38
De Vorzon, Barry 198
Dean, Laura 38
DeChant, Charlie 163
Decker, Herbert F. 144
Deco 39
Dee, Dave 147
Dee, Joey 64, 179
Dee, Joey and the Starlighters 64, 122
Dee, Kiki 33
Dee, Ruby 197
Dees, Bill 39
Dees, Rick 192
Dekker, Desmond 60, 162
Del Rio, Dolores 41
Del Vikings, The 12, 18, 179
Del-Aires, The 65
Delaney and Bonnie 29, 156, 197
Delights, The 12
Dell'Amico, Len 136, 137
Demarest, William 123
Demetrakis, Joanna 137

Demme, Jonathan 169
Demoriane, Hermine 73
Demy, Jacques 86
Dene, Terry 55
DeNiro, Robert 188
Dennen, Barry 72
Dennis, Jackie 103, 104
Denyer, Peter 82
Derek and the Dominoes 109
Dern, Bruce 88, 183, 196, 199
Des Longchamps, Ines 109
Deschanel, Caleb 154
Desmonds, Jerry 56
Desloge, Bill 185
Desmond, James 157
Detroit Spinners, The 184
Deutsch, David 182
DeVille, Mink 196
Devo 94, 191
Dexter, Maury 112, 127, 130
Di Cicco, Bobby 186
Di Laurentiis, Dino 184
di Lorenzo, Edward 66
Di Pasquale, James 184
Diamond, Neil 71, 151, 187
Diamonds, The 12, 115, 179
Dick and Dee Dee 127, 128
Dickey, Lucinda 24
Diddley, Bo 135, 153, 155, 162, 163
Didion, Joan 107
Dillard, Doug 97
Dillard, Rodney 97
Dillinger 96
Dillon, Matt 190, 192
Dillon, Robert 18, 82
Diltz, Henry 187
Dinning, Mark 179
Dion 114, 115, 122
Dixon, Dave 176
Dixon, Ivan 189, 196
Doheny, Lawrence 114
Dolenz, Mickey 61
Domino, Fats 18, 23, 50, 71, 103, 153, 162, 163, 179
Dominoes, The 12
Donahue, Tom 156
Donegan, Lonnie 103, 104
Donlan, Yolande 36
Donlevy, Brian 73
Donner, Clive 105, 186
Donovan 86, 135, 140, 143, 189, 190
Doobie Brothers, The 159, 184
Doors, The 14, 189
Dorfman, Stanley 165
Dors, Diana 86
Dorsey, Lee 179, 198
Doug Dillard Expedition, The 197
Douglas, Angela 67, 105
Douglas, Craig 68
Douglas, Donna 45
Douglas, Gordon 42, 194
Douglas, James 47
Douglas, Jo 103

Dovells, The 33
Downey, Robert 197
Doyle, Jimmy 197
Dramatics, The 173
Dreams, The 58
Dreifuss, Arthur 73, 191
Drescher, Fran 12, 186
Dreyfuss, Richard 179
Drifters, The 12, 109
Drury, David 45
Dubin, Charles 80
Dubov, Paul 103
Dumbrille, Douglas 103
Dumont, Margaret 103
Dunn, Duck 21
Dunn, Larry 21, 141
Dunn, Michael 200
Dunne, John Gregory 107
Dunne, Murphy 21
Dunne, Philip 125
Dunning, George 129
Dupin, Cleve 107
Dupont, Rene 193
Duralia, Darlene 190
Duran, Larry 56
Durand, Rudy 116
Durning, Charles 116
Dury, Ian 191, 196
Duryea, Dan 86
Duryea, Peter 28
Duvall, Shelley 190
Dvonch, Russ 94
Dye, Cameron 23
Dylan, Bob 91, 138, 140, 143, 149, 151, 183, 189, 198
Dylan, Sara 91

Eager, Brenda Lee 165
Eagles, The 91, 105, 184, 187
Earl Grant Trio, The 73
Earl Scruggs Revue 134
Earth Opera 192
Earth Wind and Fire 102, 141, 193
Eaton, Anthony 140
Eddie and the Hot Rods 94, 196
Eddy, Duane and the Rebels 17
Eden, Barbara 41, 113
Edmonds, Don 127
Edmunds, Dave 53, 109
Edwards, Henry 101
Edwards, Juma 162
Edwin Hawkins Singers, The 148
Egan, Richard 79
Eikenberry, Jill 180
Ekland, Britt 81
Elaine and Derek 56
Electric Flag 176, 196
Electric Light Orchestra 187
Electric Meatball 187
Electricians, The 109
Elegants, The 12
Elfstrom, Robert 149
Elkins, Hillard 11

INDEX OF NAMES

Eller, James   137
Elliman, Lorraine   187
Elliman, Yvonne   72, 188, 192
Elliot, Jack   91
Elliot, Ramblin' Jack   93, 134
Ellison, Andy   186
Elowe, Stephen   24
Elson, Steve   140
Ely, Joe   93
Emerson, Lake and Palmer   160
Emery, John   50
Emotions, The   173, 193, 199
Ender, Matthew   24
England, Keith   137
Englund, George   130
Eno, Brian   73, 94
Entwhistle, John   117, 150, 191
Ephron, Henry   103
Epstein, Marcelo   23
Eraminondas, Andros   53
Ericson, Leif   99
Erlich, Ken   156
Erskender, Jacob   19
Erving, Juliul   184
Esposito, Joe   42
Essex, David   109, 115, 179, 193
Esterhaus, Joe   42
Evans, Barry   186
Evans, Linda   16
Evans, Michael   191
Evans, Robert   190
Evans, Tommy   187
Eve   197
Everett, Chad   48
Everett, Kenny   33
Everly Brothers   12, 115, 162
Ewell, Tom   58
Exciters, The   18, 180
Expressos, The   81

Fabares, Shelley   30, 51, 64, 95, 107
Fabian   14, 34, 66
Fagen, Donald   199
Fagher, Tommy   110
Fahey, John   200
Fairbanks, Jay   105
Fairbanks, Lyn   78
Fairhurst, Lyn   14
Fairport Convention   146
Fairweather Low, Andy   165
Faith, Adam   17, 109, 184, 187
Family   146
Fancey, Malcolm   199
Fargas, Antonio   181
Fargnoli, Steven   91
Farina, Dick and Mimi   143
Farina, Mimi   167
Farina, Sarah   102
Farlowe, Chris   173
Farmer, Mimsey   191
Farnham, Johnny   161
Farr, Jody   50, 65
Farr-In, Dave   133

Farrar, David   17
Farrell, Glenda   76
Farrow, Tisa   186
Farryar, Cyrus   187
Fay, William   75
Feinstein, Barry   157, 176
Feldman, Phil   200
Feldshuh, Tovah   66
Felton, Felix   68
Fender, Freddie   193
Fenemore, Hilda   119
Fenton, Shane   67, 87
Fentones, The   67, 87
Ferguson, Jay   93
Ferguson, Nicholas   160
Ferris Wheel   196
Ferris, Barbera   182
Ferry, Bryan   179
Feuer, Debra   188
Field, Harry   160
Field, Shirley Ann   17
Fields, Venetta   107
Fifth Dimension, The   114, 161
Finch, Jon   25
Findlay, Seaton   148
Findley, William   84, 85, 86
Finlay, Frank   193
Finley, Bill   84, 86
Finnell, Michael   94
Fire Fox   24
Fire Inc.   111
Firesign Theater, The   130
Firth, Julian   45
Fisher, Michael   192
Fitzpatrick, Colleen   66
Five Satins, The   153, 179
Five Stairsteps, The   148
Five Stars, The   94
Fixx, The   111
Flack, Roberta   23, 165, 168
Flamingos, The   53, 95, 179
Fleetwood Mac   94, 184, 194
Fleetwoods, The   179
Fleischer, Richard   71
Flemyng, Gordon   73
Flicker, Theodore J.   107
Flo and Eddie   181
Flux Fiddlers, The   147
Flying Burrito Brothers, The   145
Fogelburg, Dan   184
Foghat   184
Fonda, Jane   183, 195
Fonda, Peter   196, 199
Fong, Benson   52
Fontaine, Eddie   50
Ford, Frankie   12
Ford, Glenn   181
Ford, Winston   111
Forde, Brinsley   180
Foreigner   43, 184
Foreman, Chris   172
Foreman, Milos   58
Forrest, Frederic   97

Forrest, Steve   41
Forster, Robert   188
Fortunes, The   109
Foster, Gloria   189
Foster, Harry   77
Foster, Jodie   182, 184
Foundations, T.J. and the   30
Four Aces, The   18
Four Amigos, The   46
Four Coins, The   71
Four Pennies, The   160
Four Seasons, The   15, 179, 180, 186, 198
Four Tops, The   183, 184, 199
Fourmost, The   40, 160
Fox, Peter   185
Fradley, Ken   155
Frame, Grazina   36, 112
Frampton, Peter   101, 102, 189
Franceschi, Antonia   38
Franchi, Franco   34
Franciosa, Anthony   199
Francis, Anne   181
Francis, Connie   43, 71, 95, 124, 180
Francis, Freddie   105
Franden, David   40
Franklin, Aretha   21, 23, 180, 183, 189
Franklin, Don   39
Franks, Michael   188
Frantz, Chris   171
Frasca, Mama Maria   91
Fraser, Jeri Lynne   122
Fraser, Liz   36, 197
Frazier, Hal   91
Frazier, Sheila   195
Freddie and the Dreamers   31, 36, 83, 124
Frederick, Jessie   66
Frederick, Vicki   23
Fredrich, John   179
Freed, Alan   33, 53, 80, 94, 95
Freeman, Alan   75
Freeman, Bobby   12, 179, 180
Freeman, Ernie   30
Freeman, Joan   39, 99
Freeman, Joel   193, 196
Freeman, Kathleen   21
Freeman, Robert   196
French, Bruce   86
French, Robert   134
Freshley, Ace   76
Friedkin, William   56, 194
Friedman, Stephen   184, 194
Friedman, Tully   188
Friedrich, John   198
Fries, Bob   150
Fripp, Robert   191
Fritts, Donnie   107
Frogg, Wynder K.   196
Frontiere, Dominic   86
Full Tilt Boogie Band, The   148
Funicello, Annette   16, 18, 61, 66, 82, 84
Fuqua, Harvey   53
Furie, Sidney J.   128, 130
Fury, Billy   69, 87, 115

INDEX OF NAMES

Gabriel, Peter 179
Gadd, Steve 83
Gage, Geoff 181
Gale, Eric 83
Galfas, Timothy 195
Gallagher, Peter 66
Gamblers, The 69
Gange, Ray 99
Ganzer, Alvin 124
Garber, Victor 54
Garcia, Jerry 146, 200
Gardner, Arthur 30
Garfield, Allen 189, 192, 199
Gariguilo, Mike 148
Garrett, Siedah 39
Garrison, Greg 64, 122
Garrity, Freddie 36
Garson, Henry 47
Gates, Tudor 33
Gaye, Lisa 94, 103
Gaye, Marvin 165, 167, 180, 189, 191, 196
Gazzo, Michael Vincent 75
Gebhardt, Steve 150
Gecks, Nicholas 45
Geer, Ellen 186
Geeson, Judy 186
Geller, Joyce 30
Generation X 139
Gennaro, Peter 77
Gentle, Lili 103
Gentry, Minnie 181
Gentrys, The 67
George Bean Group, The 87
George Mitchell Singers, The 67
George, Chief Dan 14
George, Nathan 193
Gerry and the Pacemakers 40, 109
Gershovsky, Yaron 156
Gershwin, George and Ira 124
Ghetto Fighters, The 162
Gibb, Barry 101
Gibb, Maurice 101
Gibb, Robin 101, 102, 116
Gibbons, Micky 187
Gibbs, Joe and the Professionals 96
Gibson, Brian 25
Gibson, Henry 21
Gibson, Wayne and the Dynamite Sound 68
Giftos, Elaine 48
Gilbert, Bruce 183
Gilbert, Lewis 185
Gilchrist, Connie 113
Gilling, John 66
Gilmore, Gail 15
Gilmore, Peter 69
Gilmour, David 160
Gipson, Fred 65
Gitler, Robert 27
Gladiators, The 165
Glan, Pentti 97
Gleason, Jackie 193
Glitter Band, The 82
Godard, Jean-Luc 171

Goetzman, Gary 169
Goldberg, Barry 196
Goldberg, Danny 159
Goldblum, Jeff 114, 180
Goldburg, Mel 79
Golden, Annie 58
Goldflies, David 137
Goldman, Bo 97
Good, Jack 29
Goode, Frederic 160
Goodhand-Tait, Phillip 137, 145
Gooding, Cuba 114
Goodrow, Gary 185
Goodwin, Laurel 52
Goodwin, Ron 50
Goorwitz, Allen 83
Gordon, Bert I. 198
Gordon, Gale 106
Gordon, Hannah 179
Gordon, James B. 33, 64, 94, 121
Gordon, Jim 156
Gordon, Lawrence 111, 129, 198
Gordon, Roscoe 94
Gordon, Ruth 186
Gore, Christopher 38
Gore, Lesley 38, 52, 104
Gore, Michael 38
Gormel, Randy 186
Gorney, Lynn 192
Gossett, Lou 187, 192
Gottlieb, Alex 45
Gottlieb, Carl 137
Gould, Elliot 185
Gourmet's Delight 48
Gracie, Charlie 71
Graef, Roger 167
Graham Bond Organization, The 56
Graham, Billy 122
Graham, Gerrit 84
Graham, Johnny 141
Graham, Sheilah 30
Graham, William 29, 196
Grant, Gogi 18
Grant, Lee 187
Grant, Peter 168
Grateful Dead 144, 189, 200
Graustark, Barbara 175
Gravenites, Nick 195, 196
Gray, Charles 96
Gray, Dobie 83
Graziano, Rocky 80, 114
Green, Charles 12
Green, Karl 64, 81
Green, Wolon 192
Greenburg, Dan 78
Greene, David 54
Greenwald, Robert 129
Greville, Edmond T. 17
Griffin, Chris 45
Griffith, Charles B. 93
Griffith, Hugh 195
Griffith, Melanie 187
Griffiths, Keith 191

Grillo, Nick 200
Grimes, Tammy 27
Groove, The 161
Gross, Henry 179
Gross, Larry 111
Grossman, Albert 140
Grundy, Reg 133
Guercio, James William 183
Guess Who, The 147
Guest, Christopher 115
Guest, Don 181
Guest, Val 36
Guillerman, John 193
Gunn, James 17
Gunn, Moses 193
Gurus, The 126
Guthrie, Arlo 11
Guttenberg, Steve 27, 182
Guy, Buddy 136
Guyler, Deryck 40
Gwinn, Marty 116

Haas, Charles 51, 86
Hackady, Hal 77
Hackett, Buddy 82
Hackett, Joan 83
Hackford, Taylor 66
Hackman, Gene 182
Hagar, Sammy 43, 197
Hagen, Dean 107
Hagey, Taryn 155
Hagman, Larry 109, 189
Hagmann, Stuart 195
Hahn, Archie 84, 86
Haifley, C.D. 138
Haley, Bill and His Comets 33, 94, 136, 153, 155, 162, 163, 179, 181
Hall, Daryl 163
Hall, Richard 96
Hall, Willie 21
Hallstrom, Lasse 133
Ham, Peter 187
Hamilton, Bernie 185
Hamilton, Roy and the Cues 77
Hampshire, Susan 128
Hampton, Lionel and His Orchestra 80
Hana, Miyi 198
Hancock, John 181
Handl, Irene 147, 199
Hands of Time, The 199
Hankerson, Barry 86
Harlettes, The 140
Harmon, Buddy 35
Harmon, David P. 18
Harmon, Joy 77
Harper, Jessica 84, 86
Harper, Kenneth 128, 130, 195
Harper's Bizarre 176, 186
Harris, Berkeley 58
Harris, Eddie 168
Harris, Emmylou 93, 151
Harris, Jet 75, 112, 128
Harris, Julie 200

210

INDEX OF NAMES

Harris, Julius W.   181, 195, 196
Harris, Lewis   193
Harris, Michael   141
Harris, Phil   30
Harrison, George   59, 62, 138, 143, 152, 199
Harrison, Gregory   185
Harrison, Jerry   171
Harrison, Stan   140
Harry, Deborah   197
Hart, Dolores   75
Hart, Harvey   188
Hartford-Davis, Robert   56
Hartman, Ras Daniel   59
Harvey, Laurence   36
Haskell, David   54
Haskell, James   130
Haskell, Jimmy   187
Hatcher, Harley   192
Hauser, Tim   156
Havens, Richie   29, 174, 183
Haverlock-Allen, Anthony   197
Havers, Nigel   19
Havoc, June   27
Hawkins, Ronnie   91, 151
Hawkins, Screamin' Jay   12
Hayers, Sidney   40
Hayes, Jack   39
Hayes, Isaac   173, 193, 197
Hayes, Melvyn   112, 128, 130
Hazan, Jack   99
Hazelwood, Lee   30
Head, John   149
Headon, Nicky   99
Heard, John   162, 180
Heartbeats, The   12, 179
Heatwave   193
Hedley, Tom   42
Heffron, Richard T.   144
Heflin, Martha   107
Heins, Jo   34
Heinz and the Houseshakers   155
Hell, Richard and the Voidoids   196
Heller, Paul   197
Hellman, Jerome   183
Helm, Anne   42
Hemmings, David   78, 105
Hendrix, Jimi   109, 149, 157, 161, 162, 174, 183, 190, 199
Henried, Paul   23
Henry, Jack   87
Henzell, Perry   59
Heptones, The   96
Herald, John   176
Herman's Hermits   64, 81, 124, 125, 160
Herman, Gus   133
Hernandez, Andy   155
Hernandez, Patrick   193
Herndon, Vanavle   11
Hershey, Barbara   187
Hertelandy, John   30
Hessler, Gordon   76
Hessman, Howard   115
Hewson, Richard   188

Heyman, John   87
Heyward, Louis M.   49, 84
Hickman, Dwayne   66, 104
Hickox, Douglas   67
Higgens, John C.   122
Higgins, Colin   186
Hill, Dan   188
Hill, George Roy   194
Hill, James   36
Hill, Marianna   84, 188
Hill, Walter   111, 198
Hilliard, Richard L.   64
Hills, Gillian   17
Hilton-Jacobs, Lawrence   183, 200
Hines, Justin and the Dominoes   96
Hodge, Charlie   141
Hodges, Eddie   30
Hodges, Michael   184
Hoey, Michael A.   78, 110
Hoffman, David   167
Hoffman, Dustin   185
Holbrook, Hal   126
Holden, Jennifer   69
Holden, Michael   40
Hole, William J. Jnr   121
Hollies, The   68, 110
Hollman, Bridget
Holloway, Ann   122
Holloway, Freda   71
Holloway, Stanley   81
Holloway, Sterling   103
Holly, Buddy   12, 162, 179
Holston, Rand   183
Holt, Ednah   171
Holt, John   162
Holt, Liam   45
Hondells, The   15, 16, 104, 128
Honeycombs, The   160
Hooker, James   165
Hooker, John Lee   21, 23
Hooks, Kevin   194
Hooks, Robert   196
Hopper, Dennis   192, 196
Hordern, Michael   86
Horn, James R.   138
Hornaday, Jeffrey   111
Horne, Lena   128
Horton, Gaylon   23
Hot Streak   24
Hot Tuna   144
Hounds   193
House, Son   143
Houston, David   28
Houston, Thelma   114
Houston, Tony   190
Hovis, Larry   83
Howard, Clint   94
Howard, Jerry   126
Howard, Karl   180
Howard, Mel   91
Howard, Ronny   179, 189, 198
Howe, Steve   174
Howerd, Frankie   101

Howlin' Wolf   181
Hubley, Season   29, 35
Hudie, Norman   119
Huffaker, Clair   41
Hughes, Finola   110
Hughes, Fred   180
Hughes, Geoffrey   129
Hughes, Ken   179
Hulce, Thomas   180
Hulme, Kenneth   69
Hulsey, Patrick   96
Hunter, Ian   197
Hunter, Kaki   93
Hunter, Steve   97
Hurst, Veronica   78
Hurt, John   86
Hurt, Mississippi John   143
Hurt, Wesley Ivan   190
Hurt, William   180
Husky, Ferlin   80
Hussein, Waris   188
Hutchins, Will   30
Hutchinson, J.   197
Hutton, Brian   28
Huxley, Rick   182
Huxtable, Judy   196
Hyer, Martha   18
Hyland, Brian   115
Hyman, Phyllis   184

I-Roy   180
I-Threes, The   147
Ian, Janis   184
Ice T   24
Ingram, Luther   173
Inkpen, Ron   82
Inner Circle, The   96, 165
Inwood, Steve   110
Iovine, Jimmy   111
Ireland, John   126
Ireland, John A. Jr.   194
Isaacs, Gregory   96
Isenberg, Gerald I.   153
Isley Brothers, The   148, 198
Israel, Neil   14
It's Beautiful Day   144
Ivers, Robert   47
Ivey, Ron   187

Jabara, Paul   189
Jackie and Gayle   127, 128
Jackson, Joe   116
Jackson, Michael   128
Jackson, Mick   199
Jackson, Sammy   39
Jackson, Sherry   127
Jacksons, The   193
Jacobs, Jim   56
Jacobs, Seamon   67
Jacobson, Harvey   52
Jaffe, Nichole   121
Jagger, Dean   75, 197
Jagger, Mick   154, 171

INDEX OF NAMES

Jahan, Marin 42
James Gang, The 130
James, Elmore 23
James, Etta 136
James, Harry 18
James, Sally 82
James, Sidney 66
Jan and Dean 189
Janis, Conrad 27, 77
Janni, Joseph 190
Jardine, Al 179
Jarman, Derek 72, 73
Jarre, Maurice 120
Jarreau, Al 24
Jay and the Americans 127, 128
Jays, The 96
JB Pickers, The 197
Jefferson Airplane 110, 144, 145, 157, 183
Jeffreys, Garland 116
Jeffries, Fran 60
Jeffries, Lang 33
Jeffries, Lionel 66
Jenner, Bruce 27
Jensen, Karen 83
Jepson, Warner 185
Jergens, Diana 114
Jerizmy 147
Jessie, DeWayne 180
Jewison, Norman 72, 187
Jimmy Smith Trio, The 49
Jivin' Gene 194
Joel, Billy 184
Johansen, David 116
John Barry Seven, The 103
John Mayall's Original Blues Breakers 136
John, Dr 151
John, Elton 117, 143, 179, 184, 187, 194
Johnny and the Hurricanes 115
Johnny and the Tornadoes 48
Johns, Glyn 165, 188
Johnson, Don 130
Johnson, Jed 180
Johnson, L.A. 165
Johnson, Monica 14
Johnson, Nunnally 41
Johnson, Ralph 141
Johnson, Robin 116
Johnston, Bob 182
Johnston, Johnny 94
Johnstone, Bruce 49
Jones, Booker T. 107
Jones, Carolyn 75
Jones, Davy 61
Jones, Dean 69
Jones, Freddie 82, 105
Jones, Jack 73
Jones, James Earl 182, 190, 192
Jones, Jimmy 173
Jones, John Paul 53, 168
Jones, Kenny 165
Jones, Mick 99
Jones, Paul 87
Jones, Quincy 39, 128

Jones, Sam 184
Jones, Steve 147
Joplin, Janis 14, 148, 157, 183
Jordan, Christopher 126
Jordan, Louis 23
Jordanaires, The 19, 35, 46, 52, 69, 84, 99, 107
Joy, Ron 116
Joyce, Yootha 182
Julien, Max 88
Jumonville, Jerome 97
Junior, William 49
Junkin, John 59
Jurado, Katy 110
Justis, Bill 115

K.C. and the Sunshine Band 192
Kaegi, Adriana 155
Kaff, David 115
Kahn, John 195
Kahn, Ronald J. 36
Kale, Jim 147
Kaleidoscope 181, 200
Kalem, Toni 198
Kamon, Karen 42
Kane, Chris 133
Kanin, Garson 50
Kanner, Alexis 188
Kanter, Bob 128
Kanter, Hal 19, 80
Kantor, Lenard 71
Kaplan, Gabe 184
Kaplan, Jonathan 190, 197
Karlatos, Olga 91
Karloff, Boris 49
Karlson, Phil 75
Kasdan, Lawrence 180
Kass, Ron 136
Kastner, Peter 200
Kath, Terry 183
Katt, William 180
Katzman, Sam 33, 39, 48, 60, 64, 73, 76, 94, 121, 124, 191
Kaufman, Philip 198
Kaufman, Robert 104
Kay, Janet 180
Kaye, John 11
Kaye, Suzie 30, 67, 127
Kaylan, Howard 120
Kaylor, Robert 182
Keach, Stacy 187, 197
Keaton, Buster 66, 84
Keef 169
Keitel, Harvey 181, 188, 189, 198
Kellerman, Sally 184, 198
Kelly, Gene 129
Kelly, Paula 196
Keltner, Jim 156
Kendall, Suzy 197
Kennedy, Neil 73
Kennedy, Ray 84, 86
Kenny and the Wranglers 14
Kent, Robert E. 33, 39, 48, 94, 124
Kerby, Bill 97

Kern, Ronni 14
Kerr, Jacqueline 95
Kershaw, Doug 130, 156
Kestelman, Sarah 77
Keys, Bobby 156
Kid Creole and the Coconuts 155
Kiddus-I 96
Kilmer, Val 120
King, Albert 136, 173
King, Anthony 45
King, B.B. 156, 167, 184
King, Ben E. 198
King, Bernard 184
King, Carole 180
King, Evelyn 199
King, Mabel 128
King, Perry 180
King, Philip 101
King, Zalman 199
Kingdom Come 146
Kingsmen, The 66, 180
Kinnear, Roy 62
Kirby, Bruno 179
Kircher, Peter 169
Kirgo, George 107
Kirk, Tommy 28, 49, 67, 84, 198
Kirkwood, Gene 66
Kiss 76
Klane, Robert 114
Klein, Allen 81, 124, 138
Kleiser, Randal 56
Kline, Kevin 180
Klinger, Tony 150
Knickerbockers, The 83
Knight, Gladys 86, 199
Knight, Gladys and the Pips 86, 166, 167, 182
Knox, Buddy 71, 115, 179
Koch, Howard W. Jr. 66, 122
Koerner, Spider John 143
Komikoff, Sandy 156
Kongas, John 185
Kool and the Gang 192
Korman, Harvey 14
Korn, David 181
Kortchmar, Danny 197
Kotero, Apollonia 91
Kotto, Yaphet 181, 197
Kovack, Nancy 45
Kowalski, Lech 139
Kozmic Blues Band, The 148
Kraftwerk 24, 191
Kramer, Billy J. and the Dakotas 110, 160
Kramer, Larry 186
Kramer, Michael 190
Kramer, Stanley J. 191
Kranz, Steve 183
Kreitsek, Howard B. 114
Kristofferson, Kris 107, 182
Kruschen, Jack 42
Kurland, John 19
Kurtz, Gary 179

La Plano, Frederick 198

212

INDEX OF NAMES

Ladde, Diane 199
Lagond, Charles 155
Laine, Cleo 103
Laird, Trevor 180
Lake, Alan 41
Lamas, Lorenzo 23, 56
Lamb 144
Lampert, Zohra 64
Lancaster, Alan 169
Lanchester, Elsa 34, 84,
Land, Paul 66
Landers, Lew 65
Landis, John 21, 180
Landres, Paul 53
Landsburg, Valerie 114
Lane, Brian 174
Lane, Diane 111
Lane, Jocelyn 116
Lane, Ronnie 165, 188
Langdon, Sue Ann 45, 64, 99, 124
Lange, Hope 126
Lansbury, Angela 19
Lansbury, Edgar 54
Lansing, John 195
LaRosa, Julius 77
Larson, Jack 114, 130
Larson, Nicolette 159
Lathan, Stan 165
Lauber, Ken 182
Laurel, Allen 65
Lauren, Rod 130
Lauter, Ed 182
Laven, Arnold 30
Law, John Phillip 194
Lawler, Mike 137
Lawrence, Anthony 34, 84, 99
Lawrence, Douglas 78, 106, 110
Lawry, Kook 137
Le Gault, Lance 29
Le Mat, Paul 179, 189
Le Mesurier, John 31
Leach, Mike 35
Leach, Rosemary 115
Leacock, Richard 157
Leadbelly 91
Leander, Mark 87, 112
Leaves, The 30
Lebolt, David 140
Leckenby, Derek 64, 81
Led Zeppelin 168, 186
Lederer, Charles 42
Lederer, Richard 186
Lee, Carl 195
Lee, Christopher 17, 188
Lee, James 29
Lee, Johnny 183
Leewood, Jack 113
Leiber and Stoller 69
Leiberman, Leo 28
Leigh, Suzanne 84
Lembeck, Harvey 16, 18, 49, 66, 84
Lemon, Meadowlark 184
Lenno, Jay 12

Lennon, John 59, 62, 147, 152, 175
Lennon, Kip 39
Lenska, Rula 179
Lerman, Oscar 199
Lerner, Michael 183
Lerner, Murray 143
Leslie, Avril 103
Lester, Ketty 75
Lester, Mark 188
Lester, Richard 59, 62, 68
Levay, Sylvester 23
Levey, William A. 193, 194
Levin, Sid 153
Levin, Tony 83
Levis, Bob 185
Levis, Paul 185
Levy, Jules 30
Levy, Marcy 116
Lewis, Barbara 110
Lewis, Bobby 180
Lewis, Fiona 77
Lewis, Gary and the Playboys 83, 113
Lewis, Harvey 116
Lewis, J.P. 147
Lewis, Jerry Lee 12, 71, 115, 155, 194
Lewis, Linda 146
Lewis, Ray and the Trekkers 56
Lewis, Roger 193
Leyton, John 36, 68
Liberace 124, 125
Lieberson, Sandy 109, 115, 179, 187
Lieberson, Sanford 86, 146
Liebman, Ron 197
Lightfoot, Gordon 91
Lightnin' Hopkins 195
Lile, Bobby 34
Lilley, Joseph J. 19, 46, 52, 99
Lincoln, Abbey 50, 189
Lincoln, Junior 162
Lindfors, Viveca 198
Lindsay-Hogg, Michael 152
Linhart, Buzzie 58
Linn, Roberta 49
Linnear, Claudia 156
Linson, Art 11, 181, 199
Lipman, Maureen 197
Lipscomb, Dennis 197
Liston, Sonny 61
Lithgow, John 43
Little Caesar and the Romans 188
Little Eva 180
Little Feat 190
Little Milton 173
Little Nell 73, 96
Little Richard 12, 28, 33, 50, 51, 80, 94, 115, 153, 155
Little, Cleavon 183, 197
Litto, George 190
Lloyd Webber, Andrew 72
Lloyd, Charles 179, 188
Loach, Ken 190
Locke, Peter 199
Lockhart, Anne 187

Lockwood, Gary 67, 126, 191
Lockwood, Roy 71
Lodge, David 66, 182
Logan, Robert 15
Loggins, Kenny 43
Lokey, Ben 24
Lombardo, Lou 197
Loncraine, Richard 41
London Symphony Orchestra, The 179
London, Barbera 182
London, David 27
London, Julie 50, 51
London, Mark 87
London, Tony 196
Long and the Short, The 56
Longbranch Pennywhistle 197
Lopez, Trini 180
Loren, Donna 16, 18
Losey, Gavrik 180
Love Unlimited 196
Love, Darlene 66
Love, Donna 82
Love, Mike 179
Lovich, Lena 191
Lovin' Spoonful, The 83, 110, 135, 186, 198, 200
Lowe, Arthur 189
Lowe, Nick 14, 94, 196
Lowry, Hunt 120
Lubin, Arthur 64
Lucas, George 179
Lucas, William 33
Lukas, Paul 46
Lulu and the Luvvers 56
Luman, Bob 28
Lumet, Sidney 128
Lunn, Doug 24
Lydon, Johnny 146
Lyle, Adrian 42
Lyman, Joni 128
Lymon, Frankie and the Teenagers 80, 95, 115, 179
Lymon, Lewis and the Teenchords 71
Lyneh, Joe 82
Lynes, Adrian 184
Lyngstad-Frederiksson, Anni-Frid 130
Lynley, Carol 66
Lynne, Jeff 179
Lyon, Alice 64
Lyttleton, Humphrey 119

Maben, Adrian 160
Mabley, Moms 148
Mabry, Lynn 171
MacDonald, Country Joe 48
MacDonald, Philip 172
MacDonald, Ralph 23
MacGowran, Jack 199
Machat, Martin 136, 179
MacIntosh, Jay 102
Macmillan, Keith 136
MacNee, Patrick 115
Maddern, Victor 31
Madigan, Amy 111

213

INDEX OF NAMES

Madness 139, 172
Madura 183
Magic Michael 146
Magic, Eddie 155
Magnoli, Albert 91
Maguire, Charles 186
Maher, Fred 157
Maier, Sigrid 47
Main Ingredient 166, 167
Malcolm, David 14, 52, 127
Maleeva, Irina 197
Malin, Howard 72
Mallet, David 140
Malone, Cindy 127
Malone, Dorothy 16
Malone, Tom 23
Malstead, Jack 138
Mamas and the Papas, The 110, 157
Mandrill 198
Manduke, Joe 11
Manfred Mann 110, 191, 197
Manhattan Transfer 156
Mankiewicz, Tom 189
Mankowitz, Wolf 36
Mann, Barry 126, 187
Mansfield, Jayne 50
Mansfield, Mike 155
Marathon 114
Marcels, The 122, 183
March, Timothy 39
Marciano, Rocky 30
Mardin, Glenn 141
Margolis, Herbert 95
Mariachi Aguila 46
Mariachi Los Vaqueros 46
Marin, Cheech 197
Marini, Lou 23
Mark, Tamara 39
Marks, Guy 196
Marks, Harry 156
Marks, Harvey 192
Marley, Bob and the Wailers 136, 162, 165
Marquand, Richard 19
Marre, Jeremy 164
Marriot, Anthony 36
Marriott, Steve 14, 78, 189
Marsala, James 138
Marsden, Gerry 40
Marshall, Alan 38
Marshall, Dodie 34
Marshall, Ken 116
Marshall, Peter 113
Marson, Andy 133
Martha and the Vandellas 110, 183, 186, 189
Martin, Andy 71
Martin, Ansra 18
Martin, George 53, 59, 62, 101, 129
Martin, Strother 194, 197
Martinez, Tony 94
Marucci, Robert 66
Marvellettes, The 183, 188, 189
Marvin, Hank B. 36, 112, 128
Marx, Groucho 194

Masekela, Hugh 157
Mason, Dan 192
Mason, Dave 193
Mason, Marlyn 121
Mason, Nick 160
Masser, Mike 86
Massot, Joe 139, 168, 199
Matheson, Tim 180
Matlock, Glen 147
Matos, Jeri 36
Matthau, Walter 75
Mature, Victor 61
Maughan, Susan 124
Maurice, Bob 173
Maxwell, Jenny 19
Mayfield, Curtis 58, 106, 167, 182, 190, 193, 195
Maylam, Tony 199
Maysles, Albert 145, 157
Maysles, David 145
Maytals, The 60, 162
Maytones, The 96
Mazur, Mark 155
Mazursky, Paul 107, 181
MC5, The 94
McBain, Diane 107
McBride, Joseph 94
McCall, Mary C. 73
McCambridge, Mercedes 192
McCann, Henry 50
McCann, Les 168
McCartney, Linda 53
McCartney, Paul 53, 59, 62, 152, 164, 184
McClure, Doug 79
McClure, Marc 186
McCoo, Marilyn 193
McCormack, Kevin 116
McCowan, Alec 45
McCoy, Charlie 35
McCoys, The 189
McCrane, Paul 38
McCuller, Arnold 198
McDaniels, Gene 68, 130
McDermot, Galt 58
McDonald, Christopher 24
McDowall, Fred 143
McDowell, Malcolm 189, 190
McDowell, Roddy 30
McDowell, Ronnie 35
McGee, Jerry 107
McGee, Vonetta 181, 185, 193
McGhee, Brownie 143, 144
McGoohan, Patrick 29
McGrath, Joseph 187
McGuinn, Roger 91
McGuire, Barry 110, 176
McIntire, John 103
McIntire, Tim 12
McKean, Michael 115
McKee, Lonette 106
McKenna, Stephen 19
McKensie, Scott 157
McKern, Leo 62
McLaren, Malcolm 146, 147

McLean, Don 185
McMurray, Sam 39
McNair, Barbara 29
McPhatter, Clyde 80
McQuade, Terry 99
McVie, John 139
McWilliams, David 185
Meadows, Jayne 30
Meatloaf 93, 96
Medford, Kay 71, 122
Medlin, Big Boy 93
Medwin, Michael 67, 69, 189
Meehan, Tony 75, 112, 128
Meek, Joe 78
Meisner, Randy 184
Mel and Tim 173
Melanie 146, 191
Melcher, Terry 79
Mellowmen, The 84
Melly, George 194
Melodians, The 68
Mendelsohn, Jack 129
Mendham, Mary 58
Mercury, Eric 180
Meredith, Burgess 110, 194
Merseybeats, The 191
Mersh Brother, The 198
Metton, Barry 48
Meyerson, Alan 195
MFSB 192
Michael, Gertrude 121
Middleton, Robert 79
Midler, Bette 97, 140
Mighty Diamonds, The 165
Mihasi, Tatsuta 198
Mikell, George 33
Miles, Buddy 196
Milius, John 180
Millaney, Scott 136
Miller, Barry 192
Miller, Dick 28
Miller, Jacob 96
Miller, Jacob and Inner Circle 147
Miller, Jody 113
Miller, Kenny 112
Miller, Kick 93
Miller, Mrs 30
Miller, Roger 135
Miller, Sid 48
Miller, Walter 65
Milligan, Spike 188
Millington, Mary 147
Mills Brothers, The 18
Mills, Freddie 103
Mills, Hayley 184
Mills, John 184
Mimieux, Yvette 86
Mineo, Sal 95
Mingay, David 99
Minoff, Lee 129
Mislowe, Michael 14
Mitchell, Joni 137, 151
Mobley, Mary Ann 48, 60

214

INDEX OF NAMES

Money, Eddie 14
Monkees, The 61
Monotones, The 115, 179
Montez, Chris 180
Montez, Maria 62
Montgomery, Patrick 162
Monty's Band 97
Moody, Ron 36
Moon, Keith 115, 117, 150, 179, 191
Moonglows, The 12, 80, 95
Moore, Del 28
Moore, Eulabelle 65
Moore, Joanna 42
Moore, Mary Tyler 29
Moore, Michael 39, 84
Moore, Terry 86
Morali, Jacques 27
Moran, Mike 120
Moranis, Rick 111
More, Kenneth 105
Morgan, Patrick 191
Morley, Robert 40, 130
Moroder, Giorgio 42
Morris, Garrett 181, 183
Morris, Russell 161
Morrison, Dorothy 137
Morrison, Van 151
Morrow, Jo 73
Morrow, Patricia 112
Morrow, Vic 75, 181
Morse, Robin 93
Morton, Arthur 113
Moses, Gilbert 184
Mosk, Tom 168
Mother Earth 162
Mothers of Invention, The 188
Mount, Peggy 40
Mountain 197
Moving Pictures 43
Moyle, Alan 116
Mud 82
Muldaur, Maria 185, 195
Mull, Martin 183
Mullaney, Jack 116
Mullard, Arthur 31, 68
Munich Machine 184
Munson, Art 107
Murphy, Karen 115
Murphy, Matt 34
Murphy, Roger 157
Murphy, Walter 192
Murray, Bill 199
Murray, Pete 103
Murvin, Junior 96, 165
Mutrux, Floyd 11, 186
Myrick, Don 141
Mystics, The 12

Nadel, Arthur H. 30
Nakano, Desmond 23
Nash, Graham 159
Nashville Teens, The 14, 160
Naughton, Bill 179

Neal, Peter 145, 174
Neeley, Ted 72
Nelson, Ed 28
Nelson, Gene 30, 60, 76
Nelson, Lori 122
Nelson, Sandy 127
Nelson, Tracy 134
Nelson, Willie 91
Nesmith, Michael 61
New Establishment 185
New York City Band, The 195
New York Rock'n'Roll Ensemble, The 130
Newall, Norman 67
Newborn, Ira 21
Newborn, Phineas III 24
Newbrook, Peter 56
Newley, Anthony 66
Newman, Barry 197
Newman, Laraine 12
Newman, Paul 194
Newman, Phyllis 77
Newman, Randy 79
Newman, Scott 185
Newman, Susan Kendell 186
Newman, Thunderclap 188, 195
Newton-John, Olivia 56, 129
Nicastro, Michelle 23
Nichol, Alex 186
Nicholas, Denise 190
Nicholas, Paul 71, 77, 101, 102, 117, 199
Nichols, Mike 185
Nichols, Nichelle 197
Nichols, Peter 182
Nicholson, Jack 61, 88, 117
Nicholson, James H. 15, 16, 18, 49, 66, 82, 83, 103, 126
Night 81
Nightingale, Maxine 194
Nightriders, The 192
Nightshades, The 14
Nilsson, Harry 105, 190, 193
99½ 24
Nirvana 196
Nitty Gritty Dirt Band, The 134, 182
Nitzsche, Jack 181, 198
Noel, Chris 15, 127
Nolan, Tom 182
Noonan, Tommy 113
Noone, Peter 64, 81, 82
Nooney Rickett Four, The 84, 128
North, Alex 182
North, Sheree 121
Norton, Bill L. 182, 189
Nosseck, Noel 200
Nouri, Michael 42
Numan, Gary 116, 145
Nunn, Terri 114
Nurradin, Ahmad 196
Nutmegs, The 188

O'Brien, Edmond 50, 103
O'Brien, Joan 48, 67
O'Brien, Lois 80

O'Brien, Richard 96
O'Connell, Arthur 42, 76
O'Connell, Jack 162
O'Conner, Glynnis 181
O'Connor, Hazel 25
O'Curran, Charles 19, 46, 47, 52, 75
O'Dell, Bryan 200
O'Dell, Denis 187
O'Donovan, Danny 163
O'Hara, Quinn 113
O'Horgan, Tom 101
O'Jays, The 166, 167
O'Neal, Ron 181, 195
O'Neal, Ryan 185
O'Rahilly, Ronan 185
O'Steen, Sam 106
O'Sullivan, Richard 130
Oakland, Simon 42
Oates, John 163
Oblong, Harold 84, 86
Odets, Clifford 126
Ogden, Bobby 35
Olen, Johnny 50, 51
Olivier, Laurence 71
Ollie and Jerry 24
Only Ones, The 196
Ono, Yoko 147, 175
Ontkean, Michael 194
Orbison, Roy 39, 93
Originals, The 114
Orlons, The 191
Orneals, Willie 138
Osibisa 195
Ossman, David 130
Otis, Clark 12
Otis, Johnny 12, 73
Outlaws, The 78, 184
Ove, Horace 162
Owen, Alun 59
Owen, Wilfred 36
Owens, Charles 107

P.K. Limited 185
Pacemakers, The 40
Page, Gene 196
Page, Geraldine 200
Page, Jimmy 165, 168
Page, Pamela 162
Paget, Debra 79
Paley Brothers, The 94
Palillo, Ron 193
Palk, Anna 87
Palmer, Tony 136
Paluzzi, Luciana 82
Pape, Paul 192
Paramour, Norrie 40, 128
Pare, Michael 111
Parfitt, Rick 169
Paris Sisters, The 68, 115
Parker, Alan 38, 188
Parker, Charles 23
Parker, Chris 195
Parker, Col. Tom 34, 35, 46, 52, 69, 99

INDEX OF NAMES

Parker, Graham 180
Parker, Ray Jr. 188
Parks, Gordon 192, 193, 195
Parkyn, Leslie 87
Parnell, R.J. 115
Parnes, Larry 69
Parrish, Julie 128
Parsons, Clive 25, 196
Parsons, Lindsley 56
Pasternak, Joe 51, 107
Pastine, Robert 71
Pate, Johnny 193
Patrick, Lory 112
Patten, Luana 95
Patterson, Lee 55
Patton, Bart 14, 83, 127
Paul and Paula 180, 194
Paul and the Pack 34
Paul Butterfield Blues Band, The 143
Paul, Alan 156
Paul, Stefan 162
Paul, Terry 107
Payton, Dennis 182
Peach, Mary 23
Pearson, Michael 171
Peerce, Larry 135
Pendergrass, Teddy 93
Penn, Arthur 11
Penn, Christopher 43
Pennebaker, D.A. 140, 157
Peploe, Mark 86
Percival, Lance 67, 81
Perez, Jose 193
Perkins, Carl 71, 149
Perkins, Millie 126
Perren, Freddie 183
Perrine, Valerie 27
Perry, Frank 187
Perry, Lee and the Upsetters 96
Persky, Lester 58
Peter and Gordon 160
Peter Paul and Mary 143
Peters Brock 194
Peters, Jon 107
Peters, Laurie 112
Peterson, Garry 147
Peterson, Gil 30
Peterson, Robert 17
Petit, Chris 191
Petty, Tom and the Heartbreakers 183, 188
Peyser, Arnold 121
Peyser, Lois 121
Pfeiffer, Carolyn 93
Phillips, Conrad 33
Phillips, Mackensie 189
Phillips, Michelle 181
Phillips, Phil 194
Phillips, Sam 34
Phillips, Simon 165
Phoenix Horns, The 141
Pickett, Lanny 140
Pickett, Robert (Bobby 'Boris') 67
Pickett, Wilson 168, 186

Pickles, Vivian 186
Pierce, Maggie 39
Pierson, Frank 107
Pike, Rex 143
Pims, Suzi 73
Pine, Robert 83
Pink Floyd 160, 173, 200
Pitchford, Dean 38, 43
Pitts, Zazu 114
Place, Mary Kay 180
Planotones, The 12
Plant, Robert 168
Plastic Ono Band, The 147
Platters, The 28, 50, 51, 93, 94, 115, 179, 194
Player 184
Pleasance, Donald 81, 86, 101, 102
Pointer Sisters, The 182
Poirier, Cheryl 155
Poitier, Sidney 39, 181, 190
Polan, Amy 137
Ponitails, The 115
Ponti, Carlo 200
Poole, Brian and the Tremeloes 75
Pop, Iggy 139
Porter, Don 78
Posta, Adrienne 186
Potenza, Anthony 159
Powell, Jimmy 75
Powell, Richard 42
Powell, Robert 117
Preminger, Otto 193
Prentiss, Paula 43
Presley, Elvis 19, 29, 30, 34, 41, 42, 45–47, 51, 52, 60, 67, 69, 75, 76, 78–80, 84, 99, 106, 107, 110, 116, 121, 123, 126, 141, 143, 162, 163
Presnell, Harve 124, 125
Pressman, Edward R. 84
Pressman, Lawrence 193
Preston, Billy 102, 138, 152, 184, 189
Preston, Don 156
Preston, Johnny 115, 194
Pretenders, The 116
Pretty Things, The 81
Previn, Andre 72
Price, Alan 179, 189
Price, Dennis 87, 105
Price, Jim 156
Price, Jonathan 25
Price, Lloyd 115
Price, Vincent 34, 81, 121
Price, Will 95
Priest, Pat 34
Prima, Louis 121
Prince 91
Procol Harum 110
Proctor, Phil 130
Proferes, Nick 157
Prophet, Michael 180
Prowse, Juliet 47
Pryor, Richard 126, 128, 181
Puppa, Piccola 49
Purcell, Lee 179
Pursey, Jimmy 99

PUSH Choir, The 166, 167
Puttnam, David 89, 109, 115, 146, 184, 187, 188
Pyramids, The 18, 162

Quaid, Randy 184
Quale, Anna 59
Quarrier, Ian 171
Quatro, Suzi 116
Quayle, Anthony 101
Queen 184
? and the Mysterians 189
Quickly, Tommy 160
Quicksilver Messenger Service 144, 162, 181
Quiet Riot 43
Quine, Robert 157
Quinn, Anthony 191
Quinn, Bernie 36
Quinn, Pat 11, 130
Quinones, Adolfo 24
Quintessence 146
Quo, Beulah 52

Rabal, Francisco 194
Rachmil, Lewis J. 43
Radle, Carl 156
Radnitz, Robert B. 194
Rado, James 58
Raelettes, The 23
Rafelson, Bob 61
Rafkin, Alan 104
Ragni, Gerome 58
Rain 19
Raines, Cristina 193
Raitt, Bonnie 159, 183
Rakow, Ron 146
Ramone, Joey 42
Ramone, Phil 23
Ramones, The 94, 116, 190, 196
Ramsey Lewis Trio, The 166, 167
Randall, Frankie 127
Randazzo, Teddy 64, 80, 95
Rankin, Dugald 179
Ransohoff, Martin 14, 198
Rash, Maggie 27
Rash, Steve 27
Rathbone, Basil 49
Raven, Genya 198
Ray, Aldo 191
Ray, Annita 103
Ray, Gene Anthony 38
Ray, Nicholas 58
Re-Flex 24
Red Mountain Jug Band, The 195
Redding, Otis 157, 161
Redgrave, Lynn 194
Redman, Roy 196
Redmond, Jack 107
Reed, Jerry 197
Reed, Lou 83, 116, 157, 187
Reed, Oliver 117
Reese, Della 77
Reflections, The 128
Regas, Jack 84

INDEX OF NAMES

Reichenbach, Francois 156
Reichert, Mark 197
Reid, Terry 146
Reiner, Rob 115
Reizner, Lou 179
Remar, James 198
Reno, Mike 43
Renzetti, Joe 27, 34
REO Speedwagon 183
Revolution, The 91
Rey, Alejandro 46
Reynolds, William 18
Rhodes, Cynthia 110
Rhodes, Leah 56
Rhodes, Marjorie 184
Rhone, Trevor 59
Rhythm Nation 23
Rice, Tim 72
Rich Kids 139
Rich, John 34, 99
Richard, Cliff 36, 40, 101, 112, 122, 128–130, 136, 195
Richard, Keith 154, 171
Richard, Marilyn 196
Richards, Allen 192
Richardson, Ralph 53, 189
Riche, Alan 200
Richman, Jonathan and the Modern Lovers 197
Richmond, Ted 67
Richwine, Maria 27
Rickles, Don 18
Ridge, Sam 185
Riegert, Peter 180
Righteous Brothers, The 15, 110, 113
Riley, Jeannine 183
Rip Chords, The 113
Ritchie Family, The 27
Ritchie, Michael 140
Ritt, Martin 194
Ritter, John 14
Rivers, Johnny 183
Roarke, Adam 88, 192
Roarke, Mickey 192
Robbins, Harold 75
Robbins, Tony 185
Roben, Joseph 187
Roberts, Kim 78
Roberts, Rachel 189
Robertson, Annette 130
Robertson, B.A. 81
Robertson, Lee 155
Robertson, Robbie 151
Robin, Dany 43
Robins, Jessie 80
Robinson, Baxter 23
Robinson, Dave 172
Robinson, Jay 196
Robinson, Matt 165
Robinson, Smokey and the Miracles 180, 183, 188, 189, 198
Robinson, Tom 167
Rocca and His Saints 71
Rockers All Stars, The 96
Rockin' Berries, The 160

Rod McKuen Group, The 95
Roddam, Franc 190
Rodgers, Jimmie 115
Roe, Tommy 110
Roeg, Nicholas 75
Roemer, Michael 189
Rogers, Buddy 65
Rogers, Jaime 24
Rogers, Peter 119
Rojas, Carmine 140
Roland, Cherry 75
Rolling Stones, The 145, 150, 154, 161, 171, 183, 188
Romain, Yvonne 34
Roman, Leticia 47
Romero, Alex 30, 34
Romm, Harry 64
Ronettes, The 135, 191
Rondeau, Charles 196
Ronstadt, Linda 183, 184
Ronney, Mickey 66, 86
Rosco 41, 176
Rose Band, The 97
Rose Royce 182
Rose, Alex 180, 186
Rose, Si 67
Rosenberg, Max J. 71
Rosenbloom, Richard 29
Rosenman, Howard 106
Ross, Diana 114, 128
Ross, Herbert 43
Ross, Katherine 185
Ross, Ted 128
Rossi, Francis 169
Rossington, Norman 59
Rosso, Franco 180
Roth, Joe 14
Rothchild, Paul 97
Rothman, Stephanie 67
Roundtree 96
Roundtree, Richard 193
Routers, The 113
Rowe, Annie 133
Rowland, Betty 199
Rowlands, Patsy 33
Roxy Music 116
Royal Philharmonic Orchestra 179
Royal, Teens, The 77
Royal, Billy Joe 189
Royce, Earl and the Olympics 40
Royle, Derek 80
Rubel, Marc Reid 129
Rubenstein, John 130
Rubettes, The 82
Rubin, Alan 23
Rubin, Andrew 195
Ruby and the Romantics 189
Rudolph, Alan 93, 198
Rudolph, Oscar 33, 121
Ruffalo, Joseph 91
Ruffin, Jimmy 110
Rufus 24
Rumour 191

Runacre, Jenny 73
Rundgren, Tod 94
Rush, Richard 88, 185
Rushton, William 67
Rusoff, Lou 16, 49, 65, 103
Russell, Bing 35
Russell, John 122
Russell, Ken 77, 117
Russell, Kurt 35
Russell, Leon 138, 156
Russell, Nipsey 128
Russo, Aaron 97
Ruts, The 116
Ryan, Deborah 76
Ryan, Mitchell 183
Ryan, Peter 161
Rydell, Bobby 17
Rydell, Mark 97

Saad, Sue and the Next 93
Sachson, Monroe 194
Sacks, Ezra 183
Sadler, Barry 189
Sagal, Boris 51
Sahm, Doug 189
Sailcat 185
Sainte-Marie, Buffy 143, 144, 195
Salamanca, J.R. 126
Salter, Hans J. 42
Sam and Dave 23, 83
Sam the Sham and the Pharaohs 124, 125, 189
Sampson, Annie 195
Sand, Paul 27
Sandals, The 183
Sanders, George 56
Sands, Diana 187
Sands, Jodie 71
Sands, Tommy 103
Santana 144, 168, 174
Santee, Clark 157
Saperstein, Henry G. 198
Sarafian, Richard C. 197
Sarandon, Susan 96
Sarasohn, Lane 58
Sargent, Joseph 182
Sargent, Laurie 111
Sarne, Mike 36
Sartain, Gailard 27, 93
Satterfield, Louis 141
Saunders, Denis 143, 168
Saunders, Fernando 157, 165
Saunders, Mark 137
Saunders, Merle 195
Savage, John 58, 195
Savile, Jimmy 40, 75
Saxon, John 95
Sayer, Leo 179, 194
Scaduto, Sam ('The Sham') 39
Scaggs, Boz 144, 184
Scaife, Gerald 23
Scales, Steve 171
Scardino, Don 186
Scarwid, Diane 192

217

INDEX OF NAMES

Schechtman, Jeffrey 23
Scheff, Jerry 141
Scheider, Roy 194
Schenck, Aubrey 122
Schlossberg, Julian 159
Schneider, Bert 61
Schneider, Ronald 145
Schott, Peter 155
Schrader, Paul 181
Schulman, Ivy 95
Schultz, Gloria 141
Schultz, Michael 101, 140, 141, 181, 183
Schumaker, Joel 106, 128
Schwalb, Ben 116
Schwalm, Thomas 167
Schwary, Ronald L. 154
Schwarz, Lew 31
Schwarz, Stephen 54
Schweitzer, S.S. 29
Scorcese, Martin 151, 188
Scott, Jimmy 133
Scott, John 64
Scott, Linda 33
Scott, Linda Gaye 192
Scott, Lizabeth 80
Scott, Terry 56
Scott, Tom 14, 39
Scott-Heron, Gil 159
Scotty 60
Scoular, Angela 186
Sears, Fred F. 33, 94
Sebastian, John 137, 174, 193, 200
Second Time 126
Sedaka, Neil 110, 187
Seeds, The 89
Seeger, Pete 11
Segal, Erich 129
Segarini and Bishop 197
Seger, Bob 14, 184
Selector 139
Sellars, Dale 35
Sellers, Pete 186, 188
Sembello, Cruz 23
Sembello, Michael 42
Senators, The 126
Severson, John 190
Sex Pistols, The 139, 147
Sha-Na-Na 56, 174
Shabba-Doo 24
Shadows, The 28, 38, 40, 112, 128–130
Shaffer, Paul 115
Shah, Krishna 191
Shakey, Bernard 149, 165
Shalamar 43
Shamberg, Michael 180
Shankar, Ravi 138, 157
Shannon, Del 68, 110, 115, 179
Shannon, Johnny 41
Shapiro, Helen 68, 87
Shapiro, Ken 58
Shargo, Becky 43
Sharif, Omar 121, 185
Sharkey, Ray 23, 66

Sharman, Jim 96
Sharp, Dee Dee 33
Sharp, Don 55, 67
Sharp, Mike 189
Sharp, Ray 115
Shaughnessy, Alfred 103
Shaughnessy, Mickey 30, 69
Shaw, Larry 173
Shaw, Victoria 17
Shear, Barry 126
Shearer, Harry 115
Shearing, George 18
Shelyne, Carole 83
Shenson, Walter 59, 62
Shepard, Sam 91
Shields, Brooke 116
Shigeta, James 84
Shipley, Julie 196
Shire, David 184, 192
Shirelles, The 153, 198
Shirley and Lee 153
Sholem, Lee 28
Shore, Sig 193, 195
Shrew, Bobby 107
Shrimpton, Jean 87
Shuken, Philip 106
Shullman, Irving 30
Sidney, George 123
Siegel, Don 41, 65
Siegel, Janis 156
Siepe, Ralph 80
Siberg, Joel 23
Silhouettes, The 179
Silva, Victy 25, 193
Silver, Joan Micklin 180
Silver, Joel 111
Silver, Raphael D. 180
Silver, Tracy 39
Silvers, Phil 182
Simmons, Gene 76
Simms, Frank and George 140
Simon and Garfunkel 183, 185, 189
Simon, Carly 159
Simon, Francis 182
Simon, John 176, 187
Simon, Paul 83
Simonds, Kathy 196
Simonon, Paul 99
Simpson, Don 42
Sims, Nelson 196
Sims, Sylvia 36
Sinatra Nancy 48, 49, 106, 199
Sinclair, John 115
Singer, Lori 43
Siouxsie and the Banshees 73
Six, Eva 16
Skeleton Dancers 23
Sky Oats 190
Skyliners, The 179
Skynyrd, Lynyrd 181
Slade 41
Slate, Jeremy 52
Sledge, Percy 189

Slezak, Walter 128
Slick 82
Slick, Earl 140
Slickers, The 60, 99
Sloopys, The 34
Sly and the Family Stone 174
Small Faces, The 33, 161, 173
Small, Charlie 128
Small, Edward 45
Small, Henry 181
Smash, Chas 172
Smight, Jack 184
Smith, Charles Martin 27, 179
Smith, Dawn 106
Smith, G.E. 163
Smith, Greg 82
Smith, Herbert 103, 119
Smith, Jack 62
Smith, Mike 182
Smith, O.C. 193
Smith, Patti 116, 196
Smith, Preacher and the Deacons 94
Smith, Robert 51, 86
Smith, William D. 138
Soles, P.J. 94
Solow, Herbert F. 143
Sonny and Cher 56, 127
Sonny Stewart Skiffle Group, The 55
Sorels, The 111
Soul Sisters, The 99
Sounds Incorporated 68, 75, 78, 160
Souther, J.D. 183
Southside Johnny and the Asbury Jukes 180
Spalding, Harry 112, 127, 130
Spaniels, The 12, 179
Spann, Dave 155
Spano, Vincent 190, 192
Sparks, Randy 30
Sparr, Robert 113
Specials, The 139
Spector, Phil 135, 138
Spedding Chris 53
Speechley, David 146
Spencer Davis Group, The 161, 186
Spencer, Norman 197
Spencer, Vicki 114, 122
Spielberg, Steven 186
Spinetti, Victor 59, 62, 80
Spoelstra, Mark 183
Sporup, Murray Douglas 94
Spotniks, The 75
Springfield, Buffalo 150, 183, 186
Springfields, The 68, 75
Springsteen, Bruce 159
Spungen, Nancy 147
Squire, Chris 174
Sroka Jerry 54
St Jacques, Raymond 197
St John, Barry 185
St John, Helen 42
St John, Louis 56
Stacy, James 113, 128
Stafford, Terry 34

218

INDEX OF NAMES

Stainton, Chris 156, 165
Stallone, Frank 110
Stallone, Sylvester 110
Stamp, Terence 190
Stamps Quartet, The 141
Standells, The 49, 191
Stanley, Paul 76
Stanshall, Viv 115
Stanton, Harry Dean 91, 97, 182
Stanwyck, Barbara 99
Staple Singers, The 143, 144, 168, 173, 187
Staples, Mavis 190
Stargard 102
Starlighters, The 64, 122
Starr, Edwin 199
Starr, June 30
Starr, Ringo 53, 59, 105, 115, 137, 138, 151, 152
Stathakis, Jonathan 136, 137
Status Quo 169, 179
Steagall, Red 197
Steel, John 41
Steele, Mary 55
Steele, Tommy 67, 119, 136
Steely Dan 184
Stein, Chris 197
Stein, Jeff 150
Steinberg, Diane 102
Stellman, Martin 180
Steppenwolf 183, 189
Sternberg, Scott 138
Steve Miller Band, The 162, 181, 184, 186, 190
Stevens, Cat 110, 186
Stevens, Stella 52
Stewart, David J. 28
Stewart, Eric 53
Stewart, Martin 133
Stewart, Paul 75
Stewart, Rod 179
Stewart, Sandy 53
Stigwood, Robert 56, 72, 101, 110, 117, 188, 192
Sting 191
Stockwell, Dean 88
Stokes, Simon and the Nighthawks 190
Stona, Winston 59
Stone, Harold J. 51
Stone, Jeffrey 18
Stoneground 156
Stoner, Rob 91
Storm, Gale 162
Stormy Tempest 115
Storybook, The 89
Strasberg, Susan 88, 196
Strawberry Alarm Clock 89, 186, 189
Stray Cats, The 109
Streisand, Barbra 107
Stromberg, Gary 181
Strong, Barrett 180, 183
Stroud, Don 27, 194
Strummer, Joe 99
Stuart, Mel 173
Stubbs, Una 112, 128
Styx 93
Subotsky, Milton 68, 71, 73

Suggs 172
Sullivan, Tim 192
Summer, Donna 42, 114, 184
Summers, Jeremy 33, 39
Summers, Joanie 79
Supremes, The 15, 110, 183, 189, 191
Surfaris, The 79, 186, 198
Sutch, Screaming Lord 155
Sutherland, Donald 195
Sutton, Grady 84
Swartz, Charles S. 67
Sweet Inspirations, The 66, 141, 143
Swimmer, Saul 81, 138
Swinging Medallions, The 189
Sylvers, The 184
Sylvester, Harold 184
Syreeta 114, 184

Tai Mahal 181, 194
Talking Heads 116, 171
Tamblyn, Russ 43, 192
Tams, The 189
Tamu 182
Tanaguchi, Senkichi 198
Tangerine Dream 194
Tannen, Michael 83
Taplan, Jonathan 188
Tashlin, Frank 50
Taupin, Bernie 185
Taurog, Norman 19, 34, 47, 52, 67, 78, 106, 107, 116
Tavares 192, 199
Tavel, Ronnie 62
Taylor, Andre 56
Taylor, Beloyd 141
Taylor, James 159, 184
Taylor, Johnny 173
Taylor, Kent 192
Taylor, Mick 136
Taylor, Vaughn 69
Taylor, Wilda 64
Taylor-Corbett, Lynn 43
Tebelak, John-Michael 54
Tee, Richard 83
Temple, Julian 146
Tempo, Nino 50, 51, 66
Tempos, The 179
Temptations, The 166, 167, 180, 183
10 CC 188
Ten Years After 174
Tenney, Del 64
Terrell, Tammi 189
Terry and the Idiots 139
Terry Kennedy Group, The 55
Terry, Sonny 143, 144, 182
Tewksbury, Peter 110, 121
Tharp, Twyla 58
Thigpen, Lynne 54
Third World 162, 199
13th Power 126
Thom, Robert 126
Thomas, Carla 173
Thomas, Jeremy 146

Thomas, Philip Michael 106
Thomas, Richard 187
Thomas, Rufus 173
Thompson, Lee 172
Thompson, Tony 140
Thornton, Big Mama 163, 197
Thornton, Frank 56
Thorpe, Richard 43, 46, 69
Three Chuckles, The 95, 69
Three Degrees, The 199
Three Dog Night 180
Tidyman, Ernest 193
Tiffin, Pamela 79
Tiger, J.G. 94
Till, Sonny and the Orioles 179
Tillotson, Johnny 75, 115
Tilton, Alix 94
Time, The 91
Timmy and the Tangerines 12
Tiny Tim 176
Tisch, Steve 183
Tobin, Thomas J. 185
Todd, Diane 103
Toguri, David 53
Toler, Dan 137
Toler, David 137
Tomlin, Lily 188
Toots and the Maytals 165
Tork, Peter 61
Torme, Mel 51
Torn, Rip 83, 200
Tornados, The 75
Torres, Liz 199
Tosh, Peter 96, 147, 162
Towers, Constande 39
Townes, Carol Lynn 24
Townsend, Jill 179
Townsend, Leo 16, 18, 66
Townshend, Pete 117, 119, 150, 167, 188, 191
Townshend, Simon 117
Toys, The 67
Traffic 146, 186
Tramm, Peter 43
Trammps, The 192
Travolta, Joey 195
Travolta, John 56, 110, 188, 192
Tremaine, Jerry 133
Treniers, The 33, 50, 51, 73
Trent, John 186
Tristan, Dorothy 181
Troles, The 56
Trosper, Guy 69
Trucks, Butch 137
Tu, Vicky 67
Tubes, The 129
Tubingen, Kino Aresenal 162
Tucker, Little Junior 147
Tucker, Melville 190
Tudor, Tenpole 147
Turbans, The 12
Turman, Glynn 183, 192
Turman, Lawrence 185
Turner, Ike and Tina 135, 145, 148, 168, 181

219

INDEX OF NAMES

Turner, Joe 103, 162, 163
Turner, Tina 117, 119, 138, 179
Turtles, The 83
Tushingham, Rita 194
Tutt, Ronnie 141
Twice As Much 173
Twilley, Dwight 23
Twitty, Conway 30, 86
Tyler, Bonnie 43, 199
Tyler, Judy 69
Tyler, Leon 50
Tynant, H.M. 67
Tyrell, Susan 29, 180
Tyrones, The 77
Tyson, Cicely 192, 194

U. Roy 147
UB40 81
Ulius, Betty 88
Ullman, Elwood 49, 116
Ullman, Tracey 53
Ulvaeus, Agnetha 130
Ulvaeus, Bjorn 133
Underhill, Frederic 150
Underwood, Mark 97
Usher, Gary 16, 52
Utley, Mike 107

Vacqueros, The 56
Valens, Ritchie 12, 53, 163
Valentino, Sal 156
Vallee, Rudy 78
Valli, Frankie 56
Van Doren, Mamie 30, 51, 122, 123
Van Fleet, Jo 186
Van Halen 190
Van Patten, Joyce 121, 186
Van Patten, Vince 94
Vance, Kenny 11, 199
Vance, Tommy 41
Vane, Thaddeus 81
Vanilla Fudge 161
Varhol, Michael C. 134
Varsi, Diane 126
Vashti 173
Vastano, Johnny 198
Vee, Bobby 30, 75, 87, 113, 115
Vegas, Pat and Lolly 67
Veitch, John Patrick 39
Velvet Underground, The 62, 94
Venet, Nik 49, 52
Ventura, Michael 93
Vereen, Ben 48
Vernon, Cherry 75
Vernon, John 180
Vernon, Richard 75
Verona, Steven 86
Vicious, Sid 147
Vidal, Maria 23
Viewers, The 81
Vigran, Herb 53
Village People, The 27, 28, 114
Vincent, Gene 65, 68, 78, 136

Vincent, Gene and His Blue Caps 50, 51, 65
Vincent, Jan-Michael 180
Vinton, Bobby 112, 113, 189
Visconti, Tony 25
Visitors, The 199
Vitte, Ray 114
Voices of East Harlem 167, 168
Voight, Jon 183
Volman, Mark 120
Volumes, The 198
Von Sydow, Max 184
Voorman, Klaus 138

Wachtel, Waddy 197
Wadleigh, Michael 173
Wadsworth, Derek 179
Wagner, Jane 188
Wagner, Robin 101
Wagoner, Lyle 28
Wahl, Ken 198
Wailer, Bunny 96
Waite, Ralph 196
Waites, Thomas 198
Wakeman, Rick 77, 174
Wald, Jerry 65, 125
Waldman, Ann 91
Walker Brothers, The 15
Walker, Jimmy 197
Walker, Junior and the All Stars 183
Walker, Nancy 27
Walker, Robert Jr 192
Wallace, Anthony 52
Wallace, Eugene 115
Wallace, Leroy 96
Wallace, Sippie 136
Walley, Deborah 49, 67, 104, 107
Wallis, Hal 19, 34, 46, 47, 52, 75, 80, 84, 99
Walters, Nancy 19
Walsh, Joe 184, 198
Walston, Ray 190
War 192, 200
Ware, Clyde 28
Warhol, Andy 62, 180
Warren, George 40
Warren, Mike 184
Washbourne, Mona 81
Washington, Dinah 194
Waterman, Dennis 197
Waters, Muddy 143, 151, 163
Waters, Roger 160
Waterson, Sam 188
Watkins, Peter 87
Watling, Debbie 195
Watson, Debby 30
Watson, Doc and Merle 134
Watson, Jimmy 56
Watt, Michael 147
Wattis, Richard 87
Watts, Charlie 154, 165, 171
Wayne, Jeff 180, 187
We Five, The 189
Weatherford, Pat 136
Weaver, Blue 116

Weaver, Mick 196
Webb, Peter 53
Webb, Robert D. 79
Weil, Cynthia 126
Wein, Chuck 162
Weinrib, Lennie 14, 83, 127
Weintraub, Fred 197
Weir, Alex 171
Weis, Don 49, 83
Weis, Gary 149
Weisbart, David 41, 42, 79
Weiss, Allan 34, 46, 52, 84, 99
Weiss, Danny 97
Weiss, Robert K. 21
Welch, Bob 184
Welch, Bruce 112, 128
Welch, Lenny 189
Welch, Lester 121
Welch, Raquel 113, 188
Weld, Tuesday 17, 95, 126
Weller, Michael 58
Wellman Jnr., William 107, 113, 128
Wells, Junior 136
Wells, Mary 28, 189
Wesley, Fred 181, 194
Wesley, Richard 39
West, Bryan 190
West, Keith and Tomorrow 194
West, Martin 52, 113
Westmorland, Kathy 141
Weston, Kim 173
Westwood, Patrick 119
Wexler, Haskell 188
Wexler, Norman 110
Weymouth, Tina 171
Whaley, James 72
Whatham, Claude 115
Wheeler, John 102
Wheeler, Kay 94
Whirlwind 39
Whiskey, Nancy 55, 119
White Lightnin 130
White, Alan 174
White, Barry 196
White, Carol 190
White, Fred 141
White, Judy 148
White, Kitty 75
White, Maurice 141
White, Michael 96
White, Tony Joe 29
White, Verdine 141
Whitehead, Annie 137
Whitehead, Peter 173
Whitfield, Norman 181
Whitley, Richard 94
Whitman, Slim 71
Whitman, Stuart 66
Whitwam, Barry 64, 81
Who, The 110, 117, 119, 150, 157, 174, 191
Wickes, David 193
Wiere Brothers, The 34
Wiest, Dianne 43

INDEX OF NAMES

Wiland, Harry 167
Wilcox, Toyah 73, 191
Wild, Jack 86, 188
Wilde, Marty 109, 124
Wilkinson, John 141
Wilkinson, June 121
Willard, Frank 188
Willard, Fred 14
Willard, Harry 167
Willett, E. Hunter 88
Williams, Cindy 48, 189
Williams, Clarence III 91
Williams, Deniece 43
Williams, Edy 56
Williams, Joe 71, 167
Williams, John 34, 167
Williams, Kate 190
Williams, Larry 115
Williams, Maurice & the Zodiacs 12
Williams, Narada Michael 39
Williams, Paul 84, 86
Williams, Robin 190
Williams, Treat 58
Williamson, Fred 181, 185
Willoughby, George 17
Wilson, Ann 43
Wilson, Anthony 196
Wilson, Brian 179
Wilson, Flip 193
Wilson, Frank 127
Wilson, Jackie 12, 53, 114
Wilson, Maurice J. 31, 36
Wilson, Nancy 166, 167
Winchell, Walter 30
Winfield, Paul 191, 194, 196
Winger, Deborah 194
Wingett, Mark 25, 191
Wings 94, 164

Winkler, Irwin 34, 195
Winner, Michael 87
Winningham, Marc 83
Winslow, Susan 179
Winstone, Raymond 191, 196
Winstons, The 148
Winters, David 84
Winters, Jonathan 184
Winters, Shelley 35, 126
Wintle, Julian 87
Winwood, Steve 165
Wishful Thinking 115
Witney, William M. 52
Withers, Bill 166, 167, 199
Wohl, Burton 23
Wolf, Fred 190
Wolfgang 190
Wolk, Tom T-Bone 163
Wonder, Stevie 18, 82, 110, 183, 189, 192
Wood, Charles 62
Wood, Duncan 31
Wood, John 75
Wood, Lana 52
Wood, Ronnie 151, 154, 171, 188
Wood, Roy 179
Woodard, Bronte 27, 56
Woods, Ren 200
Woolfolk, Andrew 141
Woronov, Mary 62
Worrell, Bernie 171
Worth, Irene 39
Worth, Marvin 97
Wray, Fay 95
Wreckless Eric 191, 196
Wright Brothers Flying Machine 114
Wright, Richard 160
Wunsch, Robert J. 194
Wyman, Bill 154, 165, 171, 185

Wynn, Keenan 18
Wynter, Mark 75

X-Ray Spex 139
XTC 116

Yabby U 180
Yarrow, Peter 143, 176
Yates, Peter 112, 189
Yes 174
York, Michael 194
Young Gents, The 148
Young Rascals, The 180, 189
Young, Bob 169
Young, Chip 35
Young, Dey 94
Young, Jesse Colin 159
Young, Gig 75
Young, Neil 149–151, 165, 184, 187, 195, 199
Young, Robert M. 83, 193, 199
Young, Terence 101
Youngbloods, The 156

Zadan, Craig 43
Zappa, Frank 61, 189, 192, 199
Zaremba, Jerry 27
Zemeckis, Robert 186
Zephyrs, The 14
Zerbe, Anthony 76
Zito, David 23
Zito, Richie 138
Zombies, The 110, 189
Zones, The 196
Zucker, David 120
Zucker, Jerry 120
Zugsmith, Albert 30, 51, 86
Zulema 166, 167
Zwerin, Charlotte 145

Index of Song Titles

ABC Boogie 94
ABC of Love, The 12
Abie Baby 58
Abraham Martin and John 148
Acapulco 71
Ace In the Hole 83
Acid Queen 119
Across the Universe 152
Act Naturally 157
Adam and Evil 107
Adom Olom 71
After Dark 114
After the End 198
Ain't It a Shame 103
Ain't Nobody 24
Ain't Seen Nothing Yet 147
Ain't That a Shame 163, 179
Ain't Too Proud to Beg 180
Air 58
Alaskan Pipeline 86
Albatross 94
Albert Flasher 147
Alfred Hitchins 124
Alice's Restaurant 11
All Along the Watchtower 109
All At Once 112
All Down the Line 154
All For One 130
All For the Best 54
All God's Children 137
All Good People 174
All I Need 130
All I Needed Was the Rain 110
All I Really Want To Do 143
All I Want Is You 36
All Kinds of People 128
All My Trials 143
All Night 165
All of Us 196

All On a Warm Summer Day 75
All Over the World 129
All Shook Up 143
All Summer Long 179
All That I Am 107
All That You Dream 190
All the Stars In the Sky 75
All The Things I Do for You Baby 64
All the Way Home 115
All the Young Punks 99
All Together Now 129
All You Need Is Love 80, 129
Alley Cat 94
Alley Oop 115
All's Fair In Love and War 67
Almost 121
Almost Always True 19
Almost Grown 179
Almost Human 76
Almost In Love 78
Almost Paradise 43
Almost Summer 179
Aloha Oe 19
Alright Okay You Win 121
Always Crashing the Same Car 191
Am I What I Was or Was I What I Am? 186
Amazed and Confused 71
Amazing Grace 11, 134
Amazing Journey 117
Amen 141
America 71
American Girl 183
American Trilogy 141
American Woman 147
Americana Stray Cat Blues 109
Among the Yesterdays 181
Among the Young 84
Anarchie pour le UK 147
Anarchy in the UK 139, 147

And I Love Her 59
And Me (I'm On the Outside Now) 122
Angel 42
Angel Face 53, 82
Animal House 180
Annie I'm Not Your Daddy 155
Another Girl 62
Another Girl Another Planet 196
Another Tear Falls 68
Anthem 187
Anti-Brotherhood of Man, The 195
Any Time At All 59
Anyone 76
Anyone for Tennis 192
Anyway Anyhow Anywhere 150
April Come She Will 185
Are You Lonesome Tonight? 35, 120
Are You Sleeping? 190
Are You Sure? 168
Around and Around 49, 138
Art of Heartbreak 163
Aruba Liberace 125
As Long As I Have You 75
As Time Goes By 196
As We Go Along 61
Ashbury Wednesday 89
Ashes to Ashes 140
At My Front Door 105
At the Hop 77, 153, 174
Aura Lee 121
Autumn Lake 168
Avalanche 136
Ave Maria 51
Awaiting On Your All 138

Baba O'Riley 150
Babe I'm Gonna Leave You 162
Baby 66
Baby Baby 95

INDEX OF SONG TITLES

Baby Baby Your Love Is All I Need   30
Baby Blue   65
Baby Come Back   184
Baby Don't Go   194
Baby Don't You Do It   191
Baby How I Fell For You   192
Baby I Don't Care   69
Baby I'm a Star   91
Baby I'm Yours   110
Baby If You Give Me All Your Love   34
Baby Let Me Follow You Down   151
Baby Love   110, 183, 191
Baby Lover   104
Baby Please Don't Go   83
Baby Strange   137
Baby, What You Want Me to Do?   15, 45, 136
Baby Won't You Please Come Home   122
Baby You're a Rich Man   80
Baby You're So Good To Me   40
Babylon   180
Babylon's Burning   116
Bachelor Boy   112
Back Talk   30
Back to School Blue   114
Backwoods Preacher   29
Bacon Fat   156
Bad Love   184
Bad Man   184
Bad Reputation   197
Bad Woman's Love, A   30
Bajabula Bonke   157
Baker Man   30
Ball and Chain   148, 157
Ballad in Plain D   91
Ballad of Job Cain, The   130
Ballad of the Green Berets   189
Ballad of the Savage Seven   192
Ballad of Tommy Udo   181
Ballroom Dancing   53
Band of Thieves   182
Band On the Run   53, 164
Bang Bang   56
Bang Your Head   43
Bangla Dhun   138
Bangladesh   138
Barbara Ann   150
Barbarian, The   160
Barefoot Ballad   76
Barrels of Pain   159
Battle Hymn of the Republic   35
Battle of New Orleans   134, 156
Be   187
Be a Lion   128
Be Bop a Lula   45, 51
Be My Baby   135, 176, 188, 191
Be My Guest   14
Be Not Too Hard   190
Beach Ball   15, 84
Beach Blanket Bingo   16
Beach Boy Blues   21
Beach Party   16
Beach Shack   107
Beads of Innocence   89

Beast of Burden   154
Beat Box   24
Beat Girl Song   17
Beat Goes On, The   161
Beat the Devil   197
Beautiful Boy   175
Beautiful City   54
Beautiful Ones, The   91
Beauty School Dropout   56
Because   102, 179
Because the Night   196
Because They're Young   17
Because You're You   18
Bed and Breakfast Man   172
Beechwood 4-5789   183, 189
Before the Deluge   159
Before We Say Goodbye   55
Beginner's Luck   45
Being Different Has Never Been a Crime   195
Being For the Benefit of Mr Kite   102
Believe In Yourself   128
Bell Boy   191
Bells of Rhymney, The   135
Belsen Was a Gas   147
Ben E. Wriggle   133
Berserker   145
Best of My Love   199
Best Temptation of All, The   198
Best That I Know How, The   187
Better Be Ready   66
Better Twist Now Baby   121
Beware My Love   164
Beware of Darkness   138
Beyond the Bend   67
Biding My Time   125
Big Beat, The   18
Big Boots   47
Big Bottom   115
Big Brother   25
Big City Blues   190
Big Girls Don't Cry   186, 198
Big Hunk of Love, A   141
Big Love Big Heartache   99
Big News   112
Big Noise From Winnetka   140
Bikini Beach   18
Bill Bailey   84
Billy Fehr   134
Bird On a Wire   136, 156
Bird, The   91
Birdland   156
Bitch   151
Black Arabs Medley   147
Black Dog   168
Black Juju   156
Black Limousine   154
Black Man   25
Black Mountain Rag   134
Blank Generation   196
Blast Off   77
Blazing Fire   191
Bless the Lord   54
Blitzkrieg Bop   94

Blowin' In the Wind   134, 138
Blowin' Your Mind   193
Blue Feeling   49
Blue Hawaii   21
Blue Jay Way   80
Blue Monday   50
Blue Moon   56, 122
Blue Moon of Kentucky   35
Blue Shadows   111
Blue Sky   137
Blue Suede Shoes   35, 143, 149
Blue's Theme   199
Blueberry Hill   153
Bluebird   164, 186
Blues   143
Blues For a Frog   196
Bo Diddley   33, 45, 135, 163, 195
Bodies   147
Body and Soul   156
Body Rock   23
Body Work   24
Boney Moronie   49, 115
Bongo Blues   38
Bongo Party   199
Bony Moronie   115
Boogie Children   23
Boogie Down   24
Boogie Nights   193
Boogie Shoes   192
Boogie Wonderland   193
Boogie Woogie Bugle Boy   140
Boogiest Band In Town   82
Book of Love   28, 115, 179
Book of Prophecy   29
Book of Rules   96
Bookends   183
Boppin   95
Born In Chicago   143
Born to Be Alive   193
Born to Be Wild   183
Born to Hand Jive   56
Born to Love You   181
Born Too Late   115
Born Under a Bad Sign   136
Boss Barracuda   79
Bossa Nova Baby   46
Boy and A Girl, A   66
Boy Blue   187
Boy Like Me A Girl Like You, A   52
Boy Needs a Girl, A   36, 82
Brainlock   93
Brand New Day   187
Brand New Family   195
Brave New World   186
Break It Down   193
Break, The   135
Breakdown   173, 182, 183
Breakin' Out   39
Breakin' Up Is Hard to Do   194
Breaking Glass   196
Breakthrough   189
Breathless   137
Brickhouse   114

223

INDEX OF SONG TITLES

Bridge Over Troubled Water   141, 143
Bright Green Pleasure Machine, The   185
Bristol Stomp   33
Britches   41
Broadway Rhythm   155
Broken Promise, A   71
Bron-Y-Aur   168
Brother Mary   200
Brotherhood   195
Brothers Doin' Time   181
Brown Eyed Handsome Man   138
Brown Sugar   145, 151, 154
Brumberger Duet, The   195
Bruvvers   124
Bubble Gum Girl   48
Buffalo Stomp   199
Build Up   119
Bullfighter Was a Lady, The   46
Bundle of Dreams   103
Burnin' Love   35
Burning Down the House   171
Burning Love   141
But I Don't Care   87
But Not For Me   124
Butterfingers   119
Buy For Me the Rain   182
By My Side   54
Bye Bye Baby   189
Bye Bye Johnny   169
Bye Bye Love   12, 115

C.C. Rider   136, 141
California Dreamin'   157, 181
California Sun   94
Call It Stormy Monday   136
Call Me the Entertainer   155
Call On Me   183
Calling All Comets   33
Calls the Tune   25
Camellia   97
Can Can   133
Can I Go Out   128
Can I Put You On   185
Can You Dig It?   61
Candy Floss   55
Candy Man   143, 144
Cane and a High Starched Collar, A   41
Cannibal Pot   119
Can't Buy Me Love   19, 59
Can't Explain   150
Can't Get It Out of My Head   187
Can't Give It Up   180
Can't Help Falling in Love   21, 141, 143
Can't Stop the Music   27
Can't Wait   18
Can't We Try   93
Captain Walker Didn't Come Home   117
Car Song   11
Car Wars   14
Car Wash   181
Caravan   151
Careful With That Axe Eugene   160, 200
Careless Love   23

Carnaby Street   194
Carnival Rock   28
Carny Town   99
Caroline   169
Carrie Ann   109
Carry On to Tomorrow   188
Carry That Weight   102, 179
Casey Jones   144
Casey Wake Up   79
Castles   48
Casual   77
Catalin Caper   28
Catch Us If You Can   182
Catchin' On Fast   76
Catfish   91
C'est Si Bon   122
Chance of a Lifetime   184
Change In Louise   156
Change of Habit   29
Change of Heart, A   127
Changes   189
Chantilly Lace   27, 115, 121, 179, 194
Chapel of Love   140
Chapter 33   182
Charge   50
Chariot Choogle   137
Charles Atlas Song   96
Charlie Brown   12, 152, 153
Charm   55
Chase, The   199
Cheats On You   133
Chelsea (I Don't Want to Go To)   14, 196
Chelsea Hotel   136
Chesay   45
Chest Fever   151
Chestnut Mare   91
Chicken In the Rough   95
Children of the Future   181
Children of the Revolution   137
China Star   95
Chocolate City   190
Christ the Clown   54
Chug a Lug   29
Cinnamon Sinner   50
Circle Game, The   195
Circle Sky   61
City By Night   34
City Sirens   165
Clambake   30
Clap For the Wolfman   147
Clap, The   174
Clean Up Your Own Back Yard   121
Close to the Edge   174
Close to You   166
Closest to Love, The   23
C'mon and Be Loved   55
C'mon Everybody   123, 147
C'mon Let's Go   94
C'mon Let's Live a Little   30
Cobwebs and Strange   150
Cocaine   143, 165
Codine   143
Cold War   145

College Confidential   30
College Confidential Ball   30
Colores   143
Colours   190
Combination of the Two   157
Come A-Running   130
Come Along   45
Come and Get It   66, 188
Come Back Jonee   94
Come Closer (If You're a Man)   195
Come Go With Me   18, 179
Come Into the Air   25
Come On   172, 190
Come On and Get Ready   181
Come On Let's Go   68
Come to the Party   130
Come To the Sunshine   176
Come Together   102, 179
Comin' Home   148
Comin' Home Johnny   49
Common Ground   195
Complete Control   99
Computer Blue   91
Concrete Jungle   139
Confidence   30
Contact   199
Cool Baby   71
Cool It Baby   50
Cool Jerk   189
Cool Million, A   198
Cool Ones, The   30
Coquette   197
Cordelia   187
Cosmic Dancer   137
Cotton Candy Land   67
Cottonpicker   123
Could I Fall In Love?   34
Countdown to Love   111
Country Fever   130
Country Preacher   166
Cousin Kevin   117
Coyote   151
Crack Up   113
Cracked Actor   140
Crawfish   75
Crawlin' to the USA   14
Crazy Baldhead   136
Crazy Cause I Love You   103
Crazy Crazy Lovin'   95
Crazy Horse Saloon   36
Crazy Party Crazy   77
Cream Puff War   189
Creep, The   28
Creeque Alley   157
Crippled Crow   107
Crippled Inside   147
Cross My Heart and Hope to Die   51
Cross Over   71
Cruisin'   179
Crumbling Land   200
Cry   23, 137
Cry a Little   48
Cry Baby   148

INDEX OF SONG TITLES

Cry Me a River 51
Cry My Heart Out 87
Crying in the Chapel 35, 179
Crying Time 143
Crystal Ball 93
Cucurrucucu Paloma 91
Cups and Cakes 115
Curves 39
Cut it 24
Cycle Set, The 16

Da Doo Ron Ron 109, 191
Daddy Rich 181
Daddy Wants to Do Right 103
Daddy's Song 61
Dainty Little Moonbeam 52
Daisy Chain 81
Damn Dog 116
Dance 189
Dance All Night 114
Dance In the Streets 65
Dance of Death 200
Dance to the Bop 65
Dance to the Music 174
Dancin' 129
Dancin' in the Street 110
Dancing Frog 196
Dancing In the Streets 43, 183
Dancing Queen 133
Dancing Shoes 112
Dang Me 135
Dangerous Type 116
Dark Side of Midnight, The 136
Dark Side of the Moon 160
Dark Star 200
Darling Be Home Soon 156, 200
Darling Nikki 91
Datin' 84
Dawn 15
Day By Day 54
Day In the Life, A 102, 129
Day Out 194
Daybreak 105
Daydream 137
Dazed and Confused 168
Dea Sancta 109
Dead Man's Curve 189
Dealer's Theme, The 58
Dear Father 187
Dear Jesus God 197
Deeper and Deeper 111
Deliver 23
Deliver Me From My Enemies 180
Delores Delage 140
Delta Lady 156
Desiree 188
Devil With the Blue Dress On 159
Devoted to You 115
Diamonds and Rust 91
Did We Meet Somewhere Before? 94
Diddy Doo Wop 163
Didya Ever 47
Dig It 152

Diggy Liggy Lo 134
Dirty Dirty Feeling 116
Dirty Water 169
Disco Duck 192
Disco Inferno 192
Dixie 35
Dixieland Rock 75
Dizzy 110
Do Anything You Wanna Do 196
Do I Have to Do This All Over Again? 61
Do It Again 184
Do Not Disturb 51
Do That Ski 128
Do the Clam 51
Do the New Continental 33
Do the Old Soft Shoe 69
Do the Rocksteady 139
Do Wah Diddy 110
Do You Believe In Magic? 83, 135
Do You Know Who I Am 23
Do You Love Me? 198
Do You Remember 128
Do You Wanna Dance 12, 94, 179, 180
Do You Want It Right Now 39
Do You Want To Know a Secret? 110
Doctor Jimmy 191
Dog's Life, A 84
Dogs In the Yard 38
Doin' Me Dirty 187
Doin' the Best I Can 47
Doing the Hully Gully 75
Dolly Dagger 162
Dominique 110
Donna 45, 58
Don't Ask Me Why 75
Don't Be Afraid to Love Me 53
Don't Be Cruel 141
Don't Chase Me Around 48
Don't Do It 151
Don't Do That To Me 36
Don't Knock the Rock 33
Don't Knock the Twist 33
Don't Leave Me Now 69
Don't Let Me Down 152
Don't Let the Rain Get To You 116
Don't Let the Sun Catch You Crying 109
Don't Misunderstand 193
Don't Need Your Loving 191
Don't Nobody Bring Me No Bad News 128
Don't Put It Down 58
Don't Quote Me On That 172
Don't Remind Me Now of Time 176
Don't Start Me Talkin' 136
Don't Stop 184
Don't Stop Now 16
Don't Stop the Music 116
Don't Take My Coconuts 155
Don't Take You From Me 78
Don't Talk to Me About Work 157
Don't Talk To Strangers 56
Don't Think Twice It's All Right 140
Don't Twist With Anyone Else But Me 122
Don't Wanna Be Teacher's Pet 71

Don't Worry Kyoko 175
Don't You Understand 78
Doomsday Rock 119
007 139
Double Shot of My Baby's Love 189
Double Trouble 34
Double Yellow Line 93
Down 105
Down and Out 68
Down and Out in New York City 181
Down By the River 19
Down By the Riverside 45
Down Down 169
Down In the Boondocks 188
Down In the Park 116
Down to Lovetown 114
Downed 190
Dr Goldfoot and the Girl Bombs 34
Drag 65
Drastic Measures 23
Draw Your Brakes 60
Dread Lion 96
Dream Girl 180
Dream Goes On Forever, A 94
Dream Lover 109
Dreambo 157
Drivin' Daisy 187
Driving 195
Drowned 167
Drum Dance 127
Drums of the Islands 84
Dry Your Eyes 151
Duke of Earl 33
Dyna-Mite 82

E Street Shuffle 140
Eagle 133
Earth Angel 153
Earth Blue 162
Earth Boy 52
Ease On Down the Road 128
Easy 114
Easy Come Easy Go 34
Easy Life 139
Easy Rider 162
Easy Thing 76
Easy To Be Hard 58
Eat Your Heart Out 95
Echo 4.2 133
Echoes 160
Echoes In My Mind 198
Eddie's Teddy 96
Edge of Reality 78
Eighth Day 25
El Toro 46
El-Pussycat 133
Eleanor Rigby 53, 129
Electric Blues 58
Elevator Rock 119
Elijah 130
Embraceable You 124
Emerald City Ballet 128
Energy Fools the Magician 94

INDEX OF SONG TITLES

Engine No. 9   135
England Swings   135
Evangeline   151
Eve of Destruction   110
Ever Since I Can Remember   95
Evergreen   107
Every Little Thing   186
Everybody But You   75
Everybody Come Aboard   45
Everybody Let's Get Together   137
Everybody Loves a Lover   153
Everybody Needs Someone to Love   23
Everybody Ought To Make a Change   165
Everybody Ought To Sing a Song   161
Everybody Plays the Fool   167
Everybody Rejoice   128
Everybody's Breakin'   23
Everybody's Dancin'   181
Everybody's Got 'Em   190
Everyday   27
Everyday With Your Girl   182
Everything   107
Everything Works If You Let It   93
Evil Lies   97
Excelsior Song   77
Exodus   136
Eye For an Eye, An   136
Eyesight to the Blind   117

Fade Away   96
Fall In Love   40
Fame   38, 140
Family Dog   176
Family Man   163
Family Tree   148
Famous Blue Raincoat   136
Fanny Mae   179, 180
Fantasy   141
Far Far Away   41
Far From Over   110
Fast Forward   39
Fast Speaking Woman   91
Fastest Guitar Alive, The   39
Fat Man, The   182
Faust   86
Feel Like I'm Fixin' To Die Rag   174, 189
Feel To Be Free   144
Feelin' Alright   156, 193
Feelin' Happy   103
Feeling That We Have, The   128
Feels Like the First Time   184
Feels So Good to Win   183
Fernando   133
Ferry 'Cross the Mersey   40
Fiddle About   117
Fiesta   40
Fifth of Beethoven, A   192
Fifty-two Percent   126
Find a Way   86
Find the Cost of Freedom   150
Find Your Dream   69
Finders Keepers   40
Fingers   58

Fingertips   18, 183, 189
Fire Down Below   97, 140
Fire Water   113
Firehouse Blues   187
First Love First Tears   111
First of May, The   188
First Time Last Time   48
Fish That Saved Pittsburgh, The   184
Fishin' Blues   195, 198
5-4-3-2-1   191
5.15   191
Five Hundred Miles   135
Flaming Star   41
Flesh Departures   58
Flowers In the City   116
Fly Boy   16
Fly Like An Eagle   184
Fly Too High   184
Fly, The   33
Flying   80
FM   184
Follow   183
Follow My Dreams   86
Follow That Dream   42
Follow the Boys   43
Folsom Prison Blues   149
Fool Around   121
Fool On the Hill, The   80
Fool Such As I   35
Fool That I Am   183
Fools Like Us   23
Foot Tapper   112
Footloose   43
For Granted   30
For No One   53
For What It's Worth   183, 186
For You and I   188
For You Blue   152
Forever   181
Forever Young   45, 151
Forget Me Never   126
Fort Lauderdale Chamber of Commerce   51
Forward Ever   165
Four Brothers   156
Four Faces   191
Fourscore   58
Fourteen or Fight   126
Foxy Lady   162
Fractured Mirror   76
Frank Mills   58
Frankfurt Special   47
Frankie and Johnny   45
Freak's Lament   182
Freakout   157, 176
Freakshow On the Dancefloor   24
Freddie's Dead   195
Free From the Devil   183
Free Me   87, 187
Free the Brothers   181
Free the People   156
Freedom   174
Freedom of Expression   197
Freedom Song   168

Freeze, The   73
Freight Train Boogie   134
Fresh Air   144
Friends   116, 185
Friggin' In the Riggin'   147
From the Beginning   165
Frozen Years   191
Fun In Acapulco   46
Funeral For a Friend   187
Funky Broadway   168
Funky Chicken   173
Funny How Time Slips Away   141
Funny Money   95
Funny Over You   83
Further On Up the Road   143, 151

G.I. Blues   47
Game, The   195
Garageland   99
Garden of Earthly Delights   182
Gas Man   48
Gasser, The   104
Gates of Eden   140
Gee   179
Genetic Method   151
George and Dragon, The   64
Georgia On My Mind   135
Geronimo   49, 50
Get a Job   179
Get a Move On   14
Get Away From Here   191
Get Back   102, 148, 152, 179
Get Down   199
Get It On   137
Get It Together   197
Get On the Carousel   133
Get Out and Stay Out   191
Get Out of Denver   111
Get Out of the Car   73
Get The Funk Out Ma Face   189
Get Together   137, 159
Get Up and Get On Down   96
Get Up Stand Up   136
Get Yourself a College Girl   49
Get Yourself Together   115
Gettin' Better   179
Getting Better All the Time   102
Getting Straight   185
Ghost Train   50
Giddy Up a Ding Dong   94
Gimme a Break   27
Gimme Shelter   145, 151
Gimme Some Lovin'   23, 161, 165
Gimme Some Money   115
Gimme Some Truth   147
Gimme Your Love   18
Gina Gina   155
Girl Can't Help It, The   50
Girl Gets Around, The   43
Girl Happy   51
Girl I Never Loved, The   30
Girl In Every Port, A   128
Girl Needs a Boy, A   82

226

INDEX OF SONG TITLES

Girlfriend Is Better   171
Girls Girls Girls   52
Girls On the Beach, The   52
Girls' Town   51
Give Her Lovin'   66
Give Me an Inch   25
Give Me Your Love   167
Give Peace a Chance   156, 175
Give Your Best   188
Glad All Over   71
Glad to Be Gay   167
Gloria   156
Glory Wave   113
Go   75
Go East Young Man   60
Go For It   184
Go Johnny Go   53
Go Now   164
Go On Back to Mama   185
Go Tell Aunt Rhody   143
Go To Sleep   196
God and Mama   91
God Bless the Absentee   83
God Bless the Children   187
God Save the Queen   139, 147
Goin' Up the Country   174
Going Home   110
Going to A-Go-Go   154
Gold   185
Golden Age   55
Golden Coins   60
Golden Slumbers   102, 179
Good Day Sunshine   53, 196
Good Days, The   148
Good Golly Miss Molly   153
Good Lovin'   180, 189
Good Lovin' Daddy   190
Good Morning   102
Good Morning Starshine   58
Good Rockin' Tonight   163
Good Time Party   39
Good Times   16, 56
Goodbye Eddie Goodbye   86
Goodbye Porkpie Hat   165
Goodbye Sadness   175
Goodbye So Long   181
Goodnight   179
Goodnight Irene   165
Goodnight, It's Time to Go   12
Got a Feeling   64
Got a Funny Feeling   130
Got a Lotta Livin' To Do   80
Got My Mojo Workin'   143
Got To get Moving   48
Got To Get You Into My Life   102
Got to Have Your Body   195
Gotcha Where I Want You   18
Gotta Get a Message to You   109
Gotta Get Away   64
Gotta Love   137
Gotta Stop That Feeling   192
Graduation in Zion   96
Grand Cooley Dam   104

Gratitude   141
Gravedigger   130
Gray Prison Blues   198
Grease   56
Great Balls of Fire   12, 71, 115, 194
Great Imposter, The   179
Great Pretender, The   94, 179, 194
Great Rock'n'Roll Swindle, The   147
Greatest Performance of My Life   167
Greedy Man   184
Green Grass and High Times   184
Green Light   114
Green Onions   179, 180, 191
Greenback Dollar   130
Grinding Halt   116
Guadalajara   46

Hair   58
Hallelujah   23
Hand Me Down World   147
Handful of Songs, A   119
Hands   30
Hang Fire   154
Hang On Sloopy   189
Hang on to Your Life   147
Happy Baby   94
Happy Birthday Sweet Sixteen   110
Happy Ending   67
Happy Jack   150
Happy Street   82
Happy Times   114
Hard Day's Night, A   59
Hard Knocks   99
Hard Luck   45
Hard Rain's A-Gonna Fall, A   91, 138
Hard Workin' Man   181
Hard-headed Woman   75
Harder They Come, The   60
Hare Krishna   58
Harem Holiday   60
Hashish   58
Hats Off to Larry   110
Have a Happy   29
Have You Tried Love?   161
Having a Party   180
Having a Wild Weekend   182
Hawaii USA   84
Hawaiian Sunset   21
Hawaiian Wedding Song   21
Hayfoot Strawfoot   66
He Didn't Stay   184
He Is Your Brother   133
Hear My Train A-Comin'   149, 162
Hearsay   165
Heart and Soul   179
Heart Beat Pig Meat   200
Heart Breaker   168
Heart of the Beat   24
Heart to Heart   137
Heart's In Traction   137
Heartbeats   128
Heartbreak Hotel   35, 115, 143
Heat Treatment   180

Heathen, The   136
Heatwave   150, 186, 189
Heaven Knows   41
Heaven Must Be Missing An Angel   199
Heaven On Their Mind   72
Heavenly Father   53
Heavy Duty Rock'n'Roll   115
Hell   77
Hell Hole   115
Hell Is For Children   14
Hell of It, The   86
Hellacious Acres   107
Hello Again   71
Hello Friends   144
Hello Goodbye   80
Hello Mr Dream   114
Hello There   190
Help   62, 179
Help Me   116
Help Me Jesus   144
Helpless   151, 195
Helpless Dancer   191
Here Comes Love   77
Here Comes the Nice   173
Here Comes the Sun   102, 138
Here I Come There She Goes   195
Here Is My Love   66
Here There and Everywhere   53
Here We Go Round the Mulberry Bush   186
Heroes   191
Heroes and Villains   161
He's a Dream   42
He's a Rebel   180
He's Alright   168
He's Mine   93
He's My Guy   50
He's So Fine   191
He's So Sweet   122
He's the Wizard   128
He's Your Uncle Not Your Dad   106
Hey Baby   149, 162, 194
Hey Bo Diddley   153
Hey Bulldog   129
Hey Hey Hey   30
Hey Jah Children   180
Hey Joe   161
Hey Juanita   95
Hey Jude   179, 183
Hey Let's Twist   64
Hey Little Girl   12, 60
Hey Louise   71
Hey Mama   51
Hey Paula   180, 194
Heyjorter   168
Hi Hi Hi   164
Hi Ho Silver Lining   165
Hideaway   188
Hidin' From Myself   34
High   30
High Flying Bird   157
High School   94
Higher   174
Highway 61   143, 199

INDEX OF SONG TITLES

Hilltop Song 66
Hippy From Olema 157
Hold Me, Touch Me 76
Hold On 64, 182
Hold On, I'm Comin' 23
Hold That Snake 111
Holding Out For a Hero 43
Hole In Your Sole 133
Holiday Inn 81
Holidays In the Sun 147
Hollywood 114, 184
Hollywood Blues 144
Hollywood Boulevard 188
Hollywood Waltz 91
Home 128
Home Is Where the Heart Is 42, 75
Home On the Range 199
Honey Can't You See 196
Honey Chile 103
Honey Roll 185
Honeybee 45
Honeycomb 115
Honky Tonk part 2 12
Honky Tonk Women 145, 148, 154, 156
Honky Tonkin' 134
Hook Line and Sinker 33
Hooked On Rock'n'Roll 76
Hooked On Your Love 106
Hooray For Romance 196
Hootchie Cootchie Man 163
Hopelessly Devoted to You 56
Hosanna 72
Hot Dog 80
Hot Dog Buddy Buddy 33
Hot Love 137
Hot Lunch Jam 38
Hot Rock 95
Hound Dog 56, 163
Hound Dog Man 66
House of Sand 84
House of the Rising Sun 91
House on the Beach 127
House That Has Everything, A 30
How About That 18
How Blue Can You Get? 156
How Deep Is Your Love 192
How Do You Do 39
How Do You Sleep? 147
How Does It Feel 41
How Long Can I Keep It Up? 194
How Many More Times 186
How Silly Can You Get 120
How the Heart Approaches What It Yearns 83
How the Web Was Woven 143
How to Stuff a Wild Bikini 66
How Would You Like It 49
How Would You Like To Be? 67
How? 147
However Dark the Night 66
Hula Love 71
Hurricane 91
Hurts So Good 43

Hush 188
Hushabye 12

I Am My Ideal 16
I Am the Sea 191
I Am the Walrus 80, 179
I Am What I Am 114
I Believe In Love 107
I Believe It Can Be Done 66
I Can Dream About You 111
I Can See For Miles 150
I Can Tell By the Way You Dance 183
I Can't Believe 197
I Can't Get You Out of My Heart 130
I Can't Go For That 163
I Can't Help Myself 183, 199
I Can't Stand It 182
I Can't Tell 66
I Can't Turn You Loose 148
I Cried All Night 69
I Did What You Told Me 17
I Dig a Pony 152
I Don't Know How to Love Him 72
I Don't Wanna Be Tied 52
I Don't Want To Be a Loser 52
I Don't Want To Be a Soldier 147
I Don't Want To Go Home 180
I Feel I've Known You Forever 116
I Feel It Right Here 73
I Fell In Love 193
I Fought the Law 99
I Found Jesus 29
I Found Myself 165
I Got a Woman 23, 40, 141
I Got Life 58
I Got Lucky 75
I Got Rhythm 124
I Got You 104
I Got You Babe 56, 176
I Heard It Through the Grapevine 167, 180
I Is De Daw 185
I Just Can't Help Believing 143
I Just Wanna Have Something To Do 94
I Knew From the Start 95
I Know Where You're Goin' 66
I Like 119
I Like Animals 69
I Like the Way You Work 192
I Look Away 188
I Love Her So 23
I Love How You Love Me 115
I Love Only One Girl 34
I Love to Twist 33
I Love You 198
I Love You So 188
I Love You to Death 27
I Love You Too 40
I Love You Too Much 110
I May Not Be What You Want 173
I Me Mine 152
I Meant To Do My Work Today 185
I Need Somebody to Lean On 123
I Need You 62

I Never Had a Sweetheart 95
I Only Have Eyes For You 179
I Put a Spell On You 12
I Saw the Light 141
I Second That Emotion 180
I Shall Be Released 137, 140, 151
I Shot the Sheriff 136
I Should Have Known Better 59
I Sing the Body Electric 38
I Slipped I Stumbled I Fell 126
I Smell Trouble 168
I Stole Your Love 76
I Sure Know a Lot About Love 124
I Think I'll Always Love You 193
I Think I'm Gonna Like It Here 46
I Think You Think 16
I Wait 114
I Wanna Be Free 69
I Wanna Be Sedated 94, 116
I Wanna Be Your Boyfriend 94
I Wanna Dance 114
I Wanna Get Next to You 181
I Wanna Hold Your Hand 19, 59
I Want to Take You Higher 148
I Want You 91, 102
I Want You Around 94
I Would Die 4 U 91
Iceman Comes, The 145
I'd Rather Be Sorry 182
Idle On Parade 66
Idle Rock A Boogie 66
If I Can't Have You 192
If I Fell 59
If I Were An Artist 113
If It Stops You Runnin' 184
If Loving You Is Wrong 173
If You Can Dream 185
If You Love Him 79
If You See Her Say Hello 91
If You Think I Don't Need You 123
If You Want to Be Happy 155
I'll Be Back 107
I'll Be Gone Long 144
I'll Be Seeing You 153
I'll Be Unhappy 67
I'll Be Waiting There For You 77
I'll Be Where the Heart Is 42
I'll Build a Bridge 18
I'll Cry Instead 59
I'll Love You Forever Today 122
I'll Miss You 86
I'll Play the Blues For You 173
I'll Take Love 34
I'll Try Something New 189
I'll Wait For You 40
I'm a Boy 150
I'm a Man 153, 189
I'm a Marionette 133
I'm a One Woman Man 93
I'm a Wanted Man 165
I'm a Wonderful Thing Baby 155
I'm Alive 129
I'm Black 58

INDEX OF SONG TITLES

I'm Falling In Love Tonight 67
I'm Free 117
I'm Free (Heaven Help the Man) 43
I'm Going Home 96, 174
I'm Gonna Love You 56
I'm Gonna Love You Too 27
I'm Gonna Walk and Talk With My Lord 103
I'm Gonna Wrap You Up 55
I'm Growing Up 66
I'm Happy Just to Dance With You 59
I'm Here Again 114
I'm In Love Again 103
I'm In Shape 196
I'm Looking For a World 48
I'm Not a Juvenile Deliquent 95
I'm Not Going Home 187
I'm Not the Marrying Kind 42
I'm On My Way Out 192
I'm One 191
I'm Sandra Dee 56
I'm So Cool 137
I'm Sorry 93
I'm Still Waiting 137
I'm Sweet On You 128
I'm the Kind of Sugar Daddy Likes 137
I'm Too Close to Heaven to Turn Around 167
I'm Waiting For the Man 159
I'm Walkin' 18, 23
I'm Yours 116
Imagination 42
Imagine 147
Imitation 155
Immigrant, The 187
In a Heartbeat 137
In a Silent Way 144
In From the Storm 149
In Havana 198
In My Way 126
In the City 198
In the Morning 91, 188
In the Pines 91
In the Stars 128
In the Still of the Night 153
In the Stone 141
In-Between Age 55
Incense and Peppermints 89, 189
Incident at Neshibur 144
Independence 124
Inner London Violence 133, 139
Innocent Not Guilty 116
Instant Girl 30
Intermezzo Nr I 133
Interstellar Overdrive 173
Intrigue 43
Is It Better to Have Loved and Lost? 192
Is It Love? 40
Is It Okay If I Call You Mine? 38
Is This What Feeling Gets? 128
Isis 91
Island of Love 21
It Ain't Me Babe 91
It Don't Come Easy 138
It Feels So Right 116

It Makes No Difference 151
It Only Hurts When I Cry 16
It Takes A Long Time 53
It Takes a Lot To Laugh It Takes a Train To Cry 91, 138, 157
It Was Great When It All Began 96
Italian Girls 163
Italian Lullaby 43
Itchykoo Park 161
It'll Be Me 115
Ito Eats 21
It's A Beautiful Day 14
It's a Boy 117
It's a Pity to Say Goodnight 64
It's a Wonderful World 99
It's All Over Now Baby Blue 140
It's All Too Much 129
It's Alright Ma (I'm Only Bleeding) 140
It's Always Your Fault 194
It's Been a Long Time 186
It's Carnival Time 99
It's Gonna Be All Right 40
It's Gonna Rain 127
It's Gonna Take Magic 87
It's Gonna Work Out Fine 135
It's Gotta Be You 52
It's Legal 17
It's Magic 30
It's Nice to Be Out In the Morning 81
It's Not Unusual 83
It's Only Money 195
It's Serious 114
It's So Easy 27
It's So Hard 147
It's That Kind of Day 84
It's the Little Things 56
It's Your World 30
I've Been a Bad Bad Boy 87
I've Been Loving You Too Long 145, 157
I've Been Waiting For You 133
I've Got a Feeling 152, 157
I've Got To Find My Baby 51
I've Gotta Be Me 166
I've Gotta Horse 69
I've Had Enough 141, 191
I've Just Seen a Face 164
I've Lost You 143
I've Waited So Long 66
I've Written a Letter To Daddy 97
Ivor the Engine 133

Jack O'Diamonds 104
Jah No Dead 96
Jah Works 165
Jailhouse Rock 23, 69, 172
James Dean 187
Jammin' 136
Janie Jones 99
Jay Walker 55
Jazz Odyssey 116
Je T'Aime 114
Jeanine 156
Jeepster 137

Jerusalem 73, 87
Jessica 137
Jet 164
Jet, The 114
Jody's Got Your Girl 173
Joe Hill 174
Joey's Blues 64
Johan Pa Snippen 133
Johnny B. Goode 138, 141, 144, 147, 149, 179
Johnny O 55
Johnny Too Bad 60, 99
Join the Band 195
Joker James 191
Jonah 83
Joy to the World 180
Judy 75
Juke Box Rhythm 73
Juke Box Serenade 48
Jump Children 53
Jump Into the Fire 105
Jumpin' Jack Flash 138, 145, 151, 154, 161, 183, 188
Jungle Love 91
Jupiter 141
Just a Dream Away 187
Just a Feeling 133
Just a Little Love 156
Just a Name 56
Just For Fun 75
Just For You 82
Just Like A Woman 91, 138, 183, 189
Just Like Me 186
Just My Imagination 154
Just the Way You Are 184
Just Wait and See 127
Just What I Needed 190
Just You Wait and See 124
Justice 189
Justine 113

K-Jee 192
Kaw-Liga 91
Keep It In the Family 181
Keep Moving 78
Keep On Chooglin' 199
Keep On Dancin' 75
Keep On Keepin' On 181
Keep On Rockin' 97
Keep Your Head to the Sky 141
Kelele 195
Key to My Kingdom, The 184
Key to the Highway 144
Kicking Up a Fuss 197
Kicks 196
Kill Your Sons 159
King Creole 75
King of the Mountain 128
King of the Road 135
King of the Whole Wide World 75
King Ska Far 133
Kismet 60
Kiss Me Deadly 139
Kiss On My List 163

INDEX OF SONG TITLES

Kissin' Cousins 76
Kissin' Game 114
Knife Edge 160
Knocking on Heaven's Door 91
Koala Shuffle 116
Kol Nidre 71
Koochie Koochie Koochie 190
Ku-u-i-po 21

L.B.J. 58
La Bamba 12, 52, 163, 180
La Ila I La La 195
La La Song 40
La Paloma Twist 33
Lady L 42
Lady Linda 179
Lady Loves Me, The 123
Lady Wants to Know, The 188
Laguna Salada 130
Lah Dee Dah 104
Land of a Thousand Dances 168
Last Dance, The 114
Last Night 73
Last of an Ancient Breed 198
Last Supper 72
Late In the Evening 83
Laugh It Off 189
Laughing 147
Law and Order 78
Lawdy Miss Clawdy 35, 141, 156
Lay Down Sally 143, 165
Lay It Down 41
Layabout's Lament 124
Layla 109, 143, 165
LBC Theme 180
Lead Me Guide Me 141
Leader of the Pack 140
Lean On Me 167
Leaning On the Lamppost 64
Leatherman's Theme 114
Leave Me Alone 52
Leave My Woman Alone 45
Led Boots 165
Lemon and Lime 81
Les Girls 112
Lessons In Love 130
Let 'Em In 164
Let It Be 152, 156, 179
Let It Be Me 109
Let It Bleed 154
Let Me Be 79
Let Me Call You Sweetheart 97
Let Me Go 154
Let Me Lie 55
Let Me Love You 187
Let Me Roll It 164
Let the Good Times Roll 23, 135, 153
Let the Sunshine In 58
Let Us Pray 29
Let Your Body Rock 23
Let Your Feelings Show 141
Let Yourself Go 106
Let's Be Friends 29

Let's Dance 180
Let's Do My Twist 64
Let's Get Together Again 82
Let's Go Crazy 91
Let's Go Go 30
Let's Groove 141
Let's Have a Party 80, 137
Let's Hear It For the Boys 43
Let's Make a Deal 114
Let's Spend the Night Together 154
Let's Talk About Love 68
Let's Twist Again 114, 153
Letter, The 109, 156
Letting Go 164
Liberation 27
Lido Shuffle 184
Lie to Me 181
Life 195
Life At Last 86
Life During Wartime 116, 171
Life Goes On 110
Life In the Fast Lane 184
Life Line 190
Life's Been Good 184
Lifeboat Party 155
Lift Every Voice and Sing 173
Light House, The 143
Light My Fire 189
Light Out of Darkness 23
Like a Glove 137
Like a Rolling Stone 149, 189
Lil' Lockers 24
Linda Lou 115
Lip Up Fatty 133, 139
Lipstick Powder and Paint 103
Listen People 125
Listen to Me 27
Listen to What the Flower People Say 116
Listen To What the Man Said 164
Listening to You 117
Little Altar Boy 33
Little Bit More, A 103
Little Bitty Corrine 198
Little Blue Wren 95
Little Boat 75
Little Darlin' 12, 18, 115, 179
Little Egypt 99
Little Help From My Friends, A 109, 156, 161
Little Honda 52
Little Imagination, A 128
Little Less Conversation, A 78
Little Moses 91
Little Queenie 53
Little Sister 143
Little Speedy Gonzales 127
Little Star 12
Little T and A 154
Live and Let Die 164
Live It Up 78
Lively Set, The 79
Lively Up Yourself 136, 165
Living Doll 101, 130
Livingston Saturday Night 183

Locomotion, The 45, 180
Lollipops and Rainbows 104
London's Burning 99
Lonely Afternoon 45
Lonely Boy 51, 147
Lonely City 68
Lonely Girl 122
Lonely In the Chapel 199
Lonely Life 114
Lonely Looking Sky 187
Lonely Man 126
Lonely Rider, The 199
Lonely Sea, The 52
Lonelyville 77
Loner, The 195
Lonesome 95
Lonesome Cowboy 80
Lonesome Death of Hattie Carroll, The 140
Lonesome Train 95
Long and Winding Road, The 53, 102, 152, 179
Long Legged Girl 34
Long Live Rock 115, 150
Long Lonely Highway 116
Long Long Day 83
Long Tall Sally 33, 35
Long Time Gone 174, 195
Longest River, The 165
Look At Me 56, 79
Look Into Your Heart 106
Look Out Broadway 45
Look Out For Number One 110
Look Over Yonder 162
Look Over Your Shoulder 189
Look to the Left 137
Lookin' to Spy 198
Looking Back 29
Looking For Someone 193
Looking Good 179
Lorraine 133
Lose Your Inhibition Twist 68
Lost Inside of You 107
Lots Lots More 104
Louie Louie 180
Louisiana Man 156
Love 38
Love Children, The 89
Love In a Void 73
Love In Chains 76
Love In Vain 145, 151
Love Is a Drug 165
Love Is a Fire 198
Love Is a Four-Letter Verb 137
Love Is All I Need 95
Love Is Just a Four Letter Word 140
Love Is On Our Side 180
Love Like You, A 83
Love Machine, The 34
Love Me 143
Love Me Baby 95
Love Me Tender 35, 79, 143, 183
Love Never Forgets 95
Love On the Rocks 71
Love Potion Number 9 179

INDEX OF SONG TITLES

Love Reign O'er Me 191
Love Scene 200
Love Theme in the Key of D 181
Love Theme Number One 181
Love to Be Your Man 126
Love To Love You Baby 114
Loveliness 199
Lovely Day 199
Lovely Loretta 65
Lovely Rita 179
Lover Doll 75
Love's Dream 77
Lovin' Her Was Easy 182
Lovin' Livin' and Givin' 114
Loving Me This Way 78
Loving You 80, 195
Lucille 153
Lucky Number 191
Lucy In the Sky With Diamonds 102, 129, 179
Lumberjack Song 167
Lumpy Gravy 189
Luther's Blues 183
Lyin' On the Truth 173

M386 94
Machine Gun 149
Mad 101
Mad About the Boy 188
Mad Dogs and Englishmen Theme 156
Mad Mad Mad 130
Made You 17
Mademoiselle Nobs 160
Madness 137, 139, 172
Maggie's Farm 143
Magic 129
Magic Bus 150
Magic Mona 184
Magic Night 27
Magical Mystery Tour 80, 179
Magnetic Mama 187
Magneto and Titanium Man 164
Magnificent Seven, The 133
Mahuny 42
Mail Call 124
Majestic, The 122
Make Me Good 109
Make Me Happy 64
Make Room for Joy 73
Made The Headlines 195
Make the Music Pretty 49
Make Yours a Happy Home 182
Makings of You, The 182
Malibu Run 83
Mama's Lament 91
Mambo Rock 94
Mamma Mia 133
Man at C&A 139
Man From Nowhere 75
Man Needs a Woman, A 93
Man of 1000 Faces 76
Man of Music 186
Man Smart Woman Smarter 165
Manchester 58

Maneater 163
Maniac 42
Manic Depression 183
Mannish Boy 143, 151
Many Rivers to Cross 60
Maraca Bamba 68
Marguerita 46
Maria Maria 138
Marianne 136
Martial Law 159
Mary Hamilton 143
Mary In the Morning 143
Mashed Potato Time 33
Matter of Moments, A 128
Matthew and Son 110
Maxwell's Silver Hammer 152
Maybe 148
Maybe Baby 27, 179
Maybe I'm Amazed 164
Maybe It Wasn't Really Love 48
Maybelline 162
McVicar 187
Me and Bobby McGee 134, 148
Me and My Arrow 190
Me and You 93
Meadow Mountain Top 183
Mean Woman Blues 80
Meant it For a Minute 137
Medicine Jar 164
Medicine Man 39
Mellow Out 189
Melody Fair 188
Melody Man 116
Memories 143
Memphis Tennessee 53, 176
Mercedes Benz 148
Mercedes Morning 116
Mercury Blues 162
Merry Go Round 188
Merry Twistmas 122
Messin' With the Kid 136
Mexico 46
Michelle's Song 195
Mickey's Monkey 183, 188, 189
Mickey's Tune 200
Midnight Blue 195
Midnight Hour, The 186
Midnight Rambler 151
Midnight Rendezvous 197
Midnight Rider 199
Midsummer New York 148
Mighty Mighty Pisces 184
Milkshake 28
Mind Train 148
Minnie the Moocher 23
Miracle Cure 119
Mirage 60
Mirror in the Bathroom 139
Miss You 154
Missing Words 139
Mississippi Queen 197
Mister Blue 12
Mobile Line 137

Moby Dick 168
Mocking Bird 159
Mojo 144
Moment by Moment 188
Momma Can I Go Out? 53
Monday Monday 110
Money 180, 196
Money Man 185
Money Money Money 133
Money Worries 96
Monkey See Monkey Do 125
Monster Club, The 81
Monster Rule OK 81
Monsters in Disguise 25
Moody Girls 110
Moon Rock 185
Moonbeam Song, The 105
Moonlight Swim 21
More Than a Feeling 184
More Than a Woman 192
More Than Just a Friend 184
Most Beautiful Thing In My Life, The 81
Most of All 183
Most of the Time 169
Mother and Son 117
Mother Nature 147
Move On 182
Move On Up 58
Move Over 148
Move Over Gabriel 185
Movin' On 187
Mr Lee 12
Mr Lonely 189
Mr Make Believe 76
Mr Welfare Man 182
Mrs Brown You've Got a Lovely Daughter 81
Mrs Lennon 148
Mrs Robinson 185
Mud People 185
Mule Skinner Blues 91
Muscle Beach Party 82
Muscle Bustle 82
Music For Chameleons 145
Music Lover 174
Must To Avoid, A 64
My Best Friend's Girl 190
My Blue Heaven 153
My Bonnie 75
My Boyfriend's Back 189, 198
My Buddy Seat 15
My Conviction 58
My Desert Serenade 60
My Dying Machine 145
My First Love 82
My Generation 110, 157
My Girl 180, 183
My Girl Lollipop 133
My Guy 189
My Happiness 35
My Home Town 189
My Idea of Love 51
My Little Girl 75
My Love Is True 53

My Music 116
My My Hey Hey 165
My Name Is Jack 176
My Name is Yussel 71
My Own Way to Rock 147
My Soul Is a Witness 189
My Sweet Joy 135
My Sweet Lord 138
My Time After a While 136
My Way 40, 147
Mystery Song 169
Mystery Train 35, 143, 163

Na Na Na Na Nu Nu 139
Nadine 138
Name of the Game, The 133
Nancy 136
Nashville Cats 186
Natty Takeover 96
Naughty Boy 155
Nearness of You, The 52
Need a New Sun Rising 91
Need a Shot of Rhythm and Blues 109
Needed Time 195
Needle and the Damage Done, The 150
Neighbors 154
Never 43
Never Be You 111
Never Been to Spain 143
Never Knew How Much (I Needed You) 137
Never Let Me Go 52
Never Say Yes 107
Never Together But Close Sometimes 137
New Age 159
New Clothes 194
New Life 196
New Love 16
New Orleans 75
New York City Band 195
New York Groove 76
Next Step is Love, The 143
Next Time, The 112
Ni Ni Na Na Noo 133
Night Before, The 62
Night Boat to Cairo 139
Night Fever 192
Night Has a Thousand Eyes, The 75
Night Life 123
Night Moves 14, 184
Night Rider 116
Night Run 198
Night They Drove Old Dixie Down, The 134, 151
Night Time Girl 173
Night Train 191
Night Was Not, The 116
Night We Said Goodbye, The 97
Nightclubbing 139
Nightingale Sang in Berkeley Square, A 156
Nightride 181
1967 (So Long Ago) 167
96 Tears 189
Nite Club 139

Nitro 113
No Expectations 183
No Feelings 147
No Fun 147
No Love Today 189
No More 21
No More Lonely Nights 53
No One But Me 14
No One Does It Better 184
No One Is Innocent 147
No Quarter 168
No Reason 99
No Room to Rhumba In a Sports Car 46
No Sugar Tonight 147
No Time 147
No Turning Back 101
No Woman No Cry 136
Nobody 83
Nobody But You 86
Nobody Knows 197
Not Fade Away 27
Not Such a Bad Boy 53
Nothing Can Stand In My Way 198
Nothing's Impossible 130
Now That We've Found Love 199
Nowhere Fast 111
Nowhere Man 102, 129, 179
Nowhere to Run 198
Now's the Time 68
Nut Rocker 160

O Lucky Man 189
O.K. Yesterday Was Yesterday 41
Octopus's Garden 152
Ode to Wild Bill 199
Of Whom Should I Be Afraid? 190
Oh Bondage Up Yours 139
Oh Boy 12, 27
Oh Darling 102, 152
Oh Death 181
Oh Happy Day 137, 148
Oh Marion 83
Oh Mary 114
Oh My Love 147
Oh Senorita 40
Oh What a Family 124
Oh Yoko 148
Ohm Sweet Ohm 191
Ol La Le Da 173
Ol Sol 182
Old Fashioned Melody 58
Old Landmark, The 23
Old Macdonald 34
Old Shep 35, 79
Old Souls 86
Old Time Religion 151
On a Clear Day 166
On and On 182
On My Radio 139
On the Beach 129
On the Move 182
On the Radio 184
On the Road Again 182

On the Robert E. Lee 71
On Top Of Old Smokey 43
Once Again 53
Once I Was 183
Once In a Lifetime 171, 183
Once Is Enough 76
Once Upon a Dream 87
One After 909 152
One Bad Stud 111
One Boy Two Little Girls 76
One Broken Heart 67
One Fine Day 109, 186
One More Cup of Coffee 91
One More Day 71
One More Time 25
One Night With You 143
One of These Days I'm Gonna Cut You Into Little Pieces 160
One of Us Can't Be Wrong 136
One On One 163
One Step Beyond 139, 172
One Summer Night 194
One Thing Leads to Another 23
One Too Many Mornings 91, 149
One Track Heart 99
One Two Three 135
One Way Out 137
One Way Ticket 137
One-Trick Pony 83
Only a Northern Song 129
Only Funking 133
Only One 28
Only You 94
Onward Christian Soldiers 87
Oobala Baby 123
Ooh Baby Baby 183
Ooh Child 190
Ooh My Head 53
Ooh She's Done It Again 81
Ooo-Wee Baby 66
Open All Night 163
Open Fire 137
Open Our Eyes 29
Open Sesame 192
Open Up Your Heart 14
Operator 156
Ophelia 151
Orange Blossom Special 156
Organ Music 185
Orientation 190
Orly 147
Orpheus Song 77
Othello 29
Other Side of Life, The 145
Ou-Shoo-Bla-Dee 28
Our Day Will Come 189
Our House 159, 195
Our Love's Gonna Snowball 128
Out Here On My Own 38
Out of Time 173, 183
Out On the Floor 83
Out to Lunch 113
Over and Over 30

INDEX OF SONG TITLES

Over and Over Again 95
Over at the Frankenstein Place 96
Over Me 197
Oye Mama 195

P.O.V. Waltz 190
Pack Up Your Sorrows 143
Paella 40
Pagan Knights 182
Pain 93
Paint It Black 157, 173
Painting the Town 104
Pajama Party 84
Pali Gap 162
Papa Was a Rollin' Stone 167
Paradise Hawaiian Style 84
Paranoia Paradise 73
Parker's Mood 156
Party Doll 115
Party Knox 179
Party Music 58
Pass You By 181
Pastures of Plenty 11
Patch It Up 143
Pattern Is Broken, The 185
Patty's Gone to Laredo 91
Peace At Last 77
Peace Be Still 173
Peace Pipe 130
Peanut Butter and Jam 67
Peggy Sue 27
Pennie the Poo 113
Penny Lane 80
People Are Strange 14
People Get Ready 91
People Get Up and Drive Your Funky Soul 194
People In Love 103
People Make the World Go Round 167
People of Tomorrow Are the Children of Today 196
Peppermint Twist 64, 179
Perfect Boy, The 66
Perfect Dancer 193
Perfect Strangers 77
Personality 115
Petunia the Gardener's Daughter 46
Phantom's Theme 86
Phil's Love Theme 198
Pick Up the Pieces 173
Picking Up Strangers 183
Picture of Her 186
Pictures at an Exhibition 160
Pictures of Lily 150
Piece of My Heart 148
Piece of the Action, A 190
Pinball That's All 116
Pinball Wizard 117, 150, 167
Pinhead 94
Pipe Dreams 86
Pipeline 186, 189, 198
Pissing In the River 116
Pistolero 39
Planet Schmanet 96

Play It Cool 87
Playmate 53
Playmates 30
Please Change Your Mind 133
Please Don't Bury My Soul 48
Please Don't Stop Loving Me 46
Please Give Me a Chance 124
Please Mr Johnson 53
Please Mr Postman 188
Pledging My Love 35, 188
Poachin' 195
Pocketful of Rainbows 47
Poetry In Motion 115
Poison Ivy 153
Poison Ivy League 99
Poli High 190
Police and Thieves 96, 139
Polk Salad Annie 143
Polken Gar 133
Polythene Pam 102, 179
Pony Boy 137
Pony Time 153
Poor Boy 79
Poor Jerusalem 72
Poor Love 190
Poor People 189
Poor Poor Pitiful Me 184
Poppy Girls 128
Porpoise Song 61
Possession 186
Possibility 114
Pot of Jazz 86
Pow 198
Power To the People 148
Prelude 165
Pressure Drop 60
Pretty Boys 116
Pretty Little Girl 66
Pretty Song, The 89
Pretty Vacant 139, 147
Prince, The 139
Prisoner, The 99
Privilege 87
Promise Me Anything 17
Promised Land, The 138
Prophets 195
Proud Mary 143, 148
Psych-Out 89
Psych-Out Sanatorium 89
Psychedelic Senate 126
Psycho Killer 171
Pueblo Pool, The 48
Pump (the Pump) 165
Punk and the Godfather, The 191
Puppet On a String 51
Purple Haze 149, 162, 174, 199
Purple Rain 91
Pushin' Too Hard 89
Put a Little Love In Your Heart 182
Put Out the Light 29
Put the Blame On Me 116
Put Your Money Where Your Mouth Is 181

Quarter To Three 159
Queen 56
Queen Bee 107
Queen Majesty 96
Queenie Wahine's Papaya 84
Questionly 94
Questions 122
Quick One, A 150

R.O.C.K. 94
Race Is On, The 189
Radioactive 76
Radioactivity 191
Raga Bhimpalasi 157
Ragtime 184
Railroad 169
Rain Song 168
Rainbows 68
Rained Out 182
Rainy Day Mushroom Pillow 89
Ralph and Monty 38
Ramblin' Man 137
Rambling On My Mind 165
Ranking Full Stop 139
Raunchy 45, 115
Rave On 12, 27
Razor Blade Alley 139
Razzle Dazzle 94
Reach Out I'll Be There 183
Ready Teddy 50, 143
Ready to Groove 113
Real Me, The 191
Real Thing, The 161
Reasons 141
Rebel Rebel 140, 187
Reckless 24
Record Hop Tonight 71
Record Run 18
Red Hot Roadster 113
Red House 149
Red Leather Jacket 115
Red Light 38
Red River Rock 115
Reelin' and Rockin' 12, 138, 153
Reflection 189
Relax 67
Relax Me 161
Remember 105
Remember the Children 141
Remember When 28
Remind Me to Smile 145
Resolution Rock 99
Respect 161, 189, 196
Respect Yourself 173
Respoken 198
Return to Sender 52
Revolution 162
Rhiannon 194
Rhythm of the Rain 191
Ride My Llama 165
Ride That Wave 195
Ridin' the Storm Out 183
Riding the Rainbow 75

233

INDEX OF SONG TITLES

Right Back Where We Started From   194
Right Now Right Now   95
Right On Be Free   167
Right to Work   73
Ring of Fire   93, 149
Ring Ring   133
Ring-A-Ding Day   68
Riot On Sunset Strip   191
Rip and Destroy   76
Rip It Up   33, 153
Rita Mae   165
River   39
River Boulevard   144
River, The   159
Rivers of Babylon   60
Road Rats   93
Road Runner   135, 150, 165, 183, 197
Roadhouse Blues   169
Rock   136
Rock A Beatin' Boogie   94
Rock and Roll   94, 168
Rock and Roll Is Here to Stay   12
Rock and Roll Music   138
Rock Around the Clock   94, 147, 153, 163, 179, 181
Rock Around the Rock Pile   50
Rock Around With Ollie Vee   27
Rock Hard   116
Rock Lobster   83
Rock Me   133
Rock Me Baby   149
Rock My Soul   143
Rock of Ages   188
Rock On   115
Rock Pretty Baby   95
Rock Rock Rock   95
Rock the World   127
Rock With Me   106
Rock-a Hula Baby   21
Rockaria   187
Rockaway Beach   196
Rockers   96
Rockin' All Over the World   169
Rockin' Angel   199
Rockin' Is Our Business   51
Rockin' Maybelle   95
Rockin' Saints   95
Rockin' Saturday Night   103
Rock'n'Roll   94
Rock'n'Roll All Night   76
Rock'n'Roll Boogie   95
Rock'n'Roll Choo Choo   196
Rock'n'Roll Creation   116
Rock'n'Roll Dancing   184
Rock'n'Roll High School   94
Rock'n'Roll Is Here to Stay   56
Rock'n'Roll Party   56
Rock'n'Roll Rodeo   116
Rock'n'Roll Woman   186
Roll Over Beethoven   12, 138
Roll Over Lay Down   169
Roller Girl   193
Rollin' and Tumblin'   157

Rollin' On   39
Roly-Poly   64
Romance In Durango   91
Romeo   42
Roogie Oogie   95
Room Full of Mirrors   162
Room to Breathe   163
Room to Move   136
Rose, The   97, 140
Rough Kids   172
Roughrider   139
Round and Round   112
Roundabout   174
Roustabout   99
Rubber Biscuit   188
Rubberneckin'   29
Ruby Tuesday   183
Rudi Can't Fail   99
Rudy's Rock   94
Rule Brittania   73
Rumble   111
Run Away From Him   127
Run, Shaker, Run   29, 168
Runaround Sue   115, 122
Runaway   115, 159, 179
Runaway Country   197
Runnin' Back to Saskatoon   147
Runnin' Wild   82
Running Away   136
Running Bear   115, 194
Running On Empty   159

Sad Sad Summer   179
Sad-Eyed Lady of the Lowlands   91
Safari Mary   187
Safe European Home   99
Salad Bar   133
Sally Ann   124
Sally Le Roy   126
Sally Simpson   117
Salt Park West Virginia   91
Sam's Boogie   121
Samantha   27
Same Old Scene   116
Samson and Delilah   133
San Francisco   157
Sandy   56
Sara   91
Sara Smile   163
Satan   192
Satellite of Love   159
Satisfaction   135, 154, 161, 191
Satta Amasgana   96
Satta Massagana   165
Saturday Night   45
Saturday Night Rock A Boogie   66
Saturday Night Special   181
Saucerful of Secrets, A   160
Savage, The   130
Save Me   183
Save the Children   167
Save the Last Dance For Me   153
Sawdust and G-Strings   182

Say That You Love Me   194
Scarborough Fair   185
Scary Monsters   140
School Days   94, 138, 153
School's Out   94
Science Fiction Double-Feature   96
Scuba Party   28
Sea Cruise   12
Sea of Love   194
Sea of Madness   137
Sea's Getting Rough   182
Sealed With a Kiss   115
Searchin'   45
Season of the Witch   189
Secret Path of Love   77
Secret Surfin'   16
Secret Weapon   18
Section 43   157
Seduce Me Tonight   42
See Me Feel Me   117, 150
See You In September   179
See You Later Alligator   94, 172
Sell Sell   189
Sensation   117
Sentimental Lady   184
Separate Ways   35, 143
Sermon, The   49
Set the Controls For the Heart of the Sun   160
Seven Day Weekend   68
Sex and Drugs and Rock and Roll   196
Sex Farm   116
Sex Shooter   91
Sexy Sexy Sexy   194
Sgt. Pepper's Lonely Hearts Club Band   102, 129
Sh-Boom   163, 194, 196
Shades of Gray   185
Shaft   173
Shake   157
Shake a Tail Feather   40
Shake It   184
Shake Rattle and Roll   35, 152, 153, 163
Shake the Tambourine   60
Shake Your Body   193
Shake Your Moneymaker   23
Shake Your Tailfeathers   23
Shakin' All Over   147
Shama Lang Ding Dong   180
Shame   199
Shanty Town   60
Shape I'm In   151
Shape of Things to Come   126
Sharpshooter   23
Shattered   154
Shave and a Haircut Two Bits   21
Shazam   17
She Belongs To Me   91
She Came In Through the Bathroom Window   102, 156, 179
She Caught the Katy   23
She Drives Me Out of My Mind   189
She Laughed   14
She Loves You   19, 59
She Was a Lady   179

INDEX OF SONG TITLES

Sheena Is a Punk Rocker 94
She'll Come Back 83
Shelley In Camp 126
Sherry 180, 198
She's a Machine 34
She's Gone 163
She's Got It 50
She's Leaving Home 102, 110, 179
She's Not There 110, 189
She's So Cold 154
She's So Heavy 102
She's So Modern 196
She's So Sharp 133
She's the Meanest Girl In Town 51
She's the One 94
She's the Only Girl For Me 40
Shimme Do Wah Say 188
Shining Star 141, 193
Ship of Fools 184
Ship of Love 188
Ship On a Stormy Sea 53
Shiver Me Timbers 140
Shoppin' Around 47
Short Shorts 77
Shorty George 136
Shout 60, 135, 150, 180, 198
Shout It Out 46
Shout It Out Loud 76
Show Me the Way 189
Showdown 39
Shrine On The Second Floor, The 38
Shy Ann 130
Sign of the Zodiac 121
Silly Girl 176
Silly Love Songs 53, 164
Silly Thing 147
Silver Dream Racer 193
Simon Zealots 72
Since I Don't Have You 12, 179
Since I Fell For You 189
Since I've Been Loving You 168
Sincerely 12, 153
Sing a Song 141
Sing Boy Sing 103
Sing Out For Jesus 197
Sing You Children 34
Single 66
Sip the Wine 151
Sister Surprise 145
Sisters of Mercy 136
Sitting In Limbo 60
Sitting There Standing 191
Six Days On the Road 145
Sixteen Candles 179
Sixty Minute Man 12
Skatetown USA 193
Skeet-Surfin' 120
Ski City 128
Ski Party 104
Sky Is Crying 144
Skybird 187
Slave Master 96
Sleepyland 43

Slicin' Sand 21
Slide Some Oil to Me 128
Slider, The 137
Slippery People 171
Sloppy Sue 49
Slow Down 115
Slow Ride 184
Slow Train 169
Slow Twist 33
Slowdown Sundown 165
Slowly But Surely 116
Smashing Time 194
Smoke Gets In Your Eyes 115, 179
Smokey Mountain Boy 76
Smokie 114
Smoking In the Boy's Room 94
Smooth Talker 23
Smorgasbord 107
Snap It 127
Snuggle Huggle 39
So Bad 53
So Close and Yet So Far (From Paradise) 60
So Far So Good 41
So Find 187
So Hard To Say Goodbye to Yesterday 183
So It Goes 94
So Long 133
So Sad the Spring 86
So Tired 197
Soda Pop Pop 103
Sodomy 58
Soily 164
Sold My Soul to Rock'n'Roll 97
Soldier Boy 153, 198
Some Other Guy 109
Somebody Gonna Off the Man 196
Somebody Help Me 14
Somebody Nobody Wants 114
Somebody Super Like You 86
Somebody To Hold 58
Somebody To Love 58
Somebody's Eyes 43
Someone Greater Than You and I 173
Something 138, 156
Something Else 147
Something In the Air 188, 195
Sometime Yesterday 68
Sometimes When We Touch 188
Son House Blues 143
Son of Shaft 173
Song for David 137
Song of Sad Bottles 183
Song of the Shrimp 52
Song Remains the Same, The 168
Songs of Life 71
Songs to Ageing Children 11
Sonny Boy 176
Sonuvagun 187
Soon As I Get Home 128
Soothe Me 23
Sophistication 27
Sorcerer 111
Sorry Seems to Be the Hardest Word 194

SOS 133
Soul Man 83
Soul Sacrifice 174
Soul to Soul 168
Soulsville 173
Sound Advice 43
Sound of Silence 185, 189
Sound of the City 27
Sour Suite 147
Southbound 137
Southern Man 184
Space Ball Picket 137
Space Captain 156
Space Oddity 140
Space Ship to Mars 68
Spanish Lies 107
Spanish Stroll 196
Sparkle 106
Sparks 119, 150
Speak Now Or Forever Hold Your Peace 190
Speakin' of Spoken 198
Special Brew 133
Special To Me 86
Speedway 106
Spend This Night With Me 120
Spicks and Specks 188
Spinout 107
Spirits Drifting 94
Spirits of Ancient Egypt 164
Splish Splash 12
Spooky 182, 189
Spoonful 186
Spray It On 23
Spread the Word 50
Spring Fever 51
Stagefright 151
Stairway to Heaven 165, 168
Stand and Fight 159
Stand By Me 69, 198
Stand Up and Fight 49
Standing On the Corner 41
Star Cycle 165
Star In My Life 189
Star Spangled Banner, The 149, 162, 173, 174
Stardust 109
Starship Trooper 174
Start Me Up 154
Startin' Tonight 51
Starting Over 175
Statesboro Blues 137
Station to Station 140
Stay 12, 159
Stay, Away, Stay Away Joe 110
Stay Free 99
Stay With Me 97, 140
Staying Alive 110, 192
Steadfast Loyal and True 75
Stepping Out of Line 21
Stepping Razor 96
Stoned 133
Stonehenge 116
Stool Pigeon 155
Stop In the Name of Love 183, 189

235

INDEX OF SONG TITLES

Stop Look and Listen   107
Stop the World   95
Stop Where You Are   84
Stormy   182
Straighten Out the Rug   120
Strange Brew   189
Strange Things Mystifying   72
Stranger Girl   198
Stranger In My Home Town   162
Stranger In the Crowd   143
Stranger In Town   112
Strangered In the Night   188
Strawberry Fields Forever   80, 102, 179, 183
Street Fighting Man   145, 151
Street People   24
Stripper, The   17, 81
Stroll, The   179
Stuffed Animal   84
Substitute   150
Subterranean Homesick Blues   140
Success Story   150
Such A Night   151
Such An Easy Question   116
Sucker For Your Love   81
Suddenly   129
Sugar Baby   95
Sugar Baby Love   82
Sugartime   104
Suite Judy Blue Eyes   159, 174
Summer (The First Time)   140
Summer Day Reflection   135
Summer Holiday   112
Summer In the City   110
Summer Kisses Winter Tears   41
Summer Nights   56
Summer Song   41
Summerlove   71
Summertime   14, 148, 179
Summertime Blues   12, 163, 174
Sun King   179
Sunnyside   195
Sunshine   167
Super Soul Theme   197
Super-Heroes   96
Superbyrd   162
Superfly   195
Superfly Man   195
Superstar   72
Surf Party   113
Surfer Boy   15
Surfer's Holiday   82
Surfin' and A Swingin'   16
Survive   39
Suspicious Minds   35, 143
Suzanne   91
Swamp   171
Swan Lake   139
Swayin' to the Music   183
Sweet and Dandy   60
Sweet Caroline   143
Sweet Gene Vincent   191
Sweet Home Chicago   23
Sweet Jane   159

Sweet Jesus   197
Sweet Little Lover   66
Sweet Little Sixteen   12, 138, 153
Sweet Love On My Mind   103
Sweet Memories   182
Sweet Sir Galahad   137
Sweet Sweet Spirit   143
Sweet Transvestite   96
Swim, The   49
Swing Low Sweet Chariot   121, 174
Swing With It   195
Swing-A-Ma-Thing   49
Swingin' Affair   112
Swingin' School   17
Swingin' Set, The   49
Swingin' Summer, A   113
Sword of Damocles, The   96
Sympathy For the Devil   145, 172, 183

T.N.T.   195
Tag That Twistin' Dolly   121
Take a Pebble   160
Take It Away   109
Take It Easy   87
Take Me High   195
Take Me to the Fair   67
Take Me To the River   165, 171
Take Me with U   91
Take My Baby Back   119
Take This Town   116
Takin' Care of Business   147
Takin' It to the Streets   159
Taking Out Time   186
Talk   185
Talk of the Town   116
Talkin' About Love   49
Talkin' About You   23
Tangled Up In Blue   91
Tantrum   30
Tanya   181
Taste   39
Teach Your Children   188
Tears On My Pillow   56
Teddy Bear   80
Teen Angel   179
Teenage Crush   103
Teenage Depression   94
Teenage Fair   176
Teenage Frankie and Johnny   28
Teenage Heaven   53
Teenage Lobotomy   94, 190
Teenage Millionaire   114
Teenage Party   119
Teenage Vamp   122
Telegram Sam   137
Telephone Line   187
Tell Him   180
Tell Mama   148
Tell Me   165, 183, 188
Tell Me Why   59
Tempo's Tempo   51
Temptation Baby   78
Temptation Lust and Laziness   187

Tender Feeling   76
Tenement Yard   96
Tequila   115, 133, 198
Texas   93
Thank You For the Many Things You've Done   180
Thank You For the Music   133
Thanks to the Rolling Sea   52
Thanks to You   95
That Is Rock and Roll   12
That Lovin' You Feelin' Again   93
That Lucky Old Sun   23
That'll Be the Day   27, 115, 179
That's All I Want From You   103
That's All Right   35, 115, 143, 163
That's Just the Way It Is   39
That's the Kind of Sugar Papa Likes   76
That's the Way God Planned It   138
That's the Way of the World   141, 193
That's What God Said   29
That's What I Like About My Baby   184
That's Why   12
That's Why God Made the Movies   83
Them Bellyful   136
Them Monkeys Can't Swing   41
Theme From 'The Last Waltz'   151
Theme from Rawhide   23
Theme From Young Lovers   129
There Ain't Nothing Like a Song   106
There Are Times   77
There Goes My Baby   12
There Has To Be a Reason   84
There's a Brand New Day on the Horizon   99
There's a Kind of Hush All Over the World   81
There's a New World Opening for Me   28
There's a Place In the World For a Gambler   184
There's Gold In the Mountains   76
There's No Place Without You   28
There's No Stoppin' Us   24
There's So Much World To See   34
There's Something Wrong In Paradise   155
These Are Not My People   189
They Just Don't Make 'Em Like Her Anymore   34
They Remind Me Too Much of You   67
They're Gonna Step On You   185
They're Letting Me Drive Again   195
Things We Never Said   124
Things Your Heart Needs, The   95
Think   23
Think About Your Troubles   190
Thinking of You Baby   49
This Boat   122
This Child of Mine   167
This Day   40
This Friendly World   66
This Girl   41
This I Say   34
This Is Living   75
This Is New Love   145
This Is the Beginning   48
This Is the Night   28
This Is When I Need You Most   189
This Prison Moon   145

236

INDEX OF SONG TITLES

This Thing Called Love 40
This Time It's Love 18
This Town 30
This World 165
Those Magic Changes 56
Those Oldies But Goodies 188
Thousand Miles Away, A 12, 179
Thousand Stars, A 115
3-5-0-0 58
Three Minute Hero 139
Three Steps to Heaven 191
Three Times Seven 134
Three V 24
Throw It Out of Your Mind 124
Thunder Road 159
Thunder Thumbs and Lightning Licks 189
Tibetan Jam 24
Tick a Tick a Tick 127
Ticket To Ride 62
Tiger 133
Tiger Feet 82
Tiger Man 143
Tighten Up Your Wig 189
Tightrope 187
Till Blossoms Bloom 190
Till I Kissed You 115
Time Drags By 40
Time Has Come Today 183
Time Is On My Side 154
Time of the Preacher 91
Time to Cry 51
Time To Hide 164
Time to Kill 119
Time Warp, The 96
Times They Are a Changin', The 140, 159, 198
To Be Invisible 182
To Be Young Gifted and Black 167
To Know Him Is to Love Him 45
To Love Somebody 161, 188
To Sing For You 140
To the Aisle 179
Today 157
Today Is Where 48
Today It Rained Champagne 117
Today Tomorrow and Forever 123
Tommy Can You Hear Me 150
Tommy Gun 99
Tommy's Holiday Camp 117
Tongue Tied 50
Tonight I'm Gonna Rock You 116
Tonight Is So Right For Love 47
Tonight Is What It Means to Be Young 111
Tonight's My Night 43
Tonight's the Night 30
Too Hot To Trot 114
Too Much Monkey Business 138
Too Much Pressure 139
Too Much Too Young 139
Toot Toot Tootsie Goodbye 196
Top of the Wheel 25
Tossin' and Turnin' 180
Touch Me 75
Toucha Toucha Touch Me 96

Tour De France 24
Tra La La 95
Tracks of My Tears, The 180
Train Kept A-Rollin' The 104
Train Ride 196
Trans-Europe Express 191
Treasure Dub 96
Treat Him Nicely 17
Treat Me Nice 71
Trenchtown 136
Trenchtown Rock 165
Trickle Trickle 156
Trouble 75, 194
True Love Ways 27
Trust Me 56
Try 148
Try My World Little Girl 34
Try With Your Love 114
Trying Times 168
Tulsa Time 143, 165
Tumblin' Dice 151, 154, 184
Turn Back O Man 54
Turn Me Loose 14, 180
Turn Out the Lights 159
Turn Turn Turn 135, 143, 186, 189
Turtles Berries and Gumbo 75
Tutti Frutti 12, 33, 115, 120, 137
25 Per Cent 81
Twenty Flight Rock 50, 154
24 Hours a Day 71
Twilight Zone 156
Twist Along 122
Twist and Shout 122
Twist Around the Clock 122
Twist, The 153, 180
Twistin' On a Liner 122
Twistin' the Night Away 180
Twistin' USA 122
Twist'n'Crawl 139
Two a Penny 122
Two Eyes 119
Two Fingers Pointing On You 89
Two of a Kind 128
Two of Us 152
Two Thousand Light Years From Home 161
Type Thing 193

Unchain My Heart 23
Uncle Sam's Blues 144
Unconscious Minuet 198
Under My Thumb 145, 154, 193
Undone 147
Universal Soldier 135
Unknown Rider, The 199
Until It's Time For You To Go 35, 143
Up On the Roof 109
Up Your Totem Pole With Love 30
Upholstery 86
Ups and Downs of Love 75
Uptight 110
Urban Landscape 191
USA 99
Utterly Simple 186

Valentino Had Enough 81
Vanishing Point 23
Venus and Mars 164
Veronica 191
Vicarage, The 195
Vino Dinero Y Amor 46
Virgin's Dream 186
Virginia 184
Viva Las Vegas 123
Voice In the Wilderness, A 38
Voice On the Mountain 130
Voodoo Chile 162

Wabe, The 176
Wah Wah 138
Wah Watusi 191
Wailin' and Whoopin' 182
Wait and See 71
Wait For Me 163
Waiting For a Friend 187
Waiting For a Girl Like You 43
Waiting for Billy 43
Waiting For My Friend 194
Waiting For the Bus 96
Waiting On a Friend 154
Wake Up Little Suzie 115
Walk Like a Man 198
Walk On 67
Walk On the Wild Side 116, 159, 187
Walkin' 129
Walking In Space 58
Walking In the Sunshine 133
Walking On Thin Ice 175
Walking the Backstreets and Crying 173
Walls Have Ears, The 52
Waltz for Caroline 186
Wanderer, The 122
Wanderlust 53
Wang Dang Doodle 181
Want More 165
War 136
War Drags On, The 143
Wargasm in Pornotopia 73
Warrior Charge 180
Wash Us Clean 29
Washerwoman 40
Wasn't It a Handsome Punch-Up? 124
Watch Closely Now 107
Watcha Gonna Do 14
Watcha Gonna Do About It 147
Watching the Wheels 175
Water Water 119
Waterloo 133
Watusi Surfer 130
Waves of Fear 159
Way Back Home 30
Way I Am, The 114
Way Over There 189
We a Rockers 96
We Almost Lost Detroit 159
We Are Glass 145
We Are the Future 179
We Can Be Together 144

237

INDEX OF SONG TITLES

We Can Work It Out 179
We Don't Make Each Other Laugh Anymore 199
We Go Together 56
We Gotta Get Out of Here 197
We Gotta Get Out of This Place 67
We Live For Love 197
We Love a Movie 129
We Take Mystery to Bed 145
We the People 173
We Want You Herman 64
We Will Rock You 184
Wedding Song 96
Welcome 117
Welcome to Nevada 197
Welcome to the House of Fun 172
Welfare Mother 165
Well All Right 27, 115, 162
We'll Be Together 52
Well It's Time to Go 179
We're Comin' In Loaded 52
We're Gonna Move 79
We're Gonna Rock Tonight 95
We're Gonna Teach You to Rock 94
We're Not Going to Take It 174
We're Not Gonna Take It 117
We're the Crackers 130
Whap'n'Bap'n 180
What a Big Boy 66
What a Crazy World We're Living In 124
What a Day That Was 171
What a Difference a Day Makes 194
What a Feeling 42
What a Fool Believes 159
What a Piece of Work Is Man 58
What a Waste 196
What a Wonderful Life 43
What Becomes of the Broken Hearted? 110
What Do I Have To Do? 196
What Do You Know We've Got a Show 130
What Every Woman Longs For 46
What Fool This Mortal Be 30
What In the World 115
What Kind of Fool 189
What Kind of Fool Do You Think I Am? 189
What Kind of Love Is This 122
What Will You Do When Jesus Comes? 91
What Would I Do If I Could Feel? 128
What You See Is What You Get 173
What You're Proposing 169
What'd I Say 23, 113, 115, 123, 135, 143, 186
Whatever You Want 169
What's Cooking 36
What's Goin' On 167
What's My Name 99
What's She Really Like 47
What's the Buzz? 72
What's the Name of the Game? 75
Wheels On My Heels 99
When 182
When a Man Loves a Woman 97, 189
When Doves Cry 91
When I Kissed the Teacher 133
When I Paint My Masterpiece 91

When I'm Sixty-Four 129, 179
When It Comes to Your Love 198
When the Arrow Flies 198
When the Boys Meet the Girls 124
When the Girl In Your Arms 130
When the Right Time Comes 165
When the Saints Go Marching In 46
When the Saints Go Twistin' In 121
When Will I Be Loved 109
When You Dance 12
Whenever You're Around 49
Where Are You Going? 190
Where Did I Go Wrong? 30, 84
Where Did Our Love Go? 189
Where Do I Go 58
Where Do We Go From Here 197
Where Do You Come From 52
Where Have All the Flowers Gone 141
Where May Go, Go I 18
Where Were You When I Needed You 64
Which Way? 190
While I'm Still Young 194
While My Guitar Gently Weeps 138
Whippin' Post 137
Whispering Bells 12
Whistling Tune, A 75
White Bird 144
White City Lights 187
White Light White Heat 140, 159
White Man at the Hammersmith Palais 99
White Rabbit 110, 183
White Riot 99
Whiter Shade of Pale 110
Who Are We to Say? 71
Who Are You 150
Who Baby? 103
Who Can Say? 87
Who Do You Love? 151, 181
Who Killed Bambi? 147
Who Needs It? 25
Who Needs Money? 30
Who's Sorry Now 180
Who's to Blame 165
Whole Lotta Love 168
Whole Wide World 12, 27, 196
Whose Side Are You On? 97
Why 195
Why Are You So Mean to Me? 136
Why Did It Have To Be Me 133
Why Do Fools Fall in Love? 12, 115, 179
Why Don't You Love Me? 40
Why Oh Why 40
Why You Wanna Break My Heart 23
Wigglin'n'Wobblin' 65
Wild Angels Ballad 199
Wild Angels Theme 199
Wild Horses 145
Wild In the Country 126
Wild In the Streets 126
Wild Love 64
Wild Side of Life, The 169
Wild Thing 149, 157, 161
Wild Wild Women 95

Will It Be You 119
Will You 25
Will You Still Love Me Tomorrow? 180
Willie and the Hand Jive 12, 73
Willy Willy 122
Winning 195
Winter Is Blue 173
Winter Nocturne 127
Wipe Out 186, 198
Wish It Were Me 51
Wishin' and Hopin' 191
With a Little Help From My Friends 102
With One More Look At You 109
With You I'm Born Again 184
Without Love 14, 162
Without You 105
Without Your Love 187
Wolf Call 51
Woman 198
Woman In Love 199
Woman in the Moon 109
Woman in You, The 110
Woman's Love 195
Women 159
Won't Get Fooled Again 150, 167
Won't Somebody Tell Me Why 69
Won't You Give Me a Chance? 96
Wonder of You, The 35
Wonderful Life 129
Wonderful World 78, 180
Wooden Heart 47
Wooden Ships 174
Woodstock 137, 174
Woolly Bully 133, 189
Word Is Love, The 195
Words 143, 187
Words of Love 27
Working Nine to Five A.M. 137
Working on a Building 29
Working On It Night and Day 188
World Is For You, The 81
World Is Full of Married Men, The 199
World of Our Own, A 67
World That We All Dream Of 48
World's On Fire, The 89
Would I Be Crying? 95
Would I Love You 103
Wreck a Buddy 99
Writing on the Wall 25

X Offender 197
Xanadu 129

Ya Ya 179, 198
Yakety Yak 196
Yellow Rose of Texas 123
Yellow Submarine 129
Yesiree 33
Yesterday 53, 164, 179
YMCA 28
Yo Yo 181
Yoga Is as Yoga Does 34
Yogi 114

INDEX OF SONG TITLES

You 188
You Ain't Goin' Nowhere 134
You Are Gone 168
You Are Not a Summer Love 65
You Are What You Eat 176
You Baby 71
You Better Run 93
You Can Depend On Me 156
You Can Get It If You Really Want It 60
You Can't Always Get What You Want 140, 154
You Can't Catch Me 95
You Can't Hurry Love 116
You Can't Say No In Acapulco 46
You Can't Win 128
You Didn't Have to Be So Nice 135
You Don't Have To Say You Love Me 143
You Don't Know Me 30
You Don't Love Me 137
You Gave Me a Mountain 143
You Gave Me the Answer 164
You Got to Believe 197
You Got What You Wanted 111
You Gotta Believe 181
You Gotta Go 119
You Gotta Move 145
You Gotta Stop 34
You Kept Me Waiting 109
You Know I Love You 188
You Know Who I Am? 136

You Make Me Feel Like a Natural Woman 180
You Make Me Feel Like Dancin' 194
You Make My Dreams Come True 163
You Need Hands 147
You Never Give Me Your Money 102
You Never Talk About Me 68
You Pass Me By 130
You Really Didn't Have To Do It 16
You Really Got a Hold On Me 152, 189, 198
You Really Got Me 190
You Scratch My Back 84
You Should Be Dancing 192
You To Me Are Everything 180
You Were On My Mind 189
You'd Better Know It 53
You'll Never Change Him 16
You'll Never Change Them 104
You'll Never Know 51
Young Americans 140
Young and Beautiful 71
Young Dreams 75
Young Man Blues 150
Young Ones, The 130
Youngblood 138
Younger Generation 174
Your Daughter Is One 116
Your Groovy Self 106
Your Heart Never Lies 188
Your Last Chance 71

Your Lips and Mine 122
Your Mother Should Know 80
Your Old Lady 162
Your Precious Love 93, 189
Your Smiling Face 159, 184
Your Time Hasn't Come Yet Baby 106
You're a Big Boy Now 200
You're Going To Lose That Girl 62
You're Movin' Too Slow 198
You're On My Mind 181
You're Only Lonely 183
You're Sixteen 179
You're the One That I Want 56
You're the Reason I Feel Like Dancing 114
Yours Is No Disgrace 174
Youth and Experience 129
You've Been In 190
You've Got To Hide Your Love Away 62
You've Got to Look Right For the Part 69
You've Got Your Troubles 109
You've Lost That Lovin' Feeling 110, 135, 143, 163
You've Really Got a Hold On Me 189

Zig Zag 182
Zombie Stomp, The 65
Zoom 12
Zoot Suit 191